CONTEMPORARY MACROECONOMICS

CONTEMPORARY MACROECONOMICS

Edited by

Amitava Bose
Debraj Ray
Abhirup Sarkar

OXFORD
UNIVERSITY PRESS

OXFORD
UNIVERSITY PRESS

YMCA Library Building, Jai Singh Road, New Delhi 110001

Oxford University Press is a department of the University of Oxford. It furthers the University's objective of excellence in research, scholarship, and education by publishing worldwide in

Oxford New York

Athens Auckland Bangkok Bogota Buenos Aires Calcutta Cape Town Chennai Dar es Salaam Delhi Florence Hong Kong Istanbul Karachi Kuala Lumpur Madrid Melbourne Mexico City Mumbai Nairobi Paris Sao Paolo Shanghai Singapore Taipei Tokyo Toronto Warsaw

with associated companies in Berlin Ibadan

Published in India
By Oxford University Press, New Delhi

First published by Oxford University Press 2001

ISBN 019 565369 6

Typeset in Times New Roman 10 on 12 by Urvashi Press, Meerut, UP
Printed at Pauls Press, New Delhi 110 020
Published by Manzar Khan, Oxford University Press
YMCA Library Building, Jai Singh Road, New Delhi 110 001

Mihir Kanti Rakshit
In appreciation

Mihir Kanti Rakshit

Mihir Kanti Rakshit

Professor Mihir Rakshit was an inspiration to students of Economics at Presidency College, Calcutta, but many of us have given up trying to be like him. It is hard enough to emulate his exacting academic standards, but to try and follow his personal example of self-effacing devotion to teaching is next to impossible

In his long span of teaching at Presidency College, Calcutta, Mihir Rakshit created an entire generation of Indian economists. He conveyed the excitement and depth of economic research through his classes. Moreover, he did so in a coherent, accessible way that formed the hardwiring of our basic knowledge, and left us with the desire for more.

This volume of articles, dedicated to Professor Rakshit, aspires to the same pleasing coherence. All the ten papers, classified into five sections, study contemporary issues in macroeconomic theory, a subject close to Professor Rakshit's heart. Each of the five sections is prefaced by a self-contained introduction to the papers. This leaves our preface free to include a short biography of Mihir Rakshit, which will surely be of independent interest to the reader.

Mihir Kanti Rakshit was born to Ashalata and Birendra Kumar Rakshit on 1 July 1936 in the village of Noapara in Chittagong, East Bengal (later East Pakistan, and now, Bangladesh). In 1947, the subcontinent was partitioned into India and Pakistan, and the Rakshit family moved to the expanding urban agglomerate surrounding the city of Calcutta.

In 1952, Mihir Raskhit joined the undergraduate class in the combined Department of Economics and Political Science at Presidency College. His venture into Economics, as for many young students in India seeking some form of higher learning, was largely accidental. Whatever the implications for the theory of revealed preference, the choice proved a fortuitous one for us. It is only fitting that Rakshit, in his turn, had inspiring teachers in college—Bhabatosh Datta, Dhiresh Bhattacharya, and Tapas Majumdar among them. He was also fortunate in passing through the hands of Panchanan Chakraborty while studying for his Masters degree at Calcutta University.

Professor Rakshit's first love has remained macroeconomics and monetary theory. But within this broad area, his interests have been varied. They have kept up with changing times, honed by his keen sense of relevance. What has remained constant is his deep commitment to a sound theoretical base. Beginning in the early sixties with his work on Money and the Theory of Growth (completed under the supervision of Richard Lipsey for his Ph.D. at the London School of Economics) his research work has always had strong moorings in Keynesian macroeconomic theory. However, over the years he has concentrated more and more on contemporary problems of development. Perhaps his most notable work, done over the 1970s, concerns a reworking of the notions of effective demand and financial intermediation (so far largely developed for mature economies) to suit the vastly changed context of less developed market economies.* This work has been followed by research that concentrates on specific problems of the Indian economy and, more recently, on the Asia–Pacific region. In particular, he has been stressing on the importance of trade impediments and developed markets in both real and financial sectors.

These concerns have also been reflected in his teaching. He has himself said that he spent the happiest days of his life as a teacher in the Department of Economics at Presidency College, which he joined in 1965. For many years, he ran a fortnightly workshop in which researchers in disparate themes would converge. His quick and incisive comments have helped many of us avoid unsuspected pitfalls on a number of occasions.

We are indeed blessed to have been Mihir Rakshit's students. We have learnt from him not merely Economics, but much more. His abiding concern for his students has moved us. We hope that with his customary magnanimity, he will be happy to overlook the inadequacies in this modest attempt to say thank you.

AMITAVA BOSE
DEBRAJ RAY
ABHIRUP SARKAR

*This research culminated in his book, *The Labour Surplus Economy*, Delhi, Macmillan (1982).

Contributors

ABHIRUP SARKAR, Indian Statistical Institute, Calcutta

AMITAVA BOSE, Indian Institute of Management, Calcutta

AMITAVA KRISHNA DUTT, University of Notre Dame

BHASKAR DUTTA, Indian Statistical Institute, Delhi

BHASWAR MOITRA, Jadavpur University

DEBRAJ RAY, New York University

DIPANKAR DASGUPTA, Indian Statistical Institute, Calcutta and Osaka University

GAUTAM BOSE, University of New South Wales

PRADIP MAITI, Indian Statistical Institute, Calcutta

SARBAJIT SENGUPTA, Viswa Bharati University

SUDIPTO DASGUPTA, Hong Kong University of Science and Technology

SUGATA MARJIT, Jawaharlal Nehru University and Centre for Studies in Social Sciences

SWAPAN DASGUPTA, Dalhousie University

TAPAN MITRA, Cornell University

UDO BROLL, University of Munich

Contents

NATIONAL INCOME

National Income: An Introduction

In many ways, national income is the most important concept for macroeconomics. Conceptual and measurement issues are important aspects of Mihir Rakshit's work on savings–investment estimates for India. While beginners are routinely introduced to the general definitions, concrete illustrations using the Indian national income accounts are seldom attempted. Moreover, conceptual discussions have typically stopped short of providing a precise theoretical justification for regarding national income as a measure of current and future welfare. The two papers in this section address these two deficiencies.

INCOME ACCOUNTING: THEORY AND INDIAN ESTIMATES

Students of macroeconomics are perhaps more familiar with theories of national income determination than with the *measurement* and *definition* of national income and its related aggregates. Whatever little is available in textbooks is, at best, inadequate. Moreover, textbooks generally use data from developed countries to illustrate the basic principles of national income accounting; data from less-developed countries are seldom used. Pradip Maiti's paper, which is addressed to students of macroeconomics and practitioners of national income accounting, seeks to make a contribution in these respects. The paper begins with the observation that the diverse and innumerable activities of an economy need to be summarized by constructing various accounts which reveal the magnitudes of different macro aggregates, as well as the interrelationship between these aggregates. It then proceeds to discuss at length the fundamental concepts of macroeconomics such as production, consumption, investment, gross domestic product, government final consumption, and clarifies the notion of a national account for an economic activity. Next, it illustrates these concepts and related macro relations/identities by using India's national accounts and figures of national income, as estimated by the Central Statistical Organisation. The paper also clarifies the concept of real GDP as used in the national income accounting literature and shows how it can be obtained from outputs of individual producing units. Finally, the paper builds up a theoretical structure of *flow of funds* relations for the broad sectors of the Indian economy and estimates the various aggregates in these relations for a selected year.

INCOME ACCOUNTING AND SUSTAINABLE DEVELOPMENT

The conceptual appeal of an income measure ultimately rests on its accuracy as a welfare index. It is, of course, widely appreciated that the term 'national income' is meant to indicate the contribution made by current economic activity to the current and future welfare of the society. In particular, the value of investment is generally understood as being the contribution to *future* societal welfare. How accurate is this understanding?

To be sure, in a world with changing preferences and technology, or in a situation in which agents do not predict the future perfectly, there is no reason to expect a clear connection between the two concepts. But the point goes deeper. For the sake of argument, let us assume that preferences and technology are stationary over time, and that all agents possess perfect foresight. Would the equality between the value of current investment and the present value of future welfare hold in this simplified world? The first part of the Dasgupta–Mitra paper provides an answer to this question, following the lead provided by Weitzman.[1] Contrary to expectations, the equality cannot be taken for granted. First of all, market conditions must be competitive. But that is not enough. There is a further complication arising from the open–endedness of the future. The equality is indeed satisfied if the competitive programme is also an optimal programme, or if an additional condition is met. The importance of the additional condition arises from the well-known fact that when the future is open ended, not all competitive programmes are optimal. The additional condition requires the discounted present value of future investment to become vanishingly small in the long run.

The second part of the Dasgupta–Mitra paper applies the insights from these observations to the literature on sustainable development. Sustainable development requires policies that ensure for future generations at least the same level of welfare as that of the current generation.

[1]Weitzman, M.L. (1976), 'On the Welfare Significance of National Product in a Dynamic Economy', *Quarterly Journal of Economics*, 90, pp. 156–62.

The question is particularly important in the context of consumption of non-renewable resources. A competitive programme, for which NNP is an exact measure of current and future welfare, does lead to sustainable development if and only if the value of investment, net of the depreciation of non-renewable resources, is never negative.

1

National Income Accounting
Theory and Indian Estimates

PRADIP MAITI*

> The relation between our branch (which might be called Social Accounting) and the rest of economics can be made clear by an analogy from another science. The study of the human body is divided into two main parts—anatomy and physiology. Anatomy deals with the structure of the body, the various organs and their relations, the plan of the organism as it is discovered by dissection after death. Physiology is concerned with the working of the organism—the living body as a going concern. (Social Accounting) . . . is economic anatomy, the structure of the body economic, as it can be discovered by statisticians working on figures collected *after the event* (while) . . . economic physiology (deals with) the way the economic system works.
>
> Hicks, 1972, pp. 252–3

1. INTRODUCTION

National Income is a popular phrase nowadays. In a general way, it means the income of a nation. However, if we want to appreciate its meaning fully, we have to understand many fundamental concepts of economics—concepts like 'capital', 'income', 'production', 'saving', etc. When we go to sort out these concepts, we shall see that they are very much closely related. In fact, a full understanding of these ideas is possible only when we are able to visualize the anatomy of an

*The author gratefully acknowledges his indebtedness to Professor Mihir Rakshit, Professor Dipankar Dasgupta, and Professor Robin Mukherjee, with whom he had many a discussion on the topic under consideration. Thanks are also due to the students at various levels who have contributed to the author's understanding of the subject. Of course, none of them is to be held responsible for errors which may remain.

economic system with closely interrelated parts, i.e. only when we have a clear picture of the circular flow of economic activity.

We thus begin with the concepts which are essential for understanding the theory of National Income Accounting. We then turn to some of the statistics which are regularly collected and compiled for constructing India's national accounts. These statistics will be presented mainly with a view to illustrating the basic ideas and the macro relations. They should not be looked upon as restricting the general applicability of the subject matter of the paper. This is all the more so, as the compilation of India's national accounts follows the system recommended by the United Nations for a large number of countries.

Let us then begin with some general observations. Economic activities and transactions take place round the year. Farmers sow and harvest. Shopkeepers sell all sorts of goods, or people work in factories and turn out products of numerous varieties. These and similar transactions and activities are taking place all the time. The problem is how to summarize such diverse and innumerable activities and present the same in a form which would reveal not only the magnitudes of different types of economic activities, but the interrelationship among these magnitudes as well. As well shall see later, such summarization is the major objective of the construction of various national accounts for an economy.

The paper is organized as follows. Section 2 introduces a number of important concepts and aggregates used in National Income Accounting. In particular, the concept of national accounts for an economic activity is discussed in detail. Section 3 describes alternative methods of estimating gross domestic product (GDP) of an economy. In this section, the concept and measurement of government, final consumption expenditure are explained, and the structure of the National Production Account is first outlined, and then illustrated with the Indian data. Section 4 describes the other national accounts, illustrating each with the Indian data. Section 5 introduces the concept and estimation of real GDP and presents India's real GDP for some selected years. Section 6 attempts to outline the structure of a Flow of Fund (capital finance) table and illustrate it with the Indian data. It also contains concluding observations. The estimation procedure of selected macro aggregates and financial flows of India is briefly discussed in the Appendix.

2. SOME IMPORTANT CONCEPTS

2.1 PRODUCTION: GOODS AND SERVICES

We may begin by defining some of the relevant concepts used in macroeconomics. First is the concept of production. No definition of production is comprehensive or completely satisfactory. What economists do in respect is to begin with a definition, and then qualify that definition so as to include or exclude a number of activities[1]. Let us, therefore, start with a general definition and then see how that can be modified so as to correspond to the practice followed by several countries or the procedure recommended by the United Nations for developing countries.

Production may be defined as an activity of making something which is demanded by people. A thing is demanded, because it may be used either to satisfy personal or collective needs of individuals (i.e. for the purpose of own final consumption of individuals) or as an input to make other things or even the same thing. Any institutional unit, say a household, a firm, a non-profit making organization, a government organ or a farmer who organizes such an activity, is called a *producer*.

Now, when a farmer grows wheat and sells it in the market, or the owner of a clothing factory employs workers to make cloth and then sells it in the market, he gets revenues. Such an activity of making things—material things, to be specific—is obviously production, since there are people who demand them and pay for them. But what about the activities of traders and shopkeepers? They do not make material things, but take the things already made and make them available at the places and times at which they are wanted. In other words, they provide services, but very useful services, for which people are prepared to pay. Similarly, there are other categories of workers (like

[1]This is not an uncommon practice. For instance, Hicks (1972, pp. 295–7) defines productive work 'as work done to satisfy the wants of other people *through exchange*' (p. 296), but then uses a wider definition of production to include, e.g. all agricultural production, whether produced for sale *or not.* In fact, Hicks writes, 'we are therefore driven to adopt the limited definition here used, though we must be prepared to modify it by including some particular things not produced for sale, in cases where it would be seriously misleading not to do so' (p. 296).

doctors, teachers, transport workers) whose services are wanted by people. Hence, they should count as producers; the only difference is that they produce not material goods, but services.

Thus, things produced are of two kinds—*goods* and *services*. However, apart from the fact that goods are material things, while services are immaterial, there are other differences between the two. First, goods can be used only after they are produced. On the other hand, production and use of services take place simultaneously—they are contemporaneous. Second, goods are physical objects over which ownership rights can be established, and whose ownership rights can be transferred from one person to another. On the contrary, services are not separate entities over which ownership rights can be established, and hence, the question of transfer of ownership right does not arise in this case. Of course, there are different forms in which production of services may take place. Services typically consist of changes in the condition of the users themselves or their goods, and are brought about by the activities of producers[2]. (Such changes may, however, be either temporary or permanent).

Boundary of Production

It is not very easy to define the boundary of production. Making of certain things, particularly those arising in connection with some services, is to be excluded from this boundary.

First, activities which are not capable of being carried out by one unit for the benefit of another should be excluded. Thus, such basic human activities as eating, sleeping, taking exercises are not productive in an economic sense.

Second, economic production should refer to an activity which is carried out under the control and responsibility of an institutional unit—a unit that owns any goods produced as outputs, or is entitled to be paid, or otherwise compensated for the services provided. Thus, a purely natural process without any human involvement (e.g. the natural

[2]Such changes include: (i) changes in the condition of the user's goods (which occur in cases like transportation, cleaning, repairing of goods, etc.), (ii) changes in the user's physical or mental condition (the former occur in cases of passenger transport, accommodation, medical treatment, etc. and the latter, in cases of education, entertainment, etc.), and (iii) changes in the general economic state of the users themselves (e.g. services provided by insurance companies, financial intermediaries, etc.). See C.E.C. *et al.* (1993, pp. 115–16) for a detailed discussion.

growth of stock of fish in open seas or the water flowing down a river) is not counted as production.

Third, production of domestic and personal services by members of the household for their own use (e.g. the preparation of meals, care and training of children, cleaning, etc.) has traditionally been excluded from measured production in national accounts, although the same obtained by employing paid domestic staff is included. A number of arguments are usually put forward to justify such exclusions.

One argument is that since the vast majority of such services are not produced for the market, suitable market prices are not generally available that can be used to value such services objectively. Further, if values are to be assigned to outputs, values are to be assigned to incomes and expenditure associated with such production, and that makes the whole exercise extremely difficult and arbitrary. In fact, the inclusion of large non-monetary flows of this kind in the national accounts, together with actual monetary flows, is likely to reduce the analytic usefulness of the data. Another important argument against the inclusion of such activities is that when a country collects statistics on employment or labour force, economically active persons are defined to be those who are engaged in productive activities. If the production boundary were to include production of personal and domestic services by household members for their own use, virtually the entire adult population which is usually engaged in such activities would become self-employed, and hence, unemployment would be impossible by definition. Such a description does not fit the typical charcteristics of an economy, particularly a developing economy (C.E.C. *et al.*, 1993, pp. 123–5).

The production boundary is, however, taken to include some items which do not involve any market transactions. These are: (i) production of goods for own consumption or own use (e.g. foodstuffs produced by farmers, own-account construction of dwellings, etc.), and (ii) production of housing services for own final consumption in the case of the dwelling being occupied by the owner. Although these items are not marketed, well-defined markets exist for these and it is not difficult to find prices to estimate the value of the goods or services consumed.

To sum up, the production boundary is taken to include production of those goods and services which are actually marketed against cash or for barter, or which are retained for owner's use but are capable of being marketed. And, as we shall see later, it should also include all goods and services provided free to the households by government units and non-profit making institutions serving households.

2.2 Final Consumption and Investment

Two other important forms of economic activities are final consumption and investment or accumulation. Let us now try to define these two activities. Unless mentioned otherwise, the word 'good' will henceforth be used generically to mean either a material good or a service.

Let us choose an accounting period, say, a year. A good produced currently in an economy may be used during the current accounting period in one of four alternative ways:

(A) to satisfy personal human wants (or, 'collective wants');

(B) as an input in further production, i.e. in the production of some other good or even the same good;

(C) to augment the stock of goods for use in future period(s); or

(D) as an item of export to foreign countries.

Note that this classification has been made on the basis of the *nature of use* of a good, and not on the basis of the physical nature of a good. A good may have all the four uses. For instance, wheat may be used as an input in a bakery (use B), or be consumed by a household (use A), or be exported (use D), or even be stored by a farmer to be sold in the next period (use C).

The term 'final consumption' has been used quite a number of times earlier. To define it formally, all uses of type A may be called final consumption. On the other hand, the use of type B may be subdivided into three categories as follows:

(B.1) Some inputs are such that they can be used only once (e.g. coal, petroleum)—the so-called single-use inputs, to use the Hicksian definition. Call them raw materials or simply materials. Since services are used up as soon as they are produced, any service which is used as an input in production (e.g. transport service) falls in this category.

(B.2) There are some inputs (e.g. pencil, batteries, etc.) which can be used more than once, but can be used only over a short period, i.e. a period shorter than the accounting period.

(B.3) There are some inputs which can go on being used for considerable periods; in particular, for more than one accounting period. All sorts of machines and equipments are of this variety. Call these types of goods 'fixed capital or fixed assets'.

Obviously, the classification given above is based, not on the physical durability of an input, but on the *duration of its use* in production. For instance, an input like coal is extremely durable in nature, but it is a raw material—a single-use input. In fact, the distinction between (B.1) and (B.3) is that raw materials (as well as services used as inputs) are absorbed, rather *physically absorbed*, in the goods which are made out of them, while it is the services of the machines, and not the machines themselves, which are absorbed in the production of goods. In this context, it may be noted that the value of services of fixed capital used up in production in a year can be no less (and can, in fact, be greater) than the amount of depreciation of such goods. Fixed assets (except land) cannot last forever. When they are used to produce something, they experience some wear and tear—some 'depreciation'—or loss of value during the year. (This is also called *consumption of fixed capital*).

What about inputs belonging to the category (B.2)? It possesses some features of each of the other two categories. Although such an input is not physically absorbed in any particular good and can be used repeatedly, as in the case of fixed capital, but it is fully used up during an accounting period. From the point of view of National Income estimation, such inputs are treated like inputs in (B.1). We thus combine inputs belonging to categories (B.1) and (B.2) together and call them 'intermediate goods' and the corresponding use, an intermediate use or intermediate consumption. On the other hand, each of the remaining uses of a good (viz., use A, B.3, C and D) is a *final use.* To sum up, inputs are basically of two kinds, depending on whether they depreciate fully or only partly during an accounting period. The former are *intermediate goods* and the latter, fixed capital goods.[3]

One feels that goods which are used by households to satisfy human wants during a period, i.e. type A goods, may similarly be classified into two groups as follows:

[3]It may be re-emphasized that goods of variety (B.1) and (B.2) may be extremely durable in nature. The point is that the length of the time for which they can be used is very small—smaller than the accounting period.

(A.1) goods which cannot be used for more than a period—including goods which are used up as soon as they are used (e.g. food, barber's service, etc.) as well as goods which can be used for a few days or weeks only (e.g. pencil, electric bulb, etc.); and

(A.2) goods which can go on being used for quite a number of years (e.g. houses, motor cars, television sets, electric fans or even woollen garments).

Strictly speaking, the term final consumption should mean (i) the use of goods of the type (A.1) and (ii) the value of services enjoyed from the goods (existing at the beginning of the period as well as currently produced) of the type (A.2) during the period. The goods of the variety (A.2) are called 'consumers' durables' and it is the flow of services from these durables, and not the durables themselves, which are used up, i.e. consumed during a period.

Although such a rigorous definition of consumption is what is proper, and what might be adopted in some developed countries, it is not used in general, owing to the fact that it is difficult, if not impossible, to estimate how much service households consume from different kinds of durable-use consumers' goods. Only one exception is universally made, viz., the enjoyment of services from houses, the argument being that although other consumers' durables are generally bought outright, the renting of houses is not infrequent. We shall, therefore, call all expenditure on or uses of type A goods during the year (except the expenditure incurred to buy or construct houses), *final consumption* expenditure.

On the other hand, any purchase, installation or own-account construction of fixed capital goods may be called investment in fixed assets or *fixed capital formation*. Finally, those products which have not been used within the period for intermediate or final consumption or fixed capital formation form a reserve called increase in stocks or *investment in stocks*; these will be available for use in the future. Such addition to physical wealth, whether in the shape of fixed assets or of an increase in stocks, is called (*physical*) *investment* or 'accumulation'.

In this context it may be interesting to note that neither the estimates of flows of consumption from durable-use consumer goods nor those of stocks of such goods are available in India. However, Central Statistical Organisation (CSO), the official body entrusted with the task of estimating and publishing National Income statistics in India, estimates the relative importance of such goods in the final consumption expenditure of the households. Such data are published every year for the whole of the private sector[4]. Four different categories of goods are distinguished, depending on the length of their physical lives, viz., durable, semi-durable and non-durable commodities, and services[5]. The shares of these four categories in the private final consumption expenditure in India's domestic market at current market prices ($PFCE_d$) are given in Table 1.1 for three selected years:

TABLE 1.1

Share in $PFCE_d$ by Category of Commodity

Year	$PFCE_d$ (Rs crore)	Percentage share in the $PFCE_d$ of			
		Durable Commodities	Semi-Durable Commodities	Non-Durable Commodities	Services
1980–81	99,292	1.5	12.9	67.9	17.8
1990–91	332,364	2.4	13.8	63.5	20.3
1994–95	575,335	2.6	12.8	63.9	20.5

It is observed that in any given year the total purchase of durable and semi-durable commodities constitutes less than one-sixth of the household budget.

2.3 DOMESTIC PRODUCT, ITS VALUATION AND NATIONAL INCOME

It is now high time that we introduce some other important concepts. One such important concept is, of course, domestic product.

[4]CSO defines the private sector to be composed of two subsectors: *private corporate sector* (i.e. corporate enterprises which are recognized as business entities independent of their owners) and *household sector.* The latter is defined to comprise individuals, unincorporated establishments like sole proprietorship (i.e. all producer units which cannot be separated from the person(s)/household(s) owning them) and partnership and non-profit institutions serving households (NPISH) like charitable trusts, religious bodies, educational institutions etc.

[5]Examples of durable commodities are furniture, automobiles, radios, ornaments, etc. while clothing, leather products, utensils, etc. are considered to be semi-durable. All other items are either non-durable commodities (e.g. food, medicines, etc.) or services.

Domestic Product

Domestic product is a measure (in money value) of the volume of all the goods and services which are produced within the domestic territory[6] of an economy during a period (usually a year), accounted without duplication. Two points are worth mentioning. First, the measure has to be in money value, as the physical units in which quantities of different goods (and also services) are measured are not, in general, directly additive. Second, the measure is an unduplicated value of output. A hyothetical example may clarify the point. Suppose, in an economy in a year, a farmer produces 1 kilogram of wheat and sells it to a flour mill at a price of Rs 5. The mill in trun makes 1 kilogram of wheat flour out of this wheat and sells it to a bakery at a price of Rs 6. The bakery manufactures this flour into two and a half pounds of bread and sells this bread to households at a price of Rs 6 per pound. The total production of the economy is obviously not 1 kilogram of wheat *plus* 1 kilogram of wheat flour *plus* 2½ pounds of bread, because that will be a duplicated total. The total production is the production of final-use good only, which is 2½ pounds of bread or Rs 15 (the money value of this amount of bread). However, the same total could have been obtained in an alternative way, by considering the net contribution, or what is called in economic terminology, 'value added', by a producing unit at each stage of processing, and then summing over all such values added. The term, *value added*, means the value of output less the value of all intermediate goods used up in producing that output. (The farmer, the flour mill of the bakery might have used other intermediate inputs except wheat or wheat flour, but we have ignored such details in this simple example.) The total value added is, then, the sum of the values added at each stage of processing, i.e. Rs 5 added by the farmer, Re 1 (that is, Rs 6 – Rs 5) added by the flour mill and Rs 9 (that is, Rs 15 – Rs 6) added by the bakery and the total value added (Rs 15) is exactly the same as the value of production of final-use good, bread (Rs 15).

We have just seen that the domestic product of an economy during a year is the total value added in that economy during that year. However, such a total may be computed either gross or net, and accordingly we get two different aggregates: gross domestic product (GDP) and net

[6]The domestic territory includes not only the territory lying within the political frontiers inclusive of territorial waters of a country, but such things as ships and aircrafts operated by the residents of the country between two or more countries.

domestic product (NDP). Further, the total may be computed either at factor cost or at market prices. These concepts are clarified here.

Factor Cost and Domestic Income

The first question that arises is: how to *value* the quantities produced of different items so as to arrive at a total like GDP or NDP? An illuminating discussion is given in Stone and Stone (1972, pp. 17–19):

> Goods and services have no abstract money value in themselves. We do not pay nature for accumulating large deposits of coal in the earth, or for stimulating the growth of pearls inside oysters, or for creating the human brain. When we speak, therefore, of the value of a good or of a service, we mean the price we have to pay to induce human beings to bring forth these products for the enjoyment and enrichment of the community: the price we have to pay to induce, let us say, the miner to dig the coal out, the owner of capital to finance the necessary equipment, the owner of the land to allow his field to be dug up.

Thus, for production we need inputs like labour, capital, land and enterpreneurship, the so-called *primary factors of production*. It is the rewards they receive for their inputs that constitute the first step in valuing what they produce. The sum of these rewards is the domestic income (see relation (1), Table 1.2). Production, however, involves some other costs also. As we have noted earlier, fixed capital goods, such as buildings or equipment, when used in production lose value or depreciate. The cost of such depreciation is difficult to calculate exactly and the usual practice is to estimate it and set aside whatever sum seems likely to cover it. These provisions for the *consumption of fixed capital* are to be added to the incomes of the primary factors of production to get the full cost of products (relation (2), Table 1.2).

National Income

It may be noted that the entire amount of domestic income does not necessarily accrue to the inhabitants of a country. A part (say, '*a*') may flow abroad to foreigners as factor incomes, to the extent they participate in domestic production. Similarly, inhabitants of a country may receive factor incomes from abroad (say '*b*'). The difference, '$b-a$', is called 'net factor income from abroad'.

The term 'nationals' is used in the literature to mean normal residents of a country and all such normal resident units constitute a nation. *National Income* is the factor income which accrues to the nationals of a country from their participation in world production, i.e. production which takes place either at home or abroad. In this sense, national income is the (factor) income of a nation (relation (3), Table 1.2).

TABLE 1.2
Definitions of Some Aggregates

• Domestic Income	= NDP at Factor Cost	
	= Sum of incomes accruing to the primary factors of production from their participation in the productive activity that takes place within the domestic territory of an economy	(1)
• GDP at Factor Cost	= NDP at Factor Cost + Consumption of Fixed Capital	(2)
• National Income	= Net National Product (NNP) at Factor Cost	
	= NDP at Factor Cost + Net Factor Income from Abroad	(3)
• Net Indirect Taxes	= Indirect Taxes–Subsidies	(4)
• Market Price	= Factor Cost + Net Indirect Taxes	(5)

It may be re-emphasized that national income or domestic income is *factor income*, i.e. the total of those incomes which accrue to the primary factors as rewards for their participation in production in the *current* period. No other forms of income are included here; therefore gifts, grants, old-age pensions or remittances—which are received not against participation in current production—are excluded.

However, goods and servics are not sold at factor cost. There are two other elements in an economy which affect their values, and hence, their market prices. These two are: (i) all kinds of taxes assessed on producers in respect of production, sale, purchase or use of goods and services—taxes which the producers charge to the expenses of production (like excise duties, sales tax, entertainment tax on cinema tickets, import duties, etc.), the general name being *indirect taxes*, and (ii) *subsidies* given to the producers by the government to compensate for any operating losses arising out of government policy to maintain prices at a level below costs of production (relations (4), (5), Table 1.2).

2.4 NATIONAL ACCOUNTS

In the previous sections, we have explained the concept of production and concepts of consumption and investment, the two different kinds of final uses of goods and services. The domestic production of an *open* economy is, however, supplemented by products imported from foreign countries and also not entirely absorbed domestically, as a part of it flows abroad as export, We should thus record not only transactions connecting *production*, *consumption* and *investment*, but also transactions which the *rest of the world* has with the domestic country.

Suppose, we try to record in four statements, or what are better known as *accounts*, the incoming and the outgoing monetary flows relating to the four economic activities mentioned above. How would such a network of flows look like? A simple geometry may clarify the basic features of such a structure.

Let the economy of the world be represented by the interior of a large circle. Let us draw another circle inside this interior, so as to divide it into two areas—an outer ring and the interior of the inner circle. The latter represents the domestic economy and the former, the Rest of the World (RW) vis-a-vis the domestic economy (see Fig. 1.1)

The interior of the inner circle representing the domestic economy is divided into three regions, one for each economic activity. A given region (say, the region labelled 'production') contains a large number of accounts,

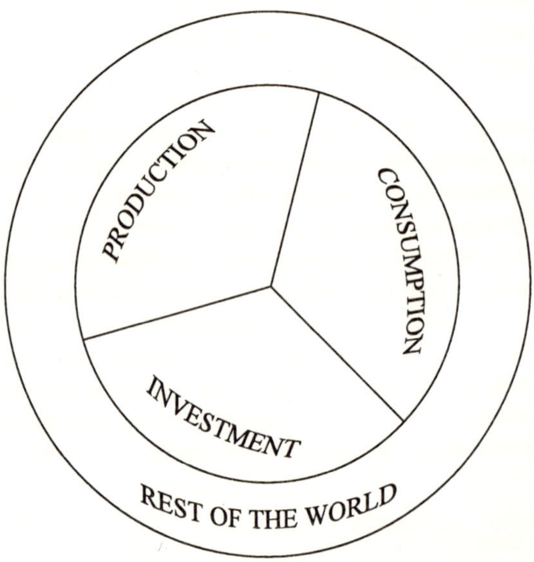

Fig. 1.1 Set of Accounts for the Domestic Economy and the RW

one for each economic entity performing the given economic activity (production activity in the present case). We may consolidate a given account across all the economic entities of the domestic economy so as to get what may be called a 'national account' for the given economic activity. Alternatively, we may consolidate it over groups of entities. For instance, we can have a production account for the private sector and a production account for the public sector separately. In this case, of course, we have to draw another boundary inside the region labeled 'production' so as to divide it into two sub-regions—production of the private sector and production of the public sector. As long as we do not want further subdivision of a region, we have to interpret it as a consolidation of the given account across all entities of the economy.

We thus have four regions inside the large circle, separated from each other by an equal number of boundaries. Since each region represents a given account, let us consider the structure of an account in detail. An account is a statement of various flows—both incomings and outgoings—which cross over the three boundaries separating the given account from the other accounts. These flows are expressed in terms of *money* (due to be) either paid (*outgoings*) or received (*incomings*), and not in terms of goods or services, which flow the other way. Thus, for instance, the sale of goods from 'production' account to 'consumption' account will be represented by a flow of money from 'consumption' to 'production', although the goods themselves flow in the opposite direction.

To summarize, we construct four accounts, one for each activity. An account has two sides—one side, say, the right-hand side (RHS) records the incoming money flows while the other side, i.e. the left-hand (LHS) records the outgoing money flows. Further, the two sides of an account should always balance.

One of the basic purposes of national accounts statistics is to provide a set of accounts for the whole nation. As we have remarked earlier, a given account for the whole nation (e.g. *national* production account) is just a consolidation of that account across all economic entities. In reality, however, national accounts are seldom derived in this way, as individual accounts are not available, or cannot even be constructed for want of requisite data. Rather, the consolidated account is normally constructed in an indirect way. Still, if one wants to understand the national accounts, it is best to think of them as if they were constructed theoretically from individual accounts of all the persons, business and other concerns which compose the national economy (Hicks, *et al.*, 1984, p. 266).

3. ALTERNATIVE METHODS OF ESTIMATING GDP

Let us now turn to a fundamental result in national income accounting, namely that the total production of an economy during a period, i.e. GDP, may be estimated by the three alternative methods at three different points—by the *income method* at the point of income generation, by the value added method (or the *product method*) at the point of production and by the *final expenditure* method at the point of final utilization. The equivalence of the last two methods is not new to us; we had already come across it in our example of the simple economy which produced bread as the only final-use good. What we have to show is that it remains valid even when the economy produces a large number of final-use goods. We show this result now, postponing a discussion on income method to Section 3.4.

3.1 AN IMPORTANT IDENTITY

We abstract from the activities of the government for the time being and assume that there are '*n*' producing units in the economy. Let us cosider the '*j*th' producing unit. We shall use the following notations to denote flows during the given accounting period:

x_j	amount of *output* of (i.e. value of goods and services produced by) the *j*th unit;
um_j	amount of intermediate inputs *used* up in *j*th unit's production;
z_j	amount of output *sold* to others by the *j*th unit (inclusive of the amount of its own final use, if any);
x_{ij}, mm_j	amount of intermediate inputs *purchased* by the *j*th unit from the *i*th domestic producer and from abroad, respectively;
Δso_j, Δsm_j	*change in the stock* of output and intermediate inputs held by the *j*th unit, respectively, during the period.

Note that:

$$\Delta\,\text{so}_j = x_j - z_j \qquad \text{(a)}$$

and

$$\Delta\text{sm}_j = \text{total amount of intermediate inputs purchased}$$
$$-\text{the amount used up}$$
$$= \Sigma_i\, x_{ij} + \text{mm}_j - \text{um}_j \qquad \text{(b)}$$

Therefore, the *value added* by the jth unit during the period (va_j) is given by:

$$\begin{aligned} \text{va}_j &= x_j - \text{um}_j \\ &= \Delta\, \text{inv}_j + z_j - \Sigma_i\, x_{ij} - \text{mm}_j \qquad (6) \end{aligned}$$

where $\Delta\, \text{inv}_j$ is the change over the period in the jth unit's inventory of outputs and intermediate inputs[7]:

$$\Delta\, \text{inv}_j = \Delta\, \text{so}_j + \Delta\, \text{sm}_j \qquad (7)$$

Let us now consider the sale of the jth unit in detail. Although it is not possible for the unit to know for what purposes a particular buyer would be buying its output, one can always enumerate all possible uses by the buyers. In general, one can write:

$$z_j = c_j + k_j + \sum_{i=1}^{n} x_{ji} + e_j \qquad (8)$$

where e_j, c_j and k_j are the amount (of the output of the jth unit) exported, bought for final consumption and bought for use as fixed capital, respectively. Obviously, for a particular producing unit, not all the items on the RHS may be present. From (6) and (8), we get[8]

$$\text{va}_j = c_j + k_j + \Delta\, \text{inv}_j + e_j - \text{mm}_j + \sum_{i=1}^{n} x_{ji} - \sum_{i=1}^{n} x_{ij} \qquad (9)$$

[7]We thus observe that we do not really have to distinguish between inventories of outputs and intermediate inputs. What is needed is the change in the aggregate stock of goods held by the jth unit over the period. The valuation of such stock might pose a problem, particularly when prices change during the period. However, the aggregate we need can be unambiguously defined. Let q^e_{kj} and q^b_{kj} be the quantity of the kth good held by the jth unit at the end and beginning of the period, respectively. Then $\Delta\, \text{inv}_j$ may be computed as:

$$\Delta\, \text{inv}_j = \sum_k p_k\, (q^e_{kj} - q^b_{kj})$$

where p_k may be some *average* price of the kth good during the period in question (see Stone and Stone, 1972, pp. 52–3).

[8]As we have explained earlier, c_j includes quantities of durable-use consumer goods, if any. Further, c_j and k_j may include amounts used by the unit itself for the respective purposes. Note that we do not have to consider a similar use of intermediate inputs, since output of a unit during a period is measured net of the amount of intermediate inputs (if any) produced and used up by itself during the period.

If we now sum over all j, the last two terms on the RHS will cancel out, since they give the same total, i.e. the aggregate *sale* of intermediate inputs and the aggregate *purchase* of the same in the domestic market. The sum of values added by all (resident) producing units, a measure of *gross domestic product* (GDP) of the economy during the period, thus becomes

$$\text{GDP} = \sum_{j=1}^{n} \text{va}_j = \sum_j c_j + \sum_j k_j + \sum_j \Delta\, \text{inv}_j + \sum_j e_j - \sum_j \text{mm}_j \tag{10}$$

All the positive terms on the RHS are final expenditure on (or final uses of) domestically produced goods and services. For instance, $\Sigma\, c_j$ is the final consumption expenditure, $\Sigma\, k_j$ is the expenditure on fixed capital goods and so on, each such expenditure being on goods and services produced at home. Each of these may be different from the total such expenditure of the nation, i.e. expenditure made by all the normal residents of the country, to the extent that (a) they import final-use goods directly/make direct purchases of such goods abroad, and that (b) a part of the expenditure in the domestic market is made by non-resident households and extraterritorial bodies. The above (a) should be treated as import of the country and (b), as export. Let the total such imports and exports be denoted by MD and ED, respectively.

What kind of adjustment do we have to make in relation (10), if we want to show on its RHS final expenditure of the country, rather than final expenditure made within the country? We subtract from each total on the RHS of (10) its corresponding amount under (b) and add the latter to the export of the country. Similarly, we add to each total the corresponding amount under (a) and subtract the latter as import of the country. The RHS will remin unchanged and we will have

$$\text{GDP} = \text{C} + \text{GFI} + \Delta\,\text{INV} + \text{EX} - \text{IM}, \tag{11}$$

where C = final consumption expenditure of the country,[9] ΔINV =

[9]The difference between final expenditure of India (i.e. by Indian nationals) and that made within India may be illustrated numerically in the case of private final consumption expenditure (PFCE). As we shall see later, C may be disaggregated into such expenditure by the private and public sectors. In Section 2.2 we have seen that private final consumption expenditure in the domestic market (PFCE_d) in 1994–95 was Rs 575,335 crore. In contrast, India's PFCE in this year was Rs 570,417 crore, which is obtained by *subtracting* direct purchases in the domestic market by non-resident households and extraterritorial bodies in the year (Rs 7420 crore) from PFCE_d and *adding* to that total, direct purchases abroad by resident households in the year (Rs 2502 crore).

change in the aggregate stock of goods held by the country, EX = aggregate exports ($= \Sigma_j e_j + \text{ED}$), IM = aggregate imports ($= \Sigma_j \text{mm}_j + \text{MD}$) and GFI = *gross* fixed investment of the country.

This is the fundamental identity in National Income accounting—an identity between the *aggregate value added* by the domestic country and the *aggregate final expenditure* made on the domestically produced goods and services (net of imports of intermediate inputs)—relation (10), or an identity between the former and the aggregate final expenditure of the nationals of the country plus net export—relation (11). We show next that this identity remains valid even when we incorporate the economic activities of the government.

3.2 Government Final Consumption

Public sector plays a crucial role in the economic growth and development of a country. Although its primary function is to protect the community against internal disturbance and external aggression, the government in all countries also takes the responsibility of producing a large number of goods and services.

Public sector comprises two sub-sectors—government *administrative departments* and government *enterprises*. Government enterprises operate like private enterprises since they provide goods and services and charge for these on a commercial basis[10].

But what do the government administrative departments do? They employ a lot of people in the police, court, army, etc., maintain law and order in the country and protect the citizens against foreign aggression. They obviously produce something, i.e. furnish to the community those *collective services* which cannot otherwise be conveniently and

[10]Central Statistical Organisation (CSO) of Government of India (GOI) makes a subdivision of government enterprises into Departmental Enterprises (DE's) and Non-Departmental Enterprises (NDE's). DE's are unincorporated enterprises which are: (i) owned, controlled and run directly by public authorities and (ii) normally do not hold or manage financial assets and liabilities apart from their working balances and business accounts payables and receivables. NDE's are government companies and statutory corporations (like ONGC, DVC, FCI, LIC, nationalized banks, electricity boards, etc.) wholly or mainly owned and/or controlled by public authorities. NDE's differ from the DE's in that the former hold and manage the financial assets involved in their business, have separate Boards of Directors and present profits and loss accounts as in the case of private corporate sector (CSO, GOI, 1989, pp. 291–2).

economically provided, and also act as an administrative agency for the economic and social policy of the country. However, these 'government services' are *not* normally *sold* to the people, and hence, three questions arise here. *First*, what kind of use is made of these services—final use or intermediate use? *Second*, who are supposed to be the users or implicit buyers of these services? And, *third*, how is the 'output' of these services to be estimated?

The first problem gives rise to an important conceptual issue, viz., whether the services of police, army, etc. are to be regarded as satisfying consumers' wants or facilitating the production of other goods and services. The measure of National Income would be different, depending on which approach is taken. The former views public services as an additional part of the National Product (i.e. final-use goods) while the latter holds that additional labours, viz., labours of government servants are needed to produce the same net output of useful goods. It is, however, impossible to say how much of the work of the public servants is directed towards protection of individuals and their assets and how much towards protection of the productive process. The convention is, therefore, to treat the entire amount of government services as consumption expenditure. But the question still remains: is this the consumption expenditure of the households? There are, however, certain difficulties in treating this as private consumption expenditure. *First*, wants satisfied by such consumption expenditure are collective wants and not individual wants and people do not generally buy these services. *Second*, there is hardly any correspondence between the amount of taxes paid by an individual (which partly finances such expenditure) and the advantage which he or she gets out of such consumption—a correspondence which definitely exists in the case of an individual's purchase of goods and services from the market. In view of these difficulties, the value of such production, to the extent that it is not sold outright, is treated as government's own final consumption.

So far as the estimation problem is concerned, the present case is different from that of other types of non-market output produced elsewhere in the economy (e.g. the housing services, foodstuffs held back by the farmers for their home consumption, etc.). Unlike in the latter cases, there are usuallly no suitable markets whose prices can be used to value the non-market services of the government under discussion. By convention, therefore, such services are valued by the sum of the costs of real resources used in their production—costs like intermediate consumption, wages, salaries, etc., paid to employees (or what is called in national accounts, 'compensation of employees'), and so on. The net operating surplus in the production of non-market goods and services by government administrative departments is naturally taken to be zero[11]. (C.E.C. *et al.*, 1993, pp. 102, 134).

At this stage it may be interesting to examine how such public consumption is estimated in India. Here government administrative departments comprise various offices of central and state governments and local bodies, i.e. those state organs which deal with not only general administrative services, like police, jails, defence services, etc. but other services as well, e.g. social and community services like education, medical and housing, etc. All such organs are called *producers of government services* (for detailed description, see CSO, GOI, 1989; pp. 152–3, 291–3). Table 1.3 shows the relevant estimates for the Indian economy for 1994–5.

The LHS shows how the value of such services (i.e. output) is obtained by adding the total cost of resources used in their production. The RHS shows how government final consumption is estimated, by subtracting from output, the small part which is sold outside.

TABLE 1.3

Production Account of Producers of Government Services in India (at current prices): 1994–5

(Rs crore)

Value of Input		Value of Output	
1. Intermediate consumption	36273	5. Governmental final consumption expenditure	100498
2. Compensation of employees	62739	6. Sale of goods and services	5200
3. Consumption of fixed capital	6686		
4. Gross Input	105698	7. Gross Output	105698

3.3 ECONOMIC ACTIVITIES OF THE GOVERNMENT AND NATIONAL PRODUCTION ACCOUNT

Let us go back to the basic identity (11) and see how it looks when we

[11]It may be mentioned that the production of NPISH is estimated in a similar way via the cost of production.

incorporate the economic activities of the government. Since public enterprises sell their products on commercial basis, the expression (9) for value added is also valid for them and any such public enterprise may be considered as one of the *n* producing units over which aggregation has been carried out in (10). For government administration, however, many of the items on the RHS of (9) would be either small or absent. The one exception is the term c_j which will include mainly[12] government final consumption expenditure.

How would the relation (11), particularly its RHS, have to be rewritten, if we consider public and private sectors separately? Aggregate final consumption would now consist of two parts—private final consumption (say, C_p) and government final consumption (say, C_g). Similarly, each term on the RHS may be disaggregated into two parts correspondig to the two sectors—private and public. Unfortunately, lack of requisite information does not allow us to carry out such disaggregation in respect of a few items in India, viz., exports, imports and net indirect taxes.

The consolidated production account of India (i.e. the empirical counterpart of the relation (11)) for 1994–5 is presented in Table 1.4, along with the division of some of the items between private and public sectors. Let us briefly explain this table. *First*, figures are given at current prices, i.e. prices prevailing during the year in question. *Second*, data on the various final expenditure flows are (usually available) at market prices. Hence, GDP on the LHS has also to be expressed at market prices. Relations (2) and (5) in Table 1.2 show how GDP at market prices may be obtained from NDP at factor cost. Exactly those computations are made on the LHS of Table 1.4. *Third*, the distribution of domestic income between the domestic sector and the rest of the world is shown in item 1. Foreigners were paid Rs 16191 crore as factor income for their participation in domestic production. Out of the factor income accruing to the domestic sector, the public sector received Rs 18671 crore in the form of property income of government departments and profits of government enterprises. *Finally*, the term 'discrepancy' is to be explained. Estimates of GDP and final expenditure flows are obtained independently in India and hence the two sides need not balance. The former is taken as the controlling total, and hence, the discrepancy term.

[12]Some private consumption expenditure may be included in c_j, as a part of the sale to the private sector (by government administration) may be used by the latter for final consumption.

3.4 Factor Income

We have seen that the net value added by a unit of production equals the sum of factor incomes generated in its process of production. The categories under which factor incomes are normally measured are: (i) compensation of employees (like wages, salaries, etc.), (ii) rent (a kind of property income defined as the actual/imputed income obtained from the letting or use of physical assets like land, buildings and other fixed capital goods), (iii) interest (another kind of property income obtained from holding of financial assets, like deposits with banks, bonds or other loans), and (iv) profits and dividends (entrepreneurial income). However, in the case of unincorporated enterprises and persons working on their own account, an entrepreneur owner works as a manager as well as a labourer, but his income cannot be apportioned into employment income and other forms of income, i.e. operating surplus (OS). Such income in India is, therefore, separately classified as 'mixed income of the self-employed' (MIS).

TABLE 1.4

National Account of India: Domestic Product Account (at current prices): 1994–5

(Rs crore)

Income				Expenditure			
1	NDP at factor cost		772680	5	Final consumption		
	of which the amount				expenditure		670915
	accuring to the				(a) private	100498	
1.1	Domestic sector	756489			(b) public	570417	
	(a) private	737818		6	Gross fixed capital		
	(b) public	18671			formation		216407
1.2	Rest of the world	16191			(a) private	129199	
2	Consumption of fixed capital		95339		(b) public	87208	
	(a) private	28445		7	Change in stocks		24972
	(b) public	23750			(a) private	11413	
3	Net indirect taxes		95473		(b) public	1974	
	(i) indirect taxes	121067		8	Exports of goods and		
	(ii) (less) subsidies	(–) 25594			services		101607
				9	(less) imports of goods		
					and services		(–) 104710
				10	Discrepancy		54301
4	GDP at market prices		963492	11	Expenditure on GDP		963492

However, India's data on factor incomes are available in two categories only—compensation of employees (CE) and a category combining OS/MIS. Such data at current prices are given in Table 1.5 for three years:

TABLE 1.5
Share of CE and OS/MIS in NDP at Factor Cost

Year	NDP at factor cost (Rs crore)	Percentage share (in NDP at factor cost) of	
		CE	OS/MIS
1980–81	110340	36.8	63.2
1990–91	425619	38.4	61.6
1994–95	772680	35.8	64.2

4. OTHER NATIONAL ACCOUNTS

We now consider flows across the boundaries of each of the remaining economic activities (Figure 1. 1) and obtain the corresponding national account. These accounts are described and illustrated with the Indian data for 1994–95 in Table 1.6. To economize space the accounts are presented in the form of relations (i.e. identities) where the RHS and the LHS of each relation show respectively the different sources of receipt and expenditure for the activity in question. We have used symbols to denote various flows during the year. Among these, the notations used to denote net current transfers, net capital transfers and net loans are respectively CT, KT and L. These three are used with two subscripts, *i* and *j*, which means the amount of net transfers/loans received by the *i*th sector from the *j*th sector.

4.1 INCOME AND EXPENDITURE ACCOUNT

The national consumption (i.e. income and expenditure) account, i.e. the consolidation of consumption accounts of all the *nationals* of the country is obtained by considering flows over the boundaries of consumption. This particular account (no. 1, Table 1.6) shows wherefrom the nationals get their income and how they dispose of it. The major source of income is, of course, *factor income* which the resident sectors receive during the period for their participation, in *domestic production* (FIDP, a flow from the production account) and, in production *abroad*

(FIA, a flow from the RW account). It may be noted that 'national income' equals the sum of FIDP and FIA, i.e. Rs 759,597 crore.

A second source of income is not factor income, but income received from the RW in the form of private remittances and grants from foreign governments, i.e. *current transfers* received by the nationals from the RW (CT_{dw}) which are shown *net*, that is, after deduction of all similar remittances and grants made by the nationals to the RW. The *last* item is a flow from the production account, viz., net indirect taxes (NIT) which is included so as to get the total at market prices. The total income received by the nationals—both factor income as well as transfers—is the *national disposable income* at market prices (Y).

The LHS of the income and expenditure account shows how a country disposes of its income. Most of it is spent on buying goods and services (flows to the production account) for the purpose of final consumption by the private sector (C_p) and by the government (C_g). The *second* item of consumers' outlay is *domestic saving* (S) whch is the excess of income over *current* expenditure, i.e. expenditure on goods and services for final consumption and transfer payments. The *last* item is statistical discrepancy (error) which, as we have explained earlier, should not have been there, if all the figures obtained independently were correctly estimated.

Can we construct separate income and expenditure accounts for the private and public sector? CSO publishes no such account for the private sector and presents this account for the public sector at some level of disaggregation. However, on the basis of the data on various aggregates published by CSO, we try to construct (with some approximation) such an account for each of the two sectors [nos. $(1)_p$ and $(1)_g$, Table 1.6].

Consider, first, the income and expenditure account for the private sector. The major part of factor income which the private sector receives is from domestic production $(FIDP)_p$—a flow from the production account, but a small part comes from participation in foreign production (FIA)—a flow from the RW account. Apart from these factor earnings, the private sector receives other kinds of income also—income received not in return for factor services provided, but as transfers—called *current transfers*. These are received from the government (like unemployment allowances, state scholarships, old age pensions, etc.: CT_{pg}) as well as from the RW (CT_{pw}). Another kind of income received from the government by the private sector is *interest on public debt* (INTPD). Government borrows from the public by

TABLE 1.6

National Account of India (at current prices): 1994–5

(Rs crore)

1 National Income and Expenditure (*IE*) Account: National disposable income at market prices (*Y*) and its appropriation

C_g	+	C_p	+	S	+	Error	=	FIDP	+	FIA	+	CT_{dw}	+	NIT		[= Y]
(100,498)		(570,417)		(151,748)		(51,230)		(756,489)		(3108)		(18,823)		(95,473)		(873,893)

$(1)_p$ Private IE Account: private income (Y_p) and its appropriation

C_p	+	DT	+	S_p	+	Error	=	$(FIDP)_p$	+	FIA	+	CT_{pg}	+	CT_{pw}	+	INTPD	[= Y_p]
(570,417)		(38,286)		(176,206)		(49,548)		(737,878)		(3108)		(29,425)		(18,823)		(45,283)	(83,445)

$(1)_g$ Government IE Account: government income (Y_g) and its appropriation

C_g	+	INTPD	+	CT_{pg}	+	S_g	+	Error	=	$(FIDP)_g$	+	DT	+	NIT		[= Y_g]
(100,498)		(45,283)		(29,425)		(–24,458)		(1682)		(18,671)		(38,286)		(95,473)		(152,430)

2 National Savings and Investment (*SI*) Account: Gross accumulation (*GAC*) and its appropriation

{GDFI	+	Δ INV	+	Error }	+	L_{wd}	=	S	+	CFC	+	KT_{dw}		[= GAC]
(216,407)		(24,972)		(17,599)		(–10,582)		(151,748)		(95,339)		(1309)		(248,396)

3 National External Transactions Account: Current and capital transactions

Current:	EX	+	FIA	+	CT_{dw}	=	{ IM	+	FIPA	+	Error }	+	CAS		[= Total]
	(101,607)		(3108)		(18,823)		(104,710)		(16,191)		(14,528)		(–11,891)		(123,538)
Capital:	CAS	+	KT_{dw}	=	L_{wd}		[= Total]								
	(–11,891)		(1309)		(–10,582)		(–10,582)								

issuing various government securities and pays interest on such public debt[13].

Coming now to the disposal of the private income [the LHS of the account $(1)_p$], a part is paid to the government as direct taxes[14]. It may be noted that direct taxes (DT) are to be paid out of income, independently of consumption or other kind of expenditure, and hence, are a charge against income of the private sector[15]. Whatever remains after making direct tax payment is the disposable income of the private sector which is partly spent as private final consumption expenditure at market prices (C_p) and partly saved (S_p). We have an extra item, viz. statistical discrepancy (error) which, as explained earlier, should not have been there, were all the figures correctly estimated.

Personal Disposable Income

We may now turn to estimation of *personal income*, i.e. income which accrues to the households (see footnote 4 for the definition of household sector). The (factor) income of the public sector $(FIDP)_g$ includes (i) income from entrepreneurship and property accruing to the government administrative departments (GAD), inclusive of savings of railways and communication and (ii) savings of non-departmental enterprises. The (factor) income of the private sector comes partly from abroad (FIA), but mainly from domestic production $(FIDP)_p$. A part of the income accruing to the private sector is, however, not paid to the households in the form of profits, dividends, etc., but is kept within the corporate sector as undistributed profits or what is also known as *savings of the private corporate sector*. Another part is paid to the

[13]Note that neither transfer payment nor INTPD is included in National Income. Transfer payments are not included because no current services are being provided against them. INTPD is not included because no capital goods are acquired by means of such public debt which could earn profit and the latter may, in turn, be used to pay for INTPD (as in the case with the debts of firms). Nor is INTPD to be treated as transfer payment, because unlike the latter, public debt may be sold to another person who will, in turn, be the recipient of the interest on such debt.

[14]Direct taxes are land revenues, income taxes on personal incomes, corporation tax (i.e. direct taxes on companies, which are levied on profits, capital or net worth of companies). Some miscellaneous receipts by the government (like fees, fines, etc.) are also included here in direct taxes.

[15]In contrast, indirect taxes are paid at the time of making expenditure, e.g. when incomes are spent on goods and services for consumption. Note that private final consumption expenditure is at market prices, and hence, includes that part of (net) indirect taxes which fall on such consumption expenditure.

government in the form of *corporation tax*. Thus *personal income*, which is the current income receipt of all persons from all sources, differs from *private income* by the sum of savings of the private corporate sector and corporation tax. *Personal disposable income* is then obtained from personal income by deducting direct taxes paid by households. In India the private sector also makes certain miscellaneous payments to GAD like fees, fines, etc. Data on such payments by the corporate sector and the household sector are not available separately, and hence, the amount paid by the entire private sector is deducted. Personal disposable income is, therefore, underestimated to this extent. The computation as well as estimates of personal disposable income for selected years are shown in Table 1.7 below.

TABLE 1.7

Relationship Among Macro Aggregates and Estimation of Personal Disposable Income of the Indian Economy at current prices for selected years

(Rs crore)

Aggregate	1980–1	1990–1	1994–5
1. GDP at market prices	136,013	535,534	963,492
2. *Net* indirect taxes (NIT)	13,586	57,720	95,473
3. GDP at factor cost (1–2)	122,427	477,814	868,019
4. Consumption of fixed capital (CFC)	12,087	52,195	95,339
5. NDP at factor cost (NDP_{fc}) (3–4)	110,340	425,619	772,680
6. *Net* factor income from abroad	345	–7545	–13,083
7. National Income (5 + 6)	110,685	418,074	759,597
8. National Income accruing to the			
(a) public sector	–266	7139	18,671
(b) private sector (7–8a)	110,951	410,935	740,926
9. Current transfers from government (CT_{pg})	2835	15,641	29,425
10. Interest on public debt (INTPD)	1524	20,233	45,283
11. Current transfers from the RW, net (CT_{pw})	2257	3711	18,823
12. Private income (8b + 9 + 10 + 11)	117,567	450,520	834,457
13. Saving of private corporate sector	584	6198	13,388
14. Corporation tax	1378	5335	13,822
15. Personal income (12 – 13 – 14)	115,605	439,987	807,247
16. Direct taxes paid by households	2197	7593	16,384
17. Miscellaneous receipts of GAD	303	2097	8080
18. Personal disposable income (15 – 16 – 17)	113,105	429,297	782,783

4.2 Savings and Investment Account

Let us now consider the flows across the accumulation boundary. The corresponding account may be called the *savings and investment* (SI) account. (In the Indian National Accounts Statistics it is called the 'capital finance account'.) This account consolidated over all the entities of the economy for the year 1994–5 is shown in account (2) of Table 1.6.

The LHS shows the different forms in which the gross accumulation of the country takes place. The most imporatant form is, of course, its gross physical investment (GI), i.e. all relevant items of (i) new capital goods produced domestically (exclusive of exports) and (ii) new and second-hand imported capital goods. Further, imports (exports) of such capital goods should include net outlays on fixed assets in foreign countries by the domestic government organizations (in the domestic country by the diplomatic bodies of the RW). However, such imports and exports cannot be estimated due to want of data. So, we have only estimates of *gross domestic investment*, i.e. additions to fixed assets and inventories made within the geographical boundary of the domestic economy, rather than gross investment (made by the nationals) of the country. GI is thus the sum of gross domestic fixed investment (GDFI) and change in inventories (Δ INV)—both being flows from the production account—and an 'Error' term (to be explained shortly). A second form of accumulation is the purchase of *intangible assets*[16] (like exclusive rights to exploit natural resources, leases, patents, copyrights, trade marks, etc.) from the RW. However, India's net purchase of such assets from the RW (that is, after subtracting sales of such assets to the RW) are nil or negligible, and hence, no figure is shown against this item. We have, therefore, dropped this item. The last item is *lending to the RW*, shown net, that is, after subtracting India's borrowing from the RW. Lending to the RW means net acquisition of foregin financial assets (i.e. acquisition of these assets net of disposition of similar assets) during the period. Similarly, borrowing from the RW means net incurrence (i.e. incurrence net of redemption) of foreign financial liabilities. The items which are included in such financial assets are monetary gold, currency, deposits, bills, bonds, equities, loans, trade credits,

[16]It may be pointed out that periodic income by way of royalties, fees, etc. from such assets is included under property income (i.e. a kind of factor income) from abroad; only the outright purchases/sales of such assets are included in the item, 'net purchase of intangible assets' (CSO, GOI, 1989, p. 331).

advances, etc. Interestingly, net lending to the RW by the domestic economy (L_{wd}) was negative in 1994–5 (and also in all other years). This means that we were a net borrower.

The RHS of account (2) shows how the gross accumulation of the country is financed. There are three such sources: (i) saving (S)—a flow from the IE account; (ii) consumption of fixed capital (CFC)—a flow from the production account; and (iii) net capital transfers received by the domestic economy from the RW (KT_{dw})—a flow from the RW account (no. 3, capital transactions, Table 1.6).

If we subtract CFC from GI (Rs 258,978 crore), we get net *domestic investment* (Rs 163,639 crore), which gives the net addition to the tangible wealth at home. On the other hand, *net foreign investment* (– Rs. 10,582 crore) gives India's net increase in claims against other countries (the figure being negative shows, in effect, net increase in claims of the RW on India). If we add these two types of investment, we get increase in India's total wealth, i.e. wealth at home and abroad.

The increase in India's total wealth was less than the additional wealth accumulated at home, as India was a net borrower. Further, *net capital flow from abroad*—the sum of net capital transfers (K_{dw}) and net borrowing from the RW ($-L_{wd}$)—is estimated to be Rs 11,891 crore.

The 'error' term may now be explained. India's GI is estimated from the sources side, which indicates types of resources (like domestic saving (S), CFC, etc.) which are available to finance investment. Such resource flows are estimated independently. Thus:

$$GI = S + CFC + \text{net capital flow from the RW (i.e. } KT_{dw} - L_{wd}) \quad (12)$$

$$= \text{Rs } 258{,}978 \text{ crore}$$

This estimate, however, exceeds the sum of GDFI and Δ INV by an amount of Rs 17,599 crore which is, therefore, the magnitude of 'error'.

4.3 External Transactions Account of the Domestic Country

Earlier we have discussed the three accounts for the nation as a whole. Let us now carry out a simple exercise. Let us consolidate the three accounts, i.e. put together *all incomings* on each of the three accounts on one side and *all outgoings* on the other side. Many items are identical on the two sides. These are transactions made between entities reckoned as internal to the economy. The identical items on both sides may be cancelled. After such a process of cancellation, we should have nothing left, if the economy were a closed one. But in an open economy we are left with a relation or account depicting all our foreign transactions, i.e. *transactions with the RW*. This account must balance, because it has been constructed from accounts which were already balanced, merely by a process of cancellation. It is this account which is the balance of payments.

To sum up, the accounts presented earlier contain some entries which depict flows across the boundary of the domestic country, i.e. incomings from or outgoings to the RW. When we bring together all these items in a single account, what we get is a condensed statement of the transactions of the RW vis-a-vis the domestic country, i.e. the balance of payments of the latter. This is actually the account of the RW vis-a-vis India. This account may, however, be presented from the point of view of the domestic country so as to get her *external transactions account*. That is how it is presented in Table 1.6 (account 3) where the current and capital transactions are shown separately. Interestingly, the current account surplus (CAS) is a large negative quantity. This means that we had a large deficit on current account which was met partly by net capital transfers (KT_{dw}), but mainly by borrowing from the RW ($-L_{wd}$). Further, while the balance of payments statement should balance, this has been achieved only with a large error term[17].

5. 'REAL' GROSS DOMESTIC PRODUCT

We have seen that gross domestic product (GDP) of a country can be regarded as the value of quantitites of goods and services produced for final use during a year. However, quantities of various items are measured in different physical units and hence, they can be added only if they are expressed in money values. In this sense, GDP is a collection of quantities of items produced domestically, multiplied by their respective current prices. Using symbols we can represent it, in year t, by $\Sigma_i P_i^t Q_i^t$ and, in year 0, by $\Sigma_i P_i^0 Q_i^0$, where P_i^r and Q_i^r are respectively the price and quantity of the i-th item produced in year r ($r = 0, t$). For instance, GDP at factor cost at current prices (i.e. at prices prevailing

[17]Such statistical adjustment was unavoidable because of the difference between the figures of merchandise exports/imports obtained from the two different sources, viz. Reserve Bank of India and Directorate General of Commercial Intelligence and Statistics.

during the year in question) was Rs 122,427 crore in 1980–81. It had increased to Rs 477,814 crore in 1990–1. In ten years then, it had increased in *value* by 290 per cent. However, the aggregate production of goods and services had obviously not increased by this percentage, as a part of this rise reflects only a rise in prices, i.e. the fact that the prices of goods and services were much higher in 1990–1 than in 1980–81. The question is: to what extent does this rise in the *value* of GDP reflect a rise in quantities of production, or what is popularly called real GDP, over this period?

The problem may be formally posed as follows. The aggregate value of production changes from a total $\Sigma_i P_i^0 Q_i^0$ in year O to a total $\Sigma_i P_i^t Q_i^t$ in year *t*. We like to decompose this change into two parts—one part representing the change in prices and the other part, the change in quantities. This is a typical index number problem and discussed in all text books on descriptive statistics. It is also known that no perfectly satisfactory method of separation exists[18]. So, people adopt the best possible solution under the given circumstances.

The procedure which is commonly used to estimate change in 'real' GDP is to value the quantities of goods and services in each year at some *constant prices*, say at the prices of a particular year (usually called the base year)[19]. This essentially means that each year quantities of different items are added by using relative prices, or a table of equivalences among them, as obtained in the base year. Thus, if in the base year the price of one metre of cloth is Rs 50 and the price of one kilogram of wheat is Rs 10, then these prices imply the following equivalence between them: 1 metre of cloth = 5 kilograms of wheat. In estimating real GDP of a year, quantities of different items in that year are added by using such a table of equivalences between items. Thus, although real GDP is a quantity measure, it measures quantity, not in the physical sense, but rather in the economic sense of 'real value'. For

[18]It may be noted that the problem of decomposing the value change into price change and quantity change does not arise, if between the two years being compared, the prices of all goods change in the same direction and same proportion (i.e. $P_i^t = \lambda P_i^0$ for all *i*, λ being a constant), or all quantities increase or decrease in the same proportion (i.e. $Q_i^t = \alpha Q_i^0$ for all *i*, α being a constant). The problem arises because some quantities and some prices rise, some quantities and some other prices fall, some quantities/prices rise in different proportions and so on.

[19]See Karmel and Polasek (1977, Ch. 12) for a brilliant discussion on procedures for estimating 'real' GDP.

example, if two varieties of almirahs are produced, an increase in the proportion of costlier variety, total number remaining constant, implies an increase in 'real' production in the economic sense.

One more question regarding real GDP remains. We have seen in Section 3.1 that either the sum of *values added* by all producing units or the sum of all *final expenditures* on domestically produced goods and services will yield GDP of a year computed at current prices, i.e. the value of GDP with quantities being evaluated at prices prevailing during the year in question. Does this equivalence hold good for real GDP as well? In other words, does the sum of values added (at constant prices) by all producing units during a year equal the sum of final expenditures (computed once again at the same set of prices) during that year? The answer is 'yes' and we show the result below.

Let us use the following notations. Capital letters will denote *quantities* of various goods in the *current* year, except P_i^0 which will denote the price of the *i*-th good in the (base) year 0.

Q_i^j = quantity of the *i*-th good produced by the *j*-th unit;

ΔS_i = change in the quantity of stock of the *i*-th good over the year;

IM_i, C_i, I_i, EX_i = quantity of the *i*-th good imported, used for the purpose of final consumption, fixed investment and export, respectively;

UM_{ir}^j = quantity of the *i*-th good used as intermediate good (raw material/service) by the *j*-th unit to produce the *r*-th good $(i, r = 1, \ldots, m; j = 1, \ldots, n)$.

With these notations we may now write

$$\sum_j Q_i^j = C_i + I_i + \Delta S_i + EX_i - IM_i + \sum_r \sum_j UM_{ir}^j \qquad (13)$$

where the RHS gives the different uses of the *i*-th good during the year. Thus we have,

GDP at constant prices (i.e. at prices of period 0)

$$= \Sigma_j (\Sigma_i P_i^0 Q_i^j - \Sigma_i \Sigma_r P_r^0 UM_{ri}^j)$$

$$= \Sigma_i P_i^0 \Sigma_j Q_i^j - \Sigma_j \Sigma_i \Sigma_r P_r^0 UM_{ri}^j$$

$$= \Sigma_i P_i^0 C_i + \Sigma_i P_i^0 I_i + \Sigma_i P_i^0 \Delta S_i + \Sigma_i P_i^0 EX_i - \Sigma_i P_i^0 IM_i$$

$$+ (\Sigma_i P_i^0 \Sigma_r \Sigma_j UM_{ir}^j - \Sigma_j \Sigma_i \Sigma_r P_r^0 UM_{ri}^j), \qquad \text{[using (13)]} \qquad (14)$$

where the expression within parentheses in the first line is the value added (during the current year) by the j-th unit at constant prices and that in the last line vanishes, as both the terms are identical. The meaning of the other terms is obvious. (For instance, $\Sigma_i P_i^0 C_i$ is the aggregate final consumption expenditure at constant prices, i.e. the *real* final consumption expenditure).

Thus, real gross domestic product equals the sum of different categories of final expenditure, when each is computed at constant prices. We illustrate this identity for the Indian data for selected years in Table 1.8. All figures are computed at 1980–81 prices. From this table we also find that during the 1980's, although nominal GDP (at factor cost) went up by as much as 290 per cent, 'real' GDP increased from Rs 122,427 crore to Rs 212,253 crore, i.e. by only 73 per cent, and that over a period of 35 years (i.e. from 1960–61 to 1994–95) per capita *Real* National Income had just doubled[20].

6. INTERSECTORAL FINANCIAL FLOWS AND CONCLUDING OBSERVATIONS

A number of interesting topics may easily be included in a course on National Income Accounting. Take, for instance, a topic like distribution of National Income among the different socio-economic groups; this topic is extremely important for a developing country. Another relevant topic is the comparison of National Income across countries. This is a much more difficult problem to deal with, compared to the comparison of National Income of a given country over different time periods. Extensive literature exists in both areas. We shall, however, turn to a different point in the concluding section.

6.1 Some Macro Relations

We shall show, first, how some of the useful macro identities follow from the various accounts presented in the preceding section. For this purpose, we shall disregard the item 'Error' term included in the various

[20]One serious limitation of the approach may be mentioned, namely, that there is no unique measure of real GDP. Real GDP is measured in terms of a set of constant prices and its movement over time depends on the set used. Thus, GDP for the years 1960–61 to 1994–95, valued at constant 1980–81 prices, may move very differently from the same GDP valued at constant 1990–91 prices, since the table of equivalences used will be different. There is no reason to prefer one set of constant prices to the other, so that if the results are very divergent, their interpretation becomes difficult, if not impossible.

accounts, recalling that such an item was needed therein just to take care of errors and omissions in measuring the various aggregates on the two sides of an account.

TABLE 1.8

Macroeconomic Aggregates of India at 1980–1 prices for selected years

(Rs crore)

Aggregate	1960–1	1970–1	1980–1	1990–1	1994–5
1. NDP at factor cost	58,974	83,172	110,340	190,218	228,964
2. Consumption of fixed capital	3930	7254	112,087	22,035	28,736
3. GDP at factor cost (1–2)	62,904	90,426	212,427	212,253	257,700
4. Net indirect taxes	5159	10,936	13,586	27,985	30,937
5. GDP at market prices (3 + 4 or 6 + 7 + 8 + 9)	68,063	101,362	136,013	240,238	288,637
6. Final consumption expenditure*	55,338	80,014	112,376	181,513	211,419
(a) Private*	51765	71,522	99,292	155,454	182,385
(b) Public	3573	8492	13,084	26,059	29,034
7. Gross fixed capital formation	10,555	16,673	26,276	51,091	63,817
8. Changes in stocks	1982	2788	2177	5794	8629
9. Exports less Imports plus Statistical discrepancy†	188	1887	–4816	1840	4772
10. Gross domestic capital formation	12,348	18,928	30,880	62,267	77,636
11. Net factor income from abroad	–378	–961	345	–3772	–5384
12. National Income (1 + 11)	58,602	82,211	110,685	186,446	223,580
13. Population (million)‡	434	541	679	839	904
14. Per capita National Income (Rs)	1350	1520	1630	2222	2734

*Figures relate to private final consumption expenditure in the domestic market only.

†Separate data on the individual items in this total are not available.

‡Relates to mid-financial year.

Consider first the relation (11) of Section 3, or its empirical counterpart given in the domestic production account of Table 1.3. One point needs to be clarified at the outset. The relation (11) is an identity implying that the *actual* level of output (GDP) is identically equal to the *actual* aggregate expenditure on domestically produced goods and services. The *actual* expenditure may be different from the planned or desired aggregate expenditure, i.e. the amount of goods and services which people *want to buy*. In particular, Δ INV in national accounts includes *unintended* or *undesired* inventory changes which occur when firms sell larger or smaller amount of goods than they had planned to sell.

Let us subtract consumption of fixed capital from both sides of Table 1.3, and combine fixed capital formation with change in stocks. We shall then have net physical investment of the private and the government sector (to be denoted by I_p and I_g, respectively) on the RHS of this table. Noting that NDP at factor cost is paid partly to the domestic private sector $(FIDP)_p$, partly to the government sector $(FIDP)_g$ and partly to the RW (FIPA), we may write from Table 1.4:

$$(FIDP)_p + (FIDP)_g + FIPA + NIT = C_p + C_g + I_p + I_g + EX - IM \quad (15)$$

Let us now consolidate accounts $(1)_p$ and $(1)_g$ of Table 1.6, so as to get

$$\begin{aligned} S_p + S_g &= (FIDP)_p + (FIDP)_g + FIA + CT_{pw} + NIT - C_p - C_g \quad (16) \\ &= I_p + I_g + (EX - IM + FIA - FIPA + CT_{pw}), \quad \text{by (15)} \end{aligned}$$

The above may be written as,

$$S_p - I_p + S_g - I_g = CAS, \quad (17)$$

where CAS is the current account surplus in the external transactions of the country (negative in our case). This is an important identity, often discussed in the textbooks ignoring some of the constituent items of the various aggregates[21]. The LHS is the aggregate savings-investment gap, shown as the sum of such gaps at the sectoral levels.

Some further analysis of the foregoing identities may be quite interesting. For instance, one may be interested to learn how a change

[21]For instance, Dornbusch and Fischer (1994, pp. 45–58) do not consider $(FIDP)_g$ and I_g and hence government dissaving $(-S_g)$ in their system is what may be called *budget deficit* of the government (BDG). In this case (17) may be rewritten as:

$$S_p - I_p = BDG + CAS.$$

See also Dornbusch (1980, pp. 22–4).

in some item in a relation might affect various aggregates in other relations or what are the possible ways in which rest of the items in a relation might adjust when one item changes. Since such discussions are usually included in text books, we turn to another interesting topic, viz., intersectoral financial flows in the economy.

6.2 Intersectoral Financial Flows

Neither CSO nor any other organization publishes flow-of-funds (FoF) tables. We shall, therefore, give a brief introduction to FoF accounts (capital financing), and try to illustrate these with the Indian data. These accounts show how the different sectors of the economy have obtained funds from various sources and used those funds to invest in physical as well as financial assets during a given period. Such accounts can be used to analyse changes in the financial assets and liabilities of each sector.

To understand properly what such FoF accounts try to depict, let us begin with the national savings-investment account (no. 2, Table 1.6). Recall that gross (physical) investment (GI) is the sum of GDFI, ΔINV and 'error' term. Subtracting CFC from both sides, this relation may be rewritten as:

$$\text{Net investment (I)} - \text{Saving (S)} - KT_{dw} = L_{dw} \qquad (18)$$

(Rs 163,639 crore) (Rs 151,748 crore) (Rs 1309 crore) (Rs 10,582 crore)

In 1994–5 net (physical) investment (I) of Rs 163,639 crore was financed mostly by S (92.7 per cent) while net capital transfers (KT_{dw}) and net loans received from the RW (L_{dw}) together financed only 7.3 per cent[22]. What the FoF accounts try to do is to depict this savings-investment imbalance at the sectoral level, i.e. present a disaggregation of the identity (18) into similar identities for the different sectors.

Thus, the primary objective of the FoF accounts is to present intersectoral financial flows, i.e. to show how surplus saving of a sector gets channelised to deficit sectors. There are units which are *net lenders* i.e. whose saving (including net capital transfers received from others) far exceeds their physical investments. Household sector is one such sector and so is the RW. On the other extreme lies the government administrative sector whose own saving is negative, i.e. which has to

[22]It is interesting to note that from the relation (18) one immediately learns that the sum of KT_{dw} and L_{dw} (i.e. Rs 11,891 crore) is the amount of saving of the RW (S_w) in excess of its net physical investment (I_w).

borrow from these even to meet its current expenditure (e.g. consumption expenditure). In between these two extremes stands the private corporate sector which is also a deficit sector, since its own saving (i.e. undistributed profit) is positive, but not sufficient to finance its physical investment.

The interesting question is: how do the savings of the surplus units flow to the deficit units? The answer is: either directly or through various banks and organizations engaged in financial intermediation. Such financial organizations mediate between ultimate lenders and ultimate borrowers, i.e. collect savings of surplus units in order to lend them on to deficit spenders. Both the surplus and deficit units belong to the 'real' sector and are engaged in buying, selling or producing productive factors and outputs. The principal economic activity of units engaged in financial intermediation is the purchase and sale of financial assets.

Financial assets are grouped under two broad heads. One is 'primary' (or direct) securities which are issued by real sector units as ultimate borrowers for raising funds (examples are: bills, bonds, equities, etc.). The other is 'secondary' (or indirect) securities which are issued by units doing financial intermediation in order to raise funds from the people (examples are: bank deposits, LIC policies, UTI units, IDBI bonds, etc.).

Primary securities are bought by both surplus real sector units and such financial organizations. When surplus units buy primary securities they are said to provide 'direct finance' to ultimate borrowers. However, this is only a small part of their total lending in a modern economy with developed money and credit markets. A large and growing part of the savings of individual units are now lent to the ultimate borrowers indirectly, i.e. are invested in secondary securities which are issued by units performing financial intermediation who, in turn, lend these funds to the deficit units[23]. Thus, these units are dealers in securities. They alone are able to produce securities (i.e. secondary securities) which are far more acceptable to surplus sectors than the primary securities issued by deficit sectors. They buy primary securities and sell secondary securities to finance them. In fact, the essence and the success of financial intermediation lies in this transformation of primary securities into secondary securities.

[23]See Gupta (1996) for a detailed discussion on financial intermediaries and financial markets.

Broadly, three types of organizations are engaged in financial intermediation[24]: banks, (non-bank) *financial institutions* (FINS) and (non-bank) *financial intermediaries* (FINT). In the field of non-bank financial intermediation, we have, on the one hand, FINS which are set up with funds from the government and banks, and specialize in providing medium and long-term loans to entrepreneurs. (Examples are various *development banks* like IDBI, IFCI, ICICI, SIDBI[25]). On the other hand, FINT attract household savings, finance ultimate users of funds and are often required to hold part of their assets in government securities. (Examples are various insurance companies, like LIC, GIC, mutual funds and pension funds, UTI, etc.) A large number of FINS and FINT are government undertakings.

In the monetary sector we have the central bank, i.e. Reserve Bank of India (RBI) and commercial and cooperative banks. So far as the monetary assets are concerned, agents are classified into two groups: *issuers of money* and *users of money*. Agents belonging to the first group are: RBI (which issues high-powered money like currency), banks (which accept demand and time deposits) and Government of India (which issues small coins and one-rupee notes and coins). The *users* of money, called the *public* are: households, firms, FINS, FINT, RW (and even the local authorities)[26].

As we have noted earlier, public sector comprises three sub-sectors: government administration, departmental enterprises and non-departmental enterprises. The last one includes nationalized banks, development banks, financial intermediaries, and the banking department of RBI. So far as the structure of financial flows is concerned, it is not very useful to disaggregate the economy into private and public sectors. Instead, we shall use the following classification.

Government administration (GAD) and departmental enterprises (DEs) will be combined[27] to form sector **G**. The banking sector will be divided into two—RBI (to be denoted by **R**) and commercial and co-opera-

[24]In the following discussion we shall leave out (due to lack of data) lending institutions in the unorganized credit markets, though their quantitative importance may be quite substantial.

[25]Of late, some development banks like IDBI, ICICI have started taking deposits from the public.

[26]See *Reserve Bank of India* (1983, 1997) for detailed discussion.

[27]Note that in India neither the income-expenditure account nor the capital finance account is available separately for GAD and DE. Each such account is published by CSO in a consolidated form—consolidated over these two sectors.

tive banks (to be dentoed by **b**).[28] Households including unincorporated enterprises and private non-profit making institutions will form another group—to be denoted by **h**. The remaining domestic sectors, viz., FINS, FINT, government non-departmental nonfinancial enterprises and private corporate sector (pf) will all be combined to form sector **F**. It is, of course, very difficult to defend such a heterogeneous group, because some of them are in the real sector while some are financial units. Further, some are in the public sector and some are private. Only lack of sufficient data has forced us to form such a heterogeneous group. Finally, RW will be another sector to be denoted by **w**.

6.3 Flow-of-Funds of the Indian Economy: 1994–5

The intersectoral financial flows are shown in Table 1.9 where each symbol denotes a flow during a year and the figure[29] in parentheses below it gives its estimated value for 1994–5. Some of the notations used are explained below while others are explained as and when they appear.

L_{ij} = additional net finance (in the form of loan/share subscription, etc.) obtained by sector *i* from sector *j*;

L_i = increase in the total (net) financial liability of sector *i*;

S_i = saving of sector *i*;

KT_{ij} = net capital transfers received by sector *i* from sector *j*;

I_i = net physical investment by sector *i*;

A_i = increase in the total (net) financial assets of sector *i*;

H_i = change in the holding of high-powered money by sector *i*;

BD_i = increase in the bank deposits of sector *i*.

Let us explain the identities for various sectors in Table 1.7. The LHS of each identity shows changes in various financial assets of the sector in question and the RHS, changes in its financial liabilities to other sectors. The symbol (with corresponding figure in brackets) on

[28]NABARD will be included in sector **b**.

[29]The theoretical structure of this table depends very much on the formulation given in Rakshit (1997). The latter presents a stock version of the asset-liability structure of a closed economy. We, however, consider here flows of assets and liabilities of different sectors in an open economy. The figures given here have been obtained/estimated from various tables in CSO, GoI (1998) and RBI (1995–6).

TABLE 1.9

Capital Finance Accounts of Different Sectors of India (at current prices): 1994–5

(Rs crore)

1 Government (Administration and Departmental Enterprises) **(G)**

$$I_G - (S_G + KT_{Gw}) + KT_{FG} = L_{GR} + L_{Gb} + L_{GF} + L_{Gh} + L_{Gw} + CLG \quad [= \mathbf{L_G}]$$

(26,836) (–31,346) (1309) (7643) (2178) (16,323) (29,090) (12,955) (3581) (389) [64,516]

2 Central Bank, i.e. Reserve Bank of India **(R)**

$$L_{GR} + L_{FR} + L_{wR} + CLG - NNML_R = H_h + H_F + H_w + H_b^u \quad [= \mathbf{H_u}]$$

(2178) (148) (23,298) (389) (3321) (15,916) (2893) (429) (3454) [22,692]

3 Commercial and Co-operative Banks **(b)**

$$H_b^u + L_{Gb} + L_{Fb} + L_{wb} - NNML_b = BD_F + BD_h \quad [= \mathbf{BD}]$$

(3454) (16,323) (54,802) (0) (–3202) (53,327) (24,454) [77,781]

4 Firms, Financial Institutions and Financial Intermediaries Combined **(F)**

$$I_F - (S_F + KT_{FG} + KT_{Fw}) = L_{FR} + L_{Fb} + L_{Fh} + L_{Fw} - L_{GF} - H_F - BD_F \quad [= \mathbf{L_F}]$$

(82,878) (20,276) (7643) (0) (148) (54,802) (55,568) (29,751) (29,090) (2893) (53,327) [54,959]

5 Households **(h)**

$$L_{Gh} + H_h + BD_h + L_{Fh} = S_h + KT_{hG} - I_h \quad [= \mathbf{A_h}]$$

(12,955) (15,916) (24,454) (55,568) (162,818) (0) (53,925) [108,893]

6 Rest of the World **(w)**

$$L_{Gw} + H_w - L_{wR} - L_{wb} + L_{Fw} - KT_{Gw} - KT_{Fw} + \text{Error} = L_{dw} \quad [= \mathbf{A_w}]$$

(3581) (429) (23,298) (0) (29,751) (1309) (0) (1428) (10,582) [10,582]

the extreme right of each identity gives the total of the RHS (or the LHS) of each identity. For sector **G**, savings inclusive of net capital transfers from the RW (KT_{Gw}) were from the negative, implying that its net increase in financial liability (L_G, the sum of the terms on the RHS) far exceeded its physical investment during the year. The government borrowed from all sectors, e.g. from the RBI (L_{GR}), from the RW (L_{Gw}), etc. The term CLG will be explained later.

Coming to the banking sectors **R** and **b**, their assets may be classified into two groups—*financial assets* (FA) and *other assets* (OA). Similarly, their liabilities are partly 'monetary liabilities' (ML) and partly *non-monetary liabilities* (NML). Since (changes in total) assets and liabilities of a sector should always match, we have for each sector:

$$\text{ML} = \text{FA} + \text{OA} - \text{NML} = \text{FA} - \text{NNML} \qquad (19)$$

where NNML = net non-monetary liability of a sector = NML – OA. The 'other assets' of a sector (OA) includes its physical assets, loans and advances granted to its staff, etc. Non-monetary liabilities of the RBI include its paid-up capital, reserve fund augmented from time to time, its contributions to various national funds, etc. while those of the banks include their owned funds (i.e. paid-up capital and reserve), net inter-bank liabilities etc.[30]

We shall consider the broad definition of money, i.e. M_3, which is the sum of currency with the (non-bank) public and bank deposits held by the public (BD). To understand how M_3 is estimated, we have to understand another important aggregate, called *high-powered money or reserve money* (H) which is the monetary liability of the RBI and the government. The relation (19) for the RBI may be written as

$$\text{FA}_R - \text{NNML}_R = \text{ML}_R$$

However, the account (2) in Table 1.9 shows, on its RHS, (increase in) the monetary liability of the RBI and the government, and not simply ML_R. It may be recalled that a small part of high powered money, viz., small coins, one-rupee notes and coins held by the public, is the *currency liability of the government to the public* (CLG). We have, therefore, added this amount to the LHS of the account (2) which gives otherwise (the increase in) the various financial assets of the RBI net of NNML_R.

The *sources* of H, which are given by the LHS of account (2), show (changes in) the financial assets which the RBI acquires as a result of its transactions with other sectors in discharge of its central banking functions.

[30]See *RBI* (1998; pp. 20–2) for a detailed discussion. See also Rakshit (1993).

The RBI provides net credit to the government[31] (L_{GR}) and credit to banks (L_{bR}), to the commercial sector, i.e. the financial institutions (L_{FR}) and to the RW in the form of net acquisition of foreign exchange assets like foreign securities, gold coin and bullion, foreign currencies, etc. (L_{wR}). As we shall see in the next paragraph, L_{bR} (Rs 7918 crore in 1994–5) will be transferred to the RHS to find 'unborrowed' deposits of banks.

The increase in the various *components* of H should be shown on the RHS of the account (2). (a) One such component is the increase in *currency with the public* (Rs. 18,380 crore in 1994–5) which was held mainly by households (H_h, Rs 15,916 crore) but partly by other domestic users of money, i.e. sector F (Rs 2464 crore). (b) A second component is the increase in the *other deposits with the RBI* (Rs 858 crore), held partly by the domestic agents like quasi-government and other financial institutions (sector **F**) and partly by the RW (e.g. foreign central banks and governments, international agencies such as the IMF, etc.).[32] For want of detailed information we assume here that one half of Rs 858 crore (i.e. Rs 429 crore) was held by **F** and the other half by **w**. Thus, the total increase in the holding of H by Sector **F** (H_F) is estimated to be Rs (2464 + 429) crore, i.e. Rs 2893 crore. (c) A third component is (additional) H held by banks (H_b), i.e. the sum of cash with banks (Rs 905 crore) and bankers' deposit with RBI (Rs 10,467 crore). We, however, consider here the change in the *unborrowed reserves of banks* with the RBI (H_b^u), obtained by subtracting their loans from it from their deposits with it ($H_b^u = H_b - L_{bR}$ = Rs 3454 crore).

The account (3) for banks has, on the RHS, (the change in) the banks' monetary liability, i.e. bank deposits (BD) which is the sum of demand deposits and time deposits with banks (respectively, Rs 22,241 and Rs 55,540 crore in 1994–5). This was held partly by the households (BD_h) and partly by the other domestic sectors, viz., sector **F** (BD_F). The LHS of this account gives various types of financial assets of banks net of their non-monetary liabilities ($NNML_b$); all notations are self-explanatory.

Coming to discuss the account (4) for the sector **F**, its net investment in excess of its saving and capital transfers received (the LHS) was financed by taking additional net loans from the various sectors. The increase in net indebtedness (L_F) equalled its additional loans from the RBI (L_{FR}), banks (L_{Fb}), households (in the form of shares and bonds, L_{Fh}) and the RW (L_{Fw}) net of its additional holding of government securities (L_{GF}), currency (H_F) and bank deposits (BD_F).

[31]Credit to central government and state governments net of their deposits with the RBI.

[32]See *RBI* (1998; p. 21) for details.

As we have remarked earlier, household sector has surplus saving—saving in excess of its net investment. Account (5) shows that in 1994–5 household sector accumulated financial assets (A_h) of the order of Rs 108,893 crore which were held in the form of claims on government (L_{Gh}), currency (H_h), bank deposits (BD_h) and shares, debentures, etc. of **F** sector (L_{Fh}).

Financial assets accumulated by the RW vis-a-vis the domestic economy during the year equalled its net lending to the domestic economy (L_{dw} = Rs 10,582 crore). The LHS of the account (6) shows how such assets were acquired. Since the estimates were built up from independent sources, there is an error term to balance the two sides.

We conclude our discussion by making some observations on Table 1.9. First, consider the account for **G**. The total of either side (L_G) gives an estimate of *fiscal deficit* of the government. Further, the RHS shows how this deficit was met by taking additional loans from the various sectors during the year. *Second*, consider accounts (2) and (3) for **R** and **b**, respectively. If we consolidate these two accounts, H_b^u will cancel out and we get a consolidated account for the monetary sector as a whole. The RHS of this account will give the *total increase* in M_3 during the year (Rs 97,019 crore), being the sum of H_h, H_F, H_w and BD while the LHS will show the various sources of this increase.[33] *Third*, since we have combined firms and financial institutions and intermediaries together, we cannot show the increase in the total credit extended to the final users (viz., government and firms). Were sufficiently disaggregated data available, we would have been able to show the total as well as the sectoral distribution of the additional credit during the year. *Finally*, if we consolidate accounts for all the domestic sectors, (1) to (5), we would obtain

$$I_G + I_F + I_h \quad - \quad (S_G + S_F + S_h) \quad - \quad KT_{dw} \quad = \quad L_{dw}$$

(Rs 163,639 crore) (Rs 151,748 crore) (Rs 1309 crore) (Rs 10,582 crore)

i.e. the relation (18), as expected.[34]

[33]RBI publishes such a consolidated account for the monetary sector as a whole. See, for example, statements 38 and 39 given on pp. 65–6 of *RBI* (1995–6).

[34]Note that NNML of **R** and **b** include non-monetary liabilities/assets owed to/owned by other sectors, and hence, will cancel out on aggregation. It may be mentioned that in our estimation/discussion we have disregarded the amount of physical assets accumulated by the monetary sector which will, in any case, be very small compared to its accumulation of financial assets.

References

Central Statistical Organisation, Government of India (CSO, GOI) (1980), *National Accounts Statistics: Sources and Methods*, April, Department of Statistics, Ministry of Planning.

——— (1989), *National Accounts Statistics: Sources and Methods*, Department of Statistics, Ministry of Planning.

——— (1989), *National Accounts Statistics (New Series), 1950–51–1979–80*, Department of Statistics, Ministry of Planning.

——— (1998), *National Accounts Statistics*, Department of Statistics, Ministry of Planning and Programme Implementation.

Commission of the European Communities (C.E.C.), International Monetary Fund, Organisation for Economic Co-operation and Development, United Nations and World Bank (1993), *System of National Accounts*; prepared under the auspices of the Inter-Secretariat Working Group on National Accounts, manufactured in U.S.A.

Datta Roy Choudhury, Uma (1995), *National Income Accounting*, Delhi: Macmillan India Ltd.

Dornbusch, Rudiger (1980), *Open Economy Macroeconomics*, New York: Harper International Edition, Basic Books, Inc., Publishers.

Dornbusch, Rudiger and Stanley Fisher (1994), *Macroeconomics*, New York: McGraw-Hill, Inc. (International Edition).

Gupta, Suraj B. (1984), *Monetary Planning for India*, Delhi: Oxford University Press.

——— (1996), *Monetary Economics: Institutions, Theory and Policy*, New Delhi: S. Chand & Co. Ltd.

Hicks, J.R. (1972), *The Social Framework: An Introduction to Economics*, Delhi: Oxford University Press.

Hicks, J.R., M. Mukherjee and Syamal K. Ghosh (1984), *The Framework of the Indian Economy: An Introduction to Economics*, Delhi: Oxford University Press (first Indian edition).

Karmel, P.H. and M. Polasek (1977), *Applied Statistics for Economists*, Australia: Pitman Publishing Pvt. Ltd.

Mukherjee, M. (1969), *National Income of India: Trends and Structure*, Calcutta: Statistical Publishing Society.

Rakshit, Mihir (1993), 'Money, Credit and Monetary Policy' in Tapas Majumdar (ed.), *Nature, Man and the Indian Economy, Delhi*: Oxford University Press.

——— (1997), 'Money, Credit and Government Finance in a Developing Economy' in Amitava Bose, Mihir Rakshit and Anup Sinha (eds), *Issues in Economic Theory and Public Policy: Essays in Honour of Professor Tapas Majumdar*, Delhi: Oxford University Press.

Reserve Bank of India (RBI) (1983), *Functions and Working*, Bombay (fourth edition).

——— (1995–6), *Report on Currency and Finance*, Vol. II, Statistical Statement.

——— (1998), *Monetary Supply: Analytics and Methodology of Compilation*, Report of the Working Group, RBI, Mumbai, June.

Stone, Richard and Giovanna Croft-Murray (1959), *Social Accounting and Economic Models*, London: Bowes & Bowes.

Stone, Richard and Giovanna Stone (1972), *National Income and Expenditure*, London: The English Language Book Society and Bowes & Bowes, (ELBS edition).

United Nations (1953), *A System of National Accounts and Supporting Tables*, Studies in Methods, Series F, No. 2, Rev. 1, New York: Statistical Office of the United Nations.

United Nations (1968), *A System of National Accounts*, Studies in Methods, Series F, No. 2, Rev. 3; Department of Economic and Social Affairs, New York: Statistical Office of the United Nations.

Appendix

A NOTE ON ESTIMATES OF SELECTED MACRO AGGREGATES AND FINANCIAL FLOWS IN INDIA

INTRODUCTION

The estimation of the data on financial flows of Table 1.9 will be described later. First, we discuss briefly how GDP and some categories of final expenditure are estimated in India. These are discussed at length in CSO, GOI (1989). A good summary may also be found in Datta Roy Choudhury (1995, pp. 222–52). A brief historical account of estimation and compilation of National Income statistics in India is available in Mukherjee (1969) and Hicks *et al.* (1984, ch. 14).

We begin with a general observation. Estimation of value of production is not much of a problem for goods and services which are bought and sold, i.e. which pass through the market. However, we have seen that the boundary of production includes some non-market items as well, e.g. (i) goods (like foodgrains) produced for own consumption and (ii) services rendered by the dwellings occupied by the owners themselves. In order to include their production in GDP, it is customary to include an estimate of the value which these items would have if they passed through the market, i.e. to *impute* values to these items.[35] Such imputation is generally sought to be carried out in the best possible way.

Unless mentioned otherwise, GDP, gross value added (GVA) or net value added (NVA) would mean the corresponding total at factor cost. It may be recalled that GVA is the value of output *net* of intermediate consumption and that NVA is obtained by subtracting consumption of fixed capital from GVA.

ESTIMATION OF GDP

Production activities of the Indian economy are classified into a number of major groups depending on the types of goods and services they

[35]It is interesting to trace the effects which the inclusion or exclusion of such items would have on GDP and other aggregates. Karmel and Polasek (1977, pp. 413–15) illustrate this with the example of owner-occupied dwellings.

produce. These groups are: (1) agriculture (including animal husbandry), forestry and fishing, (2) mining and quarrying, (3) manufacturing, (4) electricity, gas and water supply, (5) construction, (6) trade, hotel and restaurant, (7) transport, storage and communication, (8) finance and real estate, and (9) community and personal services. Groups (1) to (5) produce *material goods* and the rest, *services*. Again, groups (1) and (2) form what is generally known as *primary* sector while groups (3) to (5) constitute *secondary* sector. Each group is further subdivided into a number of sub-groups. For instance, 'manufacturing activity' is divided into two sub-groups—*registered* and *unregistered*; *construction* is divided between *pucca* construction and labour-intensive *kutcha* construction; 'finance and real estate' is subdivided into such categories as banking and insurance, ownership of dwellings, real estate services (i.e. activities of all types of dealers in real estate) and business services; *community and personal services* cover activities like public administration and defence, and other services (such as educational and medical services, recreation, legal services or personal services) and so on.

The estimate of GVA or NVA is prepared for each group/sub-group of activities mentioned above at both current and constant prices and GDP is estimated as the sum of GVA's originating in the different groups/sub-groups. So far as the method of estimation is concerned, GVA for each of the groups/sub-groups belonging to the *tertiary* sector (i.e. groups (6) to (9)) is estimated by the *income approach*. On the other hand, GVA is estimated by the *value added* method (i.e. *product* approach) for most of the sub-groups belonging to the primary and secondary sectors and by the *income approach*, for the rest.

Private Final Consumption Expenditure (PFCE)

The estimates of PFCE are obtained by following the *commodity flow* method. In this method, first the total availability of an item (of consumption) during a period is estimated by taking into account the amount of domestic production and import of the item. From the total availability, all other uses of the item (i.e. intermediate consumption in various producing sectors, change in stock, consumption on government account and export) are subtracted so as to arrive at the amount of final consumption by households and NPISH. The resulting aggregate is generally evaluated at market prices. For services, the estimate of PFCE is arrived at from the total output (as measured by the gross earnings) of the agencies providing these services to the consumers after netting out the formers' expenditure on these services during the period, if any.

Gross Domestic Capital Formation

As we have noted in the text, CSO gives estimates of India's gross domestic investment, i.e. gross additions to stocks of fixed assets and inventories made within the *domestic territory* of the country during a period. Estimates of inventories (i.e. change in stocks) are generally prepared on the basis of inventories held by industries, except for foodgrains, for which the total stocks are measured irrespective of their being held by producers and traders. Fixed assets comprise construction and machinery and equipment.

Construction

Construction activity covers all new construction; alterations and repair of buildings, streets, railroads, communication systems, etc.; improvement of land and development or extension of mining sites, timber tracts and plantations; and so on. The total expenditure on all such construction is estimated as the aggregate of the values of both material inputs used (e.g. cement, iron and steel, bricks, electrical goods, etc.) and factor income, generated in the form of payments of labour as well as to capital (i.e. rent, interest and profits) *net* of expenditure on current repairs and maintenance.

Machinery and Equipment

All types of machinery, transport equipment, etc. are included. Also included are increments in livestock in respect of breeding stock, drought animals raised for wool clipping, etc. Additions to livestock other than these are included under 'change in stock'. The estimates of expenditure on machinery and equipment at current prices are prepared by the commodity-flow approach, wherein the amount of an item available for domestic uses is first calculated and then the amount available for capital formation is estimated, taking into account other uses of the item during the period. Various items of machinery and equipment are classified into (i) capital goods, (ii) parts of capital goods, (iii) partly capital goods and (iv) parts of partly capital goods. The amount of capital formation during a period is estimated to be the total availability (for domestic uses) of the items classified under (i), 50 per cent of the total availability of the items under (ii) and varying percentages of the total availabilities of the items classified under (iii) and (iv) (the remaining percentage for a given item being taken to be the amount used for other purposes).

FLOWS IN TABLE 1.9

We now discuss how we have estimated the various flows of Table 1.9. Estimates of physical investment, saving and capital transfers of different sectors for 1994–5 have been obtained from CSO, GoI (1998).

We have observed in Section 6.2 that in 1994–95 India's net (physical) investment (I) was Rs 163,639 crore. The corresponding figure for the household sector is found to be Rs 53,925 crore (CSO, GOI (1998), Statement 19, p. 42). The balance, i.e. Rs 109,714 crore, is thus net investment by the entire non-household sector, (I_{nh}). The non-household sector includes private corporate sector (*pf*) and the public sector (*g*); the latter consists of (i) government administration and departmental enterprises (called sector **G**, in the text) and (ii) government non-departmental enterprises **(NDE)**. The (unadjusted) figures of net investment for the entire public sector (I^u_g), the sector *pf* (I^u_{pf}) and the sector **G** (I^u_G) are found to be respectively Rs 44,800, Rs 47,315 and Rs 22,531 crores. Hence, (unadjusted) net investment of NDE sector (I^u_{NDE}) is $I^u_g - I^u_{g}$, i.e. Rs 22,269 crore and that of sector **F** (I^u_F) is $I^u_{pf} + I^u_{NDE}$, i.e. Rs 69,584 crore. Since I_{nh} is 19.01 per cent higher than I^u_{nh}, we adjust net investment figures of non-household sectors, **G** and **F**, by this proportion so as to get the following estimates: $I_G =$ Rs 26,836 crore, $I_F =$ Rs 82,878 crore (the total being Rs 109,714 crore, as expected).

So far as estimates of saving for 1994–95 are concerned (net) saving of the economy (S) and that of the household sector (S_h) are found to be Rs 151,748 and Rs 162,818 crores, respectively (CSO, GOI (1998), Statement 18, p. 41). Such a figure for sector **G** is estimated to be Rs 31,346 crore (CSO, GOI (1998), Statement 41–3, pp. 127–9), the balance (i.e. Rs 20,276 crore) being saving of sector **F** (S_F).

Consider now financial flows in various accounts of Table 1.9. Various aggregates in the account (5) of the household sector are estimated by making appropriate grouping of the items in the statement (no. 73, p. 185) on financial assets and liabilities of this sector. The basic data for the accounts (2) and (3) of sector R and sector b are obtained from statement nos. 37, 39 and 42 given on pages 64, 66 and 69 of *RBI* (1995–6). The procedure has been explained in the text.

Consider now the account (1) for sector **G**. All entries on its LHS have been explained except capital transfers. We find that KT_{dw} was Rs 1309 crore in 1994–5 (CSO, GOI (1998), Statement 7, p. 15). For want of data we assume that the entire transfers from the RW were received by the sector **G**.

Further, net capital transfers made by **G** to the domestic sector were Rs 7643 crore (assumeed to be made entirely to the sector **F**, KT_{FG}) and net borrowings of **G** from abroad (L_{Gw}) were Rs 3581 cror (CSO, GOI (1998), Statement 196, p. 135)e. The other entries on the RHS of the account (1) have already been explained except L_{GF} which turns out to be Rs 29,090 crore so as to balance the RHS total with the LHS total. Finally, entries in the RW account (6) have all appeared in the accounts for the different domestic sectors (1)–(5), and hence, have already been explained.

2

National Product, Income Accounts and Sustainable Development

SWAPAN DASGUPTA and TAPAN MITRA*

1. INTRODUCTION

In recent years, there has been a renewal of interest in the concept of Net National Product (NNP) as a measure of welfare. This interest has arisen from concerns regarding exploitation of exhaustible and renewable natural resources, and regarding environmental effects of development. These concerns are to a large extent, but not solely, within the context of sustainable development. A significant body of literature has developed which seeks to promote changes in the way NNP is measured in the National Income Accounts, specifically the 'net investment' component, to better reflect the presence and the importance, in economic activity, of resources, exhaustible and renewable, and of environmental factors. It also seeks to draw some interesting connections between the notion of sustainable development on the one hand, and NNP and the pattern of investment on the other.

It is a distinctive feature of the literature mentioned in the preceding paragraph, that it is very firmly grounded in theoretical developments on a basic conceptual issue of wider interest, namely, the possibility of a current income concept being an appropriate measure of welfare in a dynamic context. In this essay we seek to provide an exposition of some of the theoretical developments in this area, and in the above mentioned literature on National Income Accounts and sustainable development,

*Research on this paper was started while the first author was on sabbatic leave at Cornell University. The first author acknowledges partial support from a NSERC grant. We also acknowledge detailed comments and suggestions by Amitava Bose which led to substantial improvements in the paper. An earlier version of the paper was presented at McGill University. Thanks are due to the participants of the seminar for their helpful comments.

which explores the implications of these theoretical developments. Along the way, we provide some critical assessments, indicate some questions of interest that arise from these developments, and outline some recent work along these lines. There is no attempt to be exhaustive in scope or in detail. The ground covered, as well as the citations provided, simply reflect our particular interest in some of the theoretical subject matter in this area, arising in the course of our investigation of certain problems. We hope that this will provide an introduction to an area which we believe is interesting, and stimulate the reader's curiosity. In the remainder of this introduction we present a brief overview of the main issues we address in the sections to follow.

It is generally accepted that if we wish to measure the economic well-being of a nation (including its current and future generations) we must determine the present discounted value of current and future utilities. However, 'Net National Income', measured by adding the value of net current investment to current consumption, is often used as an indicator of a society's welfare. A central question then is whether a theoretical justification can be provided for this practice of including 'net current investment' in a measure of welfare.

Weitzman (1976) made the fundamental observation that in theory, current Net National Product, appropriately measured, provides a precise measure of the present discounted value of current and future utilities. The observation is striking in (at least) two respects. The first is that a *current income* concept should contain all the information regarding the well-being of a society's entire future. This, of course, ceases to be a surprise when we consider the fact that Weitzman makes his observation with respect to perfect foresight competitive paths. The second, and perhaps more intriguing one, is that while it is to be expected that investment today translates in *some way* to the generation of future consumption, and therefore, to future utilities, it is quite remarkable that the current value of net investment should turn out to be such an accurate proxy for the present discounted value of future utilities.

In order to state this connection properly, we need to conduct our discussion in more precise terms. Weitzman's observation is that for a *competitive path* $\langle k(t), p(t) \rangle$ under a constant interest regime r (see following section for explanations of the fairly standard notation and definitions), for every t,

$$u(t) + p(t)\, k(t) = r \int_t^\infty e^{-r(s-t)} u(s)\, ds \tag{1}$$

Let us refer to (1) as *Weitzman's Rule*, henceforth abbreviated as WR. Interpreting the left hand side of (1) as the Net National Product (NNP) (for more on this interpretation see section 4), WR asserts that the NNP at time t is equal to the annuity equivalent of the present discounted value of utilities along the path. The second section provides the formal framework of the discussion, along with necessary defintions and notational details. The third section provides a detailed discussion of WR.

If the competitive path $\langle k(t), p(t) \rangle$ was, in fact, an *optimal* path, i.e. one which maximized:

$$\int_0^\infty e^{-rt}\, u(t)\, dt \tag{2}$$

over all paths from the same initial conditions, then WR is really an interpretation of Bellman's equation of optimality in dynamic programming; namely, for all t,

$$-V'(k(t))\, \dot{k}(t) = u(t) - rV(k(t)) \tag{3}$$

where V is the 'value function' associated with the problem of maximizing (2), assumed differentiable for convenience. The support of the value function, $V'(k(t))$, is the price vector $p(t)$ of the capital goods (for convex structures), and (3) readily yields (1). A detailed discussion of Bellman's equation (3) may be found in the third section.

But Weitzman (1976) appears to claim more, namely, that (1) holds for every *competitive* path. This turns out to be invalid in general: one can construct examples of competitive paths which violate WR. Perhaps more interesting is the observation that a competitive path satisfies WR if and only if it satisfies the *investment value transversality condition*:

$$\lim_{t \to \infty} e^{-rt} p(t)\, \dot{k}(t) = 0 \tag{4}$$

just as a competitive path is optimal if and only if it satisfies the *capital value transversality condition*:

$$\lim_{t \to \infty} e^{-rt} p(t)\, k(t) = 0 \tag{5}$$

It turns out that in the standard model of optimal intertemporal allocation, in which an exhaustible resource is a factor of production [see, e.g. Solow (1974), Hartwick (1977)], the investment value transversality condition is *always* satisfied for competitive paths (although the capital value transversality condition is not). Thus, in this framework, WR holds for every competitive path. These issues are discussed in the third section.

There is an important implication that can be drawn from WR for National Income accounting procedures. WR asserts that NNP equals the annuity equivalent of the present discounted sum of utilities. For this to be valid, the notion of capital and, therefore, of net investment has to be properly interpreted. The standard measure of net investment in the National Income Accounts, namely, the value of change in stocks of producible capital goods is too narrow and fails to capture welfare properly. The notion of capital must be interpreted very broadly and net investments should, in principle, include changes in any stock which contributes to production. In the fourth section we discuss in some detail the principle involved, in the context of a simple model of exhaustible resources.

In the fourth section we also critically survey the literature, focusing on the connection between WR and sustainable development. Here we note the most important conclusion to be drawn. The validity of WR for all competitive paths has an important implication for the discussion on investment policies ensuring *sustainable development.* Following Weitzman (1995), if we define a path of sustainable development to be one for which at each date the constant utility equivalent of the present discounted value of future utilities is at least as large as the current utility, then a competitive path generates a path of sustainable development if and only if the value of investment is never negative. This calls for an investment policy for sustainable development in which producible capital goods are augmented at a rate sufficient to offset the depletion of non-producible capital goods such as exhaustible natural resources, and produce a non-negative *aggregate* value of net investment.

Finally, in the fifth section, we make some peripheral remarks of interest, especially from the point of view of an agenda for future research.

2. PRELIMINARIES

2.1 The Framework

Consider a framework in which population and technology are unchanging, individuals are identical in all respects so that there is no harm in thinking in terms of a single representative person (and so, ignoring distribution considerations) at each date, and most importantly, that consumption level in any period can be represented by a single number. 'It might be calculated as an index number with given price weights, or as a multiple of some fixed basket of goods, or more generally, as any cardinal utility function'.[1]

Denote by $k_i \geq 0$, the stock of the ith capital good, $i = 1, \ldots, n$, and the vector $(k_1, \ldots, k_n)$ by k. Let $I = (I_1, \ldots, I_n)$ stand for the vector of quantities of the investment goods. Denote by a set T, the technologically feasible input output combinations. A typical point of T is a triplet $(U, I, -k)$, which is understood to mean that from capital input stocks[2] k, it is technologically feasible to obtain the flow of consumption U and the flow of investment I, which is net of depreciation of the existing stock of capital k. We may alternatively represent the technological possibilities by associating with each k, the combinations of consumption and net investment that is possible to realize with input stocks k. Denote this by a set $S(k)$, i.e.

$$S(k) = \{(U, I)/(U, I, -k) \in T\} \tag{6}$$

A *path*, from initial stocks k, is a triplet of functions of time, $U(t)$, $I(t)$ and $k(t)$, defined for $t \geq 0$, of consumption, investment and capital stocks, respectively, satisfying[3]:

$$\begin{aligned} (U(t), I(t)), &\in S(k(t)) \text{ for each } t \\ \dot{k}(t) &= I(t) \text{ for each } t \\ k(0) &= \underline{k} \end{aligned} \tag{7}$$

We use the notation $\langle U(t), I(t), k(t) \rangle$ to denote a path.

2.2 Competitive and Optimal Paths

We shall now elaborate what we mean by a time path of quantities and prices which evolves along an equilibrium of a competitive market economy, from an initial stock $\underline{k}$. It would be convenient, for what

[1]Weitzman (1976), pp. 156–7.

[2]Following usual convention we are using negative values for inputs.

[3]We are using conventional notation: $\dot{x}$ means time derivative. So if $x(t)$ is a vector valued function, i.e. $x(t) = [x_1(t), \ldots, x_n(t)]$, then $\dot{x}(t) = \frac{dx}{dt}(t) = \left(\frac{dx_1}{dt}, \ldots, \frac{dx_n}{dt}\right)$. If x is a vector $(x_1, \ldots, x_n)$ and $f(x)$ is a vector valued function defined from R^n to R^m, i.e. $f(x) = [f_1(x), \ldots, (f_m(x)]$ then $f'(x)$ is the '$m \times n$' matrix whose 'ijth' element is $\frac{\partial f_i}{\partial x_j}(x)$.

follows, to introduce the following notation and concepts. Let $p \geq 0$ denote the prices of the investment goods in terms of the consumption good U. Define a function $h(k, p)$ by:

$$h(k, p) = \max_{(U, I) \in S(k)} [U + p \cdot I] \tag{8}$$

Here, $h(k, p)$ is the maximum value of output which can be achieved, given input stocks k, at prices p. Let $r > 0$ denote the market rate of interest.

A *competitive* path is a path $\langle U(t), I(t), k(t) \rangle$ with associated prices, denoted by a function of time, $\langle p(t) \rangle \geq 0$, satisfying the following two conditions:

$$U(t) + p(t)\, I(t) = h(k(t), p(t)) \text{ for each } t \tag{9}$$

and

$$\frac{dp_i}{dt}(t) = rp_i(t) - \frac{\partial h}{\partial k_i}(k(t), p(t)),\ i = 1, \ldots, n, \quad \text{for each } t \tag{10}$$

Here, $p(t)$ is the vector of current prices of the investment goods, in terms of the consumption good U, prevailing along an equilibrium path at each date t. Equation (9) says that, at each date t, value of output realized on the path, $U(t) + p(t)\, I(t)$, is the maximum over the set of feasible outputs $S[k(t)]$. Equation (10) says that asset markets are in equilibrium; i.e. no gains can be made by pure arbitrage. [See Dorfman, Samuelson and Solow (1958), Weitzman (1976).]

Use the notation $\langle U(t), I(t), k(t), p(t) \rangle$ to denote a competitive path with its associated prices. Along the competitive path at time t:

$$\text{NNP}(t) = U(t) + p(t)\, I(t) \tag{11}$$

Denoting the NNP at time t by $Y(t)$, rewrite (9) as:

$$Y(t) = h(k(t), p(t)) \text{ for each } t. \tag{12}$$

We will now relate all of the above, to standard formulations of Ramsey type optimal growth models [see Benveniste and Scheinkman (1979, 1982) for example]. For this purpose define the set F by:

$$F = \{(k, I) / \text{for some } U, (U, I, -k) \in T\} \tag{13}$$

F is the set of (k, I) pairs, such that it is feasible to attain the rate of net investment I (along with some feasible consumption goods output), given the capital inputs k. Define also a function u for each feasible (k, I) pair in F by:

$$u(k, I) = \text{Max } U \quad \text{s.t. } (U, I, -k) \in T \tag{14}$$

Thus, $u(k, I)$ is the maximum utility or consumption that can be obtained from the capital stock k given the output I of the investment goods. We may note, for later use, that if we consider the efficient frontier of $S(k)$, that is, the set $\bar{S}(k)$, defined by:

$$\bar{S}(k) = \{(U, I) \in S(k) \ / \text{ there is no other } (U', I') \text{ in } S(k) \text{ satisfying } (U', I') \geq (U, I)\} \quad (15)$$

then we have

$$u(k, I) = \{U/(U, I) \in \bar{S}(k)\} \quad (16)$$

REMARK 1: Given (k, p) maximizing $U + pI$, subject to $(U, I) \in S(k)$ is equivalent to maximizing $u(k, I) + pI$ with respect to variations in I such that $(k, I) \in F$. So

$$h(k, p) = \text{Max } [u(k, I) + p{\cdot}I] \quad (17)$$
$$\text{s.t. } (k, I) \in F$$

Writing $g(k, p)$ for the maximizing value of I in (17) as a function of (k, p), we obtain

$$h(k, p) = u(k, g(k, p)) + pg(k, p) \quad (18)$$

REMARK 2: Along a competitive path $\langle U(t), I(t), k(t), p(t)\rangle$, $U(t) = u((k(t), \dot{k}(t))$ for each t; we shall sometimes write $u(t)$ to mean $u(k(t), \dot{k}(t))$ $(= U(t))$ for each t.

In view of the remark above, we can conveniently describe a competitive path from $\underline{k}$ simply as a pair of time paths of capital stocks and prices $\langle k(t), p(t)\rangle$ satisfying: $(k(t), \dot{k}(t)) \in F$ for each t; $k(0) = \underline{k}$ and (19) and (20) below:

$$u(k(t), \dot{k}(t)) + p(t)\,\dot{k}(t) = h(k(t), p(t)) \; (= Y(t)) \text{ for each } t \quad (19)$$

$$\frac{dp_i}{dt}(t) = rp_i(t) - \frac{\partial h}{\partial k_i}(k(t), p(t)),\ i = 1, \ldots, n, \text{ for each } t \quad (20)$$

Consider now the following dynamic optimization problem[4].

$$\text{Max} \int_0^\infty e^{-rt} u(k(t), I(t))\, dt$$
$$\text{s.t. } (k(t), I(t)) \in S(k(t)) \text{ for each } t$$
$$\dot{k}(t) = I(t) \text{ for each } t, \text{ and}$$
$$k(0) = \underline{k} \quad (21)$$

[4]We are taking for granted that the problem is well defined. Throughout this essay, we are presuming that regularity conditions, such as concavity, smoothness, boundedness, interiority conditions, which are necessary for the validity of arguments, are in place.

We shall say that a path from $\underline{k}$ is *optimal* if it is a solution to the above control problem.

For what follows, it is esential to note the distinction between a competitive path from $\underline{k}$ and an optimal path from $\underline{k}$. Under suitable assumptions, most important of which is convex structure on technology and utility, an optimal path is also competitive; that is, if a path $\langle k(t)\ I(t)\rangle$ from $\underline{k}$ is optimal then there is an associated time path of prices $\langle p(t)\rangle$ at which $\langle k(t), p(t)\rangle$ satisfies the competitive conditions (19) and (20) above. In other words, the competitive conditions are necessary conditions for optimality. In the literature of dynamic optimization, the necessary conditions for optimality, which correspond to the competitive conditions, are usually expressed somewhat differently and in terms of present value prices. In the appendix we formally show that these are equivalent to the competitive conditions.

While the competitive conditions are necessary, in general, they are not sufficient for optimality. From any given $\underline{k}$, typically, there will be a family of competitive paths, only one of which will be the optimal path. In addition to the competitive conditions, an optimal path must satisfy a 'transversality condition'. Usually this takes the form that, in the limit, the present value of future capital stock, i.e. $e^{-rt}p(t)\,k(t)$, goes to 0. For a competitive path, such a capital value transversality condition is both a necessary as well as a sufficient condition for it to be an optimal path.

3. NET NATIONAL PRODUCT AND WELFARE

3.1 WEITZMAN'S RULE

The concept of Net National Product (NNP) plays an important role in macroeconomics. It serves as a summary measure of the level of economic activity and is valuable on account of its close link to the level of employment. It also serves as a summary measure of the economic well being of a nation. We are interested here in the latter aspect only. Clearly, there are deficiencies in NNP as a measure of economic welfare. The size of the population which consumes the product should count and more appropriate would be NNP per capita. Inequalities in the distribution of the product over the population should also be relevant. NNP, as measured in National Income Accounts, is the sum of consumption and net investment. As is well known from the static theory of index numbers, there are problems in aggregating a heterogeneous bundle of consumption goods into a single measure of aggregate consumption. There are problems in comparison of aggregate measures of income or consumption across populations with different taste and environments. These are matters which we will not address, although they are clearly important. Instead, following Weitzman (1976), we will focus on one aspect, namely the net investment component of NNP and its role in a measure of welfare in a dynamic context.

Even if we accept the standpoint that it is consumption alone that promotes welfare and that the ultimate aim of economic activity is to provide consumption goods, the role of net capital formation in a welfare measure is unclear and indirect, at best. Intuitively, we understand that net capital formation now affects future productive potential, and hence, the consumption potential, in the future. If welfare is understood to depend on the time path of current and future consumption then, perhaps, net investment may be regarded as a proxy for the effect of this investment on welfare through its effect on consumption in the future. But it is not quite clear whether there is an exact relationship between the two, even within the confines of a drastically stripped down scenario, where it is possible to focus on this aspect of the problem alone. As Samuelson (1961) argues, a rigorous and meaningful welfare measure is a 'wealth like magnitude' such as the present discounted value of future consumption. What connection does this have, if any, with current income concepts? Weitzman sought to establish that these may be viewed as simply two sides of the same coin.

Consider the welfare achieved along a competitive path from time t onwards, using t as the origin; i.e. the discounted sum of utilities discounted to time t,

$$\int_t^{\infty} e^{-r(s-t)} u(s)\, ds \tag{22}$$

We may define a *constant utility equivalent* of this, namely, a hypothetical constant $\overline{u}$ such that if utility achieved at each date t were equal to $\overline{u}$ then the discounted sum of utility achieved would be the same as in (22).[5] So $\overline{u}$ is defined by

[5]This is similar to the device used by Milton Friedman (1957) in defining 'permanent income' in his theory of the consumption function. Of course, the horizon in his case is the finite lifetime of the individual whose consumption behaviour is being studied.

$$\int_t^\infty e^{-r(s-t)}\,\bar{u}\,ds = \int_t^\infty e^{-r(s-t)}\,u(s)\,ds \tag{23}$$

Nothing that $\bar{u}$ is a constant, we may rewrite this as:

$$\frac{\bar{u}}{r} = \int_t^\infty e^{-r(s-t)}\,u(s)\,ds \tag{24}$$

or as

$$\bar{u} = r\int_t^\infty e^{-r(s-t)}\,u(s)\,ds \tag{25}$$

Weitzman's main proposition seeks to establish that the NNP at time t, $Y(t)$, is this annuity equivalent $\bar{u}$ of the welfare along the path; that is,

$$Y(t) = r\int_t^\infty e^{-r(s-t)}\,u(s)\,ds \text{ for each } t \tag{26}$$

We refer to (26) above as *Weitzman's Rule* or WR for short. In what follows below, we shall follow through Weitzman's line of reasoning to establish (26).

Recall from the second section that $h(k, p) = u(k, g(k, p)) + pg(k, p)$ where $g(k, p)$ is the maximizing value of I in (17). Suppressing the points of evaluation of the functions involved below to save on notation,

$$\frac{\partial h}{\partial p_j}(\bullet) = \Sigma_i \frac{\partial u}{\partial I_i}(\bullet) \qquad \frac{\partial g_i}{\partial p_j}(\bullet) + I_j(\bullet) + \Sigma_i p_i \frac{\partial g_i}{\partial p_j}(\bullet)$$

Using the fact that at the optimal choice of I (assuming an interior solution),

$$\frac{\partial u}{\partial I_i}(\bullet) + p_i = 0 \tag{27}$$

it follows that

$$\frac{\partial h}{\partial p_j}(k, p) = g_j(k, p) \tag{28}$$

Along a competitive path $\langle I(t), k(t), p(t)\rangle$ from $\underline{k}$, the rate of change of NNP, $Y(t) = h(k(t), p(t))$, over time is:

$$\frac{dY}{dt}(t) = \Sigma_i \frac{\partial h}{\partial k_i}(k(t), p(t)) \bullet I_i(t) + \Sigma_i \frac{\partial h}{\partial p_i}(k(t), p(t)) \bullet \frac{dp_i}{dt}(t)$$

By (17) and (19), $I(t) = g(k(t), p(t))$. Using (20) and (28), the second term in the equation above becomes

$$r \, \Sigma \, I_i(t) \bullet p_i(t) - \Sigma \frac{\partial h}{\partial k_i} (k(t), p(t)) \bullet I_i(t)$$

So, we obtain

$$\frac{dY}{dt}(t) = r \sum_i p_i(t) \, I_i(t) = r[Y(t) - u(k(t), \dot{k}(t))] \qquad (29)$$

Clearly, (26) is a solution to this differential equation. [It is worth noting that Weitzman does not address the question of whether (26) is the *only* solution of (29), an issue we will consider in the subsection following the next one.]

3.2. Bellman's Equation and Weitzman's Rule for Optimal Paths

For *optimal* paths, WR is closely connected to the Bellman Equation in Dynamic Programming [see for instance Intriligator (1971), Sorger (1992)] derived from the Principle of Optimality. Some authors [see Hartwick (1994), Kemp and Long (1982) for instance] take this approach to establish that WR holds for *optimal* paths. We sketch this line of argument below. [For alternate derivations of this result, see Asheim (1994), Lozada (1995).]

Consider an optimal path $\langle I^*(t), k^*(t) \rangle$ from $\underline{k}$. Let $p^*(t)$ be the supporting prices at which the path is competitive. Denote the NNP at each t along the path by $Y^*(t)$. The Principle of Optimality tells us that the segment of the path from time t onwards, that is, the functions $I^*(\tau)$ and $k^*(\tau)$ for $\tau \geq t$, constitutes the optimal path, for Problem 1, from initial stock $k = k^*(t)$.

For $k \geq 0$, $t \geq 0$, define the value function $V(k, t)$ by

$$V(k, t) = \text{Max} \int_t^{\infty} e^{-rs} \, u(k(s), I(s)) \, ds \qquad (30)$$

$$\text{s.t. } (k(s), I(s)) \in F \text{ and } I(s) = \dot{k}(s) \text{ for each } s \geq 0, \text{ and } k(t) = k.$$

It is clear that

$$V(k, t) = e^{-rt} \, V(k, 0) \qquad (31)$$

The Bellman Equation for the control problem (21) is

$$-\frac{\partial V}{\partial t}(k^*(t), t) = \underset{I \text{ s.t. } (k^*(t), I) \in F}{\text{Max}} \left[e^{-rt} \, u(k^*(t), I) + \frac{\partial V}{\partial k}(k^*(t), t) \bullet I \right] \qquad (32)$$

It is also known [see Benveniste and Scheinkman (1979, Corollary 1)] that under suitable assumptions

$$\frac{\partial V}{\partial k}(k', 0) = -\frac{\partial u}{\partial I}(k', I') \tag{33}$$

where I' is the level of the control I at $t = 0$ along the optimal path from initial stocks k'.

From (31), we have that

$$\frac{\partial V}{\partial k}(k^*(t), t) = e^{-rt}\frac{\partial V}{\partial k}(k^*(t), 0)$$

$$= e^{-rt}\frac{\partial u}{\partial I}(k^*(t), I^*(t))$$

[using (33) and the Principle of Optimality]

$$= e^{-rt}p^*(t) \quad \text{[using (27)].}$$

So the right hand side expression in (32) is $e^{-rt}\,Y^*(t)$. And, the left-hand side expression in (32) is, using (31),

$$-\frac{\partial V}{\partial t}(k^*(t), t) = rV(k^*(t), t) = r\int_t^{\infty} e^{-rs}u(k^*(s), I^*(s))\,ds \tag{34}$$

Thus, WR holds for optimal paths.

3.3 Weitzman's Rule for Competitive Paths and a Transversality Condition

While it is a point of interest that WR is valid for optimal paths, it would be of far more interest if indeed it were valid for any competitive path. In fact, Weitzman's discussion of the problem, providing a motivation, seems to be along precisely such lines. Given an infinite horizon path satisfying competitive equilibrium conditions in a perfect foresight framework, the current prices and quantities carry information about the future prices and quantities. Since current net investment affects future consumption possibilities, intuitively there are grounds to explore if there is a clear cut relation between current NNP and the flow of consumption along the path. If a rule like (26) could be established for any competitive path, that would be of considerable interest. We have explored this issue elsewhere [see Dasgupta and Mitra (1999b)] and summarize the salient points below, eschewing all technical details and proofs.

It turns out that, in general, WR does not hold for every competitive path. We construct an example of a one sector neoclassical growth model of the Cass-Koopmans type [see Cass (1965) and Koopmans (1965)] with a modified golden rule and a maximum sustainable stock, where a competitive path violates WR. The competitive path chosen for the purpose of the example is one where the capital stock converges to the maximum sustainable stock. (The path is, of course, also non-optimal.)

This leads one to try to identify the competitive paths which do satisfy WR. We show that these paths can be characterized by a transversality condition involving the present value of net *investment*. Specifically, a competitive path $\langle I^*(t), k^*(t), p^*(t)\rangle$ satisfies WR if and only if

$$e^{-rt}\, p^*(t)\, k^*(t) \to 0 \quad \text{as } t \to \infty \tag{35}$$

Note that the condition is apparently different from the usual transversality condition characterizing optimal paths, namely the present value of *capital* $e^{-rt}\, p^*(t)\, k^*(t)^*(t)$, goes to zero as $t \to \infty$.

The example and the characterization result prompts one to examine closely Weitzman's line of reasoning leading to (26), which we had sketched earlier in this section.

Suppose $\langle k^*(t), I^*(t), p^*(t)\rangle$ is a competitive path from $\underline{k}$. Write $u^*(t)$ for $u[k^*(t), I^*(t)]$. Consider the differential equation.

$$\frac{d}{dt} F(t) = r[F(t) - u^*(t)] \tag{36}$$

A solution to this equation is a function of time $F\colon (0, \infty) \to R$ satisfying (36) at each $t \geq 0$. In general there is a *family* of such solutions, any two of which differ by a constant of integration. The arguments leading up to (29), starting from (19) and (20), establish that the function $Y^*(t)$, the time path of NNP associated with the given competitive path, is indeed a solution of (36). Define now a function $b(t)$ by

$$b(t) = \int_t^{\infty} e^{-r(s-t)}\, u^*(s)\, ds$$

It may be verified by direct calculation that $b(t)$ satisfies the differential equation (36). The two functions $Y^*(t)$ and $b(t)$, therefore differ by a constant. WR is valid if this constant is, in fact, zero.

In this connection it is worth noting that the arguments until this point make use of only the competitive conditions (19) and (20). As is well known, typically, in optimization problems like (21), there is more than one competitive path from each initial stock. Usually an optimal path is characterized by the competitive conditions, together with a transversality condition like

$$e^{-rt} p^*(t) k^*(t) \to 0 \quad \text{as } t \to \infty \tag{37}$$

[See Weitzman (1973) for a discrete time formulation of the problem and Benveniste and Scheinkman (1982) for a continuous time treatment.] Of course Weitzman (1976) recognizes this, but he does not clarify the role of optimality, or anything like the transversality condition (37), in deducing (26).

Finally, we show that in a specialized version of Weitzman's framework, namely, one where there is a produced good which is used both as capital input as well as consumption good, and an exhaustible resource which is 'important' in production, in the sense that its share in total output (the marginal product of the resource times its quantity divided by the output) is bounded below by some positive constant (a property of Cobb-Douglas production functions, for instance), all competitive paths satisfy WR. This is shown by verifying that the present value of net investment does go to zero along any competitive path, that is, (35) is satisfied. Furthermore, competitive paths in such a model are not necessarily optimal. This last point is noteworthy, since it can be shown for a class of multi-sector models of optimal growth, satisfying certain technological restrictions, that every competitive path is optimal [see Dasgupta and Mitra (1999a)]. In such a situation, competitive paths do indeed satisfy WR, but only 'trivially' so, by virtue of being an optimal path as well.

The results mentioned above establish that the transversality condition in terms of present value of net investment is different from the usual one involving present value of capital. Along a competitive path, the former does not imply the latter. To put it differently, within the class of competitive paths, WR is of wider validity than optimality. Along the way we also establish that in the context of models involving exhaustible resources, of a kind which is generally prevalent in the literature, under mild conditions, competitive paths do satisfy WR. Hence, the conclusions reached from it are of much wider validity than that recognized in the literature.

4. NATIONAL INCOME ACCOUNTS AND SUSTAINABLE DEVELOPMENT

4.1 Interpretation of Net National Product

Before proceeding with the discussion in this section it will be useful to briefly remark on the inclusion of a cardinal utility function in NNP as defined in (11) or (19). In National Income and Expenditure accounts, NNP is an index constructed from a heterogeneous bundle of consumption and investment good outputs evaluated at constant base year prices (alternatively, evaluated at current prices and deflated by a suitable price index). As is well known from the static theory of index numbers, there are problems with using such an index number as a welfare measure. Conceptually speaking, with more than one kind of consumption good, explicit consideration of the underlying fundamental notion of welfare, namely, a utility function defined over the heterogeneous bundle of consumption goods, becomes unavoidable. Furthermore, to be able to discuss welfare in a dynamic context, keeping separate the notion of current welfare from future welfare, it is simplest to have a cardinal utility function defined over the consumption in each period, the discounted sum of which is the accepted fundamental notion of welfare achieved along a time path of consumption. From the standpoint of theoretical consideration of NNP as a welfare measure, in contrast to its role as an aggregative measure of output which is useful because of its relationship to aggregate employment, the definition adopted in (11) or (19) is the appropriate one.

Having made the distinction between conventional measures of NNP and the notion of NNP appearing in WR, it is worth pointing out, once again, that the focus of attention in WR, and its applications to National Income accounting procedures and sustainable development, is on the welfare interpretation of the net investment component of NNP in a dynamic context. From this viewpoint, the reader may find it helpful to keep in mind a model with a single consumption good, such as Uzawa's two sector model,[6] obviating the need to distinguish between

[6]See Uzawa (1964). Instead of a two sector model one may have in mind a multi sector model so long as there is only one consumption good whose output, expressed as a product transformation function of the outputs of the many investment goods, given the stock of capital, is a non-linear function. The non-linearity is to avoid well known problems associated with optimal control

consumption and utility and, therefore, between the customary definition of NNP and that employed in WR. In such a framework prices of the investment goods are expressed in units of the consumption good and NNP is the maximum output produced (measured in units of the consumption good).

We may end this discussion by noting that the remarks above are relevant solely from the standpoint of suitable interpretation of the model and the results. From the logical standpoint there is no need for any special restriction of the kind mentioned above. The formal results are valid for standard models of capital accumulation such as Problem 1, which includes, for example, the Cass–Koopmans model.

4.2 Proposals to Revise National Income Accounts

We shall now consider some of the implications regarding National Income accounting procedures that have been drawn from WR. The principal point made appears to be as follows. For optimal programmes, WR shows that NNP is a measure of welfare. However, note that the investment component is 'all inclusive'. The concept of the capital stock, in Weitzman's formulation, is very broad. Any factor which influences the production possibilities, the menu of possible consumption and investment, which changes over time, and whose level is a matter of economic choice, is included in this.[7] The net change in such a stock, valued at the appropriate shadow price of that stock, ought to be included in the investment component in order that NNP properly measures the welfare achieved along the path, namely the annuity

problems in which the objective function is linear in the controls. This last point has been noted in the literature; see for example Hartwick (1990), Kemp and Long (1982), Brekke (1994), Hulten and Lofgren (1992), and Cairns (1997).

[7]In this regard, Weitzman follows the modern reformulation of capital theory appearing in the seminal work of Malinvaud (1953). In Malinvaud's framework, 'capital goods at time *t* include everything that has been made in preceding periods and is transferred to period *t* for further use in production'. [Malinvaud (1953, p. 235)]. In footnote 2 on p. 235, Malinvaud elaborates on the definition. 'The distinction between natural resources and produced means of production is not important as far as past activity is concerned. The only condition we need to keep in mind is the following: the available natural resources during all future periods must be independent of any present or future economic decision'. This clearly classifies non-renewable resources like mineral deposits as capital goods (produced means of production).

equivalent of future discounted sum of utility flow. If mineral resources, whose stocks can only be used up but not augmented, are used in the production processes, then the value of the change in these stocks ought to be included. Similarly, value of the changes in the stocks of renewable resources, like aquatic and forestry resources, whose harvesting, together with the underlying biological conditions, have an impact on the stocks of these resources, should also be included. Production activities generate pollution, adding to the level of pollutants. On the other hand, the level of pollutants can affect the output, given resources used in production, as for instance in fisheries and forestry products. In principle, the value of changes in the stock of pollutants should be included.

Obviously, all these are easier said than done. Very often there are difficult issues of measurement of the appropriate variables, prices and quantities. But the point being made is that to the extent that these measurement issues can be circumvented by suitable proxy measures (and in this respect similar problems are found in practice in dealing with other things like changes in quality) the value of such changes should be included in NNP. It should be emphasized that this is not an ad hoc prescription for including new items in NNP but well grounded in a clear cut theoretical link between NNP and welfare in a dynamic context.

The case of exhaustible resources brings to the fore the nature of changes that are being suggested and is worth discussing in a little more detail as typical case in point.[8]

Consider then, a very specialized version of a model of optimal exploitation of an exhaustible resource, considered quite frequently in the literature [see Dasgupta and Heal (1974), Hartwick (1990), for more elaborate versions of such a model]. Denote the stock of the exhaustible resource at date t by $S(t)$, and the flow of the resource extracted at date t by $R(t)$. A single consumption good is produced using the exhaustible resource and fixed labour as the sole inputs. Ignoring labour, which is fixed, denote the production function for the consumption good by f. Consider the following optimization problem:

[8]For more detailed discussion of this and other examples, the reader may wish to consult Dasgupta (1990), Hartwick (1990), and Maler (1991). The issues have been discussed in the context of open economies by Asheim (1995) and Sefton and Weale (1994).

$$\text{Max} \int_0^\infty e^{-rt}\, c(t)\, dt$$

such that

$$c(t) = f(R(t)) \qquad \text{for each } t$$

$$\frac{d}{dt} S(t) = -R(t) \qquad \text{for each } t$$

$$S(t), R(t) \geq 0 \qquad \text{for each } t$$

and

$$S(0) = \underline{S}$$

To avoid problems associated with linearity of the utility function [here $u(S, \dot{S}) = c = f(-\dot{S}) = f(R)$] in the control variable $\dot{S} = -R$ assume that f is a standard neoclassical production function with strictly diminishing marginal product. An appropriate 'Inada condition' like $f'(R) \rightarrow \infty \; as \; R \rightarrow 0$ would ensure an interior optimal path. Let $S^*(t)$ denote the stocks of the resource along the optimal path and $p^*(t)$ denote the associated prices supporting the optimal path. In this case $u(S, \dot{S}) + p\dot{S} = f(-\dot{S}) + p\dot{S}$ is maximized along the optimal path, for each $t \geq 0$, at $\dot{S} = \dot{S}^*(t)$. So $p^*(t) = f'[R^*(t)]$, the marginal product of the resource at time t, at the optimal quantity. This is the current price of one unit of the stock of the exhaustible resource in terms of units of the consumption good.

Under standard income accounting practices, the NNP at date t, measured from the expenditure side, equals $c^*(t) = f[R^*(t)]$. Alternatively, using the value added approach, value added in the consumption goods sector is $c^*(t) - p^*(t)\, R^*(t)$, while that in the production of the extracted resource is $p^*(t)\, R^*(t)$, providing a total of $c^*(t)$. This is to be contrasted with NNP in Weitzman's sense, which is

$$c^*(t) = p^*(t)\dot{S}^*(t) = c^*(t) - p^*(t)R^*(t) = f(R^*(t)) - f'(R^*(t))R^*(t).$$

Exhaustible resource stocks, like any other 'produced' capital stocks, are part of the productive stocks and the value of net investment in these (in this case a negative one) is also to be accounted for in this so-called 'Green' NNP. Since marginal product is decreasing, this NNP is positive but smaller than the conventional measure. [If, for example, $f(R) = R^\alpha$ where $0 < \alpha < 1$, then $f(R) - f'(R)\, R = (1 - \alpha) f(R)$, so that the new measure of NNP can be substantially smaller than the traditional measure of NNP if α is close to 1.]

It is worth noting that all this follows from the initial premise that the 'right' concept of NNP should reflect the discounted sum of future consumption and, as per WR, that is indeed the case. NNP is the annuity equivalent of the variable consumption stream over time under the discounted sum criterion. Within the limited range of possibilities in this model, consumption is decreasing over time. We can see this by using (20) of the competitive conditions which must be satisfied. This says that $\frac{d}{dt}p^*(t) = rp^*(t)$ since the stocks S do not affect the integrand. So current prices $p^*(t)$ are growing at the rate $r > 0$ and since $p^*(t) = f'(R^*(t))$, $R^*(t)$ is decreasing over time. Thus, the annuity equivalent of the consumption stream from any time t onwards is always less than $c^*(t)$. This is what is being recognized by inclusion of the term $p^*(t)\,\dot{S}^*(t)$ above.[9]

4.3 SUSTAINABLE DEVLEOPMENT

WR makes it very tempting to link NNP with some suitable notion of sustainable welfare. Various authors have examined this possibility [see Solow (1986), (1992), Hartwick (1994), Svensson (1986), Asheim (1994)]. Solow (1992), in particular, makes a very engaging heuristic case for the usefulness and possibilities of thinking along such lines, in relation to exploitation of non-renewable and renewable natural resources, and the natural environment, and seeks to link this with measurement issues in National Income Accounts, which we have sketched in the preceding sub-section.

The intuition behind seeking a connection between NNP and welfare, in the sense of the discounted sum of utilities, is that current net investment adds to future consumption potential. This could be rephrased, adopting a slightly different viewpoint. Gross Domestic Product is not suitable as an indicator of national well being, because, if two nations produce the same total final output for consumption, but one of them does so after making provisions to replace or repair worn out equipment used in production while the other does not, then we would say that the former nation is providing for its citizens better than the latter. The former can sustain this level of well being, while the latter

[9]If we incorporate extraction cost for the exhaustible resource, then the appropriate valuation per unit of the resource is its price net of cost of extraction at the margin [see Hartwick (1990)].

would be unable to do so, since it is running down its productive capacity. So, a depreciation charge needs to be deducted from GNP to arrive at a suitable measure of well being. Loosely speaking, the standpoint in this line of reasoning is that a proper notion of income, which is at one's disposal for consumption, is like an interest income on a fixed stock of capital. This is what can be consumed without depleting future earning and spending power.

Now, if we also adopt the standpoint that what is meant by sustainable development is not the preservation of specific things—natural resources, environmental riches, etc., but rather, a policy under which future generations have the possibility of ensuring for themselves and their successors at least the same level of well being as the current generation, then it seems natural to suggest that a policy of sustainable development should be one which adequately provides for depreciation of capital in a broad sense. If non-renewable mineral resource stocks are depleted to enable current productive activities to be carried out, then this 'depreciation' of stocks should be made up by the only possible way, namely, through 'appropriate' investment in produced capital goods which can substitute for the resource in production and sustain the same level of output. This, of course, presumes the possibility of such substitution between resource and produced capital. Solow (1974) analyzed a model with a produced good which is used for consumption as well as for production, together with labour and an exhaustible resource. Restricting himself to a Cobb–Douglas production function, he showed that if the share of capital exceeds the share of resource, then it is possible to maintain a minimum positive level of consumption.[10] Granted this, the interesting question is what is the *appropriate* level of investment. It is here that a connection is being made with suggested procedures for adjusting NNP to include the value of the net disinvestment of resource stocks.

The claim is that:

(a) the appropriate net investment in produced capital goods should be the value of the resource stocks which are used up; that is, the so-called *Hotelling rents* from the resource used.

This appears to be linked to two other claims:

(b) properly defined and properly calculated, this year's NNP can be regarded as this year's interest on society's total stock of capital interpreted in the broadest sense.

[10]Cass and Mitra (1991) have analyzed this in detail in a general framework.

(c) NNP indicates the largest consumption level that can be allowed this year if future consumption is never to be allowed to decrease.

Claims (b) and (c) together can be interpreted as saying that if the goal of investment policy is not to erode sustainable income then the aggregate capital stock must be maintained intact and this, presumably, leads to (a).

Below, we first sketch some arguments that have appeared in the literature which purport to provide a more precise form of these claims. Consider the framework of discussion of WR in the previous section. If a path $\langle U^*(t), I^*(t), k^*(t)\rangle$ from $\underline{k}$ is optimal then, evaluating NNP using the supporting prices $p^*(t)$, WR is valid. Suppose now that

$$p^*(t)\,\dot{k}^*(t) = 0 \quad \text{for each } t \tag{38}$$

Note that $k^*(t)$ and $p^*(t)$ are the vectors of capital stocks and their prices. If the ith component of k is an exhaustible resource then $\dot{k}_i^*(t)$ is always non-positive and $-\dot{k}_i^*(t)$ is the flow of the resource used in production. The price of this resource is $p_i^*(t)$, the 'Hotelling rent'. Then (38) states the investment rule mentioned in claim (a) above. Hartwick (1977) first stated the rule in this general form. We shall, henceforth, refer to (38) as *Hartwick's Rule* or HR for short. HR implies that $Y^*(t) = u^*(t)$. Using this in WR, and taking the time derivative on both sides of (26) yields the conclusion that $u^*(t)$ is constant [see Solow (1986) for details].

It is worth noting that the conclusion that $u^*(t)$ is constant may be derived solely from the competitive conditions (19) and (20), and HR. If a path satisfies all three conditions then, as we have seen in the second section, the competitive conditions imply [see (29)]:

$$\dot{Y}^*(t) = r(Y^*(t) - u^*(t)) = rp^*(t)\,\dot{k}^*(t) \quad \text{for all } t \tag{39}$$

HR then implies $Y^*(t)$ is constant, Finally, HR says that $Y^*(t) = u^*(t)$. This shows that if a path is competitive and satisfies HR, then utility $u^*(t)$ is a constant, say U^*. If, in addition, the path is also optimal, then clearly, it is also a *maximin* path [see (Solow (1974)];[11] i.e. there is

[11]A path $\langle U'(t), k'(t), I'(t)\rangle$ from $\underline{k}$ is a maximin path if and only if for every feasible path $\langle U(t), k(t), I(t)\rangle$ from $\underline{k}$, $\operatorname{Inf}_t U'(t) \geq \operatorname{Inf}_t U(t)$.

no other path $\langle U(t), I(t), k(t)\rangle$ from the same initial stocks $\underline{k}$ with $\inf_t U(t) > u^*$. So, there is no other path from $\underline{k}$ along which a larger utility can be sustained. This summarizes the arguments behind claim (a).

Turning now to claim (b), consider again an optimal path $\langle k^*(t), I^*(t)\rangle$ with its price support $p^*(t)$. Denote by $V(k)$ the value function at time $t = 0$ [see (30)]. Denote by $V^*(t)$ the value $V[k^*(t)]$. WR says $Y^*(t) = rV^*(t)$ for each t. Examining the time derivative of $V^*(t)$ and using standard duality theory for infinite horizon optimal growth models [see Benveniste and Scheinkman (1979)] it may be concluded that [see Hartwick (1994) for details]

$$Y^*(t) = Y^*(0) + r\int_0^t p^*(s)\,\dot{k}^*(s)\,ds \text{ for each } t \qquad (40)$$

Once again, we may observe that this equation can be derived solely from the competitive conditions (19) and (20). This is because, as noted earlier, they imply (39). Taking definite integrals on both sides we obtain

$$Y^*(t_2) - Y^*(t_1) = r\int_{t_1}^{t_2} p^*(s)\,\dot{k}^*(s)\,ds \text{ for any } t_2 \geq t_1 \geq 0 \qquad (41)$$

This, essentially, seems to be the formal statement corresponding to claim (b). Hartwick (1994) interprets (40) as showing that the current NNP, in utils, is interest on past accumulations of investments valued at the current price. It seems more accurate to state, as Solow (1986) does, that the *increment* in NNP, from t_1 to t_2, is representable as interest[12] on the accumulation of value of investment over the period t_1 to t_2.

Turning our attention now to claim (c), this is, of course, true if a path from initial stocks $\underline{k}$ is *optimal and also maintains a constant consumption* (or utility). This is because, by WR and $u(t) = u^*$ for all t, it follows that NNP, $Y^*(t)$, equals u^*. Then u^* must be the maximum

[12]Some effort has also been made to proceed from (40) to a definition of a suitable stock concept, and to the interpretation that it is such a stock which is being maintained intact under HR, and that NNP is the interest on such a stock. For details the reader should consult Solow (1986) and Svensson (1986).

[13]By maximum sustainable consumption from k we mean a level u such that there is a path $\langle U(t), I(t), k(t)\rangle$, from k satisfying $U(t) = u$ for all t, and that there is no other path $\langle U'(t), I'(t), k'(t)\rangle$ from k satisfying $\inf_t U'(t) > u$.

sustainable consumption[13] from $k^*(t)$ at each t, because otherwise there is a feasible path $\langle U(\tau), I(\tau), k(\tau)\rangle$ starting from $k^*(t)$ at time t, which provides $U(\tau) > u^*$ for $\tau \geq t$, contrary to the optimality of the given path. We may note along the way that $Y^*(t)$ constant implies, by (39), that $p^*(t)\,\dot{k}^*(t) = 0$ for all t; that is, HR is satisfied.

Claim (c), however, appears to be a lot more general than this. It seems to suggest that NNP, $Y^*(t)$, along any optimal path, measures the maximum sustainable consumption from $k^*(t)$, for each t. This, however, will not be true in general.

Consider the familiar one sector optimal growth model of the Cass–Koopmans type. Labour is assumed to be fixed and all magnitudes are in per capita form. The gross production function is denoted by f; then $y = f(k)$ is the output of the single good which can be achieved from input $k \geq 0$ (of the same good) and which is distributed over current consumption, c, and gross investment. It is assumed that f is a non-negative function, which is C^2 on the positive reals and strictly concave, with $f' > 0$ and $f'' < 0$ for $k > 0$; $f'(k) \to \infty$ as $k \to 0$ and $f'(k) \to 0$ as $k \to \infty$. Capital is assumed to depreciate at a constant exponential rate $\mu > 0$. Denote the output net of depreciation by $\phi(k) = f(k) - \mu k$. Let w denote a utility function defined over non-negative reals and C^2 on the positive reals, with $w'(c) > 0$ and $w''(c) < 0$ for $c > 0$, and $w'(c) \to \infty$ as $c \to 0$.

In the terminology adopted here, in this model,

$$S(k) = \{(U, I) \mid \text{there is } c \geq 0$$

such that $$c + I \leq \phi(k),\ I \geq -\mu k \text{ and } U = w(c)\}$$

$$F = \{(k, I)/-\mu k \leq I \leq \phi(k) \text{ and } k \geq 0\}$$

$$u(k, I) = w(c), \text{ where } c = \phi(k) - I, \text{ for } (k, I) \in F$$

It is known that there is a unique modified golden rule capital stock k^r, defined by $\phi'(k^r) = r$ which has the property that along the optimum path from k^r, denote it by $\langle k^r(t), I^r(t)\rangle$, $k^r(t) = k^r$ for all t, consumption $c^r(t) = \phi(k^r(t))$ is a constant, say c^r, and the associated prices $p^r(t)$ are also constant, say p^r. There is a unique optimum path, denote it by $\langle k^*(t), I^*(t)\rangle$, from any initial $\underline{k} \neq k^r$, with $\underline{k} > 0$, which is strictly increasing (decreasing) if $\underline{k} < k^r$ ($\underline{k} > k^r$), and along the optimal path $k^*(t) \to k^r$ as $t \to \infty$. It is straightforward to verify that if $\bar{k}$ denotes the golden rule stock [i.e. $\bar{k}$ is defined by $\phi'(\bar{k}) = 0$ and the initial stock $\underline{k} \leq \bar{k}$ then $\phi(\underline{k})$ is the maximum sustainable consumption $\underline{k}$, that the unique path which attains this is the constant path $k(t) = \underline{k}$ for all t, and that this is an efficient path.[14]

Consider such a constant path $k(t) = \underline{k}$ for all t, with $0 < \underline{k} < k^r$. Then, the maximum sustainable consumption (utility) from $\underline{k}$ is $u\,\phi(\underline{k})$. Let $u^*(t)$ denote the utility at time t along the optimal path from $\underline{k}$. Then, we have

$$\int_0^\infty e^{-rt}\, u^*(t) > u(\phi(\underline{k}))/r$$

by uniqueness of the optimal path (which is distinct from the constant path, since $k^*(t)$ converges to k^r as $t \to \infty$. But, using WR for optimal paths,

$$\int_0^\infty e^{-rt}\, u^*(t) = Y^*(0)/r$$

where $Y^*(0)$ is the NNP on the optimal path at time $t = 0$. Thus, we must have

$$Y^*(0) > u(\phi(\underline{k}))$$

so that the NNP at time $t = 0$ does *not* measure the maximum sustainable consumption (utility) from $k^*(0)$.

The above discussion also serves to underscore the fact that the kind of cases to which claim (a) may be applicable is very limited in scope, far more so, than the kind of situations where one may sensibly speak of maximum sustainable consumption through efficient allocation of resources. If we consider the class of competitive paths in this model (from any initial stock $\underline{k} > 0$), which also satisfies HR, then by (39), along a competitive path $\langle k(t), p(t) \rangle$, it follows that, since $p(t)\,\dot{k}(t) = 0$, $Y(t)$ must be a constant and $Y(t) = u(t) = w(c(t))$. Thus, $c(t)$ is a constant. It may be verified that current prices $p(t) = w'(c(t))$. So $p(t)$ is a constant, and therefore, the present value price $e^{-rt}\,p(t) \to 0$ as $t \to \infty$. As is well known, this together with the competitive conditions, implies that the path is optimal. In such a framework then, the class of paths under consideration consists only of the unique stationary path

[14]A path is efficient if there is no other path, from the same initial conditions, which provides consumption at least as large as that along the given path at all dates and strictly larger at some date (see Cass (1972)).

from k^r. The class of paths in which the maximum sustainable consumption is the constant consumption along the path, and which is also efficient, is therefore much larger than that which can be characterized by the competitive conditions (19) and (20), together with HR. In the model considered above, there is a stationary optimal path, which is the *only* path where both these conditions are satisfied. In models including exhaustible resources, where typically there are no stationary optimal paths, even though there are efficient paths in which consumption is constant, it is unclear whether there are *any* paths in which the dual sets of conditions, (19) and (20), and (38) are satisfied.

An interesting variant of these questions ought to be mentioned. We could ask whether the value of aggregate net investment is an indicator of whether or not current consumption is below or above the maximum sustainable level of consumption from the current stock of capital. In the one sector model, for example, it is easy to see that it indeed is such an indicator along optimal paths from $\underline{k} < k^r$ (the modified golden rule). Because, as we noted above, when $\underline{k} < k^r$, the optimal path is monotone strictly increasing, and so, current consumption $c^*(t)$ is below the maximum sustainable level of consumption $\phi(k^*(t))$. At the same time, $p^*(t)\,\dot{k}^*(t) > 0$, since $k^*(t)$ is strictly increasing. The reverse is true when $\underline{k} > k^r$. The sign of $p(t)\dot{k}^*(t)$ is, therefore, an indicator of whether or not current consumption is below or above the maximum sustainable level from current stocks. Asheim (1994) considers this possibility in detail in the context of an optimum growth model including an exhaustible resource. Drawing on results from Dasgupta and Heal (1974, 1979), he shows that in general the value of net investment in capital stocks (including exhaustible resource stocks) is *not* an indicator of sustainability in this sense.

The discussion above indicates that when we consider in some detail the extent of validity and the richness of interpretation of the claims surrounding the links between NNP and sustainable development, the results are not very encouraging. We will conclude on a somewhat more positive note, making the following observation due to Weitzman (1995). If, by a path of sustainable development, we do not mean maintaining the maximum sustainable consumption level at each date, but rather the weaker, but sensible, requirement that welfare, as measured by the discounted sum of consumption criteria, of future generations is at least as much as the welfare of the current generation, then, for paths satisfying WR, the value of net investment is an indicator of whether or not the path considered is one of sustainable development. The welfare of future generations can be represented by the constant consumption equivalent of the future flow of consumption and this is measured by NNP. This is larger than current consumption if and only if the value of net investment is positive.

5. SOME REMARKS AND QUESTIONS OF INTEREST

In a discrete time model of one produced good and one exhaustible resource, Dasgupta and Mitra (1983) provide a complete characterization of constant consumption paths, which are also efficient (and hence, consumption in each period along such a path is the maximum sustainable consumption from the capital stocks in that period), in terms of supporting prices. The prices are present value prices, in the sense that the price of each good is expressed in units of the single consumption good at time *0*. These are prices associated with an efficient path [see Cass (1972) and Mitra (1978)]. At these prices, intertemporal present value profit maximization conditions are satisfied along an efficient path in each period. Compared to the kind of price support properties discussed in the second and third sections, the distinguishing features of such a characterization are:

(i) the absence of any discount factor for the consumption good; and
(ii) the presence of a price support property for an appropriate value function, in the tradition of such support properties familiar from the optimal growth literature [see Weitzman (1973)]. This value function shows the level of maximum sustainable consumption which is possible from initial capital stocks.

There is no restriction on the kind of paths to which the characterization applies, other than strict positivity of initial stocks. Condition (ii), especially, makes it clear that such prices and the support properties are to be interpreted as planner's prices and planner's rules.

Solow (1974), working with a Cobb-Douglas production function, obtains closed form solution for constant consumption paths along which HR is satisfied. Hartwick (1977) extends this to general production functions and shows that paths which are price supported (by efficiency prices, no discount rate is involved) and which satisfy HR are constant consumption paths. They work in a continuous time framework and they assume efficiency of the path. Whether HR is a necessary condition for efficient constant consumption paths is a question they do not address.

In discrete time formulation, the rule that investment in produced capital equals the value of net depletion of exhaustible resource stocks, is not satisfied at any time along efficient constant consumption paths, regardless of which of the two sets of prices (beginning or end of period prices) are chosen for the valuation. However, there is an analogue of the rule in discrete time in the form of an inequality. In each period, investment in the produced capital good takes a value between an upper and a lower value, which are the values of the depletion in the resource stock during that period, evaluated according to the beginning and end of period prices, respectively. HR in its equality form may be said to hold asymptotically, since the difference between the upper and lower values in the inequality, asymptotically converges to zero [see Dasgupta and Mitra (1983) for details].

All this would suggest that a similar difference may be expected in the formulation of Weitzman's Rule, between continuous and discrete time frameworks, since the net investment component may be evaluated according to the end of period or beginning of period prices. Indeed, our analysis in a discrete time model shows that the constant consumption equivalent of an optimal path lies between the two values of NNP calculated according to the two sets of prices for the investment goods.

Throughout our discussion it was assumed that the interest rate is strictly positive. As is well known, when $r = 0$, the welfare function in *Problem 1* (see the second section) may be undefined. However, redefining the origin of measurement of utility to be the maximum sustainable utility (from arbitrary initial stocks), denote this by U^*, it may be possible to speak of optimal paths [see Gale (1967)]. Suppose that the control *Problem 1* is well defined after replacing $U(t)$ by $U(t) = U^*$ for each t, and that the turnpike theorem is valid, i.e. the capital stocks along the optimal path from $\underline{k}$, denoted by $\langle U^*(t), I^*(t), k^*(t) \rangle$, converge to k^*, the golden rule stocks from which there is a stationary path with utility equal to U^*. Along the optimal path, the Hamiltonian will be constant and equal to zero. Since the RHS of (26) is now zero, equation (26) is valid. Remembering that, in this formulation, the origin of measurement of utility is U^*, this says that the term $U^*(t) + p^*(t)\, I^*(t)$ is a constant, and equals U^* for all t, where $p^*(t)$ are the prices associated with the optimal path from $\underline{k}$. This seems to lead to an interesting observation, namely, that in a stationary framework, growth in NNP signals non-optimality and/or time preference.

We should note, however, that while WR is valid in the sense of equation (26), its main purpose, which is to show that NNP equals the constant utility equivalent $\bar{u}$, defined by (23), is not achieved here. Indeed, in general, $\bar{u}$ is not defined. This is because the LHS of (23) is finite only when $\bar{u}$ is zero. However, the RHS of (23) is well defined along an optimal path and, in general, will not be zero and will be changing over time. For example, in a one sector model, if the initial capital stock is below the level k^*, then utility and capital increase over time and the welfare along the optimal path, i.e. the RHS of (23), is increasing over time. Unlike the situation in the discounted case, this not reflected in the Hamiltonian, which, as we observed above, is a constant.

In brief then, the validity and interpretation of WR in the undiscounted case is unclear and seems to be an interesting avenue for further exploration.

Finally, throughout our discussion, the interest rate was assumed to be constant over time. Exploring the implications of allowing a variable rate of interest would be an interesting line of investigation. The interested reader may wish to consult Asheim (1997) and Long and Hartwick (1996) for some works which seek to incorporate a variable rate of interest.

References

Asheim, G.B. (1994), 'Net National Product as an Indicator of Sustainability', *Scandinavian Journal of Economics*, 96(2), pp. 257–65.

——— (1995), 'Capital Gains and Net National Product in Open Economies', *Journal of Public Economics*, 59(3), pp. 419–34.

——— (1997), 'The Weitzman Foundation of NNP with Non-Constant Interest Rates', mimeo, University of Oslo.

Benveniste, L.M. and J.A. Scheinkman (1979), 'On the Differentiability of the Value Function in Dynamic Models of Economics', *Econometrica*, 47, pp. 727–32.

——— (1982), 'Duality Theory for Dynamic Optimization Models of Economics: The Continuous Time Case', *Journal of Economic Theory*, 27, pp. 1–19.

Brekke, K.A. (1994), 'Net National Product as a Welfare Indicator', *Scandinavian Journal of Economics*, 96, pp. 241–52.

Cairns, R.D. (1997), 'A Note on the Rentier Economy', mimeo, McGill University.

Cass, D. (1965), 'Optimum Growth in an Aggregative Model of Capital Accumulation', *Review of Economic Studies*, 32, pp. 233–40.

——— (1972), 'On Capital Overaccumulation in the Aggregative, Neoclassical Model of Economic Growth: A Complete Characterization', *Journal of EconomicTheory*, 4, pp. 200–23.

Cass, D. and T. Mitra (1991), 'Indefinitely Sustained Consumption Despite Exhaustible Natural Resources', *Economic Theory*, 1, pp. 119–46.

Dasgupta, P.S. (1990), 'The Environment as a Commodity', *Oxford Review of Economic Policy*, 6, pp. 51–67.

Dasgupta, P.S. and G.M. Heal (1974), 'The Optimal Depletion of Exhaustible Resources', *Review of Economic Studies,* Symposium on the Economics of Exhaustible Resources, 41, pp. 3–28.

——— (1979), *Economic Theory and Exhaustible Resources*, Cambridge: Cambridge University Press.

Dasgupta, S. and T. Mitra (1983), 'Intergenerational Equity and Efficient Allocation of Exhaustible Resources', *International Economic Review*, 24, pp. 133–53.

——— (1999a), 'Optimal and Competitive Programmes in Reachable Multisector Models', *Economic Theory*, 14(3), pp. 565–82.

——— (1999b), 'On the Welfare Significance of Net National Product for Economic Growth and Sustainable Development', *The Japanese Economic Review*, 50(4), pp. 422–42.

Dorfman, R., P. Samuelson and R. Solow (1958), *Linear Programming and Economic Analysis*, McGraw-Hill.

Friedman, M. (1957), *A Theory of the Consumption Function*, Princeton: Princeton University Press.

Gale, D. (1967), 'On Optimal Development in a Multi-Sector Economy', *Review of Economic Studies*, 34, pp. 1–19.

Hartwick, J.M. (1977), 'Intergenerational Equity and Investing of Rents from Exhaustible Resources', *American Economic Review*, 66, pp. 972–4.

——— (1990), 'Natural Resources, National Accounting and Economic Depreciation', *Journal of Public Economics*, 43, pp. 291–304.

——— (1994), 'National Wealth and Net National Product', *Scandinavian Journal of Economics*, 96(2), pp. 253–6.

——— and N.V. Long (1999), 'Constant Consumption and the Economic Depreciation of Natural Capital: The Non-Autonomous Case', *International Economic Review, 40(1), pp. 53–62.*

Hulten, C.R. (1992), 'Accounting for the Wealth of Nations: The Net Versus Gross Output Controversy and its Ramifications', *Scandinavian Journal of Economics*, 94 (supplement), pp. 9–24.

Intriligator, M.D. (1971), *Mathematical Optimization and Economic Theory*, Englewood Cliffs, New Jersey: Prentice-Hall, Inc.

Kemp, M.C. and N.V. Long (1982), 'On the Evaluation of Social Income in a Dynamic Economy', in G.R. Feiwell (ed.), *Samuelson and Neoclassical Economics*, Boston: Kluwer Nijhoff, pp. 185–9.

Koopmans, T.C. (1965), 'On the Concept of Optimal Economic Growth', *Pontificae Academia Scientiarum*, Vatican City, pp. 225–88.

Lofgren, K.G. (1992), 'Comment on C.R. Hulten', *Scandinavian Journal of Economics*, 94 (supplement), pp. 25–8.

Lozada, G.A. (1995), 'Resource Depletion, National Income Accounting and the Value of Optimal Dynamic Programs', forthcoming in *Resource and Energy Economics.*

Mäler, K.G. (1991), 'National Accounts and Environmental Resources', *Environmental and Resource Economics*, 1, pp. 1–15.

Malinvaud, E. (1953), 'Capital Accumulation and Efficient Allocation of Resources', *Econometrica*, 21, pp. 233–68.

McKenzie, L.W. (1986), 'Optimal Economic Growth and Turnpike Theorems', in K.J. Arrow and M.D. Intriligator (eds.), *Handbook of Mathematical Economics, Vol. 3*, New York: North Holland, pp. 1281–1355.

Mitra T. (1978), 'Efficient Growth with Exhaustible Resources in a Neoclassical Model', *Journal of Economics Theory*, 17, pp. 114–29.

Pontryagin, L.S. *et al.* (1962), *The Mathematical Theory of Optimal Processes*, New York: Interscience.

Ramsey, F.P. (1928), 'A Mathematical Theory of Saving', *Economic Journal*, 38, pp. 543–59.

Samuelson, P.A. (1961), 'The Evaluation of "Social Income": Capital Formation and Wealth', in F.A. Lutz and D.C. Hague (eds.), *The Theory of Capital*, London: Macmillan, pp. 32–57.

Sefton, J.A. and M.R. Weale (1996), 'The Net National Product and Exhaustible Resources: The Effects of Foreign Trade', *Journal of Public Economics*, 61(1), pp. 21–47.

Solow, R.M. (1974), 'Intergenerational Equity and Exhaustible Resources', *Review of Economic Studies*, Symposium on the Economics of Exhaustible Resources, 41, pp. 29–45.

——— (1986), 'On the Intergenerational Allocation of Natural Resources', *Scandinavian Journal of Economics*, 88, pp. 141–49.

——— (1992), *An Almost Practical Step Towards Sustainability*, Washington, D.C.: Resources for the Future.

Sorger, G. (1992), *Minimum Impatience Theorems for Recursive Economic Models*, Berlin, Heidelberg: Springer-Verlag.

Svensson, L.E.O. (1986), 'Comment on R.M. Solow', *Scandinavian Journal of Economics*, 88, pp. 153–5.

Uzawa, H. (1964), 'Optimal Growth in a Two Sector Model of Capital Accumulation', *Review Economic Studies*, 31, pp. 1–24.

Weitzman, M.L. (1973), 'Duality Theory for Infinite Horizon Convex Models', *Management Science*, 19, pp. 783–9.

——— (1976), 'On the Welfare Significance of National Product in a Dynamic Economy', *Quarterly Journal of Economic*, 90, pp. 156–62.

——— (1997), 'Sustainability and Technical Progress', *Scandinavian Journal of Economics*, 99(1), pp. 1–13.

Appendix

Consider the dynamic optimization problem noted in section 2.2, namely,

PROBLEM 1: $$\text{Max} \int_0^{\infty} e^{-rt}\, u(k(t), I(t))\, dt$$

such that $$(k(t), I(t)) \in S(k(t)) \text{ for each } t$$

$$\dot{k}(t) = I(t) \text{ for each } t$$

and $$k(0) = \underline{k}$$

We shall verify that if a path from $\underline{k}$ is *optimal* then it satisfies the competitive conditions (19) and (20) of section 2.2. Define the associated Hamiltonian function $H(k, P, t)$ by:

$$H(k, P, t) = \text{Max}\; e^{-rt}\, u(k, I) + PI \tag{A.1}$$

such that $$(k, I) \in F$$

Given p, if we define P by: $P = e^{-rt}\, p$, and conversely, then, in view of (17), it is clear that

$$H(k, P, t) = e^{-rt}\, h(k, p) \tag{A.2}$$

It may then be verified that given a path $\langle U(t), I(t), k(t)\rangle$ from $\underline{k}$, the existence of a time path of prices $p(t)$ at which (19) and (20) are satisfied, is equivalent to the existence of a time path of prices $P(t)$ at which the path satisfies:

$$e^{-rt}\, u(k(t), \dot{k}(t)) + P(t)\, \dot{k}(t) = H(k(t), P(t), t) \text{ for each } t \tag{A.3}$$

and $$\dot{P}(t) = -\frac{\partial H}{\partial k}(k(t), P(t), t) \text{ for each } t \tag{A.4}$$

The prices $P(t)$ are present value prices, discounted from t, at the discount rate r, and are related to the current value prices $p(t)$ by:

$$P(t) = e^{-rt}\, p(t) \text{ for each } t \tag{A.5}$$

The left hand side expression in (A.3) is simply the NNP in present value form and the Hamiltonian is the maximum present value of output which can be produced, given the present value prices P and capital stock k. Equations (A.3) and (A.4) above are (19) and (20), respectively, in their present value form.

For given k, P, write the maximizing value of the control I, in (A.1), as $G(k, P)$. Define the (present value) pre-Hamiltonian function $J(k, P, I, t)$ by:

$$J(k, P, I, t) = e^{-rt}\, u(k, I) + PI \tag{A.6}$$

It is clear from the definitions that the pre-Hamiltonian is maximized at $I = G(k, P)$ for each k, P. So,

$$\frac{\partial J}{\partial I}(k, P, G(k, P), t) = 0 \quad \text{for each } k, P \text{ and } t$$

and
$$J(k, P, G(k, P), t) = H(k, P, t) \quad \text{for each } t \tag{A.7}$$

It follows that:

$$\frac{\partial H}{\partial P}(k, P, t) = \frac{\partial J}{\partial P}(k, P, G(k, P), t) + \frac{\partial J}{\partial I}(k, P, G(k, P), t)\frac{\partial G}{\partial P}(k, P)$$

$$= \frac{\partial J}{\partial P}(k, P, G(k, P), t) = G(k, P) \tag{A.8}$$

and similarly that

$$\frac{\partial H}{\partial k}(k, P, t) = \frac{\partial J}{\partial k}(k, P, G(k, P), t)$$

So, (A.3) and (A.4) are equivalent to:

$$\dot{k}(t) = G(k(t), P(t)) = \frac{\partial H}{\partial P}(k, P, t) = \frac{\partial J}{\partial P}(k, P, G(k, P), t) \text{ for each } t \tag{A.9}$$

and
$$\dot{P}(t) = -\frac{\partial J}{\partial k}(k(t), P(t), G(k(t), P(t)), t) \quad \text{for each } t \tag{A.10}$$

The existence of a price path $P(t)$, at which (A.9) and (A.10) are satisfied, is a necessary condition for a path to be optimal.[15] So, the equations (19) and (20), defining a competitive path, are precisely the necessary conditions for a path to be an optimal solution to the control *Problem 1* above. This represents the 'maximum principle' of Pontryagin *et al.* (1962).

[15]See, for example, Benveniste and Scheinkman (1982). We should note, though, that their problem is in a more general setting since they do not assume differentiability of the utility function.

DEVELOPMENT

Development: An Introduction

The papers in this section study two important aspects of the development process. Both deal with wage labour and both attempt to understand development as a structural process in which theoretical disaggregation is crucial to our understanding. The first paper is cast in the familiar dual-economy mode, the setting of some of Rakshit's finest work. The second paper focuses on the wage gap between skilled and unskilled labour, and how this gap is affected by trade, a controversial topic of great current interest.

Demand and Wage-Goods Constraints

A developing country is best not seen as a seamless homogeneous unit. A large literature has developed on the interrelations between a tradition-bound, overpopulated agricultural sector, and the more eager and dynamic sectors of the economy, elliptically clubbed together as 'industry'. Amitava Krishna Dutt concentrates on two different ways in which agricultural growth can affect industrial growth, the first through the operation of the demand constraint, the second through the wage-goods constraint. Dutt then develops a framework capable of displaying both these constraints.

Relative stagnation in agriculture could restrict industrial growth by reducing the demand for industrial goods as larger and larger portions of income get diverted to price inelastic agricultural goods. This kind of demand constraint arises from (a) slow wage dynamics leading to a significant lag between increases in the price of food and compensating increases in money wages; (b) price inelasticity in the demand for food; and (c) insufficient expenditure on industrial goods out of the increased incomes resulting from the rise in food prices. In the longer run, however, when money wages would catch up with the price of food, the basis of this demand constraint disappears. The problem then appears elsewhere. Given that agriculture dominates the wage-goods basket, the compensating increase in the industrial wages would lead to a significant squeeze in profit. This dampens industrial investment, and thereby, industrial growth. This, briefly, is the wage-goods constraint.

TRADE AND THE WAGE-GAP

Recently, a substantial literature has emerged trying to explain the growing wage-gap between skilled and unskilled labourers. A large part of this literature tries to explain the growing wage-gap through international trade. The typical practice is to model the economy in the traditional Heckscher–Ohlin framework and then, appealing to the Stolper–Samuelson theorem, to conclude that countries exporting skill intensive goods would experience a rise in the relative wage of skilled workers as international trade becomes more free. The problem with this approach is that for countries importing skill intensive goods, it would predict a decline in the skilled–unskilled wage gap.Then how could we explain the rising wage gap in less-developed countries? The paper by Marjit, Broll and Sengupta explores the implications of free trade for income distribution, especially for the relative wage between skilled and unskilled workers, in the context of a less-developed country. The authors point out that in order to understand the true implications of free trade on income distribution in less-developed countries, one has to go beyond the traditional Heckscher–Ohlin model. In particular, one has to consider the role played by the huge informal sector in these countries. In a model consisting of a formal sector and an informal sector, the authors look at the effects of changes in prices on the formal–informal as well as skilled–unskilled relative wages through a series of comparative statics exercises.

3

Demand and Wage-Goods Constraints in Agriculture–Industry Interaction in Less-Developed Countries

A Theoretical Analysis*

AMITAVA KRISHNA DUTT**

1. INTRODUCTION

Professor Mihir Rakshit has made significant contributions to the study of the macroeconomics of less-developed countries (LDCs). In these contributions [see especially Rakshit (1982, 1989)] he has stressed the importance of the interaction between agricultural and industrial sectors, which is not surprising, given the large size of the agricultural sector in most less developed countries. To analyse this interaction, he has developed models in which the industrial sector has Keynesian features, so that effective demand plays a major role in determining its output, while in the agricultural sector, output is supply constrained. Models of this type have also been developed by others [see, for instance, Chichilnisky and Taylor (1980), Taylor (1982, 1983, 1991)]. These models show how an increase in agricultural output and income

*This paper attempts to compare and synthesize models which show how the agricultural sector can constrain industrial growth in less-developed countries (LDCs) through demand and wage-goods constraints. To do so, it develops a simple framework for analyzing the macroeconomic interaction between agriculture and industry in such economies and shows how this framework can be used to construct models which formalize, in turn, the demand and wage-goods constraints. It then develops two synthesis models which include features of both demand constrained and wage-goods constrained models. It is argued that a synthesis model with inflation and conflicting claims may be a suitable basis for analyzing the macroeconomics of agriculture-industry interactions in LDCs.

**I am grateful to Amitava Bose for his insightful comments and suggestions.

can increase industrial production by increasing the demand for the industrial good, and this can increase industrial growth; conversely, agricultural stagnation reduces industrial output by reducing the demand for it.

Rakshit and others have followed a long tradition emphasizing the interaction between agriculture and industry, originating in the physiocrats, Ricardo and other classical economists, and continuing to Lewis's (1954) classical model of the dual economy.[1] Similar ideas have been discussed by Kaldor (1975, 1979), Kalecki (1976) and others. But these contributions do not introduce effective demand considerations, but instead, focus on how agriculture affects industry by changing profits through its effect on the cost side. Models in this tradition typically take the real wage in industry to be fixed in terms of a basket in which the agricultural good is strongly represented, so that if the price of the agricultural good increases, the wage in terms of the industrial good increases, implying a reduction in industrial profits which—if industrial profits are the major source of saving for industrial investment—slows down industrial growth.

These two mechanisms, by which the agricultural sector affects the industrial sector in these models, have been called the demand and wage goods constraints imposed by agriculture on industry.[2] While

[1] Lewis actually examines the interaction between a non-capitalist subsistence sector and a capitalist sector, rather than between agriculture and industry. However, in his contribution Lewis also discusses the issue of the terms of trade between food and manufactures. Subsequent contributors to the development literature identify his subsistence sector with agriculture and the capitalist sector with industry.

[2] There is no clear consensus on the formal meaning of a wage-goods constrained model. Dutta (1988), for instance, takes the view that in a wage-goods constrained model industrial employment is restricted by the need to pay workers a certain real wage, given an inelastic supply of food (which is a variant of the wages fund model). Baland (1992), however, has argued that Dutta's formalization of the wage-goods constrained model is erroneous. In this paper we return to the classical Lewis-Kaldor 'profit squeeze' idea in referring to the wage-goods constraint. The same approach is taken by Ahluwalia (1985, pp. 33–5). Though the theoretical interpretation of the demand constraint is far less controversial, its empirical relevance has been subject to a great deal of dispute. Early development economists argued that demand issues were irrelevant for less developed countries, but recently many, including Rakshit himself, have stressed its importance (see Rakshit, 1989; Dutt, 1996a).

these formal models have focused on only one or the other of these two constraints, the informal literature on constraints on industrial growth has emphasized the importance of both at the same time. For instance, in the debates on the determinants of industrial stagnation in India—which have clearly motivated the modeling efforts of Rakshit and several others—both constraints have been thought to be relevant.[3] The question naturally arises whether these constraints are relevant for two different kinds of economies, or whether the agricultural sector can actually constrain industry from both sides at the same time.

The purpose of this paper is to examine and compare these two types of models—those incorporating the demand constraint and those incorporating the wage-goods constraints—using a common analytical framework, and to attempt to synthesize them by developing models in which both constraints can simultaneously affect industrial growth.

The rest of this paper proceeds as follows. Section 2 develops a general framework with which the different constraints can be usefully discussed and compared. Sections 3 and 4 discuss how the framework can be used to present, in turn, the models with demand and wage-goods constraints. Section 5 then discusses two ways in which the two models can be synthesized. Section 6 concludes.

2. GENERAL FRAMEWORK

This section develops a general framework in terms of which simple versions of the model with demand and wage goods constraints can be examined. The framework is a simple and familiar one; similar frameworks have been used earlier by a number of writers, including Taylor (1983) and Rattso (1989). It considers a closed economy with two sectors—an agricultural sector which produces a single consumption good, and an industrial or non-agricultural sector which produces goods which can be used for both consumption purposes and for investment in the industrial sector.

[3] See Ahluwalia (1985, chap. 3) for a summary, and papers by various contributors to this literature, especially those by Sukhamoy Chakravarty and K.N. Raj [Nayyar (1994) contains a useful selection]. Formal discussions of these constraints in this literature take the two constraints to be substitutes. Dutta (1988), for instance, develops a model in which only one of the two constraints binds at any period (except by accident), and uses the technique of switching regressions to find which of the constraints was binding in India in different years.

The agricultural good is produced with labour and land. Labour is in unlimited supply and the amount of labour is irrelevant for the level of agricultural production. The amount of land is given, but agricultural output can increase over time due to land-saving technical change which requires capital investment. Assuming strict complementarity between capital and such technical change, and assuming that perfect competition in the agricultural market ensures full capacity utilization, we have,

$$Q_a = a_a K_a \tag{1}$$

where Q_i denotes output, a_i the capital-output ratio, and K_i the capital stock, all in sector i, and where the subscript a refers to the agricultural sector. A fraction θ of agricultural output goes to landlords and the rest goes to share-cropping tenant farmers. The agricultural capital good is produced only with agricultural labour, and to fix ideas, may be interpreted as irrigation facilities. Investment in agriculture depends on the agricultural terms of trade, since higher relative prices make it more worthwhile for tenant farmers to invest by expending their labour. We assume that agricultural investment, as a ratio of agricultural capital, is given by the linear equation,

$$g_a = I_a/K_a = \beta_0 + \beta_1 p \tag{2}$$

where I_i is investment in sector i, g_i is investment as a ratio of capital stock in sector $i, p = P_a/P_n$ is the agricultural terms of trade where P_i is the price of the good produced by sector i and where β_i are constants with $\beta_1 > 0$.[4] We assume that agricultural investment has no effect on income and expenditure during the current period: tenants trade off returns to labour in investment activity and the disutility of work, and invest more when their terms of trade improve by reducing their leisure.

The industrial good is produced with capital and labour with a fixed coefficients production function. With the level of industrial output given by Q_n, the employment of labour in industry is determined by

$$L_n = b_n Q_n \tag{3}$$

where L_n is employment in the industrial sector, b_n is the given labour–output ratio in the industrial sector, and subscript n refers to the industrial sector. Workers receive a money wage denoted by W_n; industrial firms are able to hire all the workers they need, given the

[4] A similar investment function is used by Rattso (1989).

presence of unlimited supplies of labour in the agricultural sector. The residual income goes to industrial capitalists in the form of profits. Industrial firms make investment to increase their capital stock, which is physically the same as the industrial output. It should be pointed out that we have so far made no assumptions about the determination of industrial output, price or investment; these issues will be discussed when the alternative models are considered below.

We assume that industrial capitalists and agricultural landlords save a constant fraction, s, of their income, and spend the rest of their income, and agricultural tenant farmers and industrial workers are assumed not to save. A fraction of the value of consumption expenditure, α, is devoted by all classes to the agricultural sector, and the rest is spent on the industrial good. For now, we assume that α is fixed, but we will later examine the implications of making it depend on the relative price. These assumptions imply that the market-clearing conditions in the industrial and agricultural sectors, respectively, are given by,

$$(1-\alpha)\{W_n b_n Q_n + (1-\theta)P_a Q_a + (1-s)[(P_n - W_n b_n)Q_n + \theta P_a Q_a]\} + P_n I_n - P_n Q_n = 0 \quad (4)$$

and

$$\alpha\{W_n b_n Q_n + (1-\theta)P_a Q_a + (1-s)[(P_n - W_n b_n)Q_n + \theta P_a Q_a]\} - P_a Q_a = 0 \quad (5)$$

Dividing these equations by $P_n K_n$ and substituting from equations (1) and (3) through (5) we get,

$$(1-\alpha)\{Vb_n u + (1-\theta)a_a pk + (1-s)[(1-Vb_n)u + \theta a_a pk]\} + g_n - u = 0 \quad (6)$$

and

$$\alpha\{Vb_n u + (1-\theta)a_a pk - (1-s)[(1-Vb_n)u + \theta a_a pk]\} - a_a pk = 0, \quad (7)$$

where $u = Q_n/K_n$, $V = W_n/P_n$, and $k = K_a/K_n$. These two equations can be added together to yield,

$$g_n = s[(1-Vb_n)u + \theta a_a pk]. \quad (8)$$

which states that total investment in the industrial sector is equal to the savings in the industrial and agricultural sectors, all of which is done by the capitalists and landlords. Agricultural investment is made by merely expending surplus labour, so that it does not enter the financial investment and saving accounts represented in equation (8). Note that equations (6), (7) and (8) are not independent equations, since any one can be derived from the other two.

Equations (2), (7) and (6) or (8) give us three equations in six variables u, p, V, g_a, g_n, and k[5]. Thus the equational system is underdetermined.

One more equation can be added to it, depending on the notion of equilibrium we wish to examine. One notion is what can be called 'short-run equilibrium', which takes the stocks of capital in each sector to be given, and which then explores equilibrium in which both goods markets clear. For this notion of equilibrium we add the equation,

$$k = k_0 \tag{9}$$

The other notion is what can be called a 'long-run equilibrium', in which k is determined as a variable, which implies that in equilibrium we have balanced growth in the two sectors (where, for simplicity, we assume away the depreciation of capital), so that,

$$g_a = g_n \tag{10}$$

Since we still have four equations and six variables, the system remains underdetermined. To close the model we need to introduce two additional equations for each of the runs we have discussed. In the next two sections, we consider two alternative models which close the model in different ways, following the method of alternative closures discussed in Marglin (1984) and Dutt (1990), to obtain simple models to formalize demand and wage-goods constraints on the industrial sector.

3. DEMAND CONSTRAINED MODEL

A demand constrained model introduces two equations which make industrial output depend on effective demand.

First, we assume that the industrial price is determined as a mark-up on prime costs, so that,

$$P_n = (1 + z)W_n b_n \tag{11}$$

[5]Note that equations (1), (3), (4) and (5) have already been incorporated into these equations.

where z is the exogenously-given mark-up rate, which is determined by the degree of monopoly *à la* Kalecki (1971). Firms set their price as a mark-up on labour costs; when demand changes they leave the price unchanged and respond by changing their level of output, and hence, capacity utilization, which can be measured by u, which is assumed to be lower than a_n, the technologically given maximum (or full capacity) output-capital ratio, implying that firms hold excess capacity. Thus, industrial output is determined by the demand for it. Equation (11) implies that,

$$V = 1/[(1 + z)b_n] \tag{12}$$

Next, we assume that industrial firms make investment plans which depend on profit expectations and market prospects. For simplicity, we assume a simple linear form of the investment function, which makes investment, as a ratio of capital stock, depend positively on the rate of capacity utilization and the share of profits in output, as proposed by Bhaduri and Marglin (1990),

$$g_n = \gamma_0' + \gamma_1 u + \gamma_2(1 - Vb_n) \tag{13}$$

Bhaduri and Marglin argue that expected future profitability depends on two factors: the expected rate of capacity utilization and the expected profit share. This formulation makes investors form such expectations from current conditions, and make these factors affect investment in linearly separable ways. As in other Keynes–Kalecki models of demand-determined output, investment plans are thus taken to be independent of savings plans.

Our demand constrained model is thus closed by adding equations (12) and (13) to our general framework.[6]

In the short run we assume that $k = k_0$ and substitute equations (12) and (13) into equations (7) and (6) or (8) to determine the short-run equilibrium values of u and p. If we assume that the level of Q_n, and hence u, changes in proportion to the level of excess demand for the industrial good, and that the level of P_a, and hence p, changes in

[6]The model is very similar to those of Chichilnisky and Taylor (1980), Rakshit (1982, 1989), Taylor (1982, 1983, 1991), Bose (1989), Rattso (1989) and others. Rakshit's own formulations generally take the more Keynesian (General Theory) route (rather than the Kaleckian one used in our general framework) of introducing factor substitution and marginal product pricing in the industrial sector.

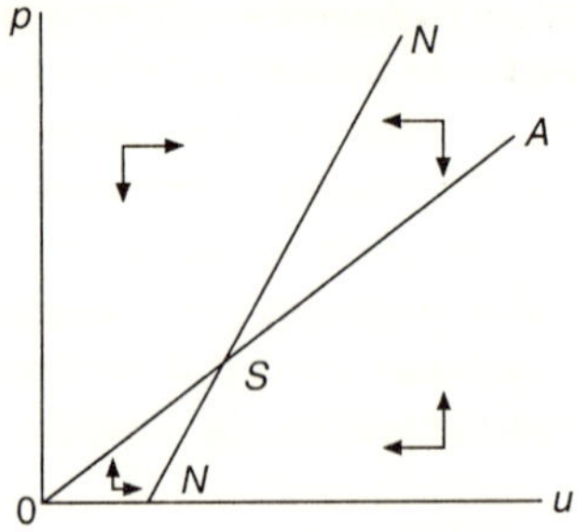

FIGURE 3.1 Demand Constrained Model: Short-run

proportion to the level of excess demand for the agricultural good, the short-run dynamics of the model, given the value of k, can be depicted in Figure 3.1. The *NN* curve shows combinations of u and p which clear the industrial goods market, and is given by,

$$-\{s[z/(1+z)] + \alpha[1 - s(z/(1+z))] - \gamma_1\}u + (1-\alpha)(1-s\theta)a_a kp$$
$$= -\gamma_0' - \gamma_2[z/(1+z)] \quad (14)$$

and the *OA* curve shows combinations of u and p which clear the agricultural goods market, and is given by,

$$\alpha[1 - s(z/(1+z))]u - [1 - \alpha(1 - s\theta)]a_a kp = 0. \quad (15)$$

Under the standard stability condition that $s[z/(1+z)] > \gamma_1$, which implies that the responsiveness of savings to changes in u exceeds that of investment, both curves are upward-rising, the horizontal and vertical arrows are as shown, and hence the short-run equilibrium at S is stable.[7] From equations (14) and (15), or equivalently, from (14) and (8), (12) and (13), we get the short-run equilibrium values of u and p, which are,

$$u = (1/\Delta)[\gamma_0' + \gamma_2(z/(1+z))][1 - \alpha(1 - s\theta)] \quad (16)$$

and

$$p = (1/a_a k\Delta)[\gamma_0' + \gamma_2(z/(1+z))]\,\alpha[1 - s(z/(1+z))] \quad (17)$$

[7] In drawing the two curves it is assumed that agricultural income is always given at full capacity output. In situations of excess supply of the agricultural good, if one assumes that realized income is given by the minimum of demand and capacity output, the curves would have to be modified.

where $\Delta = [s(z/(1+z)) - \gamma_1][1 - \alpha(1 - s\theta)] + \alpha[1 - s(z/(1+z))s\theta]$. It may be noted that the equilibrium value of u does not depend on any agricultural parameters other than θ.[8] These values can be substituted into equations (2) and (13) [with equation (12)] to determine the equilibrium values of g_i.

In this model, industrial output is constrained by demand. For instance, if γ_0'—or autonomous industrial investment—increases, u will rise with a multiplier of $[1 - \alpha(1 - s\theta)]/\Delta$. However, the model, as it now stands, does not allow conditions in agriculture to determine industrial output, and hence, g_n, other than due to changes in the parameter θ, which affects savings in agriculture. In particular, if there is an increase in a_a or in k_0 for instance, equation (17) shows that the terms of trade will move against agriculture, but there will—as equation (16) shows—be no effect on industrial output. The reason for this is the assumption that a constant fraction of consumption spending is devoted to each of the two goods, so that the fall in agricultural price results in a proportionate rise in the quantity of agricultural consumption, and no change in the value of industrial consumption.

If we wish to allow agricultural conditions to have a role in affecting industrial demand, we can assume that α increases when p increases. This implies that a rise in agricultural price leads to a greater proportion of consumption expenditure being devoted to the agricultural good, or that agricultural demand is price inelastic.[9] In this case, equations (14)

[8]This may also be seen using the Keynesian device of 'effective demand' as follows. Let us denote the level of effective demand (in real terms) for the output of sector i as D_i. Let C be aggregate consumption expenditure,

$$C = (1 - s\sigma)P_n D_n + (1 - s\theta)P_a D_a$$

where $\sigma = z/(1+z)$ is the profit share in the industrial sector. Since a constant fraction α of total consumption is spent on the agricultural good, we have $\alpha C = P_a D_a$. Substituting this into the previous equation we get $(1-\alpha)C = \zeta P_n D_n$, where $\zeta = (1 - s\sigma)/[1 - (1 - s\theta)\alpha]$. Since the effective demand for the industrial sector in nominal terms is given by $P_n D_n = (1-\alpha)C + P_n I_n$, we get $P_n D_n = \zeta P_n D_n + P_n I_n$, or $D_n = I_n/(1 - \zeta)$. For industry equilibrium with $Q_n = D_n$, we therefore get $Q_n = I_n/(1-\zeta)$. Dividing both sides by K_n we also get $u = g_n/(1-\zeta)$. With the investment function given by equation (13), and with a constant mark–up which determines σ, the right hand side of this equation is independent of p and of all agricultural parameters other than θ and the demand parameters common to the two sectors. I am grateful to Amitava Bose for suggesting this construction.

[9]The importance of this factor has been stressed by Bose (1989). See also Taylor (1983).

and (15) would still be used to determine u and p, but keeping in mind that $\alpha = \alpha(p)$ where $\alpha' > 0$. Totally differentiating equations (14) and (15) with respect to u, p, k, and a_a, we get,

$$-\{s[z/(1-z)] + \alpha[1 - s(z/(1+z))] - \gamma_1\}du + \{(1-\alpha)(1-s\theta)a_a k - \sigma\}dp$$
$$= -(1-\alpha)(1-s\theta)a_a p\, dk - (1-\alpha)(1-s\theta)pk\, da_a$$

and

$$\alpha[1 - s(z/(1+z))]\, du - \{[1-\alpha(1-s\theta)]a_a k - \sigma\}\, dp$$
$$= [1-\alpha(1-s\theta)]a_a p\, dk + [1-\alpha(1-s\theta)]pk\, da_a$$

where $\sigma = [(1 - s(z/(1+z)))u + (1-s\theta)a_a kp]\alpha' > 0$. We assume α' is small enough so that $[1-\alpha(1-s\theta)]a_a k > \sigma$ (so that a rise in p continues to reduce the excess demand for the agricultural good), which ensures that the trace of the dynamic system is negative and the determinant, $\Gamma = \Delta a_a k - [s(z/(1+z)) - \gamma_1]\sigma > 0$, ensuring the stability of short-run equilibrium. In this case we have,

$$du/dk = \sigma s\theta a_a p/\Gamma > 0$$

and

$$dp/dk = -\{[s(z/(1+z)) - \gamma_1][1-\alpha(1-s\theta)] + s\theta\alpha[1 - s(z/(1+z))]\}a_a p/\Gamma < 0$$

and analogous results hold for a_a, with identical signs. Here, an increase in k or a_a will have the effect of reducing p by increasing the supply of the agricultural good, but since this will reduce α, it will increase the share of consumption expenditure devoted to the industrial good, which will increase industrial output and u. This will also imply a rise in g_n. In this sense, the model reveals that a rise in agricultural output increases the demand for the industrial good. It should be stressed that for this result to occur, we require the assumption that the demand for agricultural goods is inelastic.[10] We now revert to the case in which $\alpha' = 0$.

[10]This is not true in general, but it is true for the specific model used here. If, for instance, increased agricultural output requires more industrial goods as intermediate goods with a fixed coefficient, there would be an agriculture-led industrial expansion even without inelastic consumption demand for the agricultural good.

In the long run we allow k to change over time, and to obtain long-run equilibrium we replace equation (9) by (10). The analysis of long-run dynamics and equilibrium can be conveniently conducted using Figure 3.2. Since equation (16) shows that u does not depend on k, from equations (12) and (13) it follows that g_n is independent of k; thus the g_n in the figure is horizontal. However, equation (17) shows that p falls with k, which follows from equation (2) and a higher k implies a lower p, and hence, a lower level of agricultural investment, explaining why the g_a curve is downward-sloping. Starting from any initial k_a, the movement in k can be seen from the diagram, since,

$$(dk/dt)/k = g_a - g_n \tag{18}$$

If g_a exceeds (is less than) g_n, k will rise (fall) over time. Given our assumptions, k will change over time until $g_a = g_n$, when balanced growth is attained and equation (10) is satisfied.

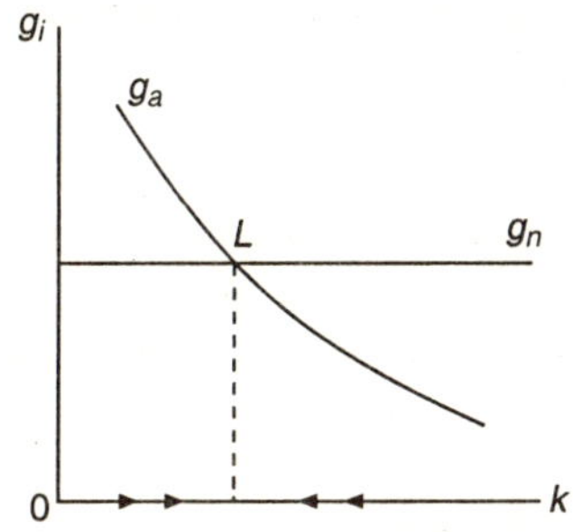

FIGURE 3.2 Demand Constrained Model: Long-run

Any change in a parameter which increases g_n will now push the g_n curve in Figure 3.2 upwards, implying a rise in long-run equilibrium levels of g_a and g_n, while an upward shift in the g_a curve (say due to a rise in β_0) will leave the long-run equilibrium level of g_n unchanged. Thus, in this version of the model, agricultural growth is not a constraint on industrial growth, although the latter is clearly demand constrained (since a rise in, say, γ_0' will clearly push the g_n curve upwards and increase industrial growth, as well as agricultural growth in long-run equilibrium). The reason for this is apparent from the earlier discussion of the short-run version of the model: the unitary price elasticity of demand. Higher industrial growth, other things constant, can push the terms of trade against industry, but this will have no adverse effect on industrial demand because given unit price elasticity, the rise in agricultural prices is compensated by a fall in the demand for food which keeps the share of agriculture in consumption constant.

If we now reintroduce our assumption that $\alpha = \alpha(p)$ with $\alpha' > 0$, as we found earlier, a rise in k will reduce p, and this will reduce α, which will increase industrial growth g_n as seen above. Thus, the g_n curve of Figure 3.2 will now become upward rising. This implies that any parametric shift which shifts upwards the g_a curve without shifting the g_n curve upwards (say due to an increase in β_0) will increase the long-run equilibrium value of g_n. In this sense, agricultural stagnation can imply industrial stagnation, and this situation can be altered (among other things) by more rapid agricultural growth.

4. WAGE-GOODS CONSTRAINED MODEL

This model, which follows Lewis (1954) and Kaldor (1975, 1979),[11] assumes that there are no demand constraints on industrial output, which is at full capacity, so that,

$$u = a_n \tag{19}$$

This could result from the assumption that the industrial market, like the agricultural market, is purely competitive, so that firms produce all that they possibly can at the going market price (which is assumed to yield positive profits). Moreover, to formalize the wage-goods constraint we need to introduce an assumption about how an increase in the price of agricultural goods increases the money wage. An extreme assumption, following Kaldor, takes the industrial wage in terms of the agricultural good to be exogenously given, so that we have[12],

$$W_n/P_a = \omega$$

which implies that,

[11]Lewis's assumptions are related, but not the same: he assumes a neoclassical production function in the industrial sector which allows for factor substitution. For Kaldorian models see Thirlwall (1986), Dutt (1992a, 1996a), and what Rattso (1989) somewhat misleadingly calls 'the neoclassical model'.

[12]If we make the alternative assumption that the real wage, ω, is fixed in terms of a basket of consumption goods, so that $\omega = W_n/P_a^{\alpha}P_n^{1-\alpha}$, we can write $\omega = Vp^{\alpha}$, so that equation (20) below has to be replaced by $V = \omega p^{1-\alpha}$. For simplicity—a procedure which may also be justified given the poltical importance of food—we assume that the basket gives all the weight to the agricultural good though the true share of the good in consumption expenditure is α. When α depends on p, of course, the true share is not constant.

$$V = \omega p \tag{20}$$

The wage-goods constrained model is thus given by appending equations (19) and (20) to our general framewok.[13]

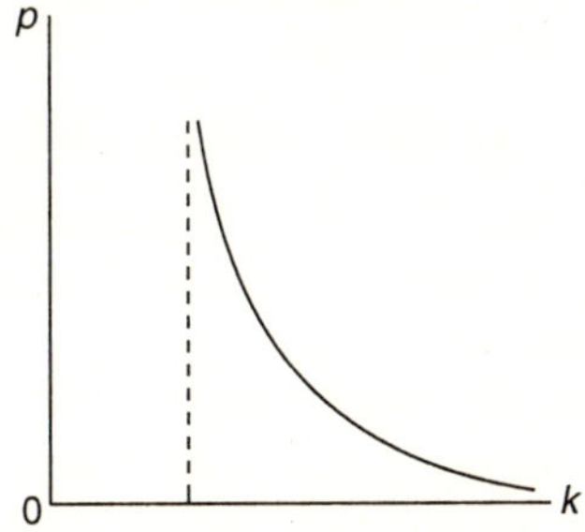

FIGURE 3.3 Wage-goods Constrained Model: Short-run

In the short-run, we can determine the market-clearing value of p from equation (7) after substituting into it from equations (19) and (20), which implies,

$$p = \alpha(1 - s)a_n / \{a_a k[1 - \alpha(1 - s\theta)] - s\omega b_n a_n\} \tag{21}$$

The determination of p is shown in Figure 3.3, which shows that as k increases (so that agricultural capital stock and output are larger relative to industrial capital stock and output), p falls. If in the short-run

[13]It should be clarified that this model does not provide the only way of modeling a wage-goods constraint. Generally, one may define a wage-goods constraint as follows. Assuming a fixed coefficients production function with (technologically) given output–capital ratio a and labour-output ratio b, and with demand (in terms of the output) given by D, we can write actual output, Q as

$$Q = \min\,[aK, L/b, D]$$

However Q is determined—by capital, labour or demand constraint, we will have $L = bQ$, and the wage bill for that (in terms of the wage good) is given by wbQ, where w is the wage in terms of the wage good, assumed to be given. The wage goods constraint can then be written as the inequality $wbQ \leq X$ where X is given, and the constraint can be said to be binding, if this is satisfied with an equality. Given this general definition, it need not be the case that a wage-goods constraint implies full capacity utilization with $Q = aK$, or that one should necessarily contrast a model with a binding wage-goods constraint with a demand constrained model. Indeed, the next section will develop a model in which both demand and wage-goods constraints operate. Nevertheless, we reserve the term wage-goods constrainted model here for the model with full capacity utilization, given the enormous influence of the Lewis and Kaldor models in the literature.

the change in p is taken to be proportional to the excess demand for the agricultural good, since the left hand side of equation (7) falls with p (after substituting from equations (19) and (20), for given k), the short-run equilibrium is stable. Also, substituting equations (19) and (20) into equation (8), we obtain,

$$g_n = s[(1 - \omega p b_n)a_n + \theta a_a pk] \qquad (22)$$

which, given the value of p from (21) determines the equilibrium value of g_n.[14] Finally, substituting equation (21) into (2) solves for the short-run equilibrium value of g_a.

To examine how this model works in the short-run it is useful to compare the assumptions of this model with those of the demand-constrained model of the previous section. There are three differences between the two models: the wage here is fixed in terms of agricultural good, while in the previous model, for a given mark-up and technology, it was given in terms of the industrial good; here the industrial output is at full capacity, whereas in the previous model there was excess capacity, and output was determined by demand; and here there is no independent investment function for the industrial sector, while in the previous model there was an independent investment function. The fact that there is no independent investment function for the industrial sector implies that for this model, industrial investment is identically equal to total saving, which implies that Say's Law must hold for the model, in the sense that if one of the goods markets is in equilibrium, the other must automatically be in equilibrium. If there is an excess demand for the agricultural goods and a corresponding excess supply for the industrial good, the relative price of the agricultural good will rise, so that there will be a squeeze in industrial profit share, since firms have to pay a higher wage in terms of the industrial good, given that the wage is fixed in terms of the agricultural good. Although this redistribution of income will increase the demand for both goods, given the rise in the relative price of the agricultural good, there will be a decline in the demand for the agricultural good in physical units, as consumers switch from agricultural goods to industrial goods. This reduces excess demand for the agricultural good and increases it for the industrial good. It should be noted that in the industrial sector, since capacity is always fully utilized, market disequilibrium leads to changes in the

[14]Since equations (7) and (8) are satisfied by equations (21) and (22), equation (6) is also satisfied, so that the industrial goods market also clears in short-run equilibrium.

relative price of the industrial good (which exactly mirrors the story told above for the agricultural good), which implies that there is a change in the industrial mark-up.

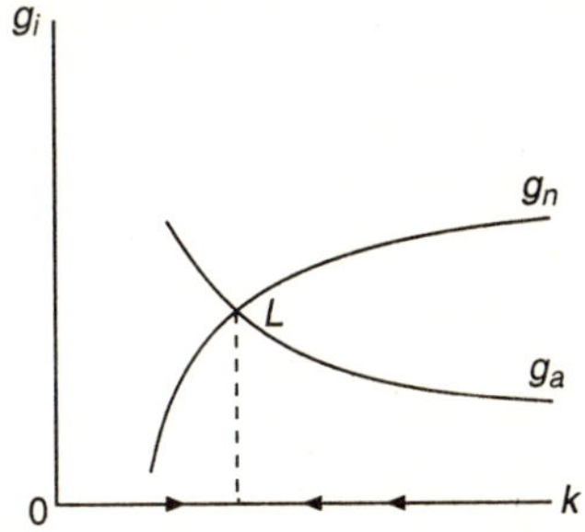

FIGURE 3.4 Wage-goods Constrained Model: Long-run

In the long-run, the dynamics of k are given by equation (18), which is depicted in Figure 3.4. Substitution of equation (21) into (22) implies that an increase in k has an ambiguous effect on g_n. On the one hand, the increase in k reduces p, which increases industrial profits, industrial savings and hence, industrial investment financed from industrial savings. On the other hand, the rise in k also reduces pk [as can be checked from equation 21], which means that savings by landlords are reduced, and therefore, industrial investment financed from agricultural savings falls. Figure 3.4 shows the more likely case, in which the first effect dominates, so that g_n rises with an increase in k. Substitution of equation (21) into (2) implies that g_a falls with k, since a decline in the agricultural terms of trade deters agricultural investment, and hence, growth. The point at the intersection of the g_a and g_n curves, L, shows the unique long-run equilibrium, which satisfies equation (10). It is simple to verify that this long-run equilibrium is stable.

If g_n, in fact, falls with k—which is empirically unlikely to be the case—so that the g_n curve is downward-sloping, as long as it is flatter in absolute slope than the g_a curve (at long-run equilibrium, assuming it exists), the long-run equilibrium will still be stable. If g_n is steeper than g_a in absolute slope, the long-run equilibrium will be unstable. In this case, an increase in k turns the terms of trade against agriculture, and therefore, reduces agricultural growth, but it reduces industrial investment and growth even more since it reduces agricultural savings for industrial accumulation, so that the rate of change of k increases.

In the case in which the g_n curve is upward rising, a parametric shift which shifts the g_a curve upwards, even without pushing up the g_n curve upwards, will imply a rise in the long-run equilibrium value of industrial growth. Note that since the signs of the effects of an increase in a_a and k are identical, the short-run effect of a rise in a_a is to cause no change in industrial output (which is given at full capacity), but an increase in g_n (in the likely case in which the industrial savings effect dominates). In the long-run in this case, higher agricultural growth (say due to an increase in β_0) implies an increase in the balanced growth rate, even without an upward shift in the g_n curve. In these senses industry can be said to be wage-goods constrained by low agricultural production and growth.

Note that for this model, unlike the case of the demand constrained model, we do not need to introduce the assumption that $\alpha = \alpha(p)$ to generate these results.[15] If, in fact, we assume that $a' > 0$, we would need to modify our model in a minor way. Now, a short-run increase in k would still have the result of reducing p, but since α falls with a reduction in p, equation (21) shows that the fall in p would be greater, which will imply—in the empirically likely case—an even greater increase in industrial capital accumulation. The g_n curve would be more steeply upward rising, so that a given upward shift in the g_a curve starting from the same long-run equilibrium position would result in a larger increase in the long-run growth rate of the economy.

5. SYNTHESIS MODELS

This section considers two models which attempt to synthesize demand and wage-goods constraints into the same model.

An obvious way to synthesize the demand and wage-goods constrained models is to add equations (13) and (20), which incorporate considerations of effective demand and real wage requirements of

[15]It should be noted that in the two models, an increase in the relative price of the agricultural good affects industrial growth through different mechanisms. In the demand constrained model (with inelastic demand for the agricultural good) the rise in the relative price chokes off industrial demand by reducing consumption spending on the industrial good (including spending by workers) and it is this which adversely affects industrial investment. In the wage-goods constrained model the rise in the relative price directly affects industrial investment by squeezing profits.

workers, respectively, into our general framework.[16] In this model, the mark-up pricing assumption is violated, so that firms are unable to realize their desired mark-up; workers, instead, are able to realize their real wage target in terms of the agricultural good.[17]

These equations imply that the short-run equilibrium conditions which clear the industrial and agricultural markets are given by,

$$-[\alpha + (1-\alpha)s - \gamma_1]u + (1-\alpha)\omega b_n spu + [(1-\alpha)(1-s\theta)a_a k_0 - \gamma_2 \omega b_n]p = -\gamma_0 \quad (23)$$

and

$$\alpha(1-s)u + \alpha\omega b_n spu - [1-\alpha(1-s\theta)]a_a k_0 p = 0 \quad (24)$$

where $\gamma_0 = \gamma_0' + \gamma_2$.

Starting with the industrial goods market, equation (23) can be written as,

$$p = [\Omega_1 u - \gamma_0]/[\Omega_2 u + \Omega_3] \quad (25)$$

where $\Omega_1 = [\alpha + (1-\alpha)s - \gamma_1]$,

$\Omega_2 = (1-\alpha)\omega b_n s > 0$, and $\Omega_3 = [(1-\alpha)(1 - s\theta)a_0 k_0 - \gamma_2 \omega b_n]$.

If we assume that the autonomous component of industrial investment is positive (that is $\gamma_0 > 0$), and that $s > \gamma_1$, which implies that

[16]An alternative route to a synthesis is to assume full capacity utilization in the industrial sector. However, this assumption—given our fixed coefficients assumptions—would remove short-run multiplier effects from our model, which are a crucial feature of demand constrained models. One could allow for two regimes—one with excess capacity and the other with full capacity in industry,—but if the demand constraint is taken to prevail in the first regime and the wage-goods constraint in the second we would not be able to show that both constraints can exist simultaneously.

[17]The structure of this model is similar to what Dutta (1988) calls the wage-goods constrained model, although she assumes that the real wage is fixed in terms of both agricultural and industrial goods and that the industrial mark-up is given and there is excess demand in the market for the industrial good. The fact that Dutta's model is not really a wage-goods constrained model, has already been argued by Baland (1992) and we therefore choose to call our variant a synthesis model; it is also one which is free of other criticisms that Baland makes about the Dutta model. In any case, Dutta only considers the short-run behaviour of the model, distinguishing between a demand constrained regime similar to the demand constrained model discussed above, and a wage-good constrained regime like the present model. The model of this section examines the long-run dynamics of capital accumulation in both agricultural and industrial sectors as well.

$\Omega_1 > 0$, the shape of the curve representing this equation depends on the sign of Ω_3. Two cases need to be distinguished—one in which the agricultural sector is relatively large enough, given the industrial real wage measured by ω and the profit squeeze parameter of the investment function, γ_2, to satisfy $(1-\alpha)(1-s\theta)a_a k_0 > \gamma_2 \omega b_n$, so that $\Omega_3 > 0$; and the other in which the opposite is true, so that $\Omega_3 < 0$. In Case I, in

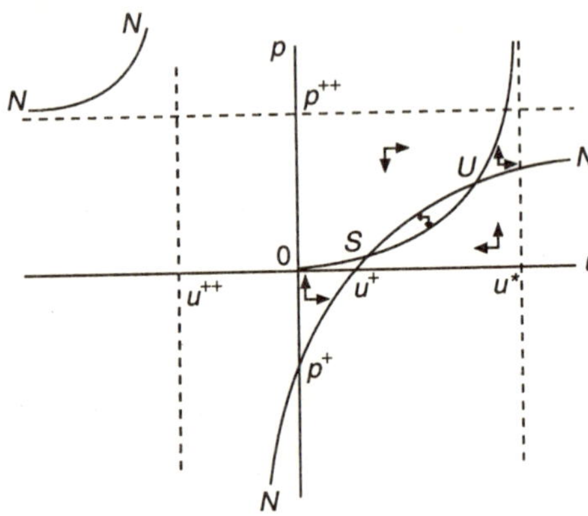

FIGURE 3.5 Synthesis Model, Case I: Short-run

which $\Omega_3 > 0$, equation (25) can be represented by the hyperbola *NN* of Figure 3.5 which intersects the *u* axis at $u^+ = \gamma_0/\Omega_1$, the *p*-axis at $p^+ = -\gamma_0/\Omega_3$ and has $u^{++} = -\Omega_3/\Omega_1$ and $p^{++} = \Omega_1/\Omega_2$ as vertical and horizontal asymptotes. With $\Omega_1 > 0$, equation (23) shows that for the region $p < p^{++}$, the excess demand for the *N* good falls with *u*, so that if we assume that the change in *u* has the same sign as the excess demand for the *N* good, the relevant horizontal arrows, showing the dynamics for *u* in the positive orthant, are as shown in Figure 3.5. In Case II, in which $\Omega_3 < 0$, two sub-cases need to be distinguished, depending on whether $\gamma_0\Omega_2 + \Omega_1\Omega_3 > 0$ (Case IIa) or $\gamma_0\Omega_2 + \Omega_1\Omega_3 < 0$ (Case IIb). Case IIa is shown in Figure 3.6 and Case IIb is shown in Figure 3.7, where the symbols in the figures are analogous to those in Figure 3.5. We find that in Case IIa the *NN* curve in the positive orthant continues to be positively sloped, but in Case IIb, in which ω is sufficiently 'large' and/or the profit squeeze effect of declining industrial terms of trade on investment—captured by γ_2—is sufficiently 'strong', the *NN* curve will have a downward-sloping portion in the positive orthant (though there will be an upward-rising segment also, for $u > u^{++}$).

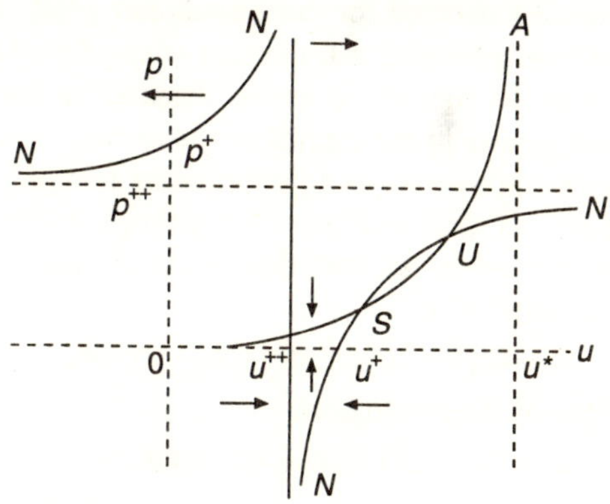

FIGURE 3.6 Synthesis Model, Case IIa: Short-run

Turning next to the agricultural goods market, equation (24) can be written as,

$$p = \alpha(1 - s)u/\{[1 - \alpha(1 - s\theta)]a_a k_0 - \alpha\omega b_n su\} \qquad (26)$$

which can be depicted by the *OA* curve in Figures 3.5 through 3.7. This curve is also a hyperbola with a vertical asymptote given by

$$u^* = [1 - \alpha(1 - s\theta)]a_a k_0/\alpha\omega b_n s$$

and a horizontal asymptote (not shown in the figures) given by $p^* = -(1 - s)/s\omega b_n$. The segment of the curve in the positive orthant

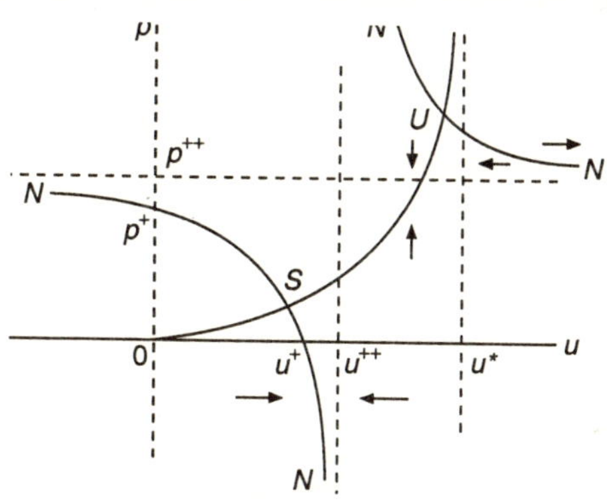

FIGURE 3.7 Synthesis Model, Case IIb: Short-run

must be upward-rising and concave upwards, and pass through the origin, as shown in the figures. Moreover, for $u < u^*$, equation (24) shows that the excess demand for the agricultural goods falls with an increase in p, so that, assuming that the sign of the direction of change in p is the same as the sign of the excess demand for the agricultural good, the vertical arrows in the figures are as shown.

We can now examine short-run equilibrium by bringing together the curves *NN* and *OA*, as done in Figures 3.5 through 3.7. In each figure we have drawn the curves so that they intersect and assuming that $u^* > u^+$, which is satisfied if,

$$(1 - \alpha)[1 - 2\alpha(1 - s\theta)]a_a k_0 > \alpha\gamma_2\omega b_n \tag{27}$$

and which can be satisfied even with

$$\Omega_3 = [(1 - \alpha)(1 - s\theta)a_a k_0 - \gamma_2\omega b_n] < 0$$

We assume for now that this condition is satisfied, and that γ_0 is small enough to allow the curves to intersect. Given these assumptions, it follows that there must be two equilibria in each case—one locally stable, marked *S* in the figures, and the other a saddle–point, marked *U*. If we are to the right of the separatrix of the saddle-point equilibrium (not shown in the figures), u and p will rise over time and the economy will be pushed to a position of full capacity, at which the present model, which assumes that excess capacity exists, will cease to apply. If we are to the left of the separatrix in the positive orthant, the economy converges to the stable short-run equilibrium at *S*.[18]

If the curves do not intersect—which is possible if γ_0 is 'too' large in Case I and IIa—then there will be no short-run equilibrium, and the economy will eventually find itself between *OA* and the right-hand segment of the *NN* curve, with monotonically increasing p and u, presumably till full capacity utilization is reached and the present model, which assumes excess capacity utilization, ceases to apply. If condition (27) is not satisfied—which is only possible in Case II—there will be only one equilibrium in the positive orthant. In Case IIa, *OA*

[18]In Figure 3.6 we have drawn Case IIa for the case in which the intersections occur on the right-hand segment (to the right of the vertical asymptote) of the *NN* curve. It is also possible to have the configurations of the curves so that the intersections occur on the left-hand segment, even with $u^* > u^{++}$. In this case, the lower equilibrium may or may not be locally stable; we require the relative price adjustment to be relatively faster than the quantity adjustment to satisfy the trace requirement for stability. The higher equilibrium will be a saddle-point, as in the cases discussed above.

will intersect *NN* on its left-hand segment and the dynamics may not be stable, but is not necessarily unstable, like the equilibrium considered in footnote 14. In case IIb there will be only one stable equilibrium. In what follows, we confine ourselves to configurations in which a stable equilibrium exists, so that at equilibrium, the determinant condition for stability is satisfied, so that,

$$\Sigma = [s - \gamma_1 - s\omega b_n p]\{[1 - \alpha(1 - s\theta)]a_a k - \alpha s b_n \omega u\}$$
$$+ \alpha[1 - s + s b_n \omega p][s\theta a_a k - s b_n \omega u + \gamma_2 b_n \omega] > 0$$

We now turn to the effects of parametric changes which can be examined by totally differentiating equations (23) and (24). The effects of autonomous changes in industrial investment (or demand, more generally) can be seen from[19],

$$\mathrm{d}u/\mathrm{d}\gamma_0 = (1/\Sigma)[1 - \alpha(1 - s\theta)]a_a k - \alpha s b_n \omega u] > 0$$

and

$$\mathrm{d}p/\mathrm{d}\gamma_0 = (\alpha/\Sigma)(1 - s + s b_n \omega p) > 0$$

As in the demand constrained model, a rise in autonomous demand implies an increase in both industrial capacity utilization and agricultural price. The effect of a rise in agricultural productivity can be seen from,

$$du/da_a = -(b_n \omega k/\Sigma)\{(1 - \alpha)su - \gamma_2[1 - \alpha(1 - s\theta)]\}$$

$$\mathrm{d}p/\mathrm{d}a_a = -(k/\Sigma)\{[s - \gamma_1 - s\omega b_n p][1 - \alpha(1 - s\theta)]$$
$$+ \alpha s\theta(1 - s + s b_n \omega p)\}.$$

The effect on *p* is most likely to be negative (if ω is not too large): the higher agricultural output turns the terms of trade against agriculture. The effect on *u* is ambiguous: the negative effect is due to the redistribution towards profits, due to the fall in the industrial product wage, caused by the fall in price, while the positive effect is due to the boost in industrial investment due to higher industrial profitability caused by the fall in the industrial product wage. This result makes clear the importance of the profitability effect on investment demand in this model: if this effect is assumed away, so that $\gamma_2 = 0$, then agricultural

[19]The positive sign follows from the fact that the equilibrium is at $u < u^*$.

expansion has a necessarily negative effect on industrial output and capacity utilization in the short-run. Thus, the Kaldor–Lewis fixed real wage (in terms of the agricultural good) assumption does not make the wage-goods constraint operate in the usual way, since its role is to redistribute industrial income to industrial capitalists when the agricultural price falls due to agricultural expansion—a redistribution which depresses industrial demand, and hence, capacity utilization and industrial investment. Capital accumulation in industry in this model is determined by investment demand and savings, and not only by industrial (and agricultural) saving alone, as in the wage-goods constrained model. To allow for the wage-goods constraint to have some role to play in affecting industrial accumulation, we made industrial investment depend on industrial profitability directly: agricultural expansion, by reducing agricultural price, now reduces the industrial product wage, turns the industrial distribution of income towards capitalists, and encourages greater investment. The effect of a rise in k is given by,

$$\mathrm{d}u/\mathrm{d}k = -(b_n \omega a_a/\Sigma)\{(1-\alpha)su - \gamma_2[1-\alpha(1-s\theta)]\}$$

and

$$\mathrm{d}p/\mathrm{d}k = -(a_a/\Sigma)\{[s-\gamma_1 - s\omega b_n p][1-\alpha(1-s\theta)] + \alpha s\theta(1-s+sb_n\omega p)\}$$

which have exactly the same sign as the effect of a rise in a_a, and which, therefore, do not require further discussion.

If α depended positively on p, the positive effect on demand would be greater, since the fall in price would reduce spending on food and increase industrial demand, so that it would become more likely that $\mathrm{d}u/\mathrm{d}k > 0$. In this case, the expansionary demand-creating that we found for the demand constrained model with an inelastic demand for food kicks in, adding to the effect of the industrial profit share on investment.

In the long-run, k moves over time according to equation (18), which, for the present model, implies that,

$$(\mathrm{d}k/\mathrm{d}t)/k = \beta_0 + \beta_1 p - \gamma_0 - \gamma_1 u + \gamma_2 \omega b_n p$$

where u and p are the short-run equilibrium values which depend on k. The long-run dynamics and equilibrium for this model are shown in Figure 3.8, which is analogous to Figure 3.4. The g_a curve shows how g_a depends on k. Its slope is given by β_1 $\mathrm{d}p/\mathrm{d}k$, and we have drawn it for the likely case in which $\mathrm{d}p/\mathrm{d}k < 0$. The g_n

curve shows how g_n depends on k, and its slope is given by $\gamma_1\, du/dk - \gamma_2 \omega b_n\, dp/dk$. Assuming $dp/dk < 0$, in the case in which $du/dk > 0$ (which is likely to occur when the investment effect is strong and α depends strongly on p), the curve is upward-rising as shown in the figure, and the long-run equilibrium is stable as shown. Even if $du/dk < 0$, g_n may rise with k because of the investment effect, and the configuration will continue to be as shown in Figure 3.8. If the capacity utilization effect is much stronger than the profitability effect on industrial investment, it is possible for g_n to fall with k. In this case the instability of long-run equilibrium cannot be ruled out. However, if the g_n curve has a smaller absolute slope than that of the g_a curve, the equilibrium will continue to be stable. In the stable cases, if there is a rise in β_0 which pushes the g_a curve upwards without shifting up the g_n curve, and in which the g_n curve is positively sloped, the long-run equilibrium balanced growth rate will increase. In the case in which the g_n curve is negatively sloped, but the equilibrium is stable, such a shift will reduce the long-run equilibrium growth rate of the economy, since the long-run increase in k depresses g_n.

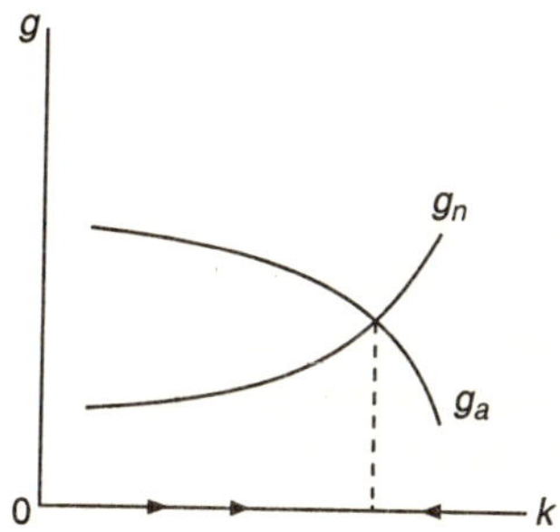

FIGURE 3.8 Synthesis Model: Long-run

Although this model synthesizes some of the characteristics of both demand constrained and wage-goods constrained models, it has the problem that it assumes that the money wage in the industrial sector always adjusts in the short-run to satisfy the wage-goods constraint, i.e., keeps the wage in terms of the agricultural good constant. If we combine the model with the demand constrained model, it has the property: as long as $p/V < \omega$, V is constant and we are in the demand-constrained model; but when k falls and p rises and we hit the constraint $p/V = \omega$, V becomes endogenous to satisfy $p/V = \omega$ and we are in the synthesis model of this section.[20] The level of k at which the switch in model occurs obviously depends on the level of ω. This assumption, that the money wage is constant as long as we are in the pure demand-constrained case and perfectly flexible when we are in the synthesis case, seems an implausible one. Another implausible feature of the model is that when the relative price of the agricultural good falls, the model assumes that the industrial money wage is instantaneously flexible in the downward direction as well. It is this feature of the model, which made it possible for agricultural expansion to have a contractionary effect on industrial output in the short-run, especially in the case in which α is a constant. It seems much more plausible to assume that a rise in p, which erodes the real wage in terms of the agricultural good, will lead to changes in the industrial money wage even without a critical value of the real wage in terms of the agricultural sector being reached, and a fall in p will contain inflationary pressures.

To develop a model which overcomes these shortcomings and introduces inflation explicitly into the model, we follow Dutt (1990) [see also Marglin, (1984)] in allowing possible deviations of the actual real wage from the real wage targets of workers (based on Kaldor-Lewis forces) and the real wage implied by the mark-up target of firms (based on Kaleckian factors), and assuming that inflation mediates the conflicting claims of workers and capitalists in the industrial labour market. In addition to providing a more plausible synthesis of the demand constrained and wage-goods constrained models, this model has the advantage that it contributes to the examination of the interaction between inflation, distribution and growth in less-developed economies with a large agricultural sector.[21]

[20]This model with two regimes is similar in spirit to the approach of Dutta (1988).

[21]There is a small, but growing literature which examines the issue of the relation between inflation and agriculture-industry interaction. Kalecki's (1976) early formulation, first published in 1963, examined the issue of increasing the growth rate of the economy with an agricultural sector and an exogenously-given rate of growth, without resorting to inflation in the price of the agricultural good. A Kaleckian model, which more formally deals with the issue of inflation and the terms of trade, is developed by Bose (1992). However, both these models abstract from demand constraints on industrial growth, which is a key issue in our synthesis model of this section. Bose also takes the industrial real wage to be fixed in terms of the industrial consumption good, thus abstracting from the wage goods constraint in our specific sense. Although he does introduce excess

For the short-run we assume that K_i, W_n and P_n are given, which implies that k and V are given, and that in the short-run the price of the agricultural good changes in response to the excess demand for it, while capacity utilization varies in the industrial sector and changes in response to the excess demand for the industrial good, with investment demand determined independently of the availability of saving, by the investment function given by (13). In short-run equilibrium we assume, as in the demand constrained model, that both goods markets clear. Thus, substituting equation (13) into equation (6) we obtain the market-clearing condition for the industrial good,

$$(1-\alpha)\{VB_n u + (1-\theta)a_a pk + (1-s)[(1-Vb_n)u + \theta a_a pk]\} + \gamma_0 + \gamma_1 u - \gamma_2 Vb_n - u = 0 \quad (28)$$

while equation (7) gives the market-clearing condition for the agricultural good. The short-run equilibrium conditions can be rewritten as,

$$-[\alpha + (1-\alpha)s(1-Vb_n) - \gamma_1]u + (1-\alpha)(1-s\theta)a_a kp = -\gamma_0 + \gamma_2 Vb_n \quad (29)$$

and

$$\alpha[1-s(1-Vb_n)]u - [1-\alpha(1-s\theta)]a_a kp = 0 \quad (30)$$

from which it follows that,

$$u = (1/\Delta)(\gamma_0 - \gamma_2 Vb_n)[1-\alpha(1-s\theta)] \quad (31)$$

and

$$p = (1/a_a k\Delta)(\gamma_0 - \gamma_2 Vb_n)\,\alpha[1-s(1-Vb_n)] \quad (32)$$

where $\Delta = [s(1-Vb_n) - \gamma_1][1-\alpha(1-s\theta)] + \alpha[1-s(1-Vb_n)]s\theta$. The determination of short-run equilibrium is the same as shown in Figure 3.1, since z was given in the demand constrained model and V is given in the short-run in the present model. The stability conditions are

---

capacity utilization in a version of his model, this is not the result of constraints on aggregate demand, but of a zero-investment policy being followed by the government, which allocates investment across sectors. Patnaik's (1992) model appears to introduce aggregate demand considerations, but assumes that the terms of trade is determined by a government policy rule, rather than by market forces, and makes a number of *ad hoc* assumptions about intersectoral investment allocation (which keeps the ratio of demand to capacity utilization the same in the industrial and agricultural sectors) and the growth rate (with the government choosing the rate of industrial capacity utilization and the indirect tax rate to maximize it). Closer to our model are the contributions by Cardoso (1981), Taylor (1982, 1983, 1991), and Balakrishnan (1991). The relationship between these contributions and the model of this section will be discussed in subsequent notes.

also the same for the two models if we replace $z/(1+z)$ by $1 - Vb_n$. Thus, the short-run version of the model is equivalent to the short-run version of the demand constrained model, and the wage-goods constrained model makes no contribution to it. The short-run comparative statics results are consequently the same as for the demand constrained model. As before, we have $\mathrm{d}u/\mathrm{d}k = 0$ and $\mathrm{d}p/\mathrm{d}k < 0$, given our assumptions. Similarly, $\mathrm{d}u/\mathrm{d}a_a = 0$ and $\mathrm{d}p/\mathrm{d}a_a < 0$. As before, if we wish to have a positive demand effect from agricultural expansion, we need to have price inelasticity of demand, i.e., making $\mathrm{d}\alpha/\mathrm{d}p > 0$ in our model. The effects of a change in V—which we need to examine for our subsequent discussion of the long-run dynamics—are given by,

$$\mathrm{d}u/\mathrm{d}V = (b_n a_a k/\Delta)\{(su - \gamma_2)[1 - \alpha(1 - s\theta)] - \alpha s^2 u\theta\} \tag{33}$$

and

$$\mathrm{d}p/\mathrm{d}V = (\alpha b_n/\Delta)\{[s(1 - Vb_n) - \gamma_1]su + [1 - s(1 - Vb_n)](su - \gamma_2)\} > 0 \tag{34}$$

where the sign of the first expression is ambiguous. A positive effect comes about due to the redistribution from capitalists to workers in the industrial sector which, on account of the higher consumption propensity of workers, increases aggregate demand, but the negative effect comes from the wage squeeze effect on investment demand. Making α depend positively on p will make the negative effect stronger, by diverting consumption spending towards the agricultural good.

In the long run, K_i, W_n and P_n are no longer constant. The long-run dynamics of the model are given by assuming that $\mathrm{d}K_i/\mathrm{d}t = g_i$ as before, and by making the following assumptions about the money wage and the industrial price. Regarding the money wage, we assume that workers have a targeted real wage given by ω_T in terms of some cost of living index, and that the money wage adjusts to close the gap between the actual real wage and the targeted real wage with a finite speed of adjustment. This is formalized with the equation,

$$W_n\hat{} = \mu[\omega_T - \omega] \tag{35}$$

where $\mu_i > 0$ is a constant and where $\omega = W_n/P_a$ as before.[22] Regarding the industrial price level we assume that firms have a targeted mark-up

[22]Changes in wages due to expected changes in relevant prices can also be incorporated into the analysis, complicating the algebra and not changing the qualitative properties of the model, if actual price changes do not lead to one-for-one changes in the money wage.

over variable costs given by z_T, which implies that they have a targeted industrial product wage given by,

$$V_T = 1/b_n(1 + z_T) \tag{36}$$

and that whenever the actual mark-up falls short of their targeted mark-up, so that the actual industrial product wage exceeds the targeted one, they increase the price of their product. We formalize this with the equation,

$$P_n\hat{} = \lambda[V - V_T] \tag{37}$$

where $\lambda > 0$ is a constant.[23]

The dynamics of our model can now be studied by examining the dynamics of the two static variables k and V. The equations of motion of these two variables in the long-run are given by,

$$k\hat{} = \beta_0 + \beta_1 p - \gamma_0 - \gamma_1 u + \gamma_2 V b_n \tag{38}$$

and

$$V\hat{} = u[\omega_T - (V/p)] - \lambda(V - V_T). \tag{39}$$

The elements of the Jacobian of this dynamic system are given by,

$$\partial\hat{k}/\partial k = \beta_1 \, dp/dk - \gamma_1 \, du/dk < 0 \tag{40}$$

$$\partial\hat{k}/\partial V = \beta_1 \, dp/dV - \gamma_1 \, du/dV + \gamma_2 b_n \tag{41}$$

$$\partial\hat{V}/\partial k = V\mu p^{-2} \, dp/dk > 0 \tag{42}$$

$$\partial V\hat{}/\partial V = -\{\lambda + (\mu/p)[1 - (V/p)](dp/dV)]\} \tag{43}$$

A rise in k, by reducing the agricultural terms of trade, unambiguously reduces the rate of change of k by reducing the agricultural rate of accumulation and leaving the industrial rate of accumulation unchanged. It also reduces the rate of change of V by reducing the growth in the money wage, since the downward pressure on the industrial real wage in terms of the agricultural good is smaller (since the agricultural terms of trade fall). The effects of a rise in V are ambiguous, however.

[23]The target real wage and mark-up rates, in turn, could be endogenized in the model, as has been discussed by a number of writers [see, for instance, Taylor (1983), Patnaik (1992)]. For an illustration of the effects of their endogenization in a one-sector model, see Dutt (1992b). It would be a simple matter to make z_T depend on u; however, the empirical evidence on the nature of this relationship is not unambiguous. Making ω_T depend on the unemployment rate would require us to introduce labour supply considerations and considerably increase the complexity of the model.

The increase in V on one hand increases p, and thus, raises g_a, which tends to increase $k^\wedge$. The increase in V reduces industrial investment through the 'direct profit share effect', and if $du/dV < 0$—which, as we have seen above, is more likely if the profitability effect on investment is strong and if α depends on p—g_n will fall with V. Thus, we will obtain $\partial k^\wedge/\partial V > 0$. But if $du/dV > 0$, if is possible—but not necessary, since the direct profitability effect is still negative—that g_n rises with V. If this effect is stronger than the effect the increase in V has on g_a, we may get $\partial k^\wedge/\partial V < 0$, but our discussion suggests that the likely case is for $\partial k^\wedge/\partial V > 0$. The increase in V will have the effect of reducing the industrial mark-up and make industrial firms increase their product price more rapidly, reducing $V^\wedge$. The rise in V will increase the real wage for a given p, and therefore, reduce the need for money wage increases for industrial workers. However, it will also increase p, and therefore, reduce the real wage in terms of the agricultural good, making the money wage increase at a more rapid rate. The net effect on the rate of growth of the money wage depends on the elasticity of p with respect to V, as shown by equation (43). If we assume that this elasticity is less than unity, we clearly have $\partial V^\wedge/\partial V < 0$. If it exceeds unity, we may still have $\partial V^\wedge/\partial V < 0$, if μ—the coefficient of money wage adjustment—is 'small' relative to λ—the coefficient of price adjustment.[24]

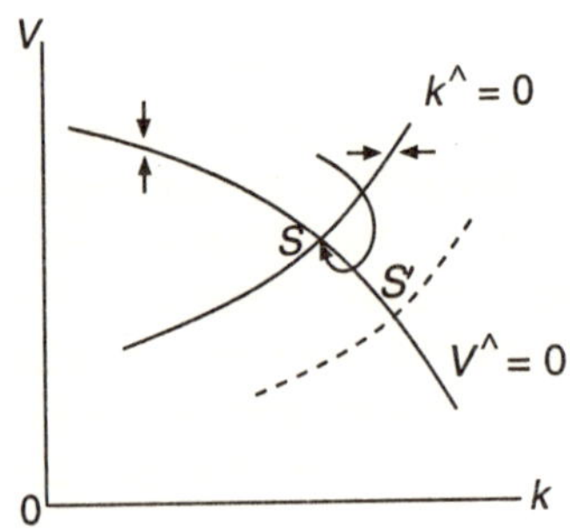

FIGURE 3.9 Synthesis Model with Inflation: Long-run

[24]Even if this is not the case, this expression is likely to be negative if the workers' target real wage is not in terms of the agricultural good alone, but some basket which gives a weight of, say, α to the agricultural good and a share $1-\alpha$ to the industrial good—which are the true shares of these goods in the consumption basket of workers.

The long-run dynamics of the model can be analyzed using the phase diagram of Figure 3.9, where we assume, as is likely, that $\partial \hat{k}/\partial V > 0$ and $\partial \hat{V}/\partial V < 0$. The $\hat{k} = 0$ line shows combinations of k and V at which k is stationary: its positive slope follows from the fact that a rise in k implies a fall in $\hat{k}$, which needs to be offset by a rise in V to restore $\hat{k} = 0$. Since $\partial \hat{k}/\partial k < 0$, above (below) the line the vertical arrows point down (up). The $\hat{V} = 0$ line shows combinations of k and V at which V is stationary: its negative slope follows from the fact that a rise in k implies a fall in $\hat{k}$, which needs to be offset by a fall in V to restore $\hat{V} = 0$. Since $\partial \hat{V}/\partial V < 0$, above (below) the line, the horizontal arrows point rightwards (leftwards). It follows that the point of intersection of the curves—assuming that it exists—is unique and one which is cyclically stable; it is shown by point S in the figure at which both k and V are stationary.

Assume now that there is an increases in β_0, which implies that there is an exogenously given increase in g_a. This implies that $\hat{k}$ will become positive at the initial equilibrium, which will require an increase in k to restore $\hat{k} = 0$, so that the $\hat{k} = 0$ curve must shift to the right, to a position shown by the dashed line in Figure 3.9. The new long-run equilibrium will be at S', which implies that the long-run equilibrium value of k will increase and that of V will fall. It follows by setting $\hat{V} = 0$ in equation (39) that the fall in V—since all parameters in equation (39) remain unchanged—implies a fall in p; this is confirmed by the results, as seen above, that $dp/dk < 0$ and $dp/dV > 0$. The effect on u, the other short-run variable, is ambiguous, for although given our assumptions $du/dk = 0$, du/dV, as equation (35) shows, is of indeterminate sign. If the profit squeeze effect on investment is strong, then it is possible that $du/dV < 0$, in which case the fall in V will imply a rise in u. It may be recalled that the likelihood of this is greater if α depends positively on p. The effect on g_n is given, from equation (13), by,

$$dg_n/dV = \gamma_1 \, du/dV - \gamma_2 b_n$$

which will necessarily be negative if $du/dV < 0$, but may be negative even with $du/dV > 0$. If $dg_n/dV < 0$, this implies that at the new long-run equilibrium g_n must be higher than at the old long-run equilibrium at S. Since at long-run equilibrium we have balanced growth of the two sectors, g_a will also be higher. It also follows from equation (37) that the fall in V implies a lower rate of price inflation in the economy. If this has an additional positive effect on industrial investment (which is not assumed in our model) by reducing uncertainty, for instance, the positive effect on growth will be even stronger. It should be noted that even with the assumption that $\partial k/\partial V < 0$, as embodied in Figure 3.9, it need not follow that g_n must increase when β_0 is increased. However, a strong demand effect following from α depending positively on p, and a strong wage-squeeze effect following from a relatively large γ_2, will make this very likely.

It should be noted that although V—or the industrial product wage—falls when β_0 is increased, this does not mean that industrial workers are worse off. First, since p also falls, it is not clear that the real wage of workers fall—as defined in terms of their consumption basket. The real wage in terms of the agricultural good, in fact, can be shown to be higher at the new long-run equilibrium than at the original one.

This can be seen as follows: we have already seen that P_n^ falls as a result of the higher β_0; this implies that at long-run equilibrium, at wich $W_n\text{^} = P_n\text{^}$, W_n^ must be lower. This, in turn, implies, from equation (35) that ω must be higher. Since the wage in terms of the industrial good falls and that in terms of the agricultural good rises, the real wage in terms of the workers' consumption basket can increase with α greater than some critical value.[25] Second, if $du/dV > 0$, there will be an expansion in industrial employment even in the short run. Finally, a higher rate of industrial capital will imply a higher rate of output growth, given that u rises over time with the fall in V (that is, if $du/dV > 0$) which, given a constant b_n (the labour-output ratio in industry) industrial employment will grow more rapidly.

Two special cases of this model are worth commenting on. In one, we make μ—the speed of industrial money wage adjustment—approach infinity, while λ—the speed of industrial price adjustment—is finite in equations (35) and (37), and in the other we assume exactly the opposite. In the first case in short-run and long-run equilibrium, we must have $W_n\text{^} = 0$, or that $\omega = \omega_T$, so that we must have $V = \omega p$. This implies that the real side of this model will be identical with the first synthesis model which assumed $V = \omega p$ in equation (20). The long-run equilibrium for this model can be depicted with a new $V\text{^} = 0$ curve with a slope given by $(V/p)(dp/dk)/[1 - (V/p)(dp/dV)]$, which will have a higher absolute slope than that of the $V\text{^} = 0$ curve shown in Figure

[25]Given the evidence that the poor spend a relatively higher proportion of their income on food, the poorest workers are likely to be benefited most by the change.

3.9 and with the economy in the long-run always being on the $V^\wedge = 0$ curve. The long-run equilibrium values of V and k will be higher than in the general case. The only role that equation (37) will have in this model is to determine the level of $P_n^\wedge$, which shows how firms push up their price because they cannot achieve their targeted mark-up. Since V and p will be constant in long-run equilibrium, W and P_a will change at the same rate as does P_n. In this special case, an increase in the speed of price adjustment, represented by an increase in λ, will only increase the rate of price and wage change, but have no real effects.[26] in our general synthesis model, however, a rise in λ will push the $V^\wedge = 0$ curve to the left, and hence, have real effects.

In the second case we have $V = V_T$, so that the mark-up equation given by equation (34) is always satisfied. In this case the $V^\wedge = 0$ curve will become a horizontal line and the economy will, in the long-run, always be on the line. The long-run equilibrium values of V and k will be lower in this model than in the general case. The real side of the model is, thus, identical to the demand constrained model of section on 'A Demand Constrained Model' and the only role that equation (35) plays is in determining the rate of change of the nominal industrial wage (and hence, the equilibrium rates of change of the absolute product prices).[27] In the special case an exogenous rise, in say, z_T will only have the effect of raising the rate of

[26]The long-run equilibrium properties of the real side of this model will be the same as a model in which, in equations (35) and (37), $\lambda = 0$ and $\mu > 0$. For this model, the dynamics can be examined with a phase diagram with the $V^\wedge = 0$ curve described in the text and the $k^\wedge = 0$ curve of the general synthesis model, but the economy will not always be on the $V^\wedge = 0$ curve in the long-run. The resulting model will be similar to the model examined by Rattsø (1989), although his is what he calls a 'medium–run model', in which the dynamics of K_n are not examined and industrial investment is taken to be autonomous, and he does not explicitly analyze inflation. Balakrishnan (1991, pp. 11–17) also considers a version of this model, although the industrial money wage there is indexed, not to the agricultural price, but to a composite of the two prices, and his analysis is conducted in a discrete time framework. Balakrishnan also does not analyze the dynamics of capital accumulation in either sector.

[27]Essentially, this model is discussed in Taylor (1982, 1983, pp. 38–48, 166–70). Taylor takes the mark-up rate to be given, and hence, although his model does allow for the profit rate to affect industrial investment, industrial investment is independent of the terms of trade. Hence, the wage-goods effect is totally absent from his model. The only avenue through which a rise in the agricultural terms of trade can cause industrial stagnation in the model is by increasing the proportion of consumption spending devoted to the agricultural

inflation without having any real effects, but our general synthesis model will allow for real effects by shifting the $V^\wedge = 0$ curve to the left.

6. CONCLUSIONS

This paper has examined some simple models of agriculture-industry interaction in less developed countries to analyze the nature of demand and wage-goods constraints that can be imposed by a stagnant agricultural sector on the industrial sector, and developed two models in which demand and wage–good constraints can co-exist. In doing so, it has argued the following:

- A relatively simple framework for analyzing the nature of agriculture-industry macroeconomic interactions can be developed, which is general enough to incorporate a number of specific and well-known models of sectoral interaction in less developed economies. Demand constrained and wage-goods constrained models in particular can be developed from this framework.

- A crucial—and obvious—feature of demand constrained models is that industrial output and growth must be determined by aggregate demand. A Kaleckian fixprice-flexprice model can be used to show how aggregate demand can affect industrial goods, by allowing industrial investment to be independent of savings. However, to demonstrate that agriculture can create a demand constraint for industrial growth, it is not enough to argue that industrial output and growth are demand determined, but one needs to show that industrial output and growth are dependent on agricultural growth. For agricultural expansion to lead to industrial epansion, additional assumptions—for instance, price-inelastic demand for food as shown in this paper—are necessary.

---

good. The model has some similarities with Cardoso's (1981) model of structuralist inflation (see also Taylor, 1983, 162–6). The difference between the Cardoso model and ours is that she allows for excess demand to exist in the agricultural goods market, with the adjustment in the agricultural price taking place in a time period comparable to adjustments in the money wage (while in our model the agricultural goods market is assumed to clear in the short-run through instantaneous variations in the price of the agricultural good, and the money wage is assumed to adjust only in the long-run). Taylor argues that this model, at best, applies to the short-run since it generates persistent macroeconomic disequilibrium. Cardoso also does not discuss the dynamics of capital accumulation.

- A Kaldor-Lewis model clearly shows how industry can be wage-goods constrained. In such a model industrial investment is driven by savings. If most investment for industry is financed by industrial saving, agricultural stagnation is seen to turn the terms of trade against industry, squeeze industrial profits, savings, and hence, investment and capital accumulation. The inelasticity of demand for food plays no significant role in showing how agriculture can create a wage-goods constraint for industry.

- Since many commentators have argued that it is possible for the agricultural sector to constrain industrial sector from the demand and wage-goods mechanisms simultaneously, the question naturally arises whether these two constraints are competing constraints on industrial goods, each one relevant for a different type of economy, or whether the two constraints can actually be shown to operate within a single model. We have shown that models synthesizing the Kalecki-Keynes tradition and the Lewis-Kaldor tradition can indeed be constructed. A simple synthesis allowed the money wage to be instantaneously flexible, and we have shown that it can incorporate some of the features of both, the demand and wage-goods constrained models. Since this model has some implausible features, a second synthesis model was developed to incorporate the phenomenon of inflation and slow money-wage dynamics. This model showed that agricultural growth in the short-run can lead to industrial growth for the same reason as it does in the demand constrained model: due to the inelastic demand for food. In the long-run, agricultural growth can lead to higher industrial growth—and even an improved distribution of income—by expanding aggregate demand from the consumption side (resulting from the inelasticity of the demand for the agricultural good), but also because of profitability effects on industrial investment, which can be interpreted as resulting in a wage-goods constraint for industry. If demand and wage-goods constraints are both relevant for the industrial sector, this synthesis model may provide a useful basis for understanding the macroeconomics of semi-industrialized less developed economies with a large agricultural sector.

References

Ahluwalia, Isher J. (1985), *Industrial Growth in India. Stagnation Since the Mid-Sixties*, Delhi: Oxford University Press.

Balakrishnan, Pulapre (1991), *Pricing and Inflation in India,* Delhi, Oxford University Press.

Baland, Jean-Marie (1992), 'The Wage-Goods Constraint on a Developing Economy: A Comment on Dutta's Model', *Journal of Development Economics*, 37, pp. 387–9.

Bhaduri, Amit and Stephen A. Marglin (1990), 'Unemployment and the Real Wage: The Economic Basis for Contesting Political Ideologies', *Cambridge Journal of Economics*, 14(4), December, pp. 375–93.

Bose, Amitava (1989), 'Short Period Equilibrium in a Less-Developed Economy', in Mihir Rakshit (ed.), *Studies in the Macroeconomics of Developing Countries*, Delhi: Oxford University Press.

——— (1992), 'Growth, Inflation and Excess Capacity in a Dual Economy', In Kaushik Basu and Pulin Nayak (eds.), *Development Policy and Economic Theory*, Delhi: Oxford University Press.

Cardoso, Eliana (1981), 'Food Supply and Inflation', *Journal of Development Economics*, 8(3), pp. 269–84.

Chichilnisky, Graciela and Lance Taylor (1980), 'Agriculture and the Rest of the Economy: Macro Connections and Policy Restraints', *American Journal of Agricultural Economics,* 62(2), pp. 303–9.

Dutt, Amitava K. (1990), *Growth, Distribution and Uneven Development,* Cambridge: Cambridge University Press.

——— (1992a), 'A Kaldorian Model of Growth and Development Revisited: Comment on Thirlwall', *Oxford Economic Papers,* 44(1), pp. 156–68.

——— (1992b), 'Conflict Inflation, Distribution, Cyclical Accumulation and Crises', *European Journal of Political Economy,* 8, pp. 579–97.

——— (1996a), 'The Role of Keynesian Policies in Semi-Industrialized Economies: Theory and Evidence from India', *International Review of Applied Economics,* 10(1), January, pp. 127–40.

——— (1996b), 'Intersectoral Capital Mobility in a Kaldorian Model of Growth and Development', *The Manchester School of Economic and Socal Studies,* 64(2), June, pp. 153–69.

Dutta, Jayashri (1988), 'The Wage-Goods Constraint on a Developing Economy: Theory and Evidence', *Journal of Development Economics,* 28(3), May, pp. 341–63.

Kaldor, Nicholas (1975), 'What is Wrong with Economic Theory?', *Quarterly Journal of Economics,* 89(3), August, pp. 347–57.

——— (1979), 'Equilibrium Theory and Growth Theory', in M.J. Boskin (ed.), *Economics and Human Welfare: Essays in Honor of Tibor Scitovsky,* New York: Academic Press.

Kalecki, Michal (1971), *Selected Essays on the Dynamics of the Capitalist Economy,* Cambridge: Cambridge University Press.

——— (1976), 'Problems of Financing Economic Development in a Mixed Economy', in M. Kalecki, *Essays on Development Economics,* Brighton: Harvester.

Lewis, W. Arthur (1954), 'Economic Development with Unlimited Supplies of Labour', *The Manchester School of Economics and Social Studies*, 22(2), pp. 139–91.

Marglin, Stephen A. (1984), *Growth, Distribution and Prices*, Cambridge, Mass.: Harvard University Press.

Nayyar, Deepak (1994), *Industrial Growth and Stagnation: The Debate in India*, Bombay: Oxford University Press.

Patnaik, Prabhat (1992), 'Terms of Trade and the Rate of Inflation', in Kaushik Basu and Pulin Nayak (eds.), *Development Policy and Economic Theory*, Delhi: Oxford University Press.

Rakshit, Mihir (1982), *The Labour Surplus Economy*, Delhi: Macmillan.

——— (1989), 'Effective Demand in a Developing Country: Approaches and Issues', in Mihir Rakshit (ed.), *Studies in the Macroeconomics of Developing Countries*, Delhi: Oxford University Press.

Rattso, Jorn (1989), 'Macrodynamic Adjustment Mechanisms in a Dual Semi-Industrialized Economy', *Journal of Development Economics*, 30, pp. 47–69.

Taylor, Lance (1982), 'Food Prices, Terms of Trade and Growth', in M. Gersovitz, C.F. Diaz-Alejandro, G. Ranis and M.R. Rosenzweig (eds.), *The Theory and Experience of Economic Development: Essays in Honor of Sir W. Arthur Lewis,* London: George Allen and Unwin.

——— (1983), *Structuralist Macroeconomics: Applicable Models for the Third World,* New York, Basic Books.

——— (1991), *Income Distribution, Growth and Inflation: Lectures of Structuralist Macroeconomic Theory,* Cambridge, MA: MIT Press.

Thirlwall, Anthony P. (1986), 'A General Model of Growth and Development on Kaldorian Lines', *Oxford Economic Papers,* 38(2), July, pp. 199–219.

Trade and Wage-Gap in Poor Countries

The Role of the Informal Sector

SUGATA MARJIT*, UDO BROLL, and SARBAJIT SENGUPTA*

1. INTRODUCTION

International trade and skilled-unskilled wage-gap has recently emerged as a topic of substantial research interest in economics. Rising income inequality in the developed part of the globe has induced trade and labour economists to seek plausible explanations for this intriguing phenomenon. A large number of studies are now available on this topic. A comprehensive summary of the issues may be found in Wood (1994), (1995) and Jones and Engerman (1996). Leamer (1995) argues that one cannot neglect the role of declining trade barriers in the north in creating the wage-gap between the skilled and unskilled. Berman *et al.* (1994) claim that the widening wage-gap is due to technological progress which has been biased in favour of skilled labour.

While there is already a substantial literature on the consequences of free trade on income inequality in the developed world, relatively few papers have focused on such implications of trade reform in the developing countries. A recent paper by Wood (1997) provides empirical evidence that the skilled-unskilled wage-gap has widened since

*This paper is a humble tribute to our respected teacher, Prof. M.K. Rakshit, who has profoundly influenced generations of students, with his teaching and research. Sugata Marjit would like to thank the Department of Economics, Erasmus University for financial support. This paper owes a lot to seminars at the CSSSC, Copenhagen Business School and University of Konstanz. Thanks are also due to Max Albert, Ronald Jones, and Guenther Schulze for helpful comments. The usual disclaimer applies.

some of the Latin-American nations went in for liberalized trade and investment regimes. Unlike the East-Asian nations, where export growth did close the wage-gap, the Latin-American nations have experienced increasing degree of income inequality. Feenstra and Hanson (1995) build up a simple and elegant trade theoretic framework to argue how 'outsourcing' through increasing foreign investment into Mexico has widened the wage-gap between the skilled and the unskilled. Foreign investment, according to their specifications, induces greater production of skill-intensive products in Mexico, thus switching demand away from the low-skill labour. If one sticks to the standard two-good structure of the Heckscher–Ohlin–Samuelson or Specific-Factors models and if the southern countries export low-skill products, rising inequality in the north should imply shrinking wage-gap in the south. This has not happened in Latin America.

The purpose of this paper is to analyse possible implications of a relatively open trade regime in the developed countries on the skilled–unskilled wage-gap in the developing world. The stage has been set recently by Feenstra and Hanson (1995), Wood (1997) and Robbins (1995a, b), (1996a, b) justifying the importance of the issue. Our purpose would be to focus on some of the structural features of a typical developing country, to incorporate them in a model of trade and production, and then look for the consequences of increasing exposure to international trade. Somehow, the discussions on the wage inequality in the southern hemisphere fail to do justice to a standard set of stylized empirical observations. It is not possible to get the right picture in this context if one ignores some of the essential features of the nature of labour markets in poor countries.

One of the most widely observed characteristics of the labour markets in developing countries is its formidable reservoir of unskilled labour employed in the 'informal' segment of the economy. This has been pointed out in numerous articles and books. A representative sample drawn from the literature contains works by Cole and Sanders (1983), Fields (1990), Mazumdar (1983), (1993), and Agenor (1996). Estimates cited in Agenor (1996) suggest that more than 50 to 60 per cent of labour force usually operates in the non-unionised sectors and often under flexible wage conditions. Urban informal sector wage is not likely to deviate much from the rural wage, given more or less unfettered mobility of labour between these sectors.

Implications of a liberalized regime for informal wage have to be analyzed closely if one has to understand the nature of the skilled-unskilled wage-gap in developing countries. Unfortunately the conventional discussion still revolves around the straight-jacket of Heckscher–Ohlin framework. For example, Wood (1997), while discussing empirical issues, seldom explores analytical structures that befit the circumstances prevailing in a developing country. The trade and wage inequality debate in East-Asia and in Latin-America do not do justice to a system which continues to have a dominant agricultural sector and a vast segment of poorly skilled people.

Wood (1997) suggests that a trade reform and wage inequality in Latin-America were conditional upon the entry of low-wage China, South-Asia and Africa in the world export market for unskilled products. This pushed down the prices of those products relative to the middle-skill intensive items, hurting the relative wage of the really unskilled. At the same time, Wood (1997) recognizes that not much is known about the possible implications of trade reform in South-Asia and Africa. If the neo-classical logic is taken at its face value, as unfortunately has been the case, the poorest countries must experience a relatively egalitarian outcome.

The purpose of this paper is to identify mechanisms through which international trade affects the wage—absolute as well as relative—of the unskilled in a developing country which exports and imports a wide range of goods. Furthermore, which has a substantial informal segment in the manufacturing sector and exhibits significant migration between the rural and urban sectors. Following Agenor and Montiel (1996) we assume that there is no 'effective' unemployment for the unskilled in the economy. If the unskilled cannot find a job in the organized sector, they find a job in the informal sector at a market adjusted wage rate.

Our conclusions suggest that a rise in agricultural exports may not affect the unskilled wage rate. Moreover, the degree to which agricultural terms of trade affects the unskilled wage depends crucially on capital mobility between the formal and informal segments of unskilled manufacturing. Rise in the prices of skilled exports naturally worsens the skilled–unskilled wage distribution. But a rise in the price of agricultural exports, which depends on unskilled labour, may not tilt the distribution in favour of the unskilled. In all these results 'informality' plays a major role.

Section 2 describes the benchmark trade model and the general equilibrium of the economy. Section 3 discusses the relevant comparative static results. Section 4 relaxes certain crucial assumptions and proves the robustness of the arguments. Section 5 concludes the study.

2. THE WAGE-GAP IN POOR COUNTRIES: BASIC FRAMEWORK

To consider the wage-gap problem for a typical developing country, we formulate a structure in a general form, incorporating the characteristics of labour markets as observed in the developing world.[1] We have a small open economy producing the following goods: a manufacturing good, *X*, produced entirely by skilled labour and capital, another good *Y* produced by unskilled labour and capital, a non-traded good, *N*, with similar resources and an agricultural product, *Z*, produced with land and unskilled labour. However, there are more sectors than goods. While there is no informal segment for the skilled labour and it is fully employed, unskilled labour is hired at a contracted nominal wage in the formal sector producing *Y*. Unskilled labour who cannot find jobs in the formal manufacturing sector, either gets a job in the informal manufacturing sector, non-traded sector or in the agricultural sector where wages are flexible and respond to competitive pressure. There is no open 'unemployment' of the unskilled labour. Everyone finds a job as wages can move up or down in the urban non-traded sector and the rural agricultural sector. Two obserservations are in order.

First, there is hard empirical evidence from many countries that 'open-unemployment' is usually observed among relatively educated people. Agenor (1996) and references there point out that job search costs are usually lower for those who are skilled and the unskilled must find a job to survive. They cannot afford the wait for a job as suggested in the standard Harris-Todaro framework (1970). This problem is well recognized and accommodated in Cole and Sanders (1983). Second, our main task is to focus on the relative well-being of the unskilled or of those who are really at the rock bottom in terms of education and skill. This befits the scenario in South-Asia and Sub-Saharan Africa. Since we are concerned with the relative wage of the unskilled, we shall not devote much attention on the 'intra-skill' distribution of wages. This justifies the assumption of a fully employed skilled factor of production.

Each sector operates with neo-classical technology of constant returns to scale and diminishing marginal productivity. Markets are competitive. These assumptions are quite standard in the existing literature. The following symbols will be used to describe the general equilibrium model:

[1]See Lindauer *et al.* (1988), Roberts (1991), Turnham (1993), Hollister and Goldstein (1994), Rama (1994), Revenga (1994), Said (1994), Banerjee and Bucci (1995) and Agenor (1996).

P_j exogenously given world price for the j-th product, $j = X, Y, Z$
P_N price of the non-traded good
W_S skilled wage rate
$\overline{W}$ fixed unskilled wage rate in the formal sector
W unskilled wage rate in the informal segment of the labour market
r return to capital
R return to land
S stock of the skilled labour
L stock of unskilled labour
K stock of capital
T stock of land
a_{ij} per unit requirement of the i-th factor of production for the j-th product

Variables with tilde refer to the informal manufacturing sector of the economy. The following equations describe the general equilibrium of the economy.

$$a_{SX}W_S + a_{KX}r = P_X, \tag{1}$$

$$a_{LY}\overline{W} + a_{KY}r = P_Y, \tag{2}$$

$$\tilde{a}_{LY}W + \tilde{a}_{KY}r = P_Y, \tag{3}$$

$$a_{LN}W + a_{KN}r = P_N, \tag{4}$$

$$a_{LZ}W + a_{KZ}r = P_Z, \tag{5}$$

$$a_{SX}X = S, \tag{6}$$

$$a_{KX}X + a_{KY}Y + \tilde{a}_{KY}\tilde{Y} + a_{KN}N = K, \tag{7}$$

$$a_{LX}X + \tilde{a}_{LY}\tilde{Y} + a_{LN}N + a_{LZ}Z = L, \tag{8}$$

$$a_{TZ}Z = T, \tag{9}$$

$$D(P_N, I) = N. \tag{10}$$

Equation (3) states the competitive pricing condition in the informal unskilled manufacturing sector. Note that the formal and the informal sector both produce the same product, and techniques of production differ as $\overline{W} > W$ (assumption A.1).

If one looks at equations (2) and (3) one may wonder why the entire capital does not flow into the informal segment with $W < \overline{W}$. The implicit assumption is that the informal segment is less productive than the formal sector. Since the informal sub-sector does not get formal institutional support and is not registered legally, there may be 'transaction costs' which are specific to this segment.[2] Hence, the benefit of lower wage is assumed to be offset by such costs. Equations (1) to (5) describe the competitive pricing conditions and (6) to (9) the full-employment requirements, while (10) is the non-traded goods market clearing condition. Also note that L is fully-employed although wage-differentials exist in the market for the unskilled. Equations (1) to (5) determine W_S, r, W, R and P_N. Equations (6) to (10) determine X, Y, $\tilde{Y}$, Z and N. Note that I is the National Income which is known once the factor prices and endowments are known.

Since we shall talk about the consequences of changes in world prices on the relative wages of the unskilled, we have not entertained the possibility of pursuing domestic policies such as tariffs, taxes or subsidies. In many cases the comparative static results should be the same, provided the internal policies are not endogenously determined. The country concerned in the model exports Z, the agricultural product, and therefore, imports at least one of X and Y. There are countries, for example India and China, which export highly skilled products such as computer software as well as primary commodities such as rice and tea. There are countries which are absolutely dependent on export of agricultural products and low unskilled manufacturing goods. In the aggregative model we describe above, agricultural exports would be common to all developing countries, with X and Y interchanging as exportables or importables as the case may be.

If the developed world starts pursuing a relatively open-door policy, as has been the case in the last twenty years or so, the world prices of X, Y and Z are likely to change. This will be reflected in the terms of trade improvement for the south. In the present context, we assume that the economy exports good X and Z and imports good Y. Therefore, we shall consider cases where prices of X and Z go up and those of Y go down in the world market. Note that as we have a fixed nominal

[2]It is possible that the informal sector gains because it does not pay 'taxes' as the formal sector does. However, these sectors do not get the 'subsidies' as well. We are assuming that such benefits and costs cancel each other and the productivity is lower in the informal segment.

unskilled wage, all nominal price movements should have real effects. One can try any combination of such price movements. But it would be instructive to try one at a time. Two types of wage movements would be interesting to analyse. First, the real-wage changes for three types of labour and the relative wage-gap between the skilled and the unskilled.

In order to evaluate the effect on the real income of labour we shall construct a price index valid for each type of labour. Let P be such an index:

$$P = P(P_X, P_Y, P_N, P_Z)$$

and we assume (assumption A.2)

$$P = \alpha \hat{P}_X + \beta \hat{P}_Y + \gamma \hat{P}_N + (1 - \alpha - \beta - \gamma)\hat{P}_Z, \tag{11}$$

where 'hat' denotes proportional change and α, β, γ, $1 - \alpha - \beta - \gamma$ are shares of expenditure on these goods. It would have been more realistic to consider a different preference structure for different classes of labour. But we abstract from such complications, noting that we may plug hypothetical values for α, β, γ to get a particular response in a particular context. For example, for very poor people at a low level of income, $\alpha + \beta + \gamma = 0$ and one should use the Stone–Geary utility function to draw realistic implications for development policies. If one conceives of N as the non-traded service, the rural workers may not have access to such products and one may incorporate that by appropriately modifying the coefficient of $\hat{P}_N$. With this in hand, we proceed to the next section.

3. TRADE AND WAGE INEQUALITY: COMPARATIVE STATICS

The first and the core proposition of the study deals with the impact of changes in P_X, P_Y, and P_Z on W the nominal wage of the informal workers, and consequently, on W_S/W. The following proposition summarizes the outcomes.

PROPOSITION 1. For a developing country with a large informal labour market as described above,

1. a rise in P_X and P_Z does not affect W;
2. a rise in P_X worsens the wage-gap while a rise in P_Z keeps it unaffected;
3. a decline in P_Y reduces W and worsens the wage-gap, provided the informal unskilled manufacturing sector is labour-intensive compared to the formal segment.

Proof. (i) Consider an increase in P_X. From equation (1) it is straightforward to argue that $\hat{W}_S > \hat{P}_X$ and $\hat{r} = 0$, as r is fixed by (2). As $\hat{r} = 0$, $\hat{W} = 0$, hence $\hat{W}_S - \hat{W} > 0$. (ii) Note that as $\hat{P}_Y = 0$, $\hat{r} = 0$. This leads $\hat{W} = 0$. Therefore, $\hat{R} = \hat{P}_Z$. Also, as $\hat{r} = \hat{P}_X = 0$, $\hat{W}_s = 0$. (iii) From equation (2) we obtain $\hat{r} = \hat{P}_Y/\theta_{KY}$. [Where θ's are the cost-shares of the factors and calculations here use the standard envelope condition for cost-minimization and follow Jones (1965).] From equation (3) we get $\hat{W} = \hat{P}_Y(1 - \tilde{\theta}_{KY}/\theta_{KY})/\tilde{\theta}_{KY}$. Hence, $\hat{W} < 0$, if and only if $\theta_{KY} > \tilde{\theta}_{KY}$, as $\hat{W}_S = 0$. This proves the claim.

In all the cases described above, including the one where only P_Z goes up, W_S/W either remains the same or moves in favour of skilled labour. The outcome of a liberal trade regime in the north is likely to generate increasing inequality. While a rise in P_X or a fall in P_Y produces conceivable outcomes, a rise in the price of *Z*, which employs unskilled labour, does not confer much benefits to the unskilled. This is guaranteed by free capital movement between the formal and informal sectors and fixed nominal wage for the unskilled. So long as capitalists want the same rate of return in the informal manufacturing as in formal manufacturing sector, *r* will dictate *W* as $\overline{W}$ is given. It is quite possible that for an expanding agriculture, reverse migration takes place without affecting the informal wage *W* and the entire benefit of a rise in P_Z goes to the landlords in the form of magnified increase in *R*.

An increase in P_X increases the real wage of the skilled labour unambiguously as $\hat{W}_S > \hat{P}_Y > 0 = \hat{P}_Y = \hat{P}_N$. As *W* remains unaffected in the process, P_N remains unaffected too. It is commonly believed that the growth in the non-traded service sector, which absorbs informal unskilled labour, helps this category of people. In this case, there are only reallocations of such labour from one sector to another, which does not improve their wages. In fact, the real wage of the unskilled declines unambigously, even with a rise in P_Z. The rise in the price of agricultural products does not necessarily help the poor working class as long as there is market induced wage suppresion in the informal manufacturing sector. A drop in P_Y would also lead to a similar outcome, except in one pathological case, where unskilled workers consume nothing except commodity *Y*, and *W* falls less than P_Y.

It is instructive to enquire the effect of an increase in P_X on the 'average' wage of the unskilled. It seems quite possible that there would be some reallocation of labour from the low wage informal to high wage ($\overline{W}$) formal manufacturing, and therefore, average wage may improve. After all, one has to work through the entire general equilibrium process to understand the complete picture. Let us look at the changes in the degree of informalization following an increase in P_X.

Since W_S is going up, a_{SX} will fall and given S, output X must increase [from (6)]. Note that as W_S is going up following the terms of trade improvement, income I must go up and given P_N, output N must increase [from (10)]. Since W and R are kept fixed, Z does not change [from (9)]. All factor proportions in Y, $\tilde{Y}$ and N do not change. From (7) it is easy to check that less capital is left to be employed in Y and $\tilde{Y}$ as a_{KX} and X both have gone up, and so has N. We now perform the familiar Rybczynski-type exercise to prove what has happened to Y. If Y goes down, then the 'average' wage of the unskilled must fall.

Differentiating (7) and (8), we obtain:

$$\lambda_{KY}\hat{Y} + \tilde{\lambda}_{KY}\hat{\tilde{Y}} = \lambda_{KN}\hat{N} - \hat{K}_X, \tag{12}$$

$$\lambda_{LY}\hat{Y} + \tilde{\lambda}_{LY}\hat{\tilde{Y}} = -\lambda_{LN}\hat{N}, \tag{13}$$

where $K_X = a_{KX}X$ (with $\hat{K} > 0$, $\hat{N} > 0$) and λ's are employment shares of each factor in different sectors, i.e., $\lambda_{LY} = a_{LY}Y/L$ etc.

$$\hat{Y} = \frac{-\tilde{\lambda}_{LY}(\lambda_{KN}\hat{N} + \hat{K}_X + \lambda_{LN}\tilde{\lambda}_{KY}\hat{N})}{|\lambda|},$$

$$= \frac{\hat{N}(\lambda_{LN}\tilde{\lambda}_{KY} - \tilde{\lambda}_{LY}\lambda_{KN}) - \tilde{\lambda}_{LY}\hat{K}_X}{|\lambda|} \tag{14}$$

Note that $\tilde{Y}$ is labour intensive compared with Y; therefore, following Jones (1965), we know $|\lambda| > 0$. It is quite likely that the non-traded sector should be labour-intensive compared to $\tilde{Y}$. In that case, there are two offsetting effects on Y. As labour is drawn into N, $\tilde{Y}$ tends to suffer as it is labour-intensive and labour is drawn into sector N. Y gets a boost on this account. But as capital is leaving the unskilled segment and Y is capital-intensive it tends to contract. If N is small, *i.e.* the rising income of the skilled does not have substantial spillover effect on the market for N, Y must contract. Since L is fully employed, people lose jobs in Y and start earning $W < \overline{W}$ instead. The average wage for the unskilled drops. As the skilled manufacturing expands, the degree of informalization also increases.

Let us define average unskilled wage as W_a as follows:

$$W_a = (\overline{W} - W)\frac{L_Y}{L} + W \tag{15}$$

where L_Y is the employment of sector Y. When P_X rises, W is held fixed and then W_a gets directly related to L_Y. A drop in L_Y will reduce W_a.

An increase in P_Z, as we have argued earlier, does not alter W. But it can alter W_a if L_Y increases, following an expansion in agriculture. Following the earlier argument one may note that initially an expansion in Z, *ceteris paribus*, draws labour away from Y to N. In the second round effect, capital leaves Y and N for X and Y. However, X cannot expand given the stock of skilled labour. This leads to an expansion in Y. If N expands because landlords spend part of their extra income on N and because unskilled employment has increased in sector Y, and these two effects outweigh the effect of a retreat of labour into the rural sector, Y expands further due to Rybcznski effect. Hence, average wage W_a tends to go up.

Note that, in real terms, both the existing insiders in the organized sector earning $\overline{W}$ lose and so do those who continue to lament in the informal sector. The only people who have their nominal income increased are those who move from low wage to high wage sector through an increase in L_Y. The ratio $(\overline{W} - W)/W$ captures the gain in percentage terms. Let us denote this as δ_W. The crucial condition turns out to be:

$$\delta_W > (1 - \alpha - \beta - \gamma)\hat{P}_Z \tag{16}$$

A substantial price increase in the agricultural sector would mean a lower real wage, even for those who now earn a higher wage.

In a typical full-employment model, higher labour-demand tends to push up nominal wage. Here, the 'average' nominal wage is pushed up without any change in the informal wage rate through the reallocation of labour. However, an increase in demand for labour may not get translated into an improvement of the real wage of the unskilled. Also note that given the supply of land, a rise in P_Z can raise agricultural production only through a decline in W/P_Z, i.e. through a decline in the marginal product of labour as more people are employed in agriculture. In any neo-classical structure where land is sector-specific and labour is the mobile factor, a rise in P_Z must reduce the real wage of the unskilled. The rise in nominal wage cannot be sufficient to outweigh the rise in z. Technically, this problem could be avoided with a multi-product agriculture, for example, with food-crop and cash-crop. An earlier structure of this type has been elaborated in the Harris-Todaro context by Marjit (1991). Let us see how such modification may work to the benefit of the unskilled, even when agriculture price rises due to a boom in the market for exports.

Consider another product which is produced in agriculture, which uses land and unskilled labour. Hence, agriculture has a 2×2 structure with a Heckscher-Ohlin nugget, as coined in Jones and Marjit (1992) and subsequently re-explored in Beladi and Marjit (1992), (1996), Marjit and Beladi (1997), (1998). Given agricultural prices, now one can determine W and R from this 2×2 structure. One W is known and $\underset{\sim}{\gamma}$ is known from (2), P_N would be known. But it would be hard for Y to survive since P_Y, W, γ all are predetermined. This sector will, in all possibility, cease to be competitive. This is a case where the entire informal segment in the urban sector is non-traded. It eliminates equation (3) for the time being. The two products in agriculture are Z_1 and Z_2. Suppose Z_1 is labour-intensive and Z_2 is land-intensive. An increase in P_{Z_1} now unambigously raises the real wage of the unskilled via the Stolper-Samuelson result.

Similarly, a rise in P_{Z_2} does exactly the opposite. This is the case where the nominal and real wage movements take place in the same direction. A rise in W induces P_N to increase. As P_N goes up, N contracts and Y expands, provided a_{KN} does not increase too much following a rise in W/P. An increase in Y improves the average wage by reallocating labour to the high wage sector. Overall, the absolute and relative real wage of the unskilled improves.

The next section deals with certain strong assumptions made in the basic framework and talks about the robustness of the results.

4. RELAXING ASSUMPTIONS

Some assumptions made in the earlier section may raise quite a few eyebrows and the likely conjecture is that the ealier results are consistent only with such a strict set of assumptions. Fortunately, this is not so.

4.1 Mobility of Capital

We shall first consider the inter-sectoral mobility of capital. It is plausible to argue that capital must earn different rates of return in the formal and informal sector. A recent study by Aryeetey *et al.* (1997) and earlier by Adams and Fitchett (1992), Binswanger and Rosenzweig (1986) suggest that informal interest rates are usually much higher than in the formal sector. In other words, the informal sector has to provide a premium to the lender. The reason for such differential, at least in the case study provided in Aryeetey *et al.* (1997), is not due to higher default rates, but more due to the oligopolistic nature of the informal capital market. As far as our experiment is concerned, what we need is that the above mentioned 'premium' does not move around much when prices and quantities adjust. The extreme case is one of absolutely no relationship between the formal and informal capital markets. We now start from the perfect immobility case and proceed to imperfect mobility with a stable differential between the formal and the informal sector.

We alter equations (3) and (4) to

$$\tilde{a}_{LY}W + \tilde{a}_{KY}\tilde{r} = P_Y \tag{17}$$

$$a_{LN}W + \tilde{a}_{KN}\tilde{r} = P_N \tag{18}$$

and furthermore

$$a_{KX}X + a_{KY}Y = K \tag{19}$$

$$\tilde{a}_{KY}\tilde{Y} + a_{KN}N = \tilde{K} \tag{20}$$

where $\tilde{r}$ is the return to capital in the informal sector and $\tilde{K}$ is the stock of capital employed in the informal sector. The model is now solved in the following manner.

Equations (1) and (2) determine W_S and r. Now fix a level of P_N, solve for W, r from (17) and (18) and R from (5). Equations (6) and (19) determine X and Y. Equation (9) determines Z.[3] Then, from (20) and (8), $\tilde{Y}$ and N are determined. We can now define a relationship between P_N and N from the supply side and then close the model by bringing in (10).

Consider an increase in P_X. It increases W_S by a magnified amount and r is kept unchanged. But X must expand and Y must fall. Labour is released into $\tilde{Y}$, N and Z. At a given P_N, W and Z do not change. The Rybczynski effect will increase N if N is labour-intensive compared to Y. N expands, P_N drops if the demand spillover effect through a rise in W_S is small. The wage rate W drops even more, like in the Stolper–Samuelson case. The drop in W is a must because either Y or

[3]Note that given P_N, all factor prices are known.

N have to be labour-intensive and the Stolper-Samuelson argument will work either through a drop in P_N or through a rise in P_N.

A decrease in P_Y reduces r and increases W_S. Again, X increases and Y contracts. W should fall if $\tilde{Y}$ is labour-intensive. If not, W rises initially. But as labour flows into the informal segment, N expands, reducing P_N and putting downward pressure on W.

If P_Z goes up, at a given P_N, then R goes up, Z expands, draws labour into agriculture. If N is labour-intensive N contracts, P_N goes up, so does W. If N is capital-intensive, N goes up, P_N goes down and W still increases via Stolper-Samuelson argument. W_S and r do not change.

One must note that the above arguments do not talk much about change in the real income in aggregate I. Given the trade pattern, a rise in P_X or P_Z, and a drop in P_Y indicate positive terms of trade effects. But we have a distortion in the system and the consequent adverse effect of a terms of trade change on L_Y will dampen the increase in National Income. We are ignoring the aggregate effect because we are concentrating on the redistributive outcomes.

The effects on W following changes in P_X, P_Y and P_Z are intuitive and quite expected, unlike the earlier ones. Sector specific capital tends to help the unskilled wage when P_Z goes up, or hurts when P_X goes up. In the earlier case, higher P_X does not affect γ, which in turn pegs W. But now, movement of labour in and out $\tilde{Y}$, N has factor-price implications. Similarly, when P_Z increases, and more labour is required, they need to be paid more, squeezing r, the return to $\tilde{K}$, which does not have any escape route through the formal segment as it is totally delinked from K.

It is instructive to postulate a relationship to capture the imperfect mobility case by (21):

$$\tilde{r} = (1 + \mu)r \tag{21}$$

where $1 + \mu$ is the premium. If $\mu = 0$, we have perfect mobility of capital between the formal and the informal segment. If $\mu > 0$, capital employed in the informal sector earns a premium over the formal sector return. The term $1 + \mu$ describes a particular relationship between $\tilde{r}$ and r. It is quite possible that $\tilde{r} > r$, yet, the premium can remain constant when relative prices alter in the system. This seems to be a more reasonable assumption than the 'zero' mobility between the formal and the informal segment. In a recent paper Aryeetey, Hettige, Nissanke and Steel (1997) provide evidence that in Ghana, Nigeria and Tanzania, most of the informal deposit mobilizers have bank accounts. This suggests the possibility that funds could be shifted towards the informal clientale, who, in turn, do not have much access to formal credit or credit from more than one source.

A theory that internalises μ as an endogenous variable should complete the picture. But the premium and mobility both can be parts of reality. In fact, Aryeetey *et al.* (1997) suggest that the premium is an outcome of monopolistic informal credit market, i.e. ability of certain groups to get access to loanable funds and supply them at an expensive rate. This seems to be the case since low default rate and small transaction costs in the informal credit market do not naturally lead to a significant premium. This type of a situation calls for some co-movement between r and $\tilde{r}$.

From the foregoing discussions it is clear that if r remains unaltered with changes in prices, all our results must hold. The wedge between r and $\tilde{r}$, *per se* does not lead to different results. Perfect immobility of capital does alter some of the results derived in the benchmark case.

4.2 Mobility of Labour

Free mobility of unskilled labour between the rural and urban sectors equates informal wage across all activities. A competing framework may be of the Harris-Todaro (1970) type structure. However, it has been pointed out repeatedly in several studies that open urban unemployment is visible among people whose search cost for a job is relatively low. The poor, with very little savings, cannot afford to be unemployed, and search for a job. This issue has been discussed in Agenor and Montiel (1996) as well as in Agenor (1996). Mazumdar (1983) mentions a few studies where the employment in the urban sector did not specifically take place from those waiting as unemployed. This casts doubts on the use of the Harris–Todaro approach. One may argue that there should be some difference between the informal manufacturing wage and the agricultural wage. Just as in the case of capital, for most of our results to hold, we need the premium or the extent of the wage-gap, if any, to remain stable.

Consider the set of equations (1) to (5). Let the informal workers be paid W and the rural workers be paid W_Z. We postulate the following relationship:

$$\tilde{W} = (1 + \rho)W_Z, \quad \rho > 0 \tag{22}$$

Replacing W_Z by $\widetilde{W}/(1+\rho)$ and reworking through the changed framework will give us similar results as in section 2. A positive movement between W and W_Z is what we need to insulate the informal sector's nominal wage from price movements in agriculture. The Harris-Todaro structure endogenises ρ in a particular fashion. But here, as the informal labour force has to be fully-employed, ρ will not be related to unemployment. ρ may be coined as 'costs of mobility' which may change with significant movement of labour. We assume a stable ρ for our initial results to hold.

This section has been developed to argue that imperfect mobility of resources between the formal-informal segment and/or between the rural and urban regions does not necessarily jeopardize the result designed in the benchmark case.

4.3 Production Structure

Let us consider certain alterations in the production structure we have been working with. First, consider the case where there is no informal traded sector, i.e. the sector producing $\tilde{Y}$ does not exist. This would eliminate equation (3) and the variable $\tilde{Y}$. Now consider an increase in P_X; then W_S increases in the first round effect. Increased income of the skilled spills over to the non-traded sector. As P_X/P_N increases, there will be a substitution effect and capital leaves Y and N to be reallocated towards X.

Let us first ignore the demand side effects. As capital leaves for X, at a given level of Z, N may expand if it is labour-intensive compared to Y, due to Rybczynski effect. Hence, P_N should fall as supply of N expands. Provided the demand side effect is weak, P_N falls, W falls [from (4)], Z expands, which again, through the Rybczynski argument, checks the increase in X. But note that if the demand side effect on N is absent or negligible, P_N must fall, notwithstanding the rise in Z, since such a rise can only be caused by a decline in W, i.e. by a decline in P_N. In this case W_S/W_a must go up.

The demand side effect will tend to increase the demand, and hence, the price for N. It would counter the downward movement in P_N. But note that as Y contracts, employment in this sector must fall. Hence, the unskilled would be reallocated from the high wage $\overline{W}$ to the low wage sector W. This negative income effect will again reinforce a decline in P_N. Hence, an increasing W_S/W is very much a possibility. The technical presentation of the result, in the full blown general equilibrium of the system, will involve lots of elasticities and coefficients. To see through the basic result, let us work out the case for the 'low' elasticity of substitution between factors in each sector.

This would make $\hat{Z} = 0$, since the only way it can change is through a change in W that affects the substitution margin between labour and capital. Similarly, the Rybczynski impact on N and Y would have two components—one through a reallocation of capital, the other through a change in the intensive margin. We ignore the latter. The following is the outcome:

Follow (11) to get,

$$(\hat{P}_N + \hat{N})(1 - \gamma) = \gamma(\hat{P}_N + \hat{X}) + \gamma\hat{Y} + \gamma\hat{Z} \tag{23}$$

From (7) and (8) we obtain,

$$\hat{Y} = \frac{\lambda_{KN}\lambda_{LN}\hat{H}}{|\lambda|} \tag{24}$$

$$\hat{N} = \frac{\lambda_{KN}\lambda_{LY}\hat{X}}{|\lambda|} \tag{25}$$

Since the elasticity of substitution is close to zero in X also, given S, $\hat{X} = 0$, even if $\hat{P}_X > 0$. Hence, $\hat{Y} = \hat{N} = \hat{X} = 0$, $\hat{Z} = 0$ (assumption A.3). Therefore, from (23),

$$\hat{P}_N = \frac{\gamma}{1 - \gamma}\hat{P}_X,$$

$$\hat{W}_S = \hat{P}_N/\theta_{SN},$$

$$\hat{W} = \frac{\gamma}{1 - \gamma}\frac{1}{\theta_{LN}}\hat{P}_N.$$

Therefore,

$$\hat{W}_S - \hat{W} = \hat{P}_X\left[\frac{1}{\theta_{SX}} - \frac{\gamma}{1 - \gamma}\frac{1}{\theta_{LN}}\right]. \tag{26}$$

This is the case where there is no quantity adjustment and there is some demand adjustment in the non-traded sector, which alters P_X/P_N,

$$\hat{W}_S - \hat{W} > 0 \quad \text{if and only if} \quad \theta_{SX} < \theta_{LN}(1 - \gamma)/\gamma \tag{27}$$

If the demand effect is weak and/or the non-traded sector is labour-intensive compared to X, W_S/W will rise in spite of an increase in W.

Suppose that the factor substitution effect in X is strong, so that $\hat{X} > 0$, but not in Y, N and Z. In that case, $\hat{X} > 0$, $\hat{N} > 0$, $\hat{Y} \lessgtr 0$, as $|\lambda| > 0$ (i.e. N is labour intensive). Again, for a low enough γ, $P_N < 0$, implying a further increase in W_S/W. In fact, even in a more general case, with a low enough γ, increase in W_S/W is quite likely to occur. Absence of a traded informal sector allows W to move around. But it can move in any direction if one carefully takes into account the possible general equilibrium response.

To summarize, free mobility of labour and capital is not necessary for the results we have reported in the earlier sections. Alterations in the production structure may not invalidate the basic arguments. However, the existence of a traded informal sector is quite crucial for unambiguous results. Since traded as well as non-traded informal segments can both be parts of reality, the extended framework seems suitable for our purpose.

5. CONCLUSIONS

The objective of this paper has been to relate the skilled–unskilled wage-gap in a developing country to its increasing exposure to international trade. We explicitly bring in fragmented labour-markets with a significant reservoir of informal, unskilled labour. The informal market determines a market clearing wage rate, which coexists with a higher contractual wage in the organized sector. In a well spelt out general equilibrium framework, relationships between relative wage of the unskilled and commodity terms of trade are examined. Intersectoral capital mobility, however imperfect it is, plays a major role in determining the impact of higher exports of agriculture on the relative wage of the unskilled.

A major motivation of this study has been to suggest that one needs to get away from the standard 2×2 Stolper–Samuelson type experiments while analyzing the case of the poor nations, which tend to have complex labour markets and multiple wages. One must bring in agriculture, with land as a specific factor; one should not ignore the fact that developing economies may export human-capital intensive goods and one should incorporate the role of intersectoral capital flows. However, the essence of international trade theory, the general equilibrium approach, must be retained to get a holistic view. This study is also an humble attempt towards this direction. It should be noted that the theoretical structure is not merely an exercise in abstraction. It has been built up in accordance with substantial empirical evidence gathered so far. Several papers cited in this study do justice to the specific analytical structure.

Two extensions will be attempted later. First, the vertical relationship between the informal and the formal sectors must be discussed. Second, the implications of foreign capital inflows on the wage-gap should be incorporated. The latter part has been recently discussed in a simpler general equilibrium structure without the informal sector in Marjit (1997). It shows that skilled-unskilled wage-gap is likely to worsen with capital mobility.

References

Adams, D.W. and D.A. Fitchett (1992), *Informal Finance in Low Income Countries*, Colorado: Westview Press, Boulder.

Agenor, P.R. (1996), 'The Labour Market and Economic Adjustment', *IMF Staff Papers,* 32, pp. 261–335.

Agenor, P.R. and P. Montiel (1996), *Development Macroeconomics*, Princeton, Princeton University Press.

Aryeety, A., H. Hettige, M. Nissanke, and W. Steel (1997), 'Financial Market Fragmentation and Reforms in Ghana, Malawi, Nigeria and Tanzania', *World Bank Economic Review*, 11, pp. 195–218.

Banerjee, B. and G.A. Bucci (1995), 'On-the-Job Search in a Developing Country: An Analysis Based on India Data on Migrants', *Economic Development and Cultural Change*, 43, pp. 565–83.

Basu, K. (1997), *Analytical Development Economics*, MIT Press.

Beladi, H. and S. Marjit (1992), 'Foreign Capital and Protectionism', *Canadian Journal of Economics*, 25, pp. 233–8.

——— (1996), 'An Analysis of Rural Urban Migration and Protection', *Canadian Journal of Economics*, 29, pp. 930–40.

Berman, E., J. Bound and Z. Grilliches (1994), 'Changes in the Demand for Skilled Labour Within U.S. Manufacturing Industries', *Quarterly Journal of Economics*, 109, pp. 367–97.

Binswanger, H. and M. Rosenzweig (1986), 'Behavioral and Material Determinants of Production Relations in Agriculture', *Journal of Development Studies*, 22, pp. 503–39.

Cole, W.E. and R.D. Sanders (1985), 'Internal Migration and Urban Employment in the Third World', *American Economic Review*, 75, pp. 481–94.

Feenstra, R. and G. Hanson (1995), 'Foreign Investment, Outsourcing and Relative Wages', R. Feenstra (ed.), *Political Economy of Trade Policy, Essays in Honor of J.N. Bhagwati*, MIT Press.

Fields, G. (1990), 'Labor Market Modeling and the Urban Informal Sector:—Theory and Evidence', D. Turnham (ed.), *The Informal Sector and Evidence Revisited*, Paris: OECD.

——— (1994), 'Changing Labour Market Conditions and Economic Development in Hong Kong, the Republic of Korea, Singapore and Taiwan, China', *World Bank Economic Review*, 8, pp. 395–414.

Harris, J.R. and M.P. Todaro (1970), 'Migration, Unemployment and Development: A Two Sector Analysis', *American Economic Review*, 60, pp. 126–42.

Hollister, R.G. and M.P. Goldstein (1994), *Reforming Labor Markets in the Far East: Implications for Structural Adjustment and Market Economies*, San Francisco: ICS Press.

Jones, R.W. (1965), 'The Structure of Simple General Equilibrium Models', *Journal of Political Economy,* 73, pp. 557–72.

Jones, R.W. and S. Marjit (1992), 'International Trade and Endogenous Production Structure', W. Neufiend and R. Riezman (eds.), *Economic Theory and International Trade: Essays in Memory of T. Rader*, Berlin, New York: Springer.

Jones, R.W. and S.L. Engerman (1996), 'Trade, Technology and Wages: A Tale of Two Countries', *American Economic Review (Papers and Proceedings),* 86, pp. 35–40.

Leamer, E. (1995), 'A Trade Economist's View of U.S. Wages and Globalization', S. Collins (ed.), *Imports, Exports and American Worker*, Washington, D.C.

Lindauer, D.L., O.A. Meesook and P. Suebsang (1988), 'Government Wage Policy in Africa: Some Findings and Policy Issues', *World Bank Research Observer*, 3, pp. 1–25.

Marjit, S. (1991), 'Agro-Based Industry and Rural-Urban Migration: A Case for an Urban Employment Subsidy', *Journal of Development Economics*, 35, pp. 393–8.

——— (1997), 'Terms of Trade and Wage-Gap in Developing Countries', Mimeo, Calcutta: Centre for Studies in Social Sciences.

Marjit, S. and H. Beladi (1996), 'Protection and Gainful Effects of Foreign Capital', *Economic Letters*, 53, pp. 311–16.

——— (1997), 'Protection, Underemployment and Welfare', EPRU Discussion Paper, Copenhagen Business School.

Mazumdar, D. (1983), 'Segmented Labour Markets in LCDs', *American Economic Review*, 73, pp. 254–9.

——— (1993), 'Labor Markets and Adjustment in Open Asian Economies: The Republic of Korea and Malaysia', *World Bank Economic Review*, 7, pp. 349–80.

Rama, M. (1994), 'Labor Markets Flexibility in Sri Lanka', Policy Research Working Paper no. 1262, World Bank.

Revenga, A. (1994), 'Employment and Wage Effects of Trade Liberalisation: The Case of Mexican Manufacturing', unpublished working paper, World Bank.

Robbins, D. (1995), *Earnings Dispersion in Chile After Trade Liberalisation*, Cambridge, Harvard Institute for International Development.

Said, M. (1992), 'Public Sector Employment and Labour Markets in Arab Countries: Recent Developments and Policy Implications', unpublished working paper, IMF.

Turuham, D. (1993), *Employment and Development: A New Review of Evidence,* Paris: OECD.

Wood, A. (1994), *North-South Trade Employment and Inequality: Changing Fortunes in a Skill-Driven World*, Oxford: Clarendon Press.

——— (1995), 'How Trade Hurt Unskilled Workers', *Journal of Economic Perspectives*, 9, pp. 57–80.

——— (1997), 'Openness and Wage-Inequality in Developing Countries: The Latin-American Challenge to East Asian Conventional Wisdom', *World Bank Research Observer*, pp. 33–57.

DYNAMICS

Dynamics: An Introduction

Modern macroeconomic theory has been characterized by a resurgence of interest in the theory of economic growth. This section brings together typical examples from two very different sub-branches of the literature which, curiously enough, proceed in very different directions. The first, 'new' growth theory, is the outcome of imposing particular structures on the growth process, bringing hitherto 'exogenous' factors such as technical progress within the ambit of deliberate decision-making. In contrast, the second branch asks just how much structure can be justified if we start with the notion of utility maximization (with conventional preferences and technology). What sort of restrictions are placed on the outcome? One might call this approach 'dynamic revealed preference'.

New Growth Theory

Three kinds of provocations have fuelled a resurgence of interest in the theory of economic growth. First, there is evidence that (savings-driven) steady growth in per capita consumption is possible. This casts doubt on the inevitability of diminishing returns to capital, a corner-stone of the 'old' growth theory. Second, and logically separate from the first, there is theoretical interest in endogenizing the factors that make for sustained growth; in particular, technical progress. Third, there is interest (both theoretical and empirical) in the nature and magnitude of dynamic externalities and in the consequent role of economic policy that arises from such externalities.

The literature that has emerged is large and technical. But the subject is too important to be left out of introductory courses. To meet the resulting pedagogic challenge of providing a unified, accessible and easy-to-remember account of the pioneering contributions is the motivation for Dipankar Dasgupta's essay. No beginner in economics can escape familiarity with demand-supply crosses, and this fact has been exploited by Dasgupta. He uses a demand-supply grouping of variables to construct a dynamic demand-supply 'cross diagram'. To simplify the exposition, Dasgupta concentrates on steady states. This device enables equalization of the rates of growth of different variables. For any 'cross diagram' there is a key equilibrating variable; in the 'Marshallian Cross', it is the market price that adjusts and in the 'Keynesian Cross', it is the level of production that adjusts. In the present case, it is the rental rate on capital that is the equilibrating variable, and this is seen as bringing the 'demand rate of growth' into equality with the 'supply rate of growth'. The demand rate of growth is that rate of growth of per capita consumption that is consistent with the representative household maximizing utility over time, given the rental on capital. A parametric increase in this rate raises the utility maximizing rate of growth of consumption (the demand rate of growth).

While the modelling of the demand side is common to different contributions, it is on the supply side that contributions differ. These differences make for differences in the slope and position of the 'supply curve' which captures the response, to parametric changes in the rental rate, of the rate of growth of consumption goods supply per capita that maintains equilibrium on the production side. Some straightforward consequences are easy to state. For example, one disturbing feature of the old growth theory was the lack of influence of demand side factors (e.g. utility functions, discount rates) on the long-run rate of growth. This situation can be seen as resulting from Dasgupta's 'supply curve' being vertical. At the other extreme is the case where the supply curve becomes horizontal on account of constant returns to capital. This is the familiar A–K model (characterized by a linear production function in capital) used in modern endogenous growth theory.

DYNAMIC REVEALED PREFERENCE

The connection between *observed* behaviour, as summarized, for instance, in a demand or supply curve, and an underlying *model* of maximization-based actions, has been of deep interest to economists. If a wide array of observed behaviours is 'rationalizable' in the sense that they could all stem from standard maximization problems with convex preferences, it would follow that maximization places too *few* restrictions on behaviour. The maximization hypothesis would not be falsifiable, or at any rate, it would be too weak.*

A celebrated paper by Hugo Sonnenschein† showed that *any* con-

*It is interesting to contrast this with the standard criticism of the maximization hypothesis, which is that it is too restrictive a description of human behaviour.

†Sonnenschein (1974), 'Market Excess Demand Functions', *Econometrica*, 40, pp. 549–63.

tinuous function, satisfying mild restrictions, could serve as the excess demand function is some exchange economy with well-behaved individual utility functions.

What about the theory of optimal growth? Can similar results be obtained there as well? It is well-known that under mild restrictions, optimal policy functions are continuous. The question arises: is continuity (or some variant thereof, such as Lipschitz continuity) all that one can hope to get? Mitra's paper is an exposition of the near-state-of-the-art in this area,* starting from a central result of Boldrin and Montrucchio.† But in doing so, Mitra raises two issues that are intrinsic to the dynamic nature of the optimal growth problem and go beyond the Sonnenschein argument.

First, if a wide range of policy functions can be accommodated as possible optima, so might functions that generate irregular or chaotic dynamics as *optimal programmes*. Informally, chaotic behaviour lies at the uneasy penumbra between deterministic and stochastic dynamics. While chaotic processes are indeed deterministic, even miniscule errors in measuring, or understanding, the initial conditions will magnify into uncontrolled degrees of imprecision as we move along the iterated sequence (generated by the policy function). If optimization can result in such behaviour, that is surely of interest.

Second, in deriving a policy function as the outcome of dynamic optimization, we constrain ourselves to 'well-behaved environments': for instance, preferences and feasible sets that are convex (just as in the Sonnenschein problem). But the dynamic nature of the question studied in Mitra's paper forces us to face additional constraints, such as a reasonable range of values for the intertemporal discount factor. Gerhard Sorger, Mitra and others have recently shown‡ that the

*For the qualification 'near-state-of-the-art' we have Mitra himself to blame—after this paper was written, Mitra and Sorger have recently obtained more definitive results along these lines. See T. Mitra and G. Sorger (1999), 'Rationalizing Policy Functions by Dynamic Optimization', *Econometrica*, 67, pp. 375–92.

†M. Boldrin and L. Montrucchio (1986), 'On the Indeterminacy of Capital Accumulation Paths,' *Journal of Economic Theory*, 40, pp. 26–39.

‡G. Sorger (1994), 'Period Three Implies Heavy Discounting', *Mathematics of Operations Research*, 19, pp. 1–16, and T. Mitra (1996), 'An Exact Discount Factor Restriction for Period-Three Cycles in Dynamic Optimization Models', *Journal of Economic Theory*, 69, pp. 281–305.

Sonnenschein-style critique of maximization may be premature as far as dynamic models are concerned—the discount factors needed for some particularly ill-behaved policies to be optimal are often unacceptably low. Mitra's contribution discusses this issue as well.

5

New Growth Theory
A Supply–Demand View

DIPANKAR DASGUPTA*

1. INTRODUCTION

The present exercise is a pedagogic attempt to summarize some of the developments in the area of *New Growth Theory (NGT)* in terms of an elementary supply-demand framework, where the object of demand as well as supply is the *rate of growth* itself. While it is not too clear if this should be viewed as a totally original approach, the matter does not seem to have been presented so far in precisely these terms. Since the literature on NGT is somewhat difficult for a beginner, it is hoped that this unified approach will serve as a quick introduction to the subject. The size of the article, however, restricts the coverage. More comprehensive treatments may be found in textbooks on the subject, such as Barro and Sala-i-Martin (1995) and Aghion and Howitt (1998).

A *Theory of Growth* is concerned with an explanation of the manner in which real macroeconomic variables, such as output, consumption, capital stock, labour force, technology, the general price level, the real rate of interest[1], etc., behave over time.

Of special interest to *Growth Theory* is the possibility that some of these variables grow at *constant* and indefinitely maintainable rates. When this happens, the economy is said to be in a state of *balanced* or *steady* growth. Balanced growth is, of course, not the only object of interest in *Growth Economics*. However, it is a useful object and the only one with which this exposition is concerned.

*The author is deeply indebted to Amitava Bose for his detailed comments on an early version that appeared as an Indian Statistical Institute, Delhi Centre Discussion Paper (# 96–08) under the title *New Growth Theory: An Expository Device*.

[1]Throughout, the 'real rate of interest' will be understood to mean the real 'rental' on capital. The expressions will be used interchangeably.

There are at least two reasons why balanced growth paths alone are emphasized. First, unbalanced or non-constant growth paths can be defined only with reference to a path along which the rate of growth is a constant. Hence, a proper appreciation of the latter would seem to be a necessary pre-requisite for discussing the former. Secondly, the technical as well as conceptual difficulties underlying unbalanced paths had best be avoided in an elementary exposition such as the present one.

A balanced growth path for an economy may be said to be in equilibrium if the rate at which the economy is *capable* of growing is indeed the rate at which it *wishes* to grow. In what follows, the first of these will be referred to as the *supply rate* of growth for the economy and the second as its *demand rate*. Thus, a growth equilibrium will be viewed as a state in which the supply and the demand rates of growth are equal.

The demand rate of growth is largely determined by the rate at which households save a part of the GDP for the purpose of capital accumulation.[2] The supply rate, by contrast, depends on the rate of growth of natural resources (such as labour) as well as technology. Ever since the publication of Ramsey's seminal paper on optimal savings [Ramsey (1928)], it has been a well-recognized fact that the demand rate of growth is an endogenous variable for any economic system. Thus, it depends on other variables, the prime example of which is the real rate of interest. The parameters describing a society's aggregate utility from consumption and the social rate of time preference affect the demand rate as well.

The thrust of NGT lies primarily in the recognition of the supply rate *also* as an endogenously determined variable. In fact, a major quest of NGT lies in the identification of variables that influence the supply rate of growth.

[2]It is assumed [as in Solow (1956)] that with perfectly flexible prices, including real wage and interest rates, household savings are automatically invested. Consequently, the Keynesian problem of a possible mismatch between savings and voluntary investment has no role to play in the analysis that follows. It is well worth noting that Growth Theory, as it began in the hands of Harrod (1939), was exclusively concerned with the savings-investment problem. The growth exercise of Domar (1946) had a bearing on the problem also. Since the ideas to be discussed below have no connection with either Harrod or Domar, it is best to abstract from Keynesian issues in the main body of the presentation. Harrod provided a very important insight into the growth process of a free enterprise economy however, and a brief discussion of his contribution is contained in the Appendix.

In this connection, the one most important variable turns out to be the real rate of interest, though theories differ as to the exact manner in which it influences the supply rate.

In the spirit of the Marshallian theory of price-quantity equilibrium under perfect competition, the equalization of the demand and supply rates of growth leads to the determination of the growth rate, and often the real rate of interest, in a dynamic equilibrium.[3]

The real rate of interest affects the demand rate of growth the same way in all the theories to be discussed below. As already noted, however, this is not true about the supply rate of growth. It is helpful, therefore, to classify some of the important ideas of NGT according to the link they establish between the real rate of interest and the supply rate. The exposition here will mostly be guided by this point of view.

There are two parts to the exposition. The first summarizes the salient issues of Old Growth Theory *à la* Solow (1956). This sets up the background as well as analytical framework for the discussion in the second part, which deals entirely with the NGT.

2. OLD GROWTH THEORY

2.1 The Solow Model

Solow's [Solow (1956)] interest revolves around the growth rate attainable *in the absence of* a Keynesian mismatch between aggregate household savings and voluntary investment carried out by the business sector. The possibility that these two may not be equal is referred to in the Keynesian literature as the effective demand problem.

In order to abstract from this problem, Solow adopts a Walrasian rather than a Keynesian view of a competitive market economy. There are only two smoothly substitutable factors of production (capital and labour), both augmentable over time. The household sector owns both these factors. The endowment of labour at each instant of time is a demographic parameter. Savings, i.e. the part of final output not demanded as consumer goods, are *assumed* to be willingly in-

[3]To avoid a possible misunderstanding, one should note that Marshall was also concerned about dynamic forces leading to an equalization of demand and supply prices under competition. The parallel that is drawn here does not stretch that far. The equality of demand and supply rates of growth is treated as the definition of equilibrium. However, the stability properties of this equilibrium, though important, fall out of the purview of the presentation.

vested, i.e. used to augment the capital stock of the household sector. The logic underlying this assumption rests on the following demand–supply story.

The household sector derives its income by supplying factor services inelastically to the business sector in perfectly competitive markets. The demand for factor services derives from profit maximization by the firms. With a flexible wage-rental ratio, there is full employment of both factors, irrespective of the size of factor endowments and this justifies the households' readiness to channel their savings into new capital formation. Since, by assumption, all output is demanded, either as consumption or as investment goods, the business sector is able to produce and sell *any* level of output, in particular, the full employment level, and the effective demand problem does not arise.

Given this analytical abstraction, Solow goes on to characterize a competitive economy under *balanced growth equilibrium*. A macro-economic system is defined to be in a state of *balanced growth* if the real rate of interest and the rates of growth of aggregate output, aggregate capital stock and aggregate consumption are constants forever. This definition will be rigorously adhered to in what follows.

The economy, however, is required not only to be in a balanced growth state, but also in *equilibrium*. To define an equilibrium, the demand and the supply rates of growth must be isolated. It is helpful to begin with the demand rate. Solow's economy is assumed to produce a single good (Y) which can be consumed (C) as well as accumulated in the form of a capital stock (K). In the absence of an effective demand problem, aggregate household income at each point of time t equals the value of the full employment output of the economy. Since income is either saved or spent on consumption, the household sector must decide on the optimal allocation of the full employment value of its income between consumption and savings at each point of time. The path of savings so chosen is also the desired path of capital accumulation. Associated with it is the path of consumption demanded over time.

Thus, while the Keynesian effective demand problem is assumed away by Solow, the notion of demand is not altogether absent in his framework. Demand for the *level* is replaced by that for a *rate of growth*.

Formally speaking, the household sector is a macro entity that assumes away differences between the constituent micro households. This is a useful abstraction, given the question Solow asks, viz., whether an equilibrium can exist between the demand and the supply rates of growth in the economy *as a whole.* How the rate may itself be affected by differences between households is of secondary importance in answering this question. As a consequence, Solow views the household as a single aggregative unit as it were, which decides about the savings path on behalf of all households. From the point of view of such a household, the economy's welfare is, logically speaking, identical with its own. The economy, however, is for all practical purposes an infinitely lived object. The macro household too must, therefore, be endowed with an infinitely long planning horizon. It is, moreover, a dynastic organization, in the sense that it makes a once for all decision, say at $t = 0$, about the savings and consumption to be undertaken by the society for all time to come.

Solow (1956) had posited a constant *ad hoc* savings rate, and hence, an arbitrary solution to the household sector's decision problem. Modern treatments of the subject, however, assume (in response to the dynamic optimization frameworks of Cass (1965) and Koopmans (1965)) the problem to be solved *optimally* by the household.[4]

Typically, the household is assumed to maximize the intertemporal welfare function given by,

$$\int_0^\infty e^{-\rho t} L(t) \frac{1}{1-\sigma} (c(t)^{1-\sigma} - 1)\, dt \tag{1}$$

where $L(t)$ is the size of the labour force at t (assumed to be equal to the population), $1/(1 - \sigma)\,(c(t)^{1-\sigma} - 1)$ is the utility from *per capita* consumption $c(t) = C(t)/L(t)$ at $t, \rho > 0$ the discount parameter and $\sigma > 0$ the constant elasticity of marginal utility from consumption.[5]

The household's budget at each instant is given by,

$$L(t)\, c(t) + \dot{K}(t) = r(t)\, K(t) + w(t)\, L(t) \tag{2}$$

where $K(t)$ is the size of the capital stock at t, $\dot{K}(t)$ is aggregate

[4]Strictly speaking, Ramsey (1928) had anticipated them. To avoid a possible misunderstanding, it is worth remarking here that Ramsey as well as Cass and Koopmans were concerned with the problems of a centrally planned economy. Such an economy is referred to below as a command economy. Although the welfare function of the aggregate household is assumed to be the same as that of a central planner, the latter will be seen to arrive at a better intertemporal allocation of resources in the presence of external effects.

[5]A utility function involving a variable elasticity of marginal utility raises problems for the existence of a balanced growth equilibrium in the presence of technical change.

investment[6] (which equals aggregate household savings, for reasons outlined above), $r(t)$ is the real rate of interest and $w(t)$ the wage rate at t. The assumption of perfectly competitive markets implies that $r(t)$ and $w(t)$ are parametrically given to the household. Thus, the household maximizes (1) subject to (2) and the values of the initial capital stock (K_0) and labour force (L_0).

The household's choice of the demand rate of growth of $c(t)$ is given by the following result:

PROPOSITION 1: The demand rate of growth of per capita consumption is a monotone increasing, linear function of r. Specifically, it has the form $g_c^d = g_c^d(r) = (r - \rho)/\sigma$.

For an informal proof[7] of the proposition, assume that $c^*(t)$ is the optimal path of per capita consumption and g_c^d its constant rate of growth. Suppose the household decides to reduce consumption by a small unit at t_0, invest the amount at the constant rate of interest[8] r and consume the entire proceeds at t_1. Along the optimal path, this perturbation should leave the household indifferent. Thus, in terms of marginal gains and losses,

$$c^*(t)^{-\sigma} = e^{(r-\rho)(t_1 - t_0)}\, c^*(t_1)^{-\sigma} = e^{(r-\rho-\sigma g_c^d)(t_1 - t_0)}\, c^*(t_0)^{-\sigma}.$$

Solving, the result follows.

On the right hand panel of Figure 5.1, the curve $g_c^d(r)$ shows the demand rate of growth as an increasing function of the rate of interest.

It is now possible to invoke the concept of the *supply rate of growth*. The supply rate of growth of $c(t)$ is simply a sustainable rate of balanced growth from supply considerations. Technology plays a crucial role in its derivation. In Solow's model, it has the form of an aggregate production function,

$$Y = F(K, AL) \tag{3}$$

where A stands for the coefficient of labour augmenting Harrod-neutral technical progress, growing over time at a constant exogenously given rate μ, i.e.,

[6]Without loss of generality, it will be assumed throughout that there is no physical depreciation of capital.

[7]The argument goes back to Ramsey (1928), who in turn quoted Keynes as its inventor. A more formal proof is relegated to the appendix.

[8]Recall that r is a constant by definition of balanced growth.

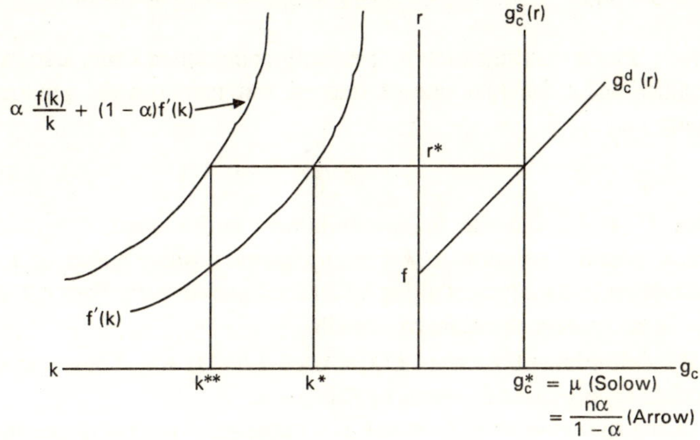

FIGURE 5.1 Equilibrium under Old Growth Theory (Solow and Arrow)

$$\frac{\dot{A}}{A} = \mu \tag{4}$$

Similarly, the labour force $L(t)$ is assumed to grow exponentially at the rate n. The aggregate production function is assumed to be governed by constant returns to scale (CRS) in K and AL and diminishing returns to both factors. Thus, (3) can be represented as,

$$y = f(k) \tag{5}$$

with $y = Y/AL$ and $k = K/AL$. The assumption of diminishing returns guarantees that $f'(k) > 0$ and $f''(k) < 0$. Further restrictions need to be imposed on f in the form of the so called 'Inada conditions'. These are $f'(k) \to 0$ as $k \to \infty$ and $f'(k) \to \infty$ as $k \to 0$. The Inada conditions imply that diminishing returns with respect to each factor are unlimited. Since both factors are fully employed and the same good serves for consumption and capital accumulation, it follows that,

$$Lc + \dot{K} = Y = F(K, AL). \tag{6}$$

Dividing both sides by K,

$$\frac{Lc}{K} + \frac{\dot{K}}{K} = \frac{f(k)}{k}. \tag{7}$$

It is now possible to prove the following result.

PROPOSITION 2: The supply rate of balanced growth $g_c^s(r)$ of c equals μ. The associated supply growth rates of K/L and Y/L are also equal to μ.

Proof: Profit maximization by perfectly competitive firms leads to an equalization of the real rate of interest and the marginal product of capital i.e.,

$$r = f'(k). \tag{8}$$

Since $f''(k) < 0$ and the Inada conditions are assumed, (8) yields a unique positive solution to k for any given positive value of r. By assumption, r is a constant along a balanced growth path. Hence, k must also be a constant in balanced growth.

By definition of k then, $\dot{K}/K = \dot{A}/A + \dot{L}/L = \mu + n$. Thus, the only possible supply rate of growth of K is $\mu + n$.

Going over now to (7), since k is a constant, it is easy to see that if K grows as $\mu + n$, then so does $C = Lc$. Alternatively, K/L and c grow at the rate μ.

Similarly, Y/L grows at the rate μ. This is seen by a total differentiation of (3) which yields,

$$\frac{\dot{Y}}{Y} = \pi \frac{\dot{K}}{K} - (1 + \pi) \frac{\dot{AL}}{AL}$$

$$= \pi \frac{\dot{K}}{K} - (1 + \pi)(\mu + n), \tag{9}$$

where π and $1 - \pi$ are respectively the shares of capital and labour in Y. Since π is a fraction, the result follows. Q.E.D.

Proposition 2 determines the supply rate of growth. However, in principle, the rate of growth is realizable for any constant value of $k \in (0, \infty)$. Hence, (8) implies that the value of r associated with μ is also indeterminate. This yields the following corollary.

COROLLARY 1: The supply rate of growth $g_c^s(r)$ of c is a perfectly inelastic function of r in the r–g_c plane.

As may be expected, the values of k and r are fixed by bringing together the supply and the demand forces. We have already noted that a growth equilibrium obtains when the demand and supply rates of growth are equal. This gives:

PROPOSITION 3: The equilibrium rate of steady state growth of c is given by $g_c^* = \mu$. Further, it is associated with a constant rate of interest r^* and a constant $k = k^*$ such that,

$$g_c^* = \frac{r^* - \rho}{\sigma} = \mu,$$

and

$$f'(k^*) = r^* = \rho + \mu\sigma \tag{10}$$

Proof: The value of g_c^* follows from Propositions 1 and 2. The implications for r and k follow from (8), i.e. profit maximization by private entrepreneurs, and Proposition 1. Q.E.D.

Proposition 3 fixes the equilibrium rate of growth for c. The next Corollary establishes that the corresponding equilibrium growth rates of K/L and Y/L are identically the same.

COROLLARY 2: The equilibrium rates of balanced growth of K/L and Y/L are both equal to μ. Moreover, they are associated with a constant savings rate $s = s^*$ such that,

$$\mu + n = \frac{\dot{K}}{K} = \frac{s^* f(k^*)}{k^*}.$$

Proof: Under CRS,

$$r(t)K(t) + w(t)L(t) = F(K, AL).$$

Thus, equations (2) and (6) are identical. Consequently, the arguments of Proposition 2 can be applied to show that the demand rates of growth of K/L and Y/L are the same as that of c. According to Proposition 2, the supply rates of growth of these variables equal μ. Hence, μ represents the *equilibrium* growth rate of K/L and Y/L. The value of s^* is definitional. Q.E.D.

The growth equilibrium is visualized in Figure 5.1 as an intersection of the two curves, $g_c^d(r)$ and $g_c^s(r)$. The unique solution to (10) is referred to as the *modified golden rule* value of k.[9] The determination of k^* is shown on the left hand panel to Figure 5.1.

Analytically speaking, the economy is visualized to be at k^* from the very beginning, no questions being asked as to how it ever went there.

[9]The qualifier 'modified' distinguishes the present exercise from the original formulation of the problem by Phelps (1961, 1965) in terms of an undiscounted welfare function.

Given $L(0)$, this constrains the initial value of $K(0)$ to be equal to $k^*L(0)$. Thus, it is being assumed that the economy has the required capital stock to ensure an instantaneous adjustment to the balanced growth path.

Even though the equilibrium rate of growth is viewed as an intersection of a demand and a supply curve, it should be obvious that it is the supply side, as brought out by Proposition 2, which dominates. For example, a change in the parameters of demand, i.e. shifts in the demand curve will leave the equilibrium rate of growth unaffected. An increase in thriftiness, caused, say, be a tax on consumption, will fail to affect the equilibrium rate of growth of the system. In other words, the equilibrium rate of growth is uncontrollable.

2.2 The Paths Ahead

Mathematically speaking, the issues surrounding the Solow exercise may be summarized as follows. The assumption that $F_{11} < 0$ is equivalent to the assumption of an invertible f'. The latter leads to a 1 : 1 correspondence between r and k under perfect competition.[10] Thus, a fixed r implies a fixed k, which causes K and AL to grow at the same rate. However, since the growth rate $\mu + n$ of AL is rigidly specified in Solow's model, this can be the only equilibrium rate of growth of capital also.

Section 3.1 introduces a class of models which allow $\dot{K}/K$ to be disentangled from a rigidly specified $\mu + n$. This is done by allowing the process of capital accumulation to generate *spill overs* affecting the level of AL, thus changing its status from an exogenous variable, as in Solow, to an endogenous one. Spill overs such as these, which are external to a firm, can co-exist with diminishing returns to capital, i.e. $F_{11} < 0$. Nevertheless, when the externalities are *strong*, a constant r will pin down k without determining the rate of growth of K from supply considerations alone.

[10]In what follows, the assumption that f' admits an inverse will be referred to as 'The Law of Diminishing Returns to Capital'. The latter implies diminishing marginal productivity of capital. However, this is somewhat misleading, because it fails to distinguish between the 'private' and the 'social' marginal product of capital. The two may often be different, as will be seen in later sections, particularly in Section on 'New Growth Theory'. Hence, it is not clear whether 'The Law of Diminishing Returns to Capital' implies a decline in private or social productivity.

Another factor that causes demand to start playing a role in the determination of the growth rate is the possible absence of diminishing returns itself ($F_{11} \geq 0$). For example, f may have a linear form (say, $y = ak$, where a is a positive constant, which is equivalent to assuming $Y = aK$). In this case, f' is not invertible. In fact, r now equals the constant marginal product of capital under competition, *independent* of the value of k. Hence $\dot{K}/K$ is once again not supply determined.[11]

Both possibilities will be seen to arise in connection with a need to rationalize the notion of technical progress. The latter is a nebulous entity in Solow's world, consisting of an *exogenously* specified growth in labour productivity from *unexplained* causes. The model fails to shed any light on the nature of economic or other resources that need to be consciously harnessed in order to bring about an improvement in productivity.

This concludes the first part of the discussion. The next part concentrates on various theoretical developments surrounding the endogenization of the equlibrium rate of growth.

3. NEW GROWTH THEORY

3.1 Arrow: A Theory of Technical Change

Solow (1960) attempts to repair the shortcomings of his earlier approach by linking technical progress to the process of capital accumulation itself. Higher productivity is *embodied* only in new equipments. The rate of increase in productivity, however, is assumed to be exogenous to the system. In the face of diminishing returns, the equilibrium growth rate remains tied up with such exogenous factors alone, while the mechanical association of new investment to technical progress fails to identify the factors responsible for a rise in productivity. Thus, from the point of view of a theory of technical progress, the approach of Solow (1960) does not qualify as an improvement over that of Solow (1956).

Arrow (1962) takes a significant step towards offering a theory of productivity growth, thereby endogenizing the equilibrium rate of

[11]Rebelo (1991) offers an important insight in this respect by restricting the linear structure to a specific sub-sector of any given economy. This is discussed in Section 3.2. The same phenomenon occurs in Lucas (1986) (Section 3.3) and Romer (1990) (Section 3.4) also.

technical progress for the economy. He attributes productivity increases over time to learning, i.e. the accumulation of experience, on the part of the labour force. Experience is gathered in workshops while producing output with the help of machinery and equipment. Hence, technical progress amounts to 'learning by doing'. Every new piece of equipment has to be 'broken in' so to speak, thus creating room for learning.[12] Since it is in the course of machinery handling that learning takes place, Arrow considers the value of cumulative *gross* investment (CGI) at any point of time to be the index of experience.[13] As he viewed it, an increase in investment today raises the size of CGI from tomorrow onwards above what it would otherwise be, thus bequeathing a more experienced and productive labour force to the future. In other words, technical change is in the nature of an *intertemporal externality* generated by the process of capital accumulation. As such, it has an *embodied* form, in the sense that later machines are more productive than earlier ones.

In what follows, however, a *disembodied* version of the Arrow exercise [suggested by Sheshinski (1967)] will be considered. Technical change is still an externality, but it is atemporal. An investment activity, irrespective of the firm in which it is located, adds to the CGI for the entire economy, and the benefit of increased labour productivity in the initiating firm *spills over* to *all* coexisting firms.[14] Thus, labour productivity goes up for all existing machinery, irrespective of their vintages.

Formally speaking, the only change this introduces in the Solow (1956) model is in the specification of $A(t)$, which is now a function of CGI at t. In the absence of physical depreciation, the latter is equal to the aggregate capital stock $K(t)$. The exact functional form assumed by Arrow and Sheshinski is,

$$A(t) = K(t)^{\alpha}, \quad \alpha > 0 \tag{11}$$

[12]In Arrow's words: 'Each new machine put to use changes the production environment, thereby inducing the workers to learn.'

[13]Thus, in the presence of physical depreciation of capital, experience is measured by the aggregate capital stock that would be in existence in its absence. Arrow also offers reasons as to why cumulative gross output is not a satisfactory index of learning.

[14]In concrete terms, it might help to think of labourers from different organizations converging to the local pub as it were, where they get a chance to exchange information.

Capital accumulation has diminishing, constant or increasing productivity in the learning activity, depending on whether $\alpha < 1, = 1$, or > 1.

The technology is therefore given by,

$$Y = F(K, K^{\alpha}L) \tag{12}$$

where $F_{11} < 0$ and $F_{22} < 0$, so that there are diminishing returns to K (if the spill over in the form of K^{α} is ignored) and $K^{\alpha}L$ taken separately. Also, the function F displays constant returns to scale in K and $K^{\alpha}L$.[15]

As compared to the Solow formulation, the social marginal productivity of capital $\partial F/\partial K = \alpha f(k)/k + (1 - \alpha) f'(k)$, is strictly greater than its 'private' marginal product $F_1 = f'(k)$. This happens because the very process of capital accumulation has a spill over effect on the level attained by AL. A private producer, in computing the profitability of an additional dose of capital, will be ignoring the gain it generates for other producers.[16] Thus, increasing returns, if any, are external to the individual firm. In such a case, the equilibrium for the system is sustainable by a Solow type competitive economy, to be called a *private* economy for brevity. In other words, the private marginal productivity of capital ($F_{11}(\cdot\,,\cdot) = f'(k)$) will still be equated to the real market rate of interest by private producers.

While the (private) marginal productivity of capital is diminishing (i.e. $F_{11} < 0$), this may not be the case for its social marginal productivity (i.e. $\partial F/\partial K$) in the presence of externalities.[17] This is evident from the expression for average social productivity of captial,

[15]As before, the function may be expressed as in (5), with no change in the definitions of y and k. The properties of $f(k)$ remain unaltered too, *vis-à-vis* the variable k.

[16]Intuitively speaking, the productive sector may be imagined to be made up of M identical firms, each producing according to $F\left(\frac{K}{M}, K^{\alpha}\frac{L}{M}\right)$. Under constant returns, this means that aggregate production is given by (12). An increase in $\frac{K}{M}$ in all firms brings about a corresponding rise in K, but each firm, being negligibly small, is aware only of the change in its own capital stock. Hence, it does not take into account the effect of the social marginal productivity of the change in the private capital stock.

[17]This indicates, as pointed out earlier, the inadequacy of the expression 'Diminishing Marginal Productivity'.

$$\frac{Y}{K} = F(1, K^{\alpha-1}L) \tag{13}$$

which decreases, remains constant or increases with K accordingly as $\alpha <, =,$ or > 1. Diminishing (private) marginal productivity of K implies $f'(k)$ is invertible. Hence, a constant r gives rise to a constant k. However, unless the externality is weak ($\alpha < 1$), a fixed k does not help determine a steady growth rate of K. As we shall see, when $\alpha = 1$, fixing k does not fix $\dot{K}/K$ at all and when $\alpha > 1$, it cannot fix $\dot{K}/K$ at a positive level.

When $\alpha < 1$, the equilibrium rate of growth of efficient labour is a blend, as it were, of an endogeneous factor, viz., the rate of growth of learning, which is a function of the rate of capital accumulation, and the exogenous population growth rate. Thus, while the rate of capital growth is determined by the rate of growth of efficient labour, the latter is itself influenced by the former. As a result, the rates of growth of capital and efficient labour are solutions to a pair of simultaneous equations, and hence, endogenously determined. In particular, the rate of technical progress is solved for by the model. As such, Arrow's view of technical change is less arbitrary than Solow's. Nevertheless, as will be seen, the growth rates of the relevant variables continue to be uncontrollable.

The discussion that follows will be divided into three parts, corresponding to $\alpha < 1, = 1$ or, > 1.

$\alpha < 1$

In Solow, the position of the perfectly inelastic g_c^s curve is determined by μ, while μ is itself exogenously specified. The important progress made by Arrow (1962) is to set up a simultaneous equation system whose solution determines the position of the inelastic g_c^s. Figure 5.1 represents Arrow's equilibrium also, but the value of μ is now specifiable in terms of other parameters of the model. This is the content of the next result.

PROPOSITION 4: The equilibrium rate of growth for an economy with learning is given by,

$$\mu = \frac{n\alpha}{1-\alpha}.$$

Proof: Although the principle of determination of equilibrium growth rate is the same as in Proposition 3, there is a difference in the determination of the supply rate of growth, which is now endogenous. Proposition 2 and equation (11) imply that,

$$\frac{\dot{K}}{K} = \mu + n$$

and
$$\mu = \alpha \frac{\dot{K}}{K}$$

Solving these simultaneous equations in μ and $\dot{K}/K$,

$$\mu = \alpha \frac{\dot{K}}{K} = \frac{n\alpha}{1-\alpha} \tag{14}$$

and
$$\frac{\dot{K}}{K} = \frac{n}{1-\alpha} \tag{15}$$

Q.E.D.

Although Arrow had a concrete theory of technical progress, his conclusions were nevertheless disappointing insofar as they failed to suggest how policy prescriptions or perturbations in preference parameters might influence the *growth* rate.

There is a role for policy in Arrow's model however, even if the *rate of growth* cannot be affected. As already noted, private entrepreneurs invest according to the private marginal productivity of capital, which underestimates its social marginal product. This leads to a sub-optimal allocation of resources and the competitive equilibrium fails to be a social optimum.

To appreciate the nature of market failure implied by the Arrow model, the equilibrium of the *private* economy, as captured by Proposition 4, needs to be compared with that of a *command* economy, where the allocation of resources is carried out by an omniscient planner. The latter, though endowed with exactly the same welfare function as the household, is aware of the true (social) productivity of capital, unlike the private entrepreneur. This has no effect on the equilibrium rate of growth of course, which, by virtue of Proposition 4, continues to be dominated by supply considerations. However, as the next proposition demonstrates, it makes the modified golden rule value of k for a *private* economy smaller than that for the *command* economy.

PROPOSITION 5: The equilibrium value k^* of k in a private economy is strictly less than its equilibrium value k^{**} in a command economy.

As in the case of Proposition 1, the formal proof of this proposition is left to the Appendix. Informally, the argument rests on the observation that the command economy computes the return from a unit of investment as the social marginal productivity of capital, i.e. $\alpha f(k)/k + (1-\alpha)f'(k)$, and not its private marginal product as in Proposition 3. Hence, replacing f' in (10) and using (14),

$$\left(\alpha\frac{f(k)}{k} + (1-\alpha)f'(k)\right) = \rho + \frac{n\alpha}{1-\alpha}\sigma$$

solves for k^{**}. The value of k^* is found on the other hand by solving

$$f'(k) = \rho + \frac{n\alpha}{1-\alpha}\sigma$$

The proposition now follows from the strict concavity of $f(k)$.

As already noted, Proposition 5 creates room for policy intervention to improve upon the competitive solution. Since the increase in wages resulting from improved labour productivity is traceable to capital, which receives less than its true marginal product in a competitive equilibrium, the obvious policy implication is to tax wage income (leaving the inelastic labour supply unaffected) and subsidize capital.

Apart from the equilibrium rate of growth turning out to be impervious to policy manipulations, a second major shortcoming of the Arrow theory is that technical progress, though endogenously generated, is viewed as an inevitable (or, unavoidable) *byproduct* of the process of capital accumulation. It is not linked to the *rational* actions of economic agents who are known in real life to innovate in search of higher profits from production.

The major diffculty of treating technical change as a choice variable of the model stems from the fact that it is not a marketable commodity. It is, in fact, both non-rival as well as non-excludable, i.e. it is a pure public good. For example, in the Arrow–Sheshinski model, it is non-rival, since all firms enjoy it simultaneously; and it is non-excludable, since it has the form of an external effect. This is an important issue addressed by Romer (1990).

$\boldsymbol{\alpha} = 1$

Arrow did not consider this case in depth, but it has a rather interesting feature as a recent study by d'Autume and Michel (1993) indicates. For the sake of continuity, the neoclassical framework will be maintained, although the original results were presented in Arrow's embodied form. For this specification of the value of the parameter α, the Arrow production function exhibits a strong spill over effect, though f' is still invertible.

The function f' being invertible, a constant r implies a constant k, but the latter does not help to determine the rate of growth. For,

$$\frac{\dot{K}}{K} = \mu + n$$

$$= \frac{\dot{K}}{K} + n, \text{ since } \alpha = 1, \tag{16}$$

and this can happen only if $n = 0$. Thus, in the present model, a necessary condition for the existence of an equilibrium balanced growth rate is a *stationary* level of population, i.e. L must be a constant, say $\bar{L}$. But this implies that the rate of growth of K is left completely free by (16). Nevertheless, the growth rate for a private economy is determinate. This follows because $L = \bar{L}$ implies a unique stationary value for $k = k^* = K/(K\bar{L}) = 1/\bar{L}$. Consequently, (10) admits a unique profit maximizing value of r, viz., $r^* = f'(1/\bar{L})$. Hence, g_c^s is a horizontal curve passing through r^*. Its intersection with the g_c^d curve determines $g^* = (r^* - \rho)/\sigma$. As can be seen, a change in ρ and σ would now have an effect on the growth rate. So would policy, such as a tax on interest income. As opposed to Arrow's case, the growth rate is controllable. The conclusions are summarized below.[18]

PROPOSITION 6: When $\alpha = 1$, equilibrium growth implies $L = \bar{L} = \text{constant}$. Further, the rate of equilibrium growth of c, $K/\bar{L}$ and $Y/\bar{L}$ is $(r^* - \rho)/\sigma$, where $r^* = f'^{-1}(1/\bar{L})$. A change in preference parameters affects the growth rate, while a change in the size of the labour force affects both the growth rate (through r^*) as well as the modified golden rule value of k.

Thus, while the equilibrium solution is no longer tied to the *rate* of population growth, it does still depend on the *size* of the labour force, since the latter determines the equilibrium rate of interest (the *level* of g^s) and hence the equilibrium growth rate via Proposition 1. Figure 5.2, demonstrates the nature of this 'demand determined' equilibrium.

[18]Note that the requirement of a zero rate of population growth follows from diminishing returns. For reasons outlined earlier, if f is linear in k, the rate of growth of K cannot be linked to the rate of population growth. In this case, the marginal product of capital is a technologically given constant. The supply rate curve is, accordingly, infinitely elastic at that level. Once again, the equilibrium rate of growth is determined by the intersection with the demand curve.

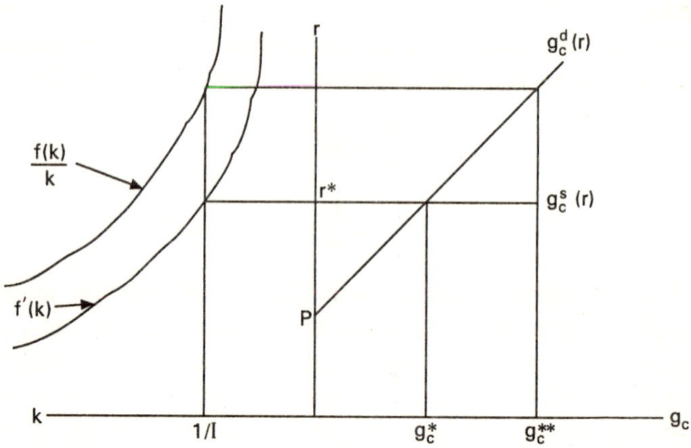

FIGURE 5.2 Equilibrium under New Growth Theory (d'Autume and Michel)

Once again, the command economy takes into account the externality factor in its optimality calculation and this shows up in the form of a higher value accorded to the social marginal productivity of capital as compared to the market economy. Since the production function can be rewritten as $K\bar{L}f(1/\bar{L})$, the social marginal productivity is a constant $\bar{L}f(1/\bar{L})$ and equals the social average productivity $f(k)/k$. As a result, the equilibrium rate of growth for the command economy is,

$$g^{**} = \frac{\bar{L}f(1/\bar{L}) - \rho}{\sigma}.$$

Since the average product is larger than the marginal product, the following proposition emerges:

PROPOSITION 7: The equilibrium value g^* of the rate of growth in a private economy is strictly less than its equilibrium value g^{**} in a command economy.

As opposed to the case $\alpha < 1$, it is now the *rate of growth* that is higher in the command economy and not the equilibrium value of k.

$\alpha > 1$

Once again, f' is invertible, but the externality is the strongest in the present case. A constant r gives rise to a constant k. Using (15),

$\dot{K}/K < 0$. In other words, the requirement of a constant k leads to a negative rate of growth of capital, which is obviously an uninteresting case. To look into the possibility of positive growth, it may be noted that the rate of growth of capital per unit of efficient labour is,

$$\frac{\dot{k}}{k} = \frac{\dot{K}}{K} - \alpha\frac{\dot{K}}{K} - n < 0 \qquad (17)$$

Hence, $\frac{\dot{K}}{K} > 0$ implies k must continuously fall over time, thereby making it necessary for the model to give up the requirement of a constant rate of interest r. This in turn means that the demand rate of growth must change over time. Thus, this system can never hope to be in balanced growth equilibrium.

Romer[19] calls for a distinction between physical and knowledge capital. Unlike Arrow, it is the accumulation of knowledge through an explicit R&D activity that contributes to an increase in labour productivity. In the changed scenario, I stands for physical investment and K for the stock of knowledge capital, though, at this stage of Romer's work, the precise nature of knowledge capital is left somewhat vague.[20] Be that as it may, in Romer (1986), (12) represents the production of Y by means of knowledge capital and efficient labour.[21]

Savings being equal to investment,

$$I = F(K, K^{\alpha}L) - C$$

On the other hand, 'new' knowledge capital (i.e. $\dot{K}$) is developed through research. Explicitly, it is assumed to be a linear homogeneous function of physical investment (i.e. I) and the *entire* stock of knowledge capital (i.e. K). The R&D production function is written $G(I, K)$. In other words,

$$\dot{K} = G(I, K) = Kg\left(\frac{I}{K}\right), \qquad (18)$$

where $g(I/K) = G(I/K, 1)$.

The fact that the whole of K is present simultaneously in both

[19] The presentation of this sub-section is a grossly simplified version of Romer (1986). The original paper is technically rather difficult.

[20] Savings (S) translates one-to-one into investment (I) as in Solow, but I does not translate into $\dot{K}$. Hence, $I \neq \dot{K}$. This constitutes an important point of departure from the models considered so far.

[21] Romer allows for physical capital also, but the latter does not play any analytically important role in his model.

F and G indicates that it is being viewed as a non-rival good.[22] The household owns K as well as L and sells these in competitive markets as in Solow (1956). The income so derived is spent wholly on C and I. The latter[23] is used in producing a non-marketed good, viz., K, with the help of the non-rival K. Thus, K is a free input as far as the production of K is concerned.

To see how the actual paths of the different variables are chosen, one must refer back to the household's optimization problem. The household still maximizes (1) subject to (2), except that it is no longer permissible to assume a constant r (or, for that matter, w). Under the assumption of perfect foresight, any possible path $r(t)$, say $\hat{r}(t)$, assumed by the household, will lead to an optimal choice of the paths of $c(t)$, $K(t)$ etc. Competition implies in turn that the chosen path of $K(t)$ is associated with a supporting profit maximizing path of $r(t)$, say $\tilde{r}(t)$. This defines a mapping of the path $r(t)$ into itself. A fixed point $r^*(t)$ of this mapping is an equilibrium path of $r(t)$.[24] The equilibrium path of $K(t)$, etc. can then be easily found. In any case, the exercise clearly reveals the endogeneity of the equilibrium growth path. It is solved for by the model. To summarize:

PROPOSITION 8: When $\alpha > 1$, the private economy is not in balanced growth equilibrium at any finite t. The household's optimization exercise has an important role to play in the choice of the paths of capital, consumption, output, etc.

While the role of demand is clear from the above result, it is not possible to represent the equilibrium as a demand-supply cross in the present case. This is a consequence of the fact that the model does not admit a balanced growth path.

It goes without saying that, on account of the externality, there would once again be a difference between the growth paths chosen by the market and the command economies.

In d'Autume and Michel (1993), there was a *logical* need for assuming the rate of population growth to be zero. Although there is

[22]The conceptual implication of this is brought out in great detail in Romer (1990).

[23]I may be viewed as necessary consumption of research workers for the production of K.

[24]Mathematically speaking, solving for $r^*(t)$ leads to a fixed point problem in a function space.

no such necessity in the remaining models, it is convenient to make the assumption in any case. Apart from simplifying the algebra, it helps to establish the fact that an exogenous specification of the population growth rate has no role to play in determining the growth rate of an economy.

3.2 Rebelo: The Role of a Linear Technology

Section 3.1 showed that in the presence of *Arrow type* externalities, the growth rate of the system is no longer exogenous, even if the technology displays diminishing returns. The present section [based on Rebelo (1991)] opens up another route for endogenization, viz., the addition of a linear sector to the one exhibiting diminishing returns.

To be precise, Rebelo divides up the factors of production into a reproducible and a non-reproducible group, say K and L. The former is a composite of physical and human capital, while the latter may be called land. For notational consistency, however, L will be referrred to as labour. Growth in the labour force is now replaced by a growth in human capital, but the latter is endogenous.[25] There are two sectors, producing respectively an investment good (I) and a consumption good (C). In the absence of labour growth, per capita consumption c is identical with C. The investment good is produced by a non-sector specific (though rival) capital good (K) using a linear technology,

$$I = a(1 - \phi)K, \tag{19}$$

where a is a technological constant, ϕ the endogenously determined share of existing capital used in producing I and, as opposed to the model of the preceding subsection, $I = K$. The consumption good is produced by a Cobb–Douglas technology using K and the non-reproducible factor L:

$$C = B(\phi\, K)^{\gamma} L^{1-\gamma}, \tag{20}$$

where B is a constant.

A decision to save is a decision to abstain from consumption, and this, in a standard one sector model, amounts to a simple diversion of a part of the output towards capital formation. In the present two sector framework, the consumption-savings choice is a more complicated

[25]In the linear version of the model considered by Rebelo, human and physical capital are inseparable. A separation is possible in his non-linear version of the problem. However, this part of the Rebelo exercise will be discussed in the next section as an extension of Lucas (1988).

problem and amounts to a decision to *produce* less of C by diverting a larger fraction of K to the production of I.[26]

In the absence of (20), i.e. if the model had a single sector with (19) as the technology, the supply curve would be infinitely elastic at the level a. On the other hand, if (20) represented an *aggregate* production function as in Solow (1956), the supply curve would be perfectly inelastic, passing through a point determined by the exogenously given rate of growth of natural resources (zero, in Rebelo's case). The simultaneous existence of the two sectors in Rebelo, however, leads to a supply curve that lies in between the two extremes.

The interesting part of Rebelo's exercise consists of deriving this supply curve based on purely economic arguments. To start with, balanced growth of capital must imply that k is increasing over time[27] and that the marginal productivity of K is continuously diminishing in the C-sector. However, unlike Romer (1986), it does not give rise to a changing rate of interest over time. This may be established from the following considerations.

In Rebelo, the rate of interest relevant for the calculation of the demand rate of growth is r_c, defined to be the rate of return on pure consumption loans.[28] As opposed to this, the own rate of return on capital is a, the constant marginal productivity of capital in the I-sector. The constancy of a allows for r_c to be maintained at a constant level also, so long as the relative price of K in units of C is adjusted appropriately.

More precisely, equilibrium in the asset markets requires that in the face of a falling (rising) price of K relative to C, the own rate a must exceed (fall short of) r_c by an amount equal to the rate of price change in order to induce the household sector to hold capital goods (IOU's denominated in units of the consumption good). In other words,

$$r_c = a + g_p, \tag{21}$$

where p is the price of K relative to C and g_p its rate of change. Thus, r_c is a constant, so long as g_p is.

[26]Thus, as opposed to Romer (1986), where $S = I$, but $I \neq \dot{K}$, Rebelo's model involves $I = \dot{K}$. However, the definition of savings being more complicated, it is not possible to write $S = I$.

[27]This follows from the fact that the supply of L is an exogenously specified constant for all time. Romer (1986), where k declined monotonically in t, represents the opposite case.

[28]In the one-sector models discussed so far, such assets were indistinguishable from pure capital loans. This is obvious from the arguments used to establish Proposition 1.

That g_p is a constant follows from the fact that for efficient production, capital must be allocated between the two sectors so that the (value of) its marginal product is equal in the two sectors, i.e.

$$a = \frac{\gamma B(\phi K)^{\gamma - 1} L^{1-\gamma}}{p} \tag{22}$$

Equation (22) shows that although the marginal productivity of K falls in the C-sector, its value measured in units of K remains a constant. For this to happen, $1/p$ rises (i.e. p declines) in the same proportion as the fall in the marginal product of K in the C-sector. Differentiation of (22) yields,

$$g_p = \frac{\dot{p}}{p} = (\gamma - 1) g_k^s , \tag{23}$$

where g_k^s is the supply rate of growth of K. The RHS of (23) represents the rate of fall of marginal productivity in the C-sector. This is a constant under balanced growth, i.e. when g_k^s is a constant. Further, g_p is a constant if g_k^s is a constant.

Putting (21) and (23) together,

$$g_k^s = g_k^s(r_c) = \frac{a - r_c}{1 - \gamma} . \tag{24}$$

Finally, (20) implies that g_c^s, the supply rate of growth of C, satisfies

$$g_c^s = \gamma g_k^s ,$$

which, using (24), gives

$$g_c^s = g_c^s(r_c) = \frac{\gamma(a - r_c)}{1 - \gamma} \tag{25}$$

This is the 'Rebelo supply curve' corresponding to C. It shows that the supply rate of growth of C is a constant whenever r_c is unchanging. Moreover, unlike the supply function in Arrow, it is not perfectly inelastic. In fact, it is a downward falling function of r_c.

The demand rate of growth g_c^d of C is given by Proposition 1. As already noted, in the presence of consumption loans, r_c is the rate of interest relevant for calculating the demand rate. Thus, $g_c^d = g_c^d(r_c) = (r_c - \rho)/\sigma$. The equilibrium value of g_c, say g_c^*, is determined by the intersection of the demand and the supply rate curves. Once this is found, (24) determines g_k^* also. Thus,

$$g_c^* = \frac{\gamma(a-\rho)}{1-\gamma(1-\sigma)}$$

$$g_k^* = \frac{(a-\rho)}{1-\gamma(1-\sigma)}.$$

The determination of equilibrium is shown in Figure 5.3.

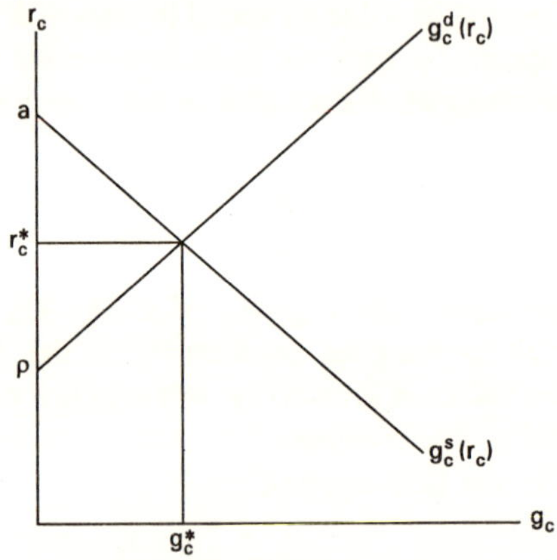

FIGURE 5.3 The Role of Linear Technology (Rebelo)

It is easy to see from the diagram that the condition for a positive rate of equilibrium growth is $a > \rho$. Writing $Y = C + pI$, the equilibrium rate of growth of Y is easily seen to be $g_y^* = g_c^* = \gamma g_k^*$. The appearance of preference parameters in the expressions for g_c^*, etc. indicates that savings behaviour plays an important role in determining the equilibrium rate of growth.

The variable ϕ showing the allocation of K between the two sectors was left indeterminate. This is found from (19), which shows that the supply rate of growth of capital satisfies,

$$g_k^s = \frac{\dot{K}}{K} = a(1-\phi)$$

Rebelo's results may be summarized as follows:

PROPOSITION 9: Even in the presence of strong diminishing returns in parts of the economy, steady state capital accumulation is possible at an 'endogenously' chosen rate so long as there is a subsector of the economy which produces capital goods by using capital goods alone and there are perfectly functioning asset markets. All other sectors into which capital goods enter as inputs and where production is carried out under diminishing returns, adjust to this rate of growth through a continuous fall in the relative price of capital goods.

In interpreting K as a composite of human and non-human capital, Rebelo is in a way offering a theory of technical change. Any tendency for diminishing returns to physical capital is being reversed by the rise in productivity on account of human capital growth, giving rise to linearity in the I sector. As a theory of technical change, this is rather vague in comparison to Arrow's, or for that matter, Rebelo's own extension of Lucas' model. Strictly speaking, it is the linear technology that is at the heart of the result and it does not seem fruitful to read any more meaning into it.

3.3 Lucas, Rebelo and Uzawa: Technical Progress as Formation of Human Capital

The logic outlined in the last section readily extends to the case of more than one accumulable factor of production. Thus, L may be replaced by H (i.e. human capital) and (19) by,

$$\dot{H} = a(1 - \phi)H. \tag{26}$$

In this case, (20) turns into,

$$Y = B(K)^{\gamma}(\phi H)^{1-\gamma}, \tag{27}$$

where K is assumed to have the same features as the physical capital in Solow (1956) and Y is either consumed (C), or saved and accumulated as K. In this framework, output is produced by means of human capital (H) (rather than pure labour) and physical capital (K). The increase in productive efficiency is traced to a conscious attempt on the part of the household sector to improve its skill level through human capital accumulation. To keep things simple, it is best to assume the rate of growth of population to be zero.[29]

From (26), the own rate of return for H is a. On the other hand, the real rate of interest r (on K) is

$$r = \gamma B(K)^{\gamma - 1}(\phi H)^{1-\gamma}. \tag{28}$$

As defined in Section 2.1, r is a constant in balanced growth. This

[29]Lucas, however, assumes a positive rate of population growth in a similar model, but this assumption has no anaytical role to play in the exercise he carries out.

means from (28) that g_k^s equals $g_h^s = \dot{H}/H$. Let p stand for the price of H relative to Y. Then, an equation similar to (22) must be satisfied. This is given by

$$a = \frac{(1-\gamma)BK^{\gamma}(\phi H)^{-\gamma}}{p} \tag{29}$$

By virtue of the equality between g_k^s and g_h^s, it follows that $g_p = 0$. Hence, the no arbitrage condition relating to loans denominated in K (which is the same as C or Y) units and H units turns out to be,

$$r = a \tag{30}$$

In other words, as in the case of a 'pure' linear model, the supply curve is horizontal at the level $r = a$. Intersection with the demand curve now determines the equilibrium rate of growth etc.

The above would seem to be a Rebelo type interpretation of Uzawa (1965). The same idea may be pushed further to elucidate Lucas (1988), who also recognizes an Arrovian external effect generated on output by the aggregate level of human capital existing in society.[30] Thus, the production function for the consumable and physically accumulable good is written as,

$$Y = BK^{\gamma}(\phi H)^{1-\gamma}H^{\alpha} \tag{31}$$

where H^{α} stands for the external effect. The accumulation of human capital continues to be governed by (26).

Defining r to be the real rate of interest as above, it follows that,

$$r = \gamma B(K)^{\gamma-1}(\phi H)^{1-\gamma}H^{\alpha} \tag{32}$$

Since r is a constant in balanced growth, it turns out from differentiation of (32) that

$$g_h^s = \frac{1-\gamma}{1+\alpha-\gamma}g_k^s \tag{33}$$

Writing the counterpart of (7) for the present model and using arguments similar to those developed in Proposition 2, equation (33) implies that the supply rate of growth of C, viz., g_c^s, satisfies the condition[31]

$$g_c^s = g_k^s .$$

[30]As is to be expected, the external effect will give rise to a divergence between the market solution and the solution for the command economy.

[31]In the absence of population growth, $C = c$ wlog.

In a *private* economy, entrepreneurs would ignore the externality caused by H^{α} in computing the marginal product of H in the Y-sector. Thus, for such an economy, the equality of the value of marginal products of H leads to,

$$pa = (1-\gamma)BK^{\gamma}\phi^{-\gamma}H^{\alpha-\gamma}, \tag{34}$$

which, on differentiation and substitution from (33), leads to,

$$g_p = \frac{\alpha}{1-\gamma+\alpha} g_c^s . \tag{35}$$

As in Rebelo, r and a must be related according to,

$$r = a + g_p.$$

Substituting this in (35), the equation for the supply rate of growth follows. Thus,

$$g_c^s(r) = \frac{(1-\gamma+\alpha)}{\alpha}(r-a).$$

Combining with the demand rate of growth, the equilibrium rate of growth of C turns out to be,

$$g_c^* = \frac{(1+\alpha-\gamma)(a-\rho)}{\sigma(1+\alpha-\gamma)-\alpha}. \tag{36}$$

Finally, using (33), it follows that,

$$g_h^* = \frac{(1-\gamma)(a-\rho)}{\sigma(1+\alpha-\gamma)-\alpha}. \tag{37}$$

To the extent that $1 \geq \phi \geq 0$, equation (26) implies that the maximum rate of growth of human captial possible in the Lucas model is given by a. This in turn, puts an upper bound on g_c also, viz., $a(1+\alpha-\gamma)/(1-\gamma)$.

The demand and supply curves as well as the equilibrium rates of interest and growth are depicted in Figure 5.4. The supply curve is drawn under the assumption of a positive externality. In case the latter is negative, the curve *could* be downward sloping.

A set of sufficient conditions for positive solutions to exist is,

(i) The slope of $g_c^s(r) >$ the slope of $g_c^d(r)$, i.e. $\alpha/(1+\alpha-\gamma) < \sigma$; and
(ii) the intercept of $g_c^s(r)$ on the r axis $>$ the intercept of $g_c^d(r)$, i.e. $a > \rho$.

The difference between the *command* and the *private* economy lies

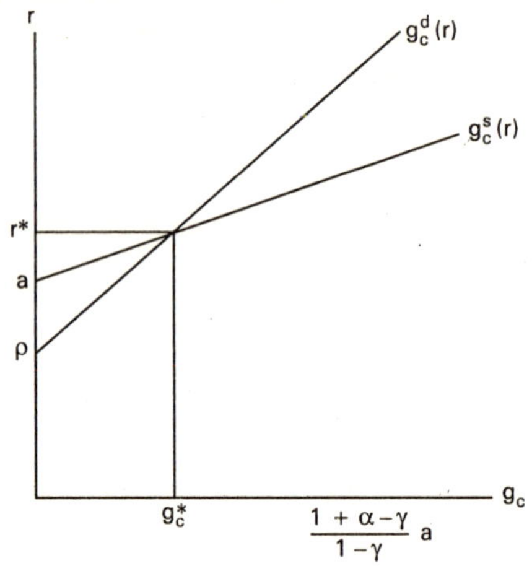

FIGURE 5.4 Lucas' Model of a Private Economy

in the fact that the planner is aware of the true social productivity of H. In other words, the planner is able to internalize the effect of H^{α} in (31). Thus, in a *command* economy, (31) may be rewritten as,

$$Y = BK^{\gamma}(\phi H^{(1+\alpha-\gamma)/(1-\gamma)})^{1-\gamma}$$

or alternatively, as,

$$Y = BK^{\gamma}(\phi H')^{1-\gamma} \tag{38}$$

where $H' \equiv H^{(1+\alpha-\gamma)/(1-\gamma)}$. Differentiating H' with respect to t and using (26), the equation governing the production of H' is given by,

$$H' = \frac{1+\alpha-\gamma}{1-\gamma}a(1-\phi)H' \tag{39}$$

Thus, *mutatis mutandis*, the *command* economy has exactly the same structure as the economy described by (26) and (27) above. The conclusions that applied to that economy must hold here also. In particular, the real rate of interest r will satisfy the condition,

$$r = \frac{1+\alpha-\gamma}{1-\gamma}a, \tag{40}$$

which is the exact counterpart of (30). Thus, in the *command* economy, the supply curve is horizontal[32] at the level $r = [(1+\alpha-\gamma)/(1-\gamma)]a$.

[32]There is now no change in the relative price. The command economy is aware of the true social productivity of H'. As a result, the marginal product of H' is unchanging along the balanced growth path.

The equilibrium growth rates of C and H are given by,

$$g_c^{**} = \sigma^{-1}\left(\frac{a(1+\alpha-\gamma)}{1-\gamma} - \rho\right) \tag{41}$$

and, using (33),

$$g_h^{**} = \sigma^{-1}\left(a - \frac{\rho(1-\gamma)}{1+\alpha-\gamma}\right). \tag{42}$$

The equilibrium is depicted in Figure 5.5.

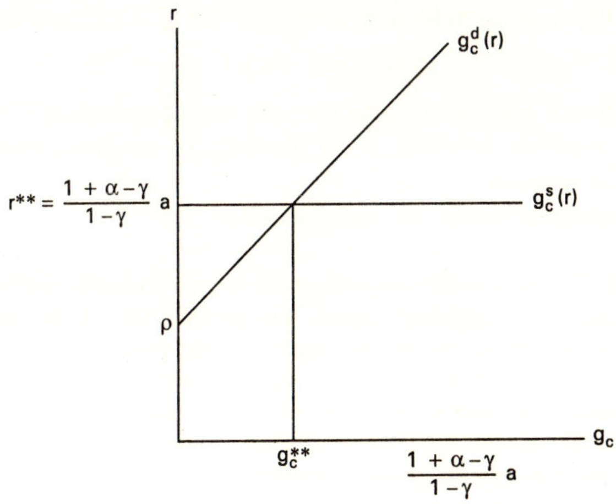

FIGURE 5.5 Lucas' Model of a Command Economy

A sufficient condition for a positive solution to g_c^{**} to exist now is that,

$$r^{**} = a\left(\frac{1+\alpha-\gamma}{1-\gamma}\right) > \rho$$

Comparing

$$g_h^{*} = \frac{(1-\gamma)(a-\rho)}{\sigma(1+\alpha-\gamma)}$$

with

$$g_h^{**} = \frac{(1-\gamma)(a-\rho)+a\alpha}{\sigma(1+\alpha-\gamma)},$$

it is straightforward that in the *command* economy, human capital accumulation will be faster than in the private economy in the presence of a positive externality, i.e. when $\alpha > 0$. The conclusion about the relative rates of growth of C is less obvious. Since,

$$g_c^{**} = \frac{(1-\gamma)(a-\rho) + a\alpha}{\sigma(1-\gamma)}$$

and

$$g_c^{*} = \frac{(1-\gamma)(a-\rho) + a\alpha - \alpha\rho}{\sigma(1-\gamma) + (\sigma - 1)\alpha}$$

it follows that a set of sufficient conditions for $g_c^{**} > g_c^{*}$ is that,

$$\alpha > 0 \quad \text{and} \quad \sigma > 1.$$

Thus, in spite of positive externalities, the rate of growth of C may be higher for a *private* economy if the elasticity of marginal utility from consumption is small.

Lucas' essential results are summarized as,

PROPOSITION 10: In a model of endogenous human capital formation along with accumulation of physical capital, the growth rate of the system is endogenously determined by the parameters of the preference function and technology. In the presence of a positive spill-over effect generated by human capital formation, the latter grows faster in the command economy. Moreover, a mild restriction on the elasticity of marginal utility ensures that the rate of growth of consumption in the market economy is less than that in the command economy.

Clearly, the rate of savings has a role to play now in determining the equilibrium rate of growth. There are two ways in which savings occur in Lucas' model. First, it has the form of physical capital accumulation. This part of savings is no different from Solow's and does not have an effect on the rate of growth. But allocating resources away from the production of final goods for the sake of human capital accumulation also constitutes savings. It is this form of savings that determines the rate of growth.

Rebelo (1991) builds on this model to make the technology for human capital generation dependent on physical as well as human capital. Thus, simultaneously with the allocation parameter ϕ, he has another parameter determining the allocation of physical capital between the two sectors. This allows him to separate out the two types of savings. Also, to the extent that both physical and human capital are used in the production of human capital, both types of savings behaviour now affect the equilibrium rate of growth. It should be clear that the source of growth in this version of the Rebelo model is different from that in his linear model.

3.4 Romer: Modelling Research

Like Lucas and Rebelo, the growth rate is traced back in Romer (1990) to a core sector unencumbered by diminishing returns.[33] He questions, however, Lucas' conclusion that there is an upper bound on an economy's achievable rate of growth. After all, an important moving force behind economic activity is the desire to break through existing barriers on growth rates.

As opposed to Lucas therefore, who locates the source of economic growth in the accumulation of human capital (by means of human capital), Romer believes that growth is not an outcome of human capital accumulation as such, but of the invention of increasingly productive techniques.

Human capital is a *sine qua non* for this activity insofar as it is a vitally important input (in the shape of research labour) into the inventive process. For a given stock of human capital, there is of course an upper bound on the achievable rate of growth in Romer also, but the bound itself is flexible upwards with a growth in this stock. To emphasise this fact, Romer assumes the stock of human capital to be at a constant level $\overline{H}$ over time.[34]

The production function for final goods[35] is chosen to be,

$$Y = H_y^{\alpha} \int_0^A x(i)^{1-\alpha}\, di \tag{43}$$

where H_y represents human capital employed in producing Y, $x(i)$ the quantity of the ith variety of specialized input used in the production

[33]As in Arrow (Case $\alpha < 1$) and Lucas, but unlike Rebelo, the absence of diminishing returns is inseparable from the theory of technical progress offered by the model.

[34]In identifying the source of technical progress in purposive research, Romer is also offering a way out of the weakness of the Arrow model, which views technical progress as an inevitable byproduct of the process of capital accumulation.

[35]Following an idea of Ethier (1982), the function is a reinterpretation of the Dixit-Stiglitz (1977) preference function for variety.

of Y and A the cardinality of a continuum of existing varieties. Specialized inputs are indexed according to the chronological order of their appearance. The proximate object of research is the ith design or idea[36], whose concrete embodiment is the input $x(i)$. Progress in research implies an increase in the value of A, and along with it, an expansion in the size of the set of ideas as well as that of the set of specialized inputs.

That (43) captures the notion of specialization may be appreciated from the following considerations. Assuming all $x(i)$'s to be used at the same level, say x, the production function reduces to,

$$Y = H_y^{\alpha} A x^{1-\alpha} \tag{44}$$

Given x, the marginal return to variety is measured by,

$$\frac{\partial Y}{\partial A} = H_y^{\alpha} x^{1-\alpha}$$

In other words, there are constant returns to variety, given the level of $x(i)$. As opposed to this, the marginal return to an increase in x, given that variety is fixed at A, behaves as follows:

$$\frac{\partial Y}{\partial x} = H_y^{\alpha} A(1-\alpha)x^{-\alpha} > 0$$

$$\frac{\partial^2 Y}{\partial x^2} = H_y^{\alpha} A(-\alpha)(1-\alpha)x^{-\alpha-1} < 0$$

Thus, given A, there are decreasing returns to a mere increase in the quantity in which the different inputs are employed. In other words, specialization offsets the tendency for diminishing returns associated with an intensive use of existing inputs.

The design underlying a specialized input is non-excludable, since it can be copied relatively costlessly.[37] This acts as a disincentive for research as a privately organized activity. Romer's model resolves the difficulty by adopting a monopolistically competitive market structure backed by patent laws. There are two ways in which an existing

[36]The two words 'design' and 'idea' will be used synonymously in what follows.

[37]It is also non-rival, since two production processes based on the *same* idea can be simultaneously operated. Unlike rival inputs, there is no sense in which the two processes can be viewed as employing two *pieces* of the same idea. Being both non-rival and non-excludable, a design has the required characteristics of a pure public good.

design may be utilized. First, it may be used to produce the specialized input based on it. Second, any idea can be utilized to create newer ideas through further research. The patent laws in Romer inhibit free access to a design by a non-patent holder in the first of these activities.

However, the laws do not preclude the free use of an existing idea to churn out new ones. In other words, a patent accords to the product of invention the status of a partially excludable commodity. The total body of knowledge incorporated in the stock of existing ideas (of size A) is a free input into new research, but the use of each individual design is excludable in producing the corresponding input.

Romer's economy consists of three parts: a perfectly competitive sector producing Y; for each i, a monopolist producing $x(i)$ by means of a non-sector specific capital good K, which (as in Solow) is physically the same as Y; and a competitive sector producing research ideas or designs with the aid of human capital H_A and the stock A of 'ideas'. Before proceeding further, it is of some help to present the social accounts of the Romer model in a schematic form:

Social Accounts for the Romer Model

Sector	Output	Input	Market Structure
Final Goods	Y	$H_y\, x(i),\, i \in (0, A]$	Competitive
Intermediate Goods	$x(i),\, i \in (0, A]$	K, ith design, $i \in (0, A]$	Monopoly
Research	$\dot{A}$	H_A, A	Competitive

Since Y is produced under perfect competition, the wages w_H^y of human capital in this sector equals its marginal product:

$$w_H^y = \alpha\, H_y^{\alpha - 1} \int_0^A x(i)^{1-\alpha}\, di \tag{45}$$

In what follows, Y will act as the numéraire. The inverse derived demand function for the input $x(i)$ is,

$$p(i) = (1 - \alpha) H_y^{\alpha} x(i)^{-\alpha} \tag{46}$$

where $p(i)$ is the price paid per unit use of $x(i)$.

We may proceed now with the details of the research technology which have to be specified along with the market structure. The production of $x(i)$ may be thought of as a two stage (but not necessarily vertically integrated) process. The lower stage consists of the creation of a design, i.e. the task of 'hitting an idea'. Human capital is an essential input in this process and calls forth a once for all payment to the inventor. At the higher stage, non-specialized or raw capital (Solow's K) is converted to specialized $x(i)$ by means of a fixed coefficient production function, each unit of $x(i)$ requiring ζ units of raw capital.

The raw capital congealed in an $x(i)$ is borrowed from the household sector. If an $x(i)$ is infinitely lived, there is an interest cost per period to be incurred by its producer for infinite time. Alternatively, $x(i)$ could also be looked upon as a consumable input, reproduced in each period. In this case too, there is an infinite stream of interest payments.[38] A patent holder of the ith idea is the monopolist supplier of $x(i)$ who earns an infinite stream of profits. The discounted present value of this infinite stream is set against the once for all payment for the design to define the rate of return on investment in research. Potential monopolists compete for this return as soon as a new design makes its appearance. This raises or depresses the price of the design, driving the rate of return to equality with the market rate of interest.

The per period profit of a monopoly producer of $x(i)$ is given by,

$$\pi(i) = p(i)x(i) - r\zeta\, x(i), \tag{47}$$

where r is the (real) market rate of interest paid on the raw capital $\zeta\, x(i)$ borrowed from the households. Using (46), the maximization of (47) yields an expression for $p(i)$ that depends only on r for each i:

$$p = p(i) = \frac{r\zeta}{1-\alpha}. \tag{48}$$

Combining this with (46), $x(i)$ is also dependent on r only. This value of $x(i)$ will be denoted simply by x. Hence, (45) reduces to,

$$w_H^y = \alpha H_y^{\alpha-1} A x^{1-\alpha}. \tag{49}$$

[38]The input $x(i)$ does not undergo obsolescence in Romer. Given the nature of the production function, there will always be positive demand for it by the competitive producers of Y. Young (1993) describes this aspect in terms of complementarity of inputs. Obsolescence related problems are recognized by Aghion and Howitt (1992) and Young.

The value of $\pi(i)$ is also dependent on r alone:

$$\pi = px - r\zeta x = \frac{r\zeta}{1-\alpha}x - r\zeta x = \alpha px. \tag{50}$$

and the infinite stream of π, discounted at the market rate of interest, equals,

$$\begin{aligned}\int_0^\infty e^{-rt}\,\pi\,dt &= \frac{\pi}{r}\\ &= \frac{\alpha px}{r}\\ &= \frac{\alpha(1-\alpha)H_y^{\alpha}x^{1-\alpha}}{r}\end{aligned} \tag{51}$$

The technology for research is given by,

$$\dot{A} = aAH_A \tag{52}$$

where a is a positive constant and H_A the human capital employed in producing new ideas (i.e. $\dot{A}$). As already indicated, this sector is perfectly competitive. Since the production function is homogeneous of degree 2 in A and H_A, payment of factors according to their marginal productivity will over-exhaust the output value. This is avoided however, A being a free input into the research process by the assumption of partial excludability. There is, thus, no difficulty in paying H_A according to the value of its marginal productivity. Denoting the price of $\dot{A}$ by P_A, the value of the marginal product of H_A is $P_A aA$.

The supply rate is determined, as Rebelo, by imposing two separate 'no-arbitrage' conditions. The first equates the marginal product of human capital in the production of final goods to the value of it in research. A second requirement is that the rate of return on investment in research is equal to the market rate of interest. Since P_A is none other than the investment in research, the second no-arbitrage condition implies that in equilibrium it equals the infinite stream of monopoly profits discounted at the *market rate of interest*, viz., (51). Thus,

$$w_H^A = P_A aA = \frac{\alpha(1-\alpha)H_y^{\alpha}x^{1-\alpha}}{r}aA \tag{53}$$

where w_H^A is the wages received by H_A.

By the first no-arbitrage requirement, $w_H^y = w_H^A$. Hence, using (49) and (53),

$$H_y = \frac{r}{a(1-\alpha)}. \tag{54}$$

Substituting (54) into (52) and recalling that $\overline{H} = H_y + H_A$,

$$\frac{\dot{A}}{A} = a\left(\overline{H} - \frac{r}{a(1-\alpha)}\right). \tag{55}$$

The last step in the derivation of the supply rate function is to identify it with (55). Going back to (43), at any fixed value of r,

$$\begin{aligned} Y &= H_y^{\alpha} A x^{1-\alpha} \\ &= H_y^{\alpha} A^{\alpha} A^{1-\alpha} x^{1-\alpha} \\ &= H_y^{\alpha} A^{\alpha} (Ax)^{1-\alpha} \\ &= H_y^{\alpha} A^{\alpha} K^{1-\alpha} \frac{1}{\zeta^{1-\alpha}}, \end{aligned} \tag{56}$$

where $K = \zeta Ax$ is the aggregate value of raw capital embodied in the specialized inputs when the rate of interest is fixed at r. Now, K/A, being equal to ζx, is a constant, given r. Using (56), the counterpart of (7) in Romer's model is,

$$\frac{C}{K} + \frac{\dot{K}}{K} = \frac{1}{\zeta^{1-\alpha}} H_y^{\alpha} \left(\frac{A}{K}\right)^{\alpha}, \tag{57}$$

Given r, the value of H_y is fixed. Hence, the RHS of (57) is a constant. This implies that the rates of growth of A, C, K and Y are the same. Thus, (55) is equivalently rewritten as,

$$g_c^s(r) = a\left(\overline{H} - \frac{r}{a(1-\alpha)}\right). \tag{58}$$

As with Rebelo, this is a declining function of r. The equilibrium is shown in Figure 5.6. The diagram shows that a positive rate of growth is achievable in equilibrium only if $\overline{H}$ is large enough.[39] Romer argues on the basis of this observation that a minimum size of the stock of human capital is a necessary pre-condition for growth. The difference

[39]To be precise, the condition is $a(1-\alpha)\overline{H} > \rho$.

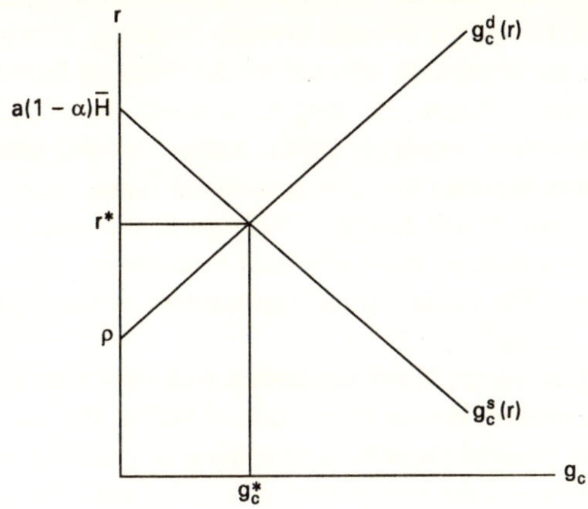

FIGURE 5.6 Equilibrium in Romer's Model of Growth through Specialization

between rich nations and poor may be explained, therefore, in terms of the differences in the size of human capital in these societies.

Finally, there would be a divergence between the social and private marginal products of x due to the facts that (i) the market economy will not internalize the intertemporal externality generated by the investment in x (an investment today raises productivity for all time to come) and (ii) a monopolistic equilibrium leads to a socially sub-optimal allocation of resources.

Romer's findings may now be summarized.

PROPOSITION 11: When technical progress assumes the form of specialized inputs into the productive process, the equilibrium growth rate of an economy can be sustained by a combination of perfectly competitive and monopolistically competitive markets, the latter backed by a legal structure recognizing patent rights. The rate of growth for the command economy is larger than that for a market economy.

3.5 AGHION AND HOWITT: OBSOLESCENCE

As in the case of Romer (1986), the work of Aghion and Howitt cannot be shown as a demand-supply cross. However, their work shares several common features with the ideas discussed so far. Besides, it captures a very important aspect of innovative research, viz., obsolescence.

Newer and more efficient techniques are known to replace the old, with the result that efforts devoted towards invention of better methods of production are negatively affected by the threat of further improvements appearing in future. So long as a newly developed technique holds sway, however, monopoly profits can be enjoyed from its use.

While Romer assumes that any specialized input, once invented, is used forever, Aghion and Howitt (1992) go to the other extreme and assume that a specialized input goes into extinction as soon as a newer variety appears. The cause behind replacement is the higher productivity of new inputs.[40]

The model, however, is not concerned with determining the rate of growth of the system. For, as in the case of Solow, the rate of increase in productivity brought about by a new input is specified exogenously. What is *not known* is the arrival time of a new input. This is a random variable. Thus, even though the growth potential of a new input is known exactly, it is possible to speak only in terms of an *expected* growth rate of the economy. The Aghion and Howitt exercise is geared towards determining this expected rate of growth. As it turns out, they are concerned with the expected value of the supply rate of growth alone, the demand rate having no role to play at all. Thus, the model is not a full equilibrium model and the real rate of interest r is exogenously given.

Time is denoted by the continuous variable τ and the arrival of inventions by the discrete variable t. Thus, x_t denotes the specialized input relevant for time *interval* t, x_{t+1} for *interval* $t+1$ and so on. The length of any such interval is a stochastic variable.

As in Romer, there are three sectors of production, the final goods sector, the intermediate goods sector and the research sector. The final good is produced according to,

$$Y = AF(x), \tag{59}$$

where A is a productivity parameter whose level is determined by the type of x in use.[41] Thus, x_t is associated with A_t, x_{t+1} with A_{t+1}, etc. Further, $A_{t+1} = \gamma A_t$, $\gamma > 1$, where γ is a nonstochastic variable. If successive generations of the inputs were to be available in a deterministic chronological sequence, the economy's growth rate would be fairly

[40] They also consider the possibility of simultaneous use of different varieties. In this context, see Young (1993) also. In Romer, the productivity differential is absent.

[41] Production of Y requires unskilled labour also, but this is a constant, and hence, ignored.

transparent. However, as noted already, the arrival time of a new input is a stochastic variable.

The entire quantum of Y is consumed, so that there is no direct savings out of Y. Nevertheless, savings enter through the back door since the level of Y depends on that of x and the latter is determined by the allocation of skilled labour to the production of x. The larger (smaller) the allocation in favour of x, the larger (smaller) is current consumption. Thus, a decision to produce less of x amounts to a decision to save more.

The input x is produced by means of skilled labour, but the latter has a competitive use in research also. A fixed quantity N of skilled labour is allocated between these alternative uses. (In Romer, it is allocated between research and the final good).

The two activities will be described in turn and it is simpler to begin with x. Any x is produced by the linear technology,

$$x = L. \tag{60}$$

As with Romer, the producer of x_t is a monopolist, with the price p_t of x_t satisfying the inverse demand relationship,

$$p_t = A_t F'(x_t).$$

The equilibrium condition for this sector is given by the equality of marginal cost (i.e. the wage rate w_t expressed in Y units) and marginal revenue, viz.,

$$w_t = A_t(F'(x_t) + x_t F''(x_t)), \tag{61}$$

or,

$$\omega_t = (F'(x_t) + x_t F''(x_t)) = \tilde{\omega}(x_t), \tag{62}$$

where ω_t stands for the productivity adjusted wage rate during t. Combining with (61), the last equation can be written as,

$$w_t = A_t \tilde{\omega}(N - n_t), \tag{63}$$

where n_t stands for the employment of research labour at each τ in t.

By assumption, only one specialized input is in use at any time. The equilibrium profit accruing at τ to the monopolist producing x_t is written as π_t, while $\tilde{\pi}(\omega_t)$ $[= \tilde{\pi}\{\tilde{\omega}(x_t)\}]$ represents the optimal value of π_t/A_t as a function of ω_t. As w_t increases, the profit maximizing value of x_t falls, thus reducing the quantum of labour used in this sector. Equation (63) shows that relation between w_t and the residual labour left for research, given that x_t satisfies (61). Relationship (63), which may be looked upon as the supply of n_t as a function of ω_t, is shown as the upward rising curve n_t^s in Figure 5.7. The intercept of the curve on the vertical axis is given by $w_t = A_t\tilde{\omega}(N)$. At any wage rate below this, N is entirely devoted to producing x_t.

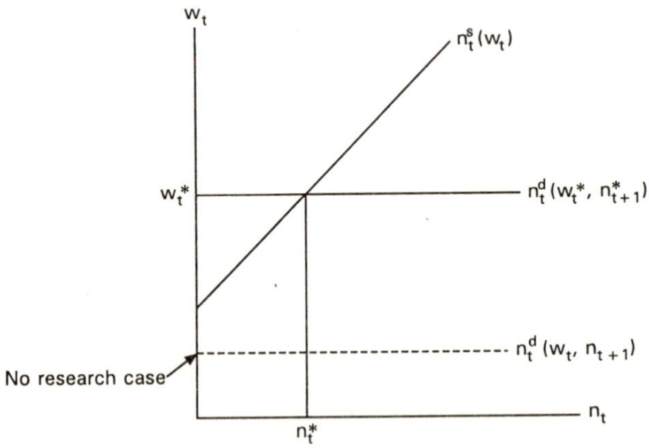

FIGURE 5.7: Equilibrium in the Aghion and Howitt Model

The next step consists of defining the demand for research labour. As noted above, the arrival time of new ideas is a random variable. The probability of success (in research) at any point of time has a Poisson distribution with parameter $\lambda\phi(n)$, where ϕ will be *assumed* to be a linear[42] function of n, with $\phi' > 0$. There is perfect competition in the research sector and V_{t+1} is the price of the $(t+1)$th innovation, i.e. the *idea* behind the specialized input x_{t+1}. A firm engaged in producing this idea faces a probability $\lambda\phi$ of success at any τ, so that $1 - \lambda\phi$ is the probability that the innovation does not occur. In case of success, the revenue earned is V_{t+1}, otherwise the revenue is zero. In either case, however, it has to incur a wage cost equal to $w_t n_t$.[43] Thus,

[42]This is done for simplicity. Aghion and Howitt deal with the more general case, viz., $\phi'(\cdot) \leq 0$.

[43]It is worth emphasizing that n_t stands for labour engaged in producing the $t+1$th innovation.

$\lambda\phi(n_t)V_{t+1} + (1 - \lambda\phi(n_t)) \cdot 0 = \lambda\phi(n_t)V_{t+1}$ stands for the 'expected' revenue and $w_t n_t$ for the *non-stochastic* cost at each τ in t. Hence, the objective function of a firm engaged in research is given by,

$$V_{t+1}\lambda\phi(n_t) - w_t n_t \tag{64}$$

Maximization of (64) yields,

$$w_t = V_{t+1}\lambda\phi'(n_t). \tag{65}$$

Equation (65) gives the demand for n_t as a function of w_t and V_{t+1}, where V_{t+1} stands for the investment made by a potential monopolist of period $t+1$ in buying the output of research carried out in period t. Equilibrium requires this investment to yield the same rate of return as the market rate of interest r. Thus, V_{t+1} must equal the present value of the expected stream of returns from the investment, discounted at the market rate of interest r.

The stream of expected returns associated with the investment V_{t+1} depends on the expected length of the interval $t+1$ for which x_{t+1} yields returns and this, in turn, depends on n_{t+1}, the labour engaged in inventing x_{t+2}. The profit associated with x_{t+1} being π_{t+1}, the expected return from V_{t+1} at any τ in $t+1$ is $e^{-\lambda\phi(n_{t+1})\tau}\pi_{t+1} = e^{-\lambda\phi(n_{t+1})\tau}A_{t+1}\tilde{\pi}[\tilde{\omega}(N - n_{t+1})]$. Thus, in equilibrium,

$$\begin{aligned} V_{t+1} &= \int_0^\infty e^{-r\tau}\, e^{-\lambda\phi(n_{t+1})\tau} A_{t+1}\tilde{\pi}(\tilde{\omega}(N - n_{t+1}))\, d\tau \\ &= \frac{A_{t+1}\tilde{\pi}(\tilde{\omega}(N - n_{t+1}))}{r + \lambda\phi(n_{t+1})}. \end{aligned} \tag{66}$$

Substituting in (65),

$$w_t = \lambda\phi'(n_t) = \frac{A_{t+1}\tilde{\pi}(\tilde{\omega}(N - n_{t+1}))}{r + \lambda\phi(n_{t+1})}, \tag{67}$$

where, by assumption, $\phi'(n_t)$ is a constant. Thus, for any given n_{t+1}, equation (67) gives an infinitely elastic[44] demand curve for n_t. Figure 5.7 shows this as horizontal lines such as $n_t^d(w_t, n_{t+1})$. Equilibrium in period t occurs where n_t^s intersects n_t^d. The equilibrium wage rate and employment for t is shown by the pair (w^*, n_t^*).

[44]In Aghion and Howitt, the curve could be downward falling, since $\phi'(\cdot) \leq 0$.

Clearly, the equilibrium described above depends on the assumed value of n_{t+1}. For a dynamic equilibrium, n_{t+1} must itself be the equilibrium value n_{t+1}^* pertaining to period $t+1$ and so on. In Figure 5.7, the equilibrium demand curve for period t is thus indicated by $n_t^d(w_t^*, n_{t+1}^*)$.

Figure 5.7 also depicts the possibility of a zero research, and hence, zero growth equilibrium. This happens when the demand and the supply curves fail to intersect, as is the case with the broken curve $n_t^d(w_t, n_{t+1})$.

Given the equilibrium sequence of $\{n_1^*\}$, a stochastic growth path emerges through the random shocks generated on A in (59). A very special equilibrium can involve $\ldots = n_t^* = \hat{n} = n_{t+1}^* = \ldots$. This is typically a fixed point of the mapping $n_{t+1} \rightarrow n_1^*$. Aghion and Howitt compute the expected growth rate and its variance for the case where a fixed point $\hat{n}$ exists.

An interesting feature of the model arises from the fact that research produces a revenue only when its output, say, the $t+1$th innovation, actually arrives. Prior to that point of time, research labour cannot be paid for from the value of its produce. The problem may be resolved by assuming that the monopoly firm producing x_{t+1} is owned by the labourers producing the $t+1$th idea. They are paid in terms of shares in the profits of their firm, once the innovation is successful. As already discussed, the discounted present value of their expected earning is V_{t+1}, which is exactly the same as their expected wage earnings during the interval t as labourers in the research firm. This is shown as follows.

In equation (64), $\lambda\phi(n_t)$ may be looked upon as a *linear* production function for 'ideas'. Under perfect competition, wages must equal the value of labour's marginal product. Thus, *had the research workers been actually paid their wages*, the earnings at each τ in t would be $V_{t+1}\lambda\phi'(n_t)$, the value of their marginal product in research. A marginal increase in labour raises the probability or success in each 'trial' by $\lambda\phi'(n_t)$. This implies that the expected waiting time of success associated with the injection of an extra unit of research labour is $1/(\lambda\phi'(n_t))$. Thus, the wages expected to be earned during this interval is $(1/(\lambda\phi'(n_t)))V_{t+1}\lambda\phi'(n_t) = V_{t+1}$.

The question nevertheless remains as to how the research labour n_t

is actually sustained during t, since the wages cannot be paid. One must assume then that there is a source of finance for research labour which is replenished later as soon as the innovation is successful. One can also try and add a market for loans to remove the lacuna.

Although the rate of growth is supply determined, it is amenable to policy manipulations. In particular, since the rate of interest r is exogenous to the model, it is possible to think of it as a policy instrument and carry out comparative statics exercises with respect to its variations. In particular, it is not hard to see that a rise in r leads to a fall in research employment.

Finally, as opposed to the previous models, a social optimum may involve a *lower* rate of growth than the market equilibrium. This happens because in a market economy, researchers do not internalize the negative effect of inventions on existing profits.

Thus, the major results of Aghion and Howitt may be summed up as follows:

PROPOSITION 12: In the presence of obsolescence, the appearance of more productive inputs has a depressing effect on the rate of private investment into research. However, since the arrival time of new inputs is uncertain, the growth rate of the economy is a stochastic variable. Moreover, the expected rate of growth of a market economy might exceed that of the command economy, since the latter internalizes the destructive effect of the arrival of new ideas on existing productive processes.

3.6 BARRO: PUBLIC SECTOR AND GROWTH

Barro (1990) attempts to capture the effect of introducing public services as an input into the growth process.

These services are merely a part of the current *flow* of output that is taxed away from households by the government and supplied free of charge to the firms.[45] Aggregate output (Y) has therefore *three* different uses. First, it can be (privately) consumed (Solow's C). Secondly, it can

[45]The government's participation in the productive process often takes the form of a provision of infrastructural services, such as roadways, telecommunications etc. When this is the case, the services in question are generated by corresponding stocks of infrastructure which, like K, need to be accumulated. Also, physical capital may itself be an input into this accumulation process. A two sector model incorporating such infrastructural stocks as well as the fact that the services of infrastructure are often non-rival in nature may be found in Dasgupta (1998).

be privately accumulated (Solow's K). Finally, it can be used as a publicly provided free input (say, G) into the productive process. Thus, the production function is,

$$Y = F(K, G). \tag{68}$$

which shares all the properties of the Solow production function.

The public sector input G is financed by a proportional income tax ν, i.e.,

$$\nu Y = G. \tag{69}$$

Since (68) reduces to (5), where $y = Y/G$ and $k = K/G$, equation (69) fixes k, once ν is given. This, in turn, fixes $r = f'(k)$ and gives rise to an infinitely elastic supply curve. Hence, the rate of growth is entirely demand determined in this model as in the case of d'Autume and Michel.

It is natural to look into the possibility of an optimal ν and Barro goes on to compare the walfare maximizing ν with the growth rate maximizing ν. He shows that in general, the two may well be unequal.

A divergence arises between the social and the market equilibrium once again, since in calculating the marginal product of capital, the market fails to take note of the proportionate relationship between K and G on account of a given ν. As a result, the command economy will grow at a higher rate than the market economy.

The essential features of Barro's conclusions are:

PROPOSITION 13: When the government taxes private sector income and transfers the proceeds entirely in the form of infrastructural support, the endogenous rate of growth of the economy is a function of the tax rate. The growth maximizing tax rate may fall short of the welfare maximizing one. The command economy chooses a higher growth rate than the market economy for any given tax rate.

4. CONCLUSIONS

Economists from the third world are naturally interested in models of growth and development. The important question to them is whether some of the models covered here have a bearing on the everyday problems which concern developing economies. Or at least, whether these models might be made to focus on a few of these issues. A belief shared by many policy planners saddled with a low level growth trap is that the panacea lies in an increase in the savings rate.

Such a viewpoint suggests that there is no immediate prospect of capital saturation, as in the core sector of Rebelo's model. However, for this to be true, it must also be the case that the process of capital accumulation can itself reverse all tendencies for diminishing returns. If so, the capital in question cannot be a simple one-to-one transformation of savings as in Solow. Rebelo's explanation lies in identifying a part of it as human capital.

A message from NGT that is relevant for developing economies then, is that a mere effort to raise the saving rate is not going to be of help. One must, at the same time, be able to transform savings into increasingly sophisticated capital 'equipment'.

On the negative side, a crucial policy problem facing a society such as ours is that of unemployment. A perceptive reader would have noticed that the entire literature on NGT is based on the assumption of full employment. Given its concern for steady states, this is perhaps a natural assumption to make. But the nagging question then is whether an excessive concern with maintainable long-term growth rates is the real issue for developing economies. A model of endogenous growth with unemployment would be a welcome addition to the existing literature.

There are other issues of contemporary interest. For example, developed economies are becoming increasingly conscious of the tradeoff between growth and environmental quality. Is growth necessarily a desirable objective? The question that arises here is whether a developing economy can afford the luxury of a low growth rate in pursuit of a better environment. Going by the example of India, higher growth rates are taken to be indices of successful government policy. It seems unlikely that a government with a concern for environment at the cost of growth would have the sympathy of the electorate. There is an increasing body of literature on growth and environment that is of interest in this connection. It could not be covered here, given the limited purpose of the paper.

References

Aghion, P. and P. Howitt (1992), 'A Model of Growth through Creative Destruction', *Ecnometrica*, pp. 323–51.

——— (1998), *Endogenous Growth Theory*, MIT, USA.

Arrow, K.J. (1962), 'The Economic Implications of Learning by Doing', *Review of Economic Studies*, pp. 155–73.

Barro, R. (1990), 'Government Spending in a Simple Model of Endogenous Growth', *Journal of Political Economy*, pp. S103–S125.

Barro, R. and X. Sala-i-Martin (1995), *Economic Growth*, New York: McGraw-Hill.

Cass, D. (1965), 'Optimum Growth in an Aggregative Model of Capital Accumulation', *Review of Economic Studies*, pp. 233–40.

Dasgupta, D. (1999), 'Growth vs. Welfare in a Model of Nonrival Infrastructure', *Journal of Development Economics*, pp. 359–85.

d'Autume, A. and P. Michel (1993), 'Endogenous Growth in Arrow's Learning by Doing Model', *European Economic Review*, pp. 1175–84.

Dixit, Avinash K. and Joseph E. Stiglitz (1977), 'Monopolistic Competition and Optimum Product Diversity', *American Economic Review*, pp. 297–308.

Domar, Evsey D. (1946), 'Capital Expansion, Rate of Growth and Employment', *Econometrica*, 14, pp. 137–47.

Ethier, Wilfred J. (1982), 'National and International Returns to Scale in the Modern Theory of International Trade', *American Economic Review*, pp. 389–405.

Harrod, Roy (1939), 'An Essay in Dynamic Theory', *Economic Journal*, pp. 14–33.

Keynes, John M. (1936), *The General Theory of Empolyment, Interest and Money*, Harcourt, Brace and World, Inc., 1965.

Koopmans, T.C. (1965), 'On the Concept of Optimal Economic Growth', *Study Week on the Econometric Approach Planning, Pontificiae Scientiarum Scripta Varia*, XXVIII, Chicago: Rand McNally.

Lucas, R.E. Jr. (1988), 'On the Mechanism of Economic Development', *Journal of Monetary Economics*, pp. 3–42.

Phelps, E.S. (1961), 'The Golden Rule of Accumulation: A Fable for Growthmen', *American Economic Review*, pp. 638–43.

——— (1965), 'Second Essay on the Golden Rule of Accumulation', *American Economic Review*, pp. 739–814.

Ramsey, Frank P. (1928), 'A Mathematical Theory of Saving', *Economic Journal*, pp. 543–59.

Rebelo, S. (1991), 'Long-Run Policy Analysis and Long-Run Growth', *Journal of Political Economy*, pp. 501–21.

Romer, P.M. (1986), 'Increasing Returns and Long-Run Growth', *Journal of Political Economy*, pp. 1002–37.

——— (1990), 'Endogenous Technical Change', *Journal of Political Economy*, pp. S71–S102.

Shell, Karl (ed.) (1967), *Essays on the Theory of Optimal Economic Growth*, MIT, USA.

Sheshinski, Eytan (1967), 'Optimal Accumulation with Learning by Doing', in *Shell*, pp. 31–52.

Solow, Robert (1956), 'A Contribution to the Theory of Economic Growth', *Quarterly Journal of Economics*, pp. 65–94.

——— (1960), 'Investment and Technical Progress', in K.J. Arrow, S. Karlin and P. Suppes (ed.) *Mathematical Methods in the Social Sciences*, Stanford, pp. 89–104.

Uzawa, H. (1965), 'Optimum Technical Change in an Aggregative Model of Economic Growth', *International Economic Review*, pp. 19–31.

Young, A. (1993), 'Substitution and Complementarity in Endogenous Innovation', *Quarterly Journal of Economics*, pp. 775–807.

Appendix

HARROD

Harrod takes off from Keynesian macro-theory, which dealt with the equilibrium level of output and income $Y(t)$ for an economy at a given point of time t. By contrast, Harrod was concerned with the *growth rate* g of $Y(t)$ that kept the economy in Keynesian equilibrium at all t.

The condition for $Y(t)$ to be in Keynesian equilibrium at t is that,

$$S(t) = sY(t) = I(t) \tag{A.1}$$

where s represents the (constant) marginal and average savings propensity of households, $S(t)$ their aggregate real savings at t and $I(t)$ the real investment demand by business. This condition is equivalent to the statement that $Y(t)$, *if produced by the entrepreneurs and received by the households as income*, will be matched by an equal level of demand. In other words, entrepreneurs and households would be satisfied respectively with the production and income level $Y(t)$ if and only if equation (A.1) is satisfied. In Keynesian terminology, the level of output and income satisfying (A.1) is known as *effective demand* [Keynes (1936), pp. 25]. By an *effective demand problem*, one usually refers to a shortfall of investment below savings at any given volume of output.

Harrod took his cue from this idea and suggested that a *constant rate of growth* g to $Y(t)$ *would leave the entrepreneurs satisfied* if, along the associated growth path of output, (A.1) holds at each t. The link between g and (A.1) is provided in his theory by the *entrepreneurs*' investment demand function. At all t, this depends on their expectation about the *rate of change* $\dot{Y}(t)$ (= $dY(t)/dt$) of $Y(t)$, i.e. the expected rate of change of aggregate demand for final goods and services. Choosing a particularly simple representation of this relationship, viz.,

$$I(t) = v\frac{dY(t)}{dt} = v\dot{Y}(t), \qquad v \text{ constant} \tag{A.2}$$

Harrod proved the following result:

PROPOSITION: A constant rate of growth g leaves all agents satisfied if $g = s/v$.

Proof: Any constant growth rate g must equal,

$$g = \frac{\frac{dY(t)}{dt}}{Y(t)} = \frac{\dot{Y}(t)}{Y(t)} \quad \forall\ t.$$

Suppose now that $g = \frac{s}{v}$. Then,

$$S(t) = sY(t) = v\dot{Y}(t) = I(t).$$

Hence, (A.1) is satisfied at all t, so that all agents are satisfied.

Conversely, suppose that g keeps all agents satisfied. Then, (A.1) holds at all t. Since g is the rate of growth of the economy, entrepreneurs must expect the rate of change of output at t to be,

$$\dot{Y}(t) = gY(t) \quad \forall\ t.$$

Hence, using (A.2),

$$sY(t) = S(t) = I(t) = v(gY(t)) \quad \forall\ t, \tag{A.3}$$

or,

$$g = \frac{s}{v}.$$

Q.E.D.

Harrod referred to the rate of growth derived above as the 'warranted' rate of growth, g^w. As opposed to g^w, the rate of growth of output that would fully utilize all resources is the natural rate of growth, g^n. If $g^n > g^w$, an effort to grow at the rate g^n will generate an inflationary spiral.[46] A similar argument holds if $g^n < g^w$. In this case, the full employment growth path will lead to demand deficiency, and eventually, to unemployment. The important point in both cases is that market forces cannot be depended upon to arrest the destabilizing movements.

[46]Thus,

$$g^n = \frac{\dot{Y}(t)}{Y(t)} > \frac{s}{v},$$

implies that

$$I(t) = v\dot{Y}(t) > sY(t) = S(t).$$

In other words, an excess of g^n over g^w leads to a state of excess demand for final goods and services. Since excess demand is a signal for buoyant markets, entrepreneurs would conclude that the rate of growth g^n is too small and attempt to grow at an even higher rate. However, since g^n is already the full employment rate, this will lead to inflation.

Given that the factors that determine g^n, are unrelated to the ones determining g^w, a discrepancy between the two rates is normally unavoidable. Thus, Harrod predicted that a free enterprise system is unlikely to be characterized by sustained growth with full employment and price stability.

Demand Rate of Growth

Proof of Proposition 1: The path of optimal consumption and savings is obtained by maximizing (1) subject to (2). The problem is solved by maximizing the current value Hamiltonian

$$H(K(t), c(t), \eta(t)) = L(t)\frac{1}{1-\sigma}(c(t)^{1-\sigma} - 1) + \eta(t)(r(t)K(t) + w(t)L(t) - L(t)c(t)) \quad \text{(A.4)}$$

at each t with respect to $c(t)$. Dropping the t's for notational convenience, this yields[47],

$$c^{-\sigma} = \eta \quad \text{(A.5)}$$

At the same time, the costate variable η is required to satisfy the condition,

$$\dot{\eta} = -\eta r + \eta\rho \quad \text{(A.6)}$$

Differentiating (A.5) logarithmically,

$$\frac{\dot{\eta}}{\eta} = -\sigma\frac{\dot{c}}{c}. \quad \text{(A.7)}$$

Writing $g^d = \frac{\dot{c}}{c}$, equations (A.6) and (A.7) imply,

$$r = \rho + \sigma g^d. \quad \text{(A.8)}$$

Thus,

$$g^d = g^d(r) = \frac{r-\rho}{\sigma}. \quad \text{(A.9)}$$

Q.E.D.

[47]It is being assumed that the optimal path is interior. There is no loss of generality here, since the assumption is fulfilled in a steady state. Also, the model permits the household to bring down the capital stock by consuming it away. In steady state, no such consumption will actually take place. A constant fraction of the capital stock could be assumed to undergo physical depreciation at each t also. However, this does not add any analytical insight and is avoided for notational simplicity.

Proof of Proposition 5: Plugging (14) in (10), the value of k^* is seen to satisfy,

$$f'(k^*) = \rho + \frac{n\alpha}{1-\alpha}\sigma.$$

The solution or the command economy is found by writing the Hamiltonian as

$$H(K(t), c(t), \theta(t)) = L(t)\frac{1}{1-\sigma}(c(t)^{1-\sigma} - 1)$$
$$+ \theta(t)(F(K(t), K(t)^{\alpha}L) - L(t)c(t)) \qquad \text{(A.10)}$$

Equation (A.7) stays unchanged, except for the replacement of η by θ. Equation (A.6) transforms to,

$$\dot{\theta} = -\frac{\partial F}{\partial K} + \rho\theta$$
$$= -\theta\left(\alpha\frac{f(k)}{k} + (1-\alpha)f'(k)\right) + \rho\theta \qquad \text{(A.11)}$$

As with Proposition 4, it is easily seen that the equilibrium rate of growth g^{**} for the command economy is still given by (14). Equation (A.11) then implies

$$\left(\alpha\frac{f(k)}{k} + (1-\alpha)f'(k)\right) = \sigma\frac{\dot{c}}{c} + \rho$$
$$= \frac{n\alpha}{1-\alpha}\sigma + \rho \qquad \text{(A.12)}$$

Denoting the solution of (A.12) by k^{**}, and noting that assumption $F_{11} < 0 \Rightarrow f(k)/k > f'(k)\ \forall\ k$, the result follows from a comparison of the solution for k^{**} with that for k^*. Q.E.D.

6

On the Nature of Policy Functions of Dynamic Optimization Models*

TAPAN MITRA

1. INTRODUCTION

Dynamic optimization models are currently in use in a number of different areas in economics, to address a wide variety of issues. The relationship between the dynamic optimization model and the (optimal) policy function associated with it is central to such applications. The purpose of this paper is to present a selective survey of results relevant to understanding this relationship.

As a backdrop to this survey, one should recall that two well-known characterizations of optimality have figured prominently in the literature on dynamic optimization. The first uses a primal approach, and characterizes optimality in terms of the existence of *value function* satisfying the functional equation of dynamic programming (often referred to as *Bellman's optimality principle*). The second (known as the *price characterization of optimality*) is based on a dual approach, and is developed for convex structures, where separation theorems for convex sets play a crucial role. Here an optimal programme is characterized in terms of existence of a sequence of dual variables or shadow prices, in terms of which (generalized) profit is maximized at the programme at each date compared to any alternative activity available at that date and, in addition, an asymptotic transversality condition is satisfied.

These characterizations are certainly useful in some respects. However, if we are given a function, h, from the state space, X, to itself,

*This paper is dedicated, with respect, to Professor Mihir Rakshit. I would like to thank Robert Becker, Jess Benhabib, Mukul Majumdar, Lionel McKenzie, Luigi Montrucchio, Kazuo Nishimura and Gerhard Sorger for conversations and comments, which have improved my understanding of the issues dealt with in this paper. The present version has benefited from suggestions by Debraj Ray.

and want to know whether h could be the policy function of some dynamic optimization model, we do not see how to answer this directly with Bellman's principle of optimality. Similarly, given an intertemporal sequence $(x_0, x_1, \ldots)$ of the state variable (with x_t in X for $t \geq 0$), if we want to know whether $(x_0, x_1, \ldots)$ is the optimal programme from x_0 generated by some dynamic optimization model, the price characterization of optimality result does not help us to resolve this issue.

The kinds of questions posed above arise quite naturally in the literature on *chaotic* economic dynamics, which has been developed primarily over the last decade. This literature has been concerned with the issue of whether chaotic behaviour is possible in the context of dynamic optimizaton models (and, if so, how 'likely' is it that it would occur). One could answer the possibility question in the affirmative if one could show, for example, that the *logistic* map $h(x) = 4x(1 - x)$ on $X = [0, 1]$ is the optimal policy function of *some* dynamic optimization model, since the logistic map is well-known to generate chaotic dynamics. Similarly, one could answer the question in the affirmative if one could show that the sequence $(x_0, x_1, x_2, x_0, x_1, x_2, \ldots)$, with x_0, x_1 and x_2 distinct, is the optimal programme from x_0, generated by some dynamic optimization model, since this establishes the existence of a period-three cycle, and the Li–Yorke theorem tells us that the model must generate optimal programmes (from other initial states) which exhibit (topological) chaos.

At the same time, it is worth emphasizing that while the question under discussion arose specifically in the context of studying chaotic economic dynamics, it is clearly of broader interest. It is useful, therefore, to pose the more general problem at this point. It is known that, given a standard dynamic optimization model, the policy function, h (from the state space X to itself) is continuous on X (and satisfies $h(0) = 0$, if one assumes, as we do, that the dynamic optimization model allows inaction and postulates impossibility of free production). We can now ask whether there are any *additional* restrictions that the exercise of dynamic optimization imposes on the policy function, or equivalently, whether any continuous function is *rationalizable* as a policy function of some dynamic optimization model. The problem is, of course, similar in spirit to the issue resolved in the Sonnenschein–Mantel–Debreu result in general equilibrium theory, where it has been shown that, given any continuous function, f, satisfying homogeneity of degree zero and Walras Law (and a compact subset, A, of the set of positive price vectors), one can construct an exchange economy so that the market excess-demand of this economy coincides with f (on the set A of positive price vectors).

Boldrin and Montrucchio (1986) took a significant step in addressing the problem posed above when they showed that any *twice continuously differentiable* function can be obtained as a policy function of an appropriate dynamic optimization model. Their demonstration raises two issues which we will discuss in this paper.

First, since policy functions are known to be continuous, the question arises whether their result can be extended to the class of all *continuous* functions. Neumann *et al.* (1988) showed that any continuously differentiable function, whose derivative satisfies a Lipschitz condition, can be rationalized as a policy function of a dynamic optimization model, thereby obtaining a slight weakening of the C^2 restriction used by Boldrin and Montrucchio. However, such a result clearly falls short of the mark since there are robust examples of dynamic optimization models which generate policy functions with a kink in the interior of the state space (similar to *tent map*). Specifically, Nishimura and Yano (1994) have shown that if the (reduced-form) utility function, u, is twice continuously differentiable in the interior of the transition possibility set, Ω, and the cross partial (u_{12}) of the utility function is negative throughout, then policy functions will have a shape similar to a tent-map. Further, a standard two-sector model of optimal growth, with Cobb–Douglas production functions (and fully depreciating capital), such that the consumption-goods sector is always more capital intensive than the investment-goods sector, will give rise to such a reduced-form utility function [see Benhabib and Nishimura (1985)]. Thus, differentiability (and so, continuous differentiability and Lipschitz continuity of the derivative) is not a general property of the policy function. [The contributions of Araujo (1991) and Santos (1991), which demonstrate differentiability of the policy function, but only under additional restrictive assumptions on the dynamic optimization model, complement this observation.] Thus, if one is interested in a *complete* characterization, the extension of the Boldrin-Montrucchio result must be addressed for a broader class of functions, which are continuous, but not necessarily differentiable.

We provide two results in this context that show that the required extension is not to be had free of charge. First, we establish a result on the behaviour of the optimal policy function at a boundary fixed point, from which it follows that the class of continuous functions is given by,

$$h(x) = \mu x^{\alpha}(1 - x^{\alpha}) \quad \text{for } x \text{ in } [0, 1] \tag{1}$$

(where the class is parametrized by μ and α, with $0 < \alpha < 1$, and $0 < \mu \leq 4$) is not rationalizable. Since differentiability of h fails here, precisely at the boundary, one may be tempted to conclude that the obstacle one encounters here is a *boundary problem*, reminiscent of a similar difficulty in the Sonnenschein–Mantel–Debreu result in general equilibrium theory. However, we establish another result on the behaviour of the optimal policy function at an interior fixed point, which compels us to be more cautious. From this second result, it follows that the continuous, *increasing*, function, given by,

$$h(x) = 1 + (x - 1)^{1/3} \quad \text{for } x \text{ in } [0, 2] \tag{2}$$

is not rationalizable. This example shows that the obstacle with the extension is not a boundary problem. It also shows that the problem is not intrinsically related to *chaotic* functions, since an increasing, continuous function can only display *simple dynamics*.The two results convincingly demonstrate that dynamic optimization places non-trivial restrictions on the nature of policy functions, besides continuity.

A similarity between the two examples mentioned above is that these continuous functions are infinitely steep at a fixed point. It might, therefore, be conjectured that the 'correct' extension of the Boldrin–Montrucchio result should be to the class of Lipschitz-continuous functions. While we leave this as an open question, we note that even the simple one-sector model of capital accumulation (*á la* Cass-Koopmans) can generate robust examples, in which the policy function is infinitely steep at a fixed point and is, therefore, not Lipschitz continuous.

The second issue stemming from the Boldrin–Montrucchio result is concerned with the restriction on the magnitude of the discount factor at which a given C^2 function is rationalized. This turns out to be particularly important in rationalizing chaotic functions, the context in which these problems arose in the first place.

Clearly, the Boldrin–Montrucchio result can be applied to rationalize the quadratic family of functions, given by,

$$h(x) = \mu x(1 - x) \quad \text{for } x \text{ in } [0, 1] \tag{3}$$

where the family is parametrized by μ, with $0 < \mu \leq 4$. But, it turned out that the dynamic optimization model (Ω, u, δ) constructed by them, to yield the logistic map [given by (3) when $\mu = 4$] as its policy function, had a very low discount factor (about 0.01). This raised the question of whether chaotic optimal policy functions can be ruled out when more 'reasonable' discount factors prevailed, or whether this feature of the dynamic optimization model was simply a shortcoming of the particular method used in its construction.

It is now known that these discount factors restrictions observed in the Boldrin–Montrucchio construction are, in fact, inescapable in rationalizing chaotic functions. The logistic map, for instance, cannot be rationalized at any discount factor exceeding 0.25, and the tent-map, given by,

$$h(x) = \begin{cases} 2x & \text{for } 0 \leq x \leq 0.5 \\ 2 - 2x & \text{for } 0.5 \leq x \leq 1 \end{cases} \tag{4}$$

cannot be rationalized for any discount factor exceeding 0.5. Both of these observations can be obtained quite simply from the two results mentioned above, as we show in this paper.

More generally, following the contributions of Sorger (1992a, 1992b, 1994), it has been demonstrated by Mitra (1996) and Nishimura and Yano (1996) that if a continuous function exhibits Li–Yorke chaos (equivalently a period-three cycle), then it can be rationalized only if the associated discount factor satisfies,

$$\delta < [(\sqrt{5} - 1)/2]^2 \tag{5}$$

Furthermore, if the discount factor satisfies the restriction in (5), then one can construct a transition possibility set, Ω, and a reduced-form utility function, u, such that the dynamic optimization model (Ω, u, δ) exhibits Li–Yorke chaos.

It is worth making a remark about our approach to the class of problems discussed above. We indicated that two distinct characterizations (a 'primal' and a 'dual') have figured prominently in the literature on dynamic optimization models. Weitzman (1973) combined the two approaches to show the existence of shadow prices associated with an optimal programme, such that (generalized) profit was maximized at each date at the optimal program, a transversality condition was satisfied, and in addition, these shadow prices also supported the value function at each date. The results established in this paper follow quite simply from an application of his characterization of optimality.

2. PRELIMINARIES

2.1 DYNAMICAL SYSTEMS

Let I be an interval in $\Re$, the set of reals. Let $f: I \rightarrow I$ be a continuous map of the interval I into itself. The pair (I, f) is called a *dynamical system*; I is called the *state space* and f the *law of motion* of the dynamical system.

We write $f^0(x) = x$ and for any integer $n \geq 1, f^n(x) = f[f^{n-1}(x)]$. If $x \in I$, the sequence $\tau(x) = \{f^n(x)\}_0^\infty$ is called the *trajectory* from (the initial condition) x. The *orbit* from x is the set $\gamma(x) = \{y : y = f^n(x)$ for some $n \geq 0\}$.

A point $x \in I$ is a *fixed point* of f if $f(x) = x$. A point $x \in I$ is called a *periodic point* of f if there is $k \geq 1$ such that $f^k(x) = x$. The smallest such k is called the *period* of x. [In particular, if $x \in I$ is a fixed point of f, it is periodic with period 1.] If $x \in I$ is a periodic point with period k, we also say that the orbit of x (or trajectory from x) is periodic with period k.

The following fundamental result on the existence of periodic orbits is due to Sarkovskii (1964).

PROPOSITION 1 (Sarkovskii): Let the positive integers be totally ordered in the following way:

$$3 \prec 5 \prec 7 \prec 9 \prec \ldots \prec 2 \bullet 3 \prec 2 \bullet 5 \prec \ldots \prec 2^2 \bullet 3 \prec 2^2 \bullet 5 \prec \ldots \prec 2^3 \prec 2^2 \prec 2 \prec 1$$

If f has a periodic orbit of period n and if $n \prec m$, then f also has a periodic orbit of period m.

In order to study the nature of trajectories which are not periodic, it is useful to define a *scrambled* set. A set $S \subset I$ is called a *scrambled set* if it possesses the following two properties.

(i) If $x, y \in S$ with $x \neq y$, then,

$$\limsup_{n \to \infty} |f^n(x) - f^n(y)| > 0$$

and

$$\liminf_{n \to \infty} |f^n(x) - f^n(y)| = 0$$

(ii) If $x \in S$ and y is any periodic point of f,

$$\limsup_{n \to \infty} |f^n(x) - f^n(y)| > 0$$

Thus trajectories starting from points in a scrambled set are not even 'asymptotically periodic'. Furthermore, for any pair of initial states in the scrambled set, the trajectories move apart and return close to each other infinitely often.[1]

The following theorem, due to Li and Yorke (1975), is fundamental in establishing a connection between the existence of period-three cycles and the existence of an uncountable scrambled set.

PROPOSITION 2. (Li and Yorke): Assume that there is some point x^* in I such that:

$$f^3(x^*) \leq x^* < f(x^*) < f^2(x^*) \ (\text{or } f^3(x^*) \geq x^* > f(x^*) > f^2(x^*)) \tag{6}$$

Then (i) for every positive integer $k = 1, 2, \ldots,$ there is a periodic point of period k;

(ii) there is an uncountable scrambled set $S \subset I$.

We will say that the dynamical system (I, f) exhibits *Li–Yorke chaos* if conditions (i) and (ii) of Proposition 2 are satisfied.[2] It is easy to check that (I, f) exhibits Li-Yorke chaos if and only if (I, f) has a periodic point of period three.

[1]Property (ii) is meant to capture the aspect of 'irregular' or 'erratic' behaviour. It means that long-run behaviour of this dynamical system cannot be approximated by regular periodic motion, however long the period of the cycles. Property (i), on the other hand, is meant to capture the aspect of sensitive dependence of the system to initial conditions. Thus, small (computation or estimtion) errors in initial conditions can be transformed into large errors over time, making 'intermediate-run' predictions inaccurate.

The reader is referred to Block and Coppel (1992) and Devaney (1989) for further discussion of these issues.

[2]The reason for including condition (i) in the definition of chaos should be explained. The point of view being expressed here (as in much of the literature on 'topological' chaos) is that the concept of chaos should involve 'complicated behaviour' but also a certain amount of 'regularity'. The existence of a scrambled set is meant to capture the first aspect, and the presence of the periodic points the second.

There are, of course, variations on condition (i) that have been used. It has been suggested that one could use, instead of (i), 'there is a positive integer k^* such that for every positive integer $k \geq k^*$, there is a periodic point of period k'. Or, one could use, instead of (i), 'there are infinitely many periodic points of different periods'. From the point of view of obtaining discount factor restrictions assocated with chaotic optimal behaviour (discussed in Section 5), these alternate definitions do, of course, make a difference. The first variation mentioned above continues to impose strong discount factor restrictions for chaotic optimal behaviour [see Mitra (1996)], the second variation does not [see Nishimura and Yano (1995)].

2.2 Dynamic Optimization

The standard framework of dynamic optimization is described by a triplet (Ω, u, δ), where Ω, a subset of $\Re_+ \times \Re_+$, is a 'transition possibility set', $u : \Omega - \Re$ is a *utility function* defined on this set, and δ is the *discount factor* satisfying $0 < \delta < 1$.

The transition possibility set describes the states $z \in \Re_+$ that it is possible to go to tomorrow, if one is in the state $x \in \Re_+$ today. We define a correspondence $\Gamma : \Re_+ \to \Re_+$ by $\Gamma(x) = \{y \in \Re_+ : (x, y) \in \Omega\}$ for each $x \in \Re_+$.

A programme $\{x_t\}_0^\infty$ from $x \in \Re_+$ is a sequence satisfying,

$$x_0 = x \text{ and } (x_t, x_{t+1}) \in \Omega \quad \text{for } t \geq 0$$

If one is in state x today and one moves to state z tomorrow [with $(x, y) \in \Omega$] then there is an immediate utility (or 'reward' or 'return') generated, measured by the utility function, u.

The discount factor, δ, is the weight assigned to tomorrow's utility (compared to today's) in the objective function. The *discount rate* (associated with the discount factor, δ) is given by $\rho = (1/\delta) - 1$.

The following assumptions are imposed on the transition possibility set, Ω:

(A.1) (i) $(0, 0) \in \Omega$, (ii) $(0, z) \in \Omega$ implies $z = 0$.
(A.2) Ω is (i) closed, and (ii) convex.
(A.3) There is $\xi > 0$ such that $(x, z) \in \Omega$ and $x \geq \xi$ implies $z < x$.
(A.4) If $(x, z) \in \Omega$ and $x' \geq x$, $0 \leq z' \leq z$ then $(x', z') \in \Omega$.

Clearly, we can pick $0 < \zeta < \xi$, such that if $x > \zeta$ and $(x, z) \in \Omega$, then $z < x$. It is straightforward to verify that if $(x, z) \in \Omega$, then $z \leq \max(\zeta, x)$. It follows from this that if $\{x_t\}_0^\infty$ is a programme from

[3]The distinction between ξ and ζ should be explained. Clearly ζ can be a 'maximum sustainable stock', while ξ cannot. Thus $Y = [0, \xi]$ is a somewhat larger closed interval than the state space $X = [0, \zeta]$, where the important dynamics will take place.

The distinction is made with assumption (A.7) in mind. It would have been nice to simply assume the monotone property of u on Ω. But this creates problems in establishing (the sufficiency part of) Theorem 3. The assumption (A.7) states that the monotone property of u holds on Ω, when x, x' are restricted to the closed interval, Y. The point about Y instead of X appearing in this definition is that the sufficiency part of Theorem 3 can be established even when u is required to be monotone on Y, rather than merely on X. [The necessity part of Theorem 3 is valid even when X is used instead of Y in the statement of assumption (A.7).]

$x \in \Re_+$ then $x_t \leq \max(\zeta, x)$ for $t \geq 0$. In particular, if $x \leq \zeta$, then $x_t \leq \zeta$ for $t \geq 0$. This leads us to choose the closed interval $[0, \zeta]$ as the natural state space of our model, which we will denote by X. We denote the interval $[0, \xi]$ by Y.[3]

The following assumptions are imposed on the utility function, u:

(A.5) u is concave on Ω; further if (x, z) and (x', z') are in Ω, and $x \neq x'$, then for every $0 < \lambda < 1$, $u[\lambda(x, z) + (1 - \lambda)(x', z')] > \lambda u(x, z) + (1 - \lambda)u(x', z')$.

(A.6) u is upper semi-continuous in Ω.

(A.7) If $x, x' \in Y$, $(x, z) \in \Omega$, $x' \geq x$ and $0 \leq z' \leq z$, then $u(x', z') \geq u(x, z)$.

We will refer to a triplet (Ω, u, δ) satisfying (A.1)–(A.7) as a *dynamic optimization model*. A programme $\{\hat{x}_t\}_0^\infty$ from $x \geq 0$ is an 'optimal programme' if,

$$\sum_0^\infty \delta^t u(x_t, x_{t+1}) \leq \sum_0^\infty \delta^t u(\hat{x}_t, \hat{x}_{t+1})$$

for every programme $\{x_t\}_0^\infty$ from x.

2.3 Two Examples

We now provide two examples of dynamic optimization problems in economics which can be studied by converting them to the 'reduced-form' problem described in the previous sub-section.

Example 1. Optimal Exploitation of a Renewable Resource

The state variable, x, here is to be interpreted as the *resource stock*. The future population of the stock is determined from the present population by means of a 'reproduction' or 'recruitment' function, f.

If we denote the harvest of the resource (the control variable) by c, then the *return* at any date is dependent on the harvest, c, and the stock, x, through a function, w. Given a discount factor, δ, the problem of resource management is to determine the sequence of harvests which will maximize the discounted sum of returns.

Formally, the model[4] is specified by (f, w, δ), where,

(a) $f: \Re_+ \to \Re_+$ is a *stock-recruitment function* satisfying, $f(0) = 0$, f is increasing, strictly concave and continuous with

$$\lim_{x \to \infty} [f(x)/x] < 1;$$

[4]Majumdar and Mitra (1994) have established the possibility (and robustness) of chaotic behaviour in this aggregative model.

(b) $w : \Re_+^2 \to \Re$ is a *return function* satisfying,

   (i) $w(x, c)$ is continuous in (x, c);

   (ii) $w(x, c)$ is non-decreasing in c (given x) and in x (given c); also it is increasing in c if $x > 0$;

   (iii) $w(x, c)$ is concave in (x, c); also it is strictly concave in c if $x > 0$;

(c) $0 < \delta < 1$ is a *discount factor*.

A *programme* from x is a sequence $\{x_t\}$ such that:

$$x_0 = x, 0 \leq x_{t+1} \leq f(x_t) \quad \text{for } t \geq 0$$

Associated with a programme $\{x_t\}$ is a sequence of harvests $\{c_{t+1}\}$:

$$c_{t+1} = f(x_t) - x_{t+1} \quad \text{for } t \geq 0$$

A programme $\{x_t^*\}$ from x is optimal if,

$$\sum_0^\infty \delta^t w(x_t^*, c_{t+1}^*) \leq \sum_0^\infty \delta^t w(x_t, c_{t+1})$$

for every programme $\{x_t\}$ from x.

If we define $\Omega = \{(x, z) \text{ in } \Re_+^2 : 0 \leq z \leq f(x)\}$, and for all (x, z) in Ω, $u(x, z) = w(x, f(x) - z)$, then the *reduced-form model* (Ω, u, δ) satisfies assumptions (A.1)–(A.7), and programmes (optimal programmes) in the reduced-form model correspond exactly to programmes (optimal programmes) in the primitive form of the model.

Notice that we allow for a 'stock effect' in the return function, but our assumptions allow us to consider the special case in which the return, w, is independent of the stock, x. In that case, the above model is formally equivalent to the one-sector neoclassical optimal growth model, *à la* Cass–Koopmans.

EXAMPLE 2. Two Sector Model of Optimal Economic Growth

Formally, the model is specified by (f, g, μ, δ) where,

(a) the *production function* in the *consumption good sector*, $f : \Re_+^2 \to \Re_+$, satisfies;

   (i) f is continuous on $\Re_+^2$,

   (ii) f is non-decreasing on $\Re_+^2$ and increasing on $\Re_{++}^2$,

   (iii) f is concave on $\Re_+^2$, and strictly concave in the first argument (capital) when the second argument (labour) is positive;

(b) the *production function* in the *investment good sector,* $g : \Re^2_+ \rightarrow \Re_+$, satisfies;

(i) g is continuous on $\Re^2_+$,

(ii) g is non-decreasing on $\Re^2_+$ and increasing on $\Re^2_{++}$

(iii) g is concave on $\Re^2_+$, and strictly concave in the first argument (capital) when the second argument (labour) is positive,

(iv) $\lim_{K \rightarrow \infty} [g(K, 1)/K] < 1$;

(c) the *depreciation factor*, μ, satisfies $0 \leq \mu < 1$;

(d) the *discount factor*, δ, satisfies $0 < \delta < 1$.

A *programme* from x is a sequence $\{k_t, n_t, x_t\}$ such that,

$$x_0 = x, \text{ and } 0 \leq n_t \leq 1, 0 \leq k_t \leq x_t \quad \text{for } t \geq 0$$

$$x_{t+1} = \mu x_t + g(x_t - k_t, 1 - n_t) \quad \text{for } t \geq 0$$

Associated with a programme $\{k_t, n_t, x_t\}$ from x is a *consumption sequence* $\{c_{t+1}\}$ given by,

$$c_{t+1} = f(k_t, n_t) \quad \text{fo } t \geq 0$$

A programme $\{k_t^*, n_t^*, x_t^*\}$ is *optimal* if

$$\sum_0^\infty \delta^t c_{t+1}^* \geq \sum_0^\infty \delta^t c_{t+1}$$

for every programme $\{k_t, n_t, x_t\}$ from x.

If we define,

$$\Omega = \{(x, z) \text{ in } \Re^2_+ : z \leq \mu x + g(x, 1)\},$$

and for all (x, z) in Ω, define,

$$u(x, z) = \max f(k, n)$$

subject to

$$0 \leq k \leq x$$

$$0 \leq n \leq 1$$

$$z \leq \mu x + g(x - k, 1 - n)$$

then the 'reduced form model' (Ω, u, δ) satisfies assumptions (A.1)–(A.7) and optimal programmes in the reduced-form model correspond exactly to optimal programmes in the primitive form of the model.[5]

[5]Boldrin and Montrucchio (1986) have established the possibility of chaotic behaviour in a two-sector model similar to this one.

3. DYNAMIC PROGRAMMING AND DUALITY THEORY

3.1 The Dynamic Programming Approach

Under the maintained assumptions of the previous section [(A.1)–(A.7)], it is standard exercise to show that there is a unique optimal programme from every $x \in \Re_+$. This leads us to define the value and policy functions as follows.

The *value function* $V : \Re_+ \to \Re$ is defined by,

$$V(x) = \sum_{0}^{\infty} \delta^t u(\hat{x}_t, \hat{x}_{t+1})$$

where $\{\hat{x}_t\}_0^\infty$ is the optimal programme from $x \in \Re_+$.

The 'policy function' $h : \Re_+ \to \Re_+$ is defined by,

$$h(x) = \hat{x}_1$$

where $\{\hat{x}_t\}_0^\infty$ is the optimal program from $x \in \Re_+$.

The properties of the value and policy functions can be summarized in the following result. This is based on Dutta and Mitra (1989) and Stokey, Lucas and Prescott (1989).

Proposition 3:

(i) The value function V is strictly concave and continuous on $\Re_+$ and non-decreasing on Y. Further, V is the unique continuous function on $Y \equiv [0, \xi]$ which satisfies the functional equation of dynamic programming,

$$V(x) = \max_{y \in \Gamma(x)} [u(x, y) + \delta V(y)]$$

(ii) The policy function h satisfies the following property: for each $x \in \Re_+$, $h(x)$ is the unique solution to the constrained maximization problem,

Maximize $\quad u(z, y) + \delta V(y)$

Subject to $\quad y \in \Gamma(x)$

Further, h is continuous on $\Re_+$, and $h(0) = 0$.

Remarks:

(i) In view of the definition of the policy function h, the optimal programme from $x \in X$ is the trajectory $\{h^t(x)\}_0^\infty$ generated by the policy function. Thus, an optimal programme from $x \in X$ can be called *periodic* (with period k) if x is a periodic point of h (with period k).

(ii) Since V is concave on $\Re_+$, it has well-defined left-hand and right-hand derivatives for all $x > 0$, which we denote by $\mu(x)$ and $\nu(x)$ respectively. If $x > y > 0$, then we have $\mu(y) \geq \nu(y) > \mu(x) \geq \nu(x)$, the strict inequality following from the strict concavity of V.

We will find it convenient to state a result here [see Mitra (1996) for a proof] which compares the value and policy functions of two dynamic optimization models. To proceed more formally, let us refer to a triplet (Ω, u, δ) satisfying (A.1)–(A.7) as a *dynamic optimization model*. Now, let $\Im = (\Omega, u, \delta)$ be a dynamic optimization model, with value function V and policy function h. We can then construct another dynamic optimization model $\Im^* = (\Omega^*, u^*, \delta^*)$ with $\delta^* = \delta^2$, such that the policy function, h^* of $\Im^*$ is h^2 and the value function, V^*, of $\Im^*$ is V.

PROPOSITION 4: Let $\Im = (\Omega, u, \delta)$ be a dynamic optimization model, with value function V and policy function h. Then, there exists Ω^* and u^* satisfying (A.1)–(A.7) such that with $\delta^* = \delta^2$, (i) the value function V^*, of the dynamic optimization model $\Im^* = (\Omega^*, u^*, \delta^*)$ is given by V, and (ii) the policy function, h^*, of $\Im^*$ is given by h^2.

3.2 DUALITY THEORY

Optimality can be characterized in terms of dual variables or shadow prices. At the shadow prices supporting an optimal programme, there is no activity which yields a higher 'generalized profit' at any date (value of utility plus value of terminal stocks minus value of initial stocks at that date) than the activity chosen along the optimal programme at that date. It was observed by Weitzman (1973) that these shadow prices support the value function as well.[6] The basic result of the theory, describing this characterization, can be stated as follows. [A full discussion can be found in Weitzman (1973) and McKenzie (1986).]

PROPOSITION 5: (Weitzman)

(a) If $\{x_t\}_0^\infty$ is an optimal programme from $x \in X$ and $x > 0$, and there is some $(\bar{x}, \bar{y}) \in \Omega$ with $\bar{y} > 0$ then there is a sequence $\{p_t\}_0^\infty$ of non-negative prices such that for $t \geq 0$,

(i) $\delta^t V(x_t) - p_t x_t \geq \delta^t V(x) - p_t x$ for all $x \geq 0$

[6]Weitzman's *proof* of this price characterization of optimality also fully exploited Bellman's principle of optimality.

(ii) $\delta^t u(x_t, x_{t+1}) + p_{t+1}x_{t+1} - p_t x_t \geq \delta^t u(x, y) + p_{t+1}y - p_t x$ for all $(x, y) \in \Omega$

(iii) $\lim_{t \to \infty} p_t x_t = 0$

(b) If $\{x_t\}_0^\infty$ is a programme from $x \geq 0$, and there is a sequence $\{p_t\}_0^\infty$ of non-negative prices such that for $t \geq 0$, (ii) and (iii) above are satisfied, then $\{x_t\}_0^\infty$ is an optimal programme from x.

If $\{x_t\}_0^\infty$ is a programme from $x \geq 0$, and $\{p_t\}_0^\infty$ is non-negative sequence of prices satisfying (i), (ii) and (iii) of Proposition 5(a), we will say that the program $\{x_t\}_0^\infty$ is price supported by $\{p_t\}_0^\infty$. When $\{x_t\}_0^\infty$ is price supported by $\{p_t\}_0^\infty$, we refer to $\{p_t\}_0^\infty$ as a sequence of *present-value prices*. Associated with $\{p_t\}_0^\infty$ is a sequence $\{p_t\}_0^\infty$ of *current value prices* defined by,

$$P_t = (p_t/\delta^t) \quad \text{for } t \geq 0$$

This price characterization of optimality leads to a basic tool for analyzing the nature of policy functions which we state in the following proposition.[7]

PROPOSITION 6: Let (Ω, u, δ) be a dynamic optimization model. Suppose $\{x_t\}_0^\infty$ is an optimal programme with price support $\{p_t\}_0^\infty$ and $\{y_t\}_0^\infty$ is an optimal programme with price support $\{q_t\}_0^\infty$. Denoting (p_t/δ^t) by P_t and (q_t/δ^t) by Q_t for $t \geq 0$, we have,

(i) $\delta(P_{t+1} - Q_{t+1})(y_{t+1} - x_{t+1}) \leq (P_t - Q_t)(y_t - x_t)$ for $t \geq 0$

(ii) $(P_t - Q_t)(y_t - x_t) \geq 0$ for $t \geq 0$

Furthermore, if $y_t \neq x_t$ for some t, then the inequalities in (i) and (ii) are strict for that t.

Proof: Let $\{x_t\}_0^\infty$ be an optimal programme with price support $\{p_t\}_0^\infty$, and $\{y_t\}_0^\infty$ be an optimal programme with price support $\{q_t\}_0^\infty$. Then using (ii) of Proposition 5, we get,

$$\delta^t u(x_t, x_{t+1}) + p_{t+1}x_{t+1} - p_t x_t \geq \delta^t u(y_t, y_{t+1}) + p_{t+1}y_{t+1} - p_t y_t \quad (6)$$

[7]The inequalities of Proposition 6 are very familiar objects from the point of view of the turnpike theory literature, where they suggest a natural choice of a Lyapunov function for the study of global asymptotic stability of optimal growth paths; see especially Cass and Shell (1976) and McKenzie (1986). The same inequalities have figured prominently in the literature on the intertemporal decentralization of the transversality condition; see Brock and Majumdar (1988), and Dasgupta and Mitra (1988).

and

$$\delta^t u(y_t, y_{t+1}) + q_{t+1}y_{t+1} - q_t y_t \geq \delta^t u(x_t, x_{t+1}) + q_{t+1}x_{t+1} - q_t x_t \quad (7)$$

Adding (6) and (7) and cancelling common terms,

$$(q_t - p_t)(x_t - y_t) \geq (q_{t+1} - p_{t+1})(x_{t+1} - y_{t+1}) \quad (8)$$

Denoting (p_t/δ^t) by P_t and (q_t/δ^t) by Q_t, we get (i). By (A.5), the inequality in (i) is strict when $x_t \neq y_t$.

Using (i) of Proposition 5, we get,

$$\delta^t V(x_t) - p_t x_t \geq \delta^t V(y_t) - p_t y_t \quad (9)$$

and

$$\delta^t V(y_t) - q_t y_t \geq \delta^t V(x_t) - q_t x_t \quad (10)$$

Adding (9) and (10) and cancelling common terms,

$$(q_t - p_t)(x_t - y_t) \geq 0 \quad (11)$$

which yields (ii), upon dividing (11) by δ^t. By the strict concavity of V, the inequality in (ii) is strict when $y_t \neq x_t$.

4. THE NATURE OF POLICY FUNCTIONS

4.1 The Boldrin–Montrucchio Result

We know (from Proposition 3) that given a dynamic optimization model (Ω, u, δ) satisfying (A.1)–(A.7), the policy function, $h : \Re_+ \to \Re_+$, is continuous on $\Re_+$ and $h(0) = 0$. We now ask the following question: Are these the only restrictions on the policy function that the exercise of dynamic optimization imposes?

The starting point of the discussion regarding an answer to this question is, of course, the result of Boldrin and Montrucchio (1986), who showed that if h is any, twice continuously differentiable function, then one can always construct a dynamic optimization model, such that h is the policy function of that model. We state the result here in a slightly modified form, since the maintained assumptions on a dynamic optimization model that we use differ from theirs.

Propositon 7: (Boldrin and Montrucchio) Let h: $\Re_+ \to \Re_+$ be any C^2 function on $\Re_+$ satisfying $h(0) = 0$. Then, there is dynamic optimization model (Ω, u, δ), such that its policy function, H, coincides with h on the state space X, associated with it.

This result has sometimes been interpreted as showing that dynamic optimization imposes no non-trivial restrictions on the nature of the policy function. The rest of this section is devoted to examining the validity of this claim.

We should observe at this point that differentiability of the policy function of a dynamic optimization model has been obtained only under quite strong restrictions [see Araujo (1991), Santos (1991)]. This indicates that it is not a 'natural' restriction imposed by the optimization exercise. Indeed, if we consider the standard, two-sector model of optimal economic growth (see Example 2 in Section 'Preliminaries'), with fully-depreciating capital ($\mu = 0$) and with Cobb–Douglas production functions [$f(k, n) = k^a n^{1-a}$ and $g(K, N) = K^{\alpha} N^{1-\alpha}$], such that the consumption goods sector is more capital-intensive than the capital goods, sector [$a > \alpha$], then the policy function will be a tent-like map with a kink in the interior of the associated state space [see Nishimura and Yano (1994) for a demonstration of this interesting result].

This means that there is no hope of strengthening Proposition 3 to conclude differentiability (and certainly, twice continuous differentiability) of the policy function, *even if the primitives of the model (utility and production functions) were smooth.*[8]

Recognition of this fact compels us to consider the C^2 restriction in the Boldrin–Montrucchio result as a strong one, and consequently, it becomes important to examine whether their result can be extended to the class of continuous functions. Neumann et al. (1988) have shown that we can replace the C^2 restriction in Proposition 7 with the restriction that h be C^1 and the derivative of h be Lipschitz continuous.[9] As we have already argued, we have to address the problem where h is continuous, but not necessarily differentiable, and so, this extension result is not useful in this regard.

One route to a possible extension of the Boldrin–Montrucchio result is to uniformly approximate the given continuous function (using the famous Weierstrass theorem) by polynomials (which are, of course,

[8]The differentiability of the *value function* (in the interior of the state space) can be considered to be a 'natural restriction' imposed by the optimization exercise; see Benveniste and Scheinkman (1979).

[9]Unlike the Boldrin-Montrucchio paper, where the state space is a subset of $\mathbb{R}^n$, the paper of Neumann et al. (1988) deals entirely with the special framework, in which the state space is a subset of $\mathbb{R}$. However, the result of Neumann et al. has been established in the more general framework, by using a different method of proof, in Montrucchio (1994).

C^2 functions), and use the Boldrin–Montrucchio result on the sequence of approximating functions. But, obtaining a dynamic optimization model as the limit of the associated sequence of dynamic optimization models, which will yield the limiting function as its policy function, turns out to be a major obstacle, even under uniform approximation.

In fact, we will show below, by examining the nature of policy functions at their *fixed points* (boundary or interior) that the Boldrin–Montrucchio result *cannot* be extended to the class of continuous functions. We turn to this demonstration in the next sub-section.

4.2 Behaviour of a Policy Function Near a Fixed Point

We will present two results in this sub-section which will show that the optimization exercise imposes non-trivial restriction on the nature of the policy function near fixed points.[10] Our first result explores such restrictions at a boundary fixed point, and the second at an interior fixed point.[11]

Theorem 1: Suppose $h : \mathfrak{R}_+ \to \mathfrak{R}_+$ is a continuous function, and there is $b > 0$, such that,

$$h(0) = 0 = h(b) \tag{12}$$

If h is the optimal policy function of a dynamic optimization model (Ω, u, δ), then,

$$\delta\omega \leq 1 \tag{13}$$

where,

$$\omega \equiv \limsup_{x \to 0} [h(x)/x] \tag{14}$$

Proof: Since (13) is clearly satisfied when $\omega \leq 1$, we consider only the case $\omega > 1$. This means, in particular, that there is some $a > 0$ such that $h(a) > 0$.

Since h is the optimal policy function of a dynamic optimization model (Ω, u, δ), and $h(b) = 0$, the sequence $(b, 0, 0, \ldots)$ is the optimal

[10]By Proposition 4, and its obvious extension to (h^n, δ^n) where $n \geq 2$ [see Sorger (1992b) for a version of such a result], we conclude that the optimization exercise also imposes non-trivial restrictions on the nature of the policy function near periodic points.

[11]Sorger (1992a, 1992b) obtains a discount factor restriction under a condition like (12), but he also requires h to be surjective, which makes it less widely applicable than our result.

programme from b. By Proposition 5, it can be price-supported by $(r_0, r_1, r_2, \ldots)$ since $h(a) > 0$. Then the sequence $(0, 0, \ldots)$ is price supported by $(p_0, p_1, p_2 \ldots)$ where $p_t = r_{t+1}$ for $t \geq 0$.

We claim that there is $\hat{p}$ such that p_t can be chosen to be $\delta^t \hat{p}$ for $t \geq 0$. To see this, denote the current-value price sequence associated with $(p_0, p_1, p_2, \ldots)$ by $(P_0, P_1, P_2, \ldots)$ and note that for all $t \geq 0$,

$$u(x, y) + \delta P_{t+1} y - P_t x \leq u(0, 0) \quad \text{for all } (x, y) \in \Omega$$

and

$$V(x) - P_t x \leq V(0) \quad \text{for all } x \geq 0$$

We divide our analysis into two sub-cases.

Case (i): Suppose $P_{t+1} \geq P_t$ for some $t = \tau$. Then, it follows that,

$$u(x, y) + \delta P_\tau y - P_\tau x \leq u(0, 0) \quad \text{for all } (x, y) \in \Omega$$

and

$$V(x) - P_\tau x \leq V(0) \quad \text{for all } x \geq 0$$

Thus, choosing $\hat{P} = P_\tau$, the claim is established.

Case (ii): Suppose $P_{t+1} < P_t$ for all $t \geq 0$. Then P_t converges to some $P \geq 0$, and so,

$$u(x, y) + \delta P y - P x \leq u(0, 0) \quad \text{for all } (x, y) \in \Omega$$

and

$$V(x) - P x \leq V(0) \quad \text{for all } x \geq 0$$

Thus, choosing $\hat{P} = P$, the claim is established again.

Since $\omega > 1$, there is a sequence $x^s \to 0$ such that $h(x^s) > x^s > 0$ for $s = 1, 2, 3, \ldots$, and $\omega = \lim_{s \to \infty} [h(x^s)/x^s]$. Using Proposition 5, for each s, the optimal programme can be price-supported by $(p_0^s, p_1^s, \ldots)$, with associated current price sequence $(P_0^s, P_1^s, \ldots)$. Using Proposition 6, we then have,

$$\delta(\hat{P} - P_1^s)(h(x^s) - 0) \leq (\hat{P} - P_0^s)(x^s - 0)$$

Now, we have, by the strict concavity of V, $\hat{P} > \mu(x^s) \geq P_0^s \geq \nu(x^s) > \mu(h(x^s)) \geq P_1^s$, where $\mu(\nu)$ denotes the left (right) hand derivative of V. Thus, we get,

$$\delta[h(x^s)/x^s] \leq (\hat{P} - P_0^s)/(\hat{P} - P_1^s) < 1$$

and letting $s \to \infty$, we obtain $\delta\omega \leq 1$.

Theorem 1 allows us to write down a family of continuous functions, h, with $h(0) = 0$, which cannot be policy functions of any dynamic optimization model.

COROLLARY 1: Suppose $h(x) = \mu x^a(1 - x^a)$, where $0 < \mu \leq 4$, $0 < a < 1$, and $x \in [0, 1]$, then there is no dynamic optimization model (Ω, u, δ), whose optimal policy function is given by h on $[0, 1]$.

Corollary 1 raises the question of whether the difficulty in extending the Boldrin–Montrucchio result to continuous functions is a 'boundary phenomenon' similar to that in the Sonnenschein–Mantel–Debreu theorem on market excess-demand functions [see Shafer and Sonnenschein (1982)]. Our next result on the behaviour of a policy function near an interior fixed point indicates that this is not the case.[12]

Theorem 2: Suppose $h : \Re_+ \to \Re_+$ is a continuous function, and there is $b > 0$, such that,

$$b = h(b) \tag{15}$$

If h is the optimal policy function of a dynamic optimization model (Ω, u, δ), then,

$$\delta\theta \leq 1 \tag{16}$$

where,

$$\theta \equiv \limsup_{x \downarrow b} \{[h(x) - h(b)]/[x - b]\} \tag{17}$$

Proof: Since (16) is clearly satisfied when $\theta \leq 1$, we consider only the case in which $\theta > 1$. This means that there is a sequence $\{x^s\}_{s=1}^{\infty}$ such that $h(x^s) > x^s > b$ and $[h(x^s) - h(b)]/(x^s - b)$ converges to θ as $s \to \infty$.

Since $h(b) = b$, the sequence $(b, b, b, \ldots)$ is the optimal programme from b, and can be price-supported by $(p_0, p_1, \ldots)$. Using the method of Sutherland (1967) and McKenzie (1986), we can find $\hat{P}$ such that p_t can be chosen to be $\delta^t \hat{P}$ for $t \geq 0$.

Using Proposition 5, for each $s = 1, 2, 3, \ldots$, the optimal programme from x^s can be price-supported by $(p_0^s, p_1^s, \ldots)$, with associated current price sequence $(P_0^s, P_1^s, \ldots)$. Using Proposition 6,

$$\delta(\hat{P} - P_1^s)(h(x^s) - b) \leq (\hat{P} - P_0^s)(x^s - b)$$

[12]A similar result is established in Hewage and Neumann (1990), by using methods different from ours.

By the strict concavity of V, we have $\hat{P} > \mu(x^s) \geq P_0^s \geq \nu(x^s) > \mu(h(x^s)) \geq P_1^s$, where $\mu(\nu)$ denotes the left (right) hand derivative of V. Thus, we get,

$$\delta(h(x^s) - b)/(x^s - b) \leq (\hat{P} - P_0^s)/(\hat{P} - P_1^s) < 1$$

and so, letting $s \to \infty$, we obtain $\delta\theta \leq 1$.

Theorem 2 allows us to write down a continuous, increasing, function, h, with $h(0) = 0$, which cannot be the policy function of any dynamic optimization model, even on a restricted domain which excludes the boundary of the natural state space.

COROLLARY 2: Suppose $h(x) = 1 + (x - 1)^{1/3}$ for $x \in [0, 1]$. Given any $0 \leq \varepsilon < 1$, there is no dynamic optimization model (Ω, u, δ) whose optimal policy function is given by h on $[\varepsilon, 2 - \varepsilon]$.

Both Corollary 1 and Corollary 2 provide examples of continuous functions, with unbounded steepness at some point of the relevant domain. One might, therefore, conjecture that the Boldrin–Montrucchio result might be extended to the class of Lipschitz continuous policy functions. We leave this as an open question.

We note, however, that even Lipschitz-continuity of the policy function can be ensured only under fairly stringent conditions on the dynamic optimization model [see Montrucchio (1987)]. In fact, if we take the standard neoclassical one-sector model of economic growth [obtained as a special case of Example 1, where there is a function $g : \mathfrak{R}_+ \to \mathfrak{R}_+$ such that $w(x, c) = g(c)$ for all $(x, c) \in \mathfrak{R}_+^2$], it is fairly straightforward to obtain policy functions which do not satisfy Lipschitz-continuity.

To see this let $f(x) = 2x^{1/2}$ for $x \in \mathfrak{R}_+$; $g(c) = 2c^{1/2}$ for $c \in \mathfrak{R}_+$; and $0 < \delta < 1$. We claim that the policy function, h, of this dynamic optimization model satisfies,

$$\limsup_{x \to 0} \, [h(x)/x] = \infty \tag{18}$$

For, suppose there is $0 < M < \infty$, such that,

$$\limsup_{x \to 0} \, [h(x)/x] < M \tag{19}$$

Then, there is $\varepsilon_0 > 0$ such that on $Z = (0, \varepsilon_0)$, $[h(x)/x] \leq M$. Choose $0 < \varepsilon < \varepsilon_0$, such that $(1/\varepsilon^{1/2}) \geq \max\,[M, 2^{1/2}M^{3/4}/\delta]$.

Choose any $x \in (0, \varepsilon)$. We know that an optimal programme from x is interior ($x_t > 0$ and $c_{t+1} > 0$ for $t \geq 0$), and so, the following

Ramsey-Euler equation holds,

$$[g'(c_1)/g'(c_2)] = \delta f'(x_1) \tag{20}$$

Using (19), we get

$$f(x_1) = f[h(x)] \leq f(Mx) \leq 2M^{1/2}x^{1/2},$$

so that

$$c_2 = f(x_1) - x_2 \leq f(x_1) \leq 2M^{1/2}x^{1/2}.$$

Also,

$$c_1 = f(x) - x_1 = f(x) - h(x) \geq 2x^{1/2} - Mx \geq x^{1/2} + (x^{1/2} - Mx) > x^{1/2}$$

since $(1/x^{1/2}) > M$. Thus, we get,

$$[g'(c_1)/g'(c_2)] < 2^{1/2}M^{1/4} \tag{21}$$

Using (19), we also get $x_1 = h(x) \leq Mx$, so that,

$$\delta f'(x_1) \geq [\delta/x_1^{1/2}] \geq [\delta/M^{1/2}x^{1/2}] \tag{22}$$

Combining (20), (21), and (22), we obtain,

$$2^{1/2}M^{1/4} > [\delta/M^{1/2}x^{1/2}]$$

so that,

$$[2^{1/2}M^{3/4}/\delta] > [1/x^{1/2}] > [1/\varepsilon^{1/2}]$$

But this contradicts the definition of ε, and establishes our claim (18).

5. DISCOUNT FACTOR RESTRICTIONS FOR CHAOTIC POLICY FUNCTION

When Boldrin and Montrucchio applied their result to the logistic function,

$$h(x) = 4x(1 - x) \quad \text{for } x \in [0, 1]$$

they found a dynamic optimization model $[\Omega, u, \delta]$ whose policy function coincides with h on $[0, 1]$, and the discount factor, δ, of this constructed dynamic optimization model was approximately 0.01. This discount factor was considered to be 'low'. Let us follow Nishimura and Sorger (1996) to explain what we mean by this.

Let the model's time period be equal to $m > 0$ years. Let r be the long-run annual real interest rate. Then the discount factor, δ, is related to r and m by the usual formula,

$$\delta = [1/(1 + r)^m]$$

Suppose $r = 5\%$. Then the model's time period is 1 year if $\delta = 0.952$; 10 years if $\delta = 0.614$; 20 years if $\delta = 0.377$.

Thus, if $\delta < 0.5$, then the model's time period (which represents the decision-making time) is longer than 14 years, which is much too long to be realistic.

In the case of the logistic function, a very low discount factor of about 0.01 raised the question of whether the logistic function had actually been 'rationalized'. Of course, it was not clear whether this feature of the dynamic optimization model was simply a shortcoming of the particular method used in its construction, or whether chaotic policy functions could never be rationalized when 'reasonable' discount factors prevailed.

Sorger (1992a, 1992b) began a systematic study of discount factor restrictions that must be satisfied by any dynamic optimization model, which generates a chaotic policy function. These were followed by more definitive results by Sorger (1994), Mitra (1996) and Nishimura and Yano (1996).

We will not try to do justice to all the contributions. Instead, we will show how the two theorems of the previous section, which were used there to obtain restrictions on policy functions generated by dynamic optimization models, can be conveniently used also to obtain discount factor restrictions on the dynamic optimization model generating a logistic, or a tent map as its policy function.

COROLLARY 3: Suppose $h(x) = \mu x(1 - x)$, where $0 < \mu \leq 4$, and $x \in [0, 1]$, and h is the optimal policy function of any dynamic optimization model (Ω, u, δ), then $\delta \leq (1/\mu)$.

Corollary 3 readily follows from Theorem 1, since $h(0) = 0 = h(1)$, and $\omega = \limsup_{x \to 0} [h(x)/x] = \mu$.

The class of functions covered by Corollary 3 is called the 'quadratic family'. The logistic function is a member of this family (obtained when $\mu = 4$), and so, the discount factor restriction on any dynamic optimization model, which generates it as a policy function, is 0.25.

COROLLARY 4: Suppose h_a: [0, 1] – [0, 1] is given by the following family of tent-maps,

$$h_a(x) = \begin{cases} ax & \text{for } 0 \leq x \leq (1/a) \\ [a/(a-1)] - [a/(a-1)]x & \text{for } (1/a) \leq x \leq 1 \end{cases}$$

where $a > 1$, and h_a is the optimal policy function of any dynamic optimization model (Ω, u, δ), then,

$$\delta \leq \min\left[(a-1)/a, 1/a\right]$$

Corollary 4 follows from Theorems 1 and 2. Since $h(0) = 0 = h(1)$, and $\omega \equiv \limsup_{x \to 0} [h(x)/x] = (1/a)$, Theorem 1 implies that,

$$\delta \leq (1/a) \tag{23}$$

The interior fixed point of h_a is at $x_a = a/(2a-1)$. Clearly h_a is decreasing in x at this fixed point, with slope $= -[a/(a-1)]$. Thus, the second iterate of h_a, denoted by h_a^2, is increasing at x_a with slope $a^2/(a-1)^2 > 1$.

Since h_a is the policy function of the dynamic optimization model (Ω, u, δ), using Proposition 4, we can find a dynamic optimization model $(\Omega^*, u^*, \delta^*)$, such that $\delta^* = \delta^2$ and h_a^2 is the policy function of $(\Omega^*, u^*, \delta^*)$. Applying Theorem 2 to h_a^2, and noting that,

$$\theta \equiv \limsup_{x \downarrow x_a} \{[h_a^2(x) - h_a^2(x_a)]/[x - x_a]\} = a^2/(a-1)^2$$

we obtain $\delta^2[a^2/(a-1)^2] \leq 1$, so that,

$$\delta \leq (a-1)/a \tag{24}$$

Combining (23) and (24) yields the corollary.

Note that the symmetric tent-map,

$$h(x) = \begin{cases} 2x & \text{for } 0 \leq x \leq 0.5 \\ 2 - 2x & \text{for } 0.5 \leq x \leq 1 \end{cases}$$

is a member of the family of tent-maps covered by Corollary 4 (obtained when $a = 2$). Thus, the discount factor restriction on any dynamic optimization model, which generates the symmetric tent-map as its policy function, is 0.5. For the non-symmetric cases, the discount factor restriction is more severe than 0.5, for if $a > 2$, then $\delta \leq (1/a) < 0.5$, while if $1 < a < 2$, then $\delta \leq (a-1)/a = 1 - (1/a) < 1 - 0.5 = 0.5$.

While the discount factor restrictions obtained above are very strong indeed, they are derived for specific chaotic functions (logistic or tent-maps). The question arises whether there are uniformly strong restrictions on the discount factor for every dynamic optimization model, whose policy function exhibits Li-Yorke chaos (equivalently, an optimal period-three cycle). Sorger (1994) showed that 'period three implies heavy discounting', and his discount factor restriction was refined independently by Mitra (1996) and Nishimura and Yano (1996) to obtain the following definitive result.

THEOREM 3: Let (Ω, u, δ) be a dynamic optimization model, with a policy function h. If h exhibits Li–Yorke chaos, then,

$$\delta < [(\sqrt{5} - 1)/2]^2 \approx 0.3819 \tag{25}$$

Further, if $0 < \delta < [(\sqrt{5} - 1)/2]^2$, then one can construct (Ω, u) such that (Ω, u, δ) is a dynamic optimization model whose policy function exhibits Li–Yorke chaos.

References

Araujo, A. (1991), 'The Once but not Twice Differentiability of the Policy Function', *Econometrica*, 59, pp. 1383–93.

Benhabib, J. and K. Nishimura (1985), 'Competitive Equilibrium Cycles', *Journal of Economic Theory*, 35, pp. 284–306.

Benveniste, L.M. and J.A. Scheinkman (1979), 'On the Differentiability of the Value Function in Dynamic Models of Economics', *Econometrica*, 47, pp. 727–32.

Block, L.S. and W.A. Coppel (1992), *Dynamics in One Dimension, Lecture Notes in Mathematics 1513*, Berlin: Springer-Verlag.

Boldrin, M. and L. Montrucchio (1986), 'On the Indeterminacy of Capital Accumulation Paths', *Journal of Economic Theory*, 40, pp. 26–39.

Brock, W.A. and M. Majumdar (1988), 'On Characterizing Optimal Competitive Programs in Terms of Decentralizable Conditions', *Journal of Economic Theory*, 45, pp. 262–73.

Cass, D. and K. Shell (1976), 'The Structure and Stability of Competitive Dynamical Systems', *Journal of Economic Theory*, 12, pp. 31–70.

Dasgupta, S. and T. Mitra (1988), 'Characterization of Intertemporal Optimality in Terms of Decentralizable Conditions: The Discounted Case', *Journal of Economic Theory*, 45, pp. 274–87.

Devaney, R.L. (1989), *An Introduction to Chaotic Dynamical Systems*, 2nd edition, New York: Addison-Wesley.

Dutta, P.K. and T. Mitra (1989), 'Maximum Theorems for Convex Structures with an Application to the Theory of Optimal Intertemporal Allocation', *Journal of Mathematical Economics*, 18, pp. 77–86.

Hewage, T.U. and D.A. Neumann (1990), 'Functions not Realizable as Policy Functions in an Optimal Growth Model', Working Paper, Bowling Green State University, Bowling Green OH.

Li, T.Y. and J.A. Yorke (1975), 'Period Three Implies Chaos', *American Mathematical Monthly*, 82, pp. 985–92.

Majumdar, M. and T. Mitra (1994), 'Periodic and Chaotic Programs of Optimal Intertemporal Allocation in an Aggregative Model with Wealth Effects', *Economic Theory*, 4, pp. 649–76.

McKenzie, L.W. (1986), 'Optimal Economic Growth, Turnpike Theorems and Comparative Dynamics', in K.J. Arrow and M.D. Intriligator (eds), *Handbook of Mathematical Economics*, Vol. III, Amsterdam: North-Holland.

Mitra, T. (1996), 'An Exact Discount Factor Restriction for Period-Three Cycles in Dynamic Optimization Models', *Journal of Economic Theory*, 69, pp. 281–305.

Montrucchio, L. (1987), 'Lipschitz Continuous Policy Functions for Strongly Concave Optimization Problems', *Journal of Mathematical Economics*, 16, pp. 259–73.

——— (1994), 'Dynamic Complexity of Optimal Paths and Discount Factors for Strongly Concave Problems', *Journal of Optimization Theory and Applications*, 80, pp. 385–406.

Neumann, D.A., T. O'Brien, J. Hoag and K. Kim (1988), 'Policy Functions for Capital Accumulation Paths', *Journal of Economic Theory*, 46, pp. 205–14.

Nishimura, K. and G. Sorger (1996), 'Optimal Cycles and Chaos: A Survey', *Studies in Nonlinear Dynamics and Econometrics*, 1, pp. 11–28.

Nishimura K and M. Yano (1994), 'Optimal Chaos, Nonlinearity and Feasibility Conditions', *Economic Theory*, 4, pp. 689–704.

——— (1995), 'Nonlinear Dynamics and Chaos in Optimal Growth: An Example', *Econometrica*, 63, pp. 981–1001.

——— (1996), 'On the Least Upper Bound of Discount Factors that are Compatible with Optimal Period-Three Cycles', *Journal of Economic Theory*, 69, pp. 306–33.

Santos, M.S. (1991), 'Smoothness of the Policy Function in Discrete-Time Economic Models', *Econometrica*, 59, pp. 1365–82.

Sarkovskii, A.N. (1964), 'Coexistence of Cycles of a Continuous Map of a Line into Itself', *Ukr. Math. Zh.*, 16, pp. 61–71.

Shafer, W. and H. Sonnenschein (1982), 'Market Demand and Excess Demand Functions', in K.J. Arrow and M.D. Intriligator (eds), *Handbook of Mathematical Economics*, vol. II, Amsterdam: North-Holland, pp. 671–93.

Sorger, G. (1992a), 'On the Minimum Rate of Impatience for Complicated Optimal Growth Paths', *Journal of Economic Theory*, 12, pp. 11–30.

——— (1992b), *Minimum Impatience Theorems for Recursive Economic Models*, Berlin: Springer-Verlag.

——— (1994), 'Period Three Implies Heavy Discounting', *Mathematics of Operations Research*, 19, pp. 1–16.

Stokey, N.L. R.E. Lucas, Jr., and E.C. Prescott (1989), *Recursive Methods in Economic Dynamics*, Harvard University Press, Cambridge.

Sutherland, W.R.S. (1967), 'On Optimal Development Programs when Future Utility is Discounted', Ph.D Thesis, Brown University.

Weitzman, M.L. (1973), 'Duality Theory for Infinite Horizon Convex Models', *Management Science*, 19, pp. 783–9.

Finance

Finance: An Introduction

The two papers in this section review important issues in finance. The first emphasizes the relationship between the 'form' of finance (e.g. debt or equity) and the subsequent behaviour of firms in the product market. The second paper studies incentive issues associated with repayment in the context of sovereign debt.

FINANCING DECISIONS AND PRODUCT MARKETS

Is there a relationship between the mode of financing adopted by a firm and its subsequent product market decisions? Sudipto Dasgupta's paper explores this question by surveying some of the recent literature dealing with this issue. The starting point is the work of Brander and Lewis* where it is shown that firms having a higher debt-equity ratio tend to produce more output in oligopolistic equilibrium. Dasgupta questions the robustness of the Brander–Lewis result, which studies firms engaged in Cournot competition. In particular, he shows that if firms choose prices rather than quantities, the effect of an increase in leverage depends crucially on the nature of uncertainty. If there is demand uncertainty, the effect of increased leverage is to raise product prices, contrary to the Brander–Lewis result. If, on the other hand, the uncertainly is with respect to cost, the effect on prices is reversed; they fall. The maturity period of debt is also shown to matter. When debt is long-term, increased leverage may increase prices (in the short-run) even with Cournot competition. Indeed, even short-term debt (as in Brander–Lewis) may have different implications for product market behaviour, once the future profits are incorporated in a dynamic setting. In particular, predation is an interesting possibility in such a context. Finally, the paper briefly discusses the relationship between the choice of leverage and the choice of product quality. The paper concludes with a discussion of the empirical work on the interaction between financing choices and product market outcomes.

*J. Brander and T. Lewis (1988), 'Oligopoly and Financial Structure: The Limited Liability Effect', *American Economic Review*, 76, pp. 956–70.

PRIVATE LENDING TO SOVEREIGN DEBTORS

Bhaswar Moitra's paper discusses some basic issues related to *sovereign debt.* It begins by explaining a fundamental difference between 'private' and 'sovereign' debt. While private debts are typically subject to well-defined laws regarding bankruptcy and enforcement of collateral, sovereign debts are not governed by regulations that are enforceable in court. Indeed, one can regard the power to abrogate commitments without having to answer to a higher authority to be the essential property of sovereignty. It is, therefore, more difficult to enforce repayment in sovereign debt contracts. Why do private lenders then willingly lend to governments of other countries? The paper reviews a simple intertemporal model to provide an answer to this question. In this standard setup, if the borrower defaults at any point in time, it cannot get a loan in the international market in future. This is the cost of default. On the other hand, the benefit from default increases with the amount of loan already taken. Indeed, there is a critical level of loan at which the borrower is just indifferent between default and repayment. The borrower can raise a loan no greater than this critical level in the international market. Finally, the paper goes on to discuss issues related to a debt crisis. First, in terms of a simple model, it identifies possible situations where a debt crisis might arise. It then proceeds to examine possible ways out of the crisis. In particular, it looks at remedial measures like *debt forgiveness* by creditors and *collective lending* which pushes back the day of reckoning.

7

How Firms' Financing Decisions Impact Product Markets

A Selective Survey

SUDIPTO DASGUPTA*

1. INTRODUCTION

Recent empirical evidence on how financing decisions affect product market competition among firms has stimulated interest in the area. The predictions of existing models were seemingly at variance with these new empirical findings, and new models have been suggested to reconcile theory and facts. This paper attempts to survey this recently emerging literature. At least two other recent surveys of the same literature exist [Zechner (1996) and Maksimovic (1996)]. Obviously, the surveys differ in the importance given to specific contributions, reflecting, perhaps, the tastes of the authors. However, the present survey differs from the others, primarily in examining more closely the particular assumptions underlying the various models, and the extent to which the models are consistent with empirical evidence.

The following pedagogical point also needs to be noted at the outset. Much of the recent literature on financial structure of firms is a response to Modigliani and Miller's classic result that under some 'ideal' conditions (in particular, if there are no corporate taxes and bankruptcy costs), financial structure is irrelevant.[1] As a consequence, there is a tendency in corporate finance models to isolate particular costs and benefits of financing decisions and show the existence of an 'optimal capital structure'. In practice, of course, there are a myriad

*I wish to thank Murray Frank and Sheridan Titman for helpful comments. The usual disclaimer applies.

[1]Throughout this survey, I shall use the terms 'financial structure' or 'capital structure' to mean the ratio of the market value of debt to that of equity.

different factors determining financing decisions of firms, and it may not necessarily be so important to learn, for example, that an (interior) optimal capital structure exists in a particular model of product market competition. Reflecting this point of view, this survey focuses mainly on the effect of financing decisions on product market outcomes, and not so much on the optimality of the financing decision itself.[2] Not surprisingly, this is also the aspect of the problem on which empirical research has the most to say.

Finally, a point about the mathematical notation used in this survey. There is clearly something to be said in favour of a uniform set of notations. However, when discussing particular models, the notation that the authors have used has been followed, in the belief that this facilitates later reading of these contributions.

The survey is organized as follows. Section 2 introduces two well known channels through which debt affects investment choices by firms. It is argued that most models of the interaction between financing choices and product market outcomes are extensions of these ideas to the product market. In section 3, the major theoretical models have been surveyed. In section 4, the empirical evidence is presented, and the models are evaluated in the light of this evidence. Section 5 concludes.

2. HOW DEBT AFFECTS INVESTMENT DECISIONS

Most of the models of interaction between a firm's financing and product market decisions have built on two basic ideas of how debt affects investment decisions of firms. These are, respectively, the 'asset substitution problem' attributed to Jensen and Meckling (1976), and the 'underinvestment problem' attributed to Myers (1977). Before proceeding, it would be helpful to review briefly these two ideas.

2.1 The Asset Substitution Problem

Suppose that a firm must choose between two mutually exclusive projects, *A* and *B*. Each project requires an investment outlay of 90 units

[2]Although in most models, the optimality of the financing decision based solely on the product market considerations can be established.

[3]Cash flows are the difference between sales revenue and production costs. In the balance sheets of a company, this differs from net income or profits, because of interest payments, depreciation and taxes. We abstract from taxes and depreciation throughout this survey.

of money, and generates a single cash flow[3] one period later. There are two states of the economy, which we label as 'good' and 'bad'. The probability that each state occurs is 0.5. The cash flows from each project in each state of the economy are described below:

Project	Good	Bad	Expected
A	120	80	100
B	160	30	95

Assume now that the projects can only be financed through issuing debt. The standard debt contract takes the form of a fixed repayment F that the firm will make to the lenders one period later. In the event of default, debt holders are residual claimants and will own the entire cash flow. Assume also that the actual choice of project is not verifiable, so that debt holders cannot force the firm to choose a particular project.

Which project will be chosen in equilibrium? Suppose lenders believed that project A will be chosen. Then, assuming that the market for loans is competitive and setting the risk-free rate of interest to zero for convenience, the fixed payment F will be set to satisfy,

$$90 = (0.5)F + (0.5)80 \tag{1}$$

since it is easily checked that for lenders to break even, F must necessarily exceed 80, the cash flow in the 'bad' state. Solving, we get

$$F = 100.$$[4]

If the firm can get debt financing at these terms, will it choose project A? The payoff to the *equity holders* of the firm from choosing project A is given by,

$$\begin{aligned} E_A &= (0.5)(120 - F) + (0.5)(0) \\ &= (0.5)(120 - 100) = 10 \end{aligned} \tag{2}$$

On the other hand, the equity holders' payoff, if project B is chosen, is given by,

$$E_B = (0.5)(160 - 100) = 30 \tag{3}$$

[4]We shall refer to the fixed payment obligation associated with a debt contract, i.e. F, as the 'face value of debt'. This is different from the amount of funds raised, which is the left hand side of equation (1). The latter is called the 'market value of debt'.

Thus, equity holders will prefer to choose project B. Consequently, project A will not be chosen in equilibrium. However, it can be checked exactly as above that if lenders anticipate that project B will be chosen and price the debt accordingly, then B will indeed be chosen. Notice that project B has the lower net present value of the two investment projects. The reason why the better project is not chosen in equilibrium is that debt gives equity holders an incentive to shift profits from the bad states, in which the debt holders are the residual claimants, to the good states, in which debt holders have a fixed claim. The *ex-ante* pricing of debt reflects this incentive, but this makes the better project unattractive.[5]

2.2 The Underinvestment Problem

Consider the following situation described in the table below,

State	Cash w/o project	Cash with project
Good	6000	7200
Bad	1000	2200

Column 1 gives the cash flows from assets in place for a firm, for each state of the economy—good and bad (assumed equally likely)—that will result next period. The firm is currently considering an investment project. The project will require an investment of 1000 units of money. If undertaken, the project will provide a cash flow of 1200 units of money next period, in either state of the economy. Thus, the investment project has a net present value of 200 (ignoring interest costs). Also, the firm currently has debt outstanding that will need to be repaid next period. Suppose the repayment obligation is 3000 units of money. This debt is senior, i.e. will have a prior claim on cash flows to any new debt that may be issued to finance the investment project. We consider below the case where the new investment is financed through newly issued junior debt; however, the analysis is very similar if, instead, we assumed that equity is issued to finance the project.

If the project is not undertaken, equity holders obviously get $6000 - 3000 = 3000$ in the good state, and nothing in the bad state, as the debt holders get everything. Thus, the payoff to equity holders is

[5]For a formal treatment of the asset substitution problem, see Green (1984).

(0.5)(3000) = 1500. On the other hand, suppose that the new investment is financed through the issue of junior debt. Since the existing debt holders have senior claim, the junior debt holders will get anything at all only in the good state. Thus, the face value of junior debt will be given by,

$$1000 = (0.5)F$$

so that $F = 2000$. Thus, the payoff to the equity holders is $(7200 - 3000 - 2000)(0.5) = 1100$. Consequently, the payoff to the equity holders is higher if the project is not undertaken.

The underinvestment problem has been called the problem of 'debt overhang'. The basic reason why the firm is willing to give up a positive net present value investment project has to do with the presence of senior debt. Since the existing debt holders have senior claim, the benefit of the new investment goes partly to the debt holders (they now get an extra 1200 if the bad state materializes). Thus, equity holders do not get enough to be willing to bear the full cost of the investment.

3. THE BRANDER–LEWIS MODEL

Brander and Lewis (1986), extending ideas from strategic trade theory [e.g. Brander and Spencer (1984)], argued that pre-commitment to debt could provide strategic advantages to firms in an oligopoly.[6] The basic avenue through which this works is very similar to the 'asset substitution' problem discussed above. Suppose we have a Cournot duopoly, and there is uncertainty about the state of demand. If a firm has debt in its capital structure, then it will be bankrupt in the low states of demand. Thus, it has an incentive to shift profits from the low states of demand to the high states. It does this by producing an output that is more appropriate for the high states, i.e. for any given output of its rival, the firm now optimally produces more.

This leads to higher profits in the high states of demand, but lower profits in the low states of demand, and the effect is similar to choosing a riskier project, as in the asset substitution problem.[7] Therefore, debt has the effect of shifting the firm's reaction function outwards, and the

[6]Maksimovic (1986) independently developed a similar model.

[7]Another way to think about this is to notice that debt makes the payoff of the firm a convex function of its profit, since the payoff is zero if profits are lower than the fixed payment obligation. The convexity of the payoff induces a preference for riskier outcomes.

firm gains market share at the expense of the rival and moves closer to its optimal (Stackelberg) point on the rival's reaction function. Of course, the rival has exactly the same incentive, so that in equilibrium, the firms end up with higher outputs and lower prices and profits compared to the case in which they are equity financed.

Let us consider things a bit more formally. There are two firms, labelled A and B, which are Cournot competitors. The firms are owned by risk neutral entrepreneurs, or equivalently, are managed for the benefits of risk neutral shareholders, and thus, act to maximize the expected value of their profits. To produce their product the firms must make a fixed investment of I dollars, which allows them to produce an unlimited amount (i.e. capacity restrictions will not be binding). The financing decision is assumed independent of the investment decision in that the firms can choose any level of debt to 'finance' the investment. In particular, the firm may raise more debt than the investment requirement. In this case, it will be assumed that any excess funds are paid off to shareholders as dividends.

The sequence of events is as follows. At time $t = 0$, the firms finance their fixed investment. At time $t = 1$, they then simultaneously choose their quantities: the financing choices of the previous stage are common knowledge at this point. However, the firms are uncertain about some random parameters of their profit functions at this point (e.g. the demand intercept or costs of production). At time $t = 2$, the uncertainty is resolved, the firm's output is sold, and debt holders are paid off. There is limited liability: if the firm is unable to meet the debt payments, the debt holders become the residual claimants and the firm's equity holders get nothing. Importantly, there are no bankruptcy costs.

We focus first on the decisions of the firm at $t = 1$, taking the financing choices of the previous stage as given. At this point, the objective of the firm is to maximize equity value. The equity value of firm i can be expressed as,

$$V^i(q_i, q_j) = \int_{\hat{z}_i}^{\bar{z}} \{R^i(q_i, q_j, \tilde{z}_i) - D_i\}\, dF(\tilde{z}_i) \tag{4}$$

where $R^i(q_i, q_j, \tilde{z}_i)$ is profit gross of payments to debt holders for firm i, D_i is the face value of firm i's debt, $q_i(q_j)$ is firm i's (j's) quantity, and $\tilde{z}_i$ is a random variable with a c.d.f. $F(\tilde{z}_i)$ defined over $[0, \bar{z}]$.

We define $\hat{z}_i$ implicitly from the equation,

$$R^i(q_i, q_j, \hat{z}_i) = D_i, \tag{5}$$

and assume that the firm is bankrupt and its equity is worthless if $\tilde{z}_i$ is less than $\hat{z}_i$, i.e. we define $\tilde{z}_i$ in such a way that the firm's profit is increasing in $\tilde{z}_i$.

In order to maximize equity value, firms select quantities that solve the following first-order condition.

$$V_i^i = 0 \Leftrightarrow \int_{\hat{z}_i}^{\bar{z}} R_i^i(q_i, q_j, \tilde{z}_i)\, dF(\tilde{z}_i) = 0 \tag{6}$$

The second-order condition for an interior optimum is,

$$V_{ii}^i < 0 \tag{7}$$

which, we assume, holds.

To examine how debt affects a firm's output decision, we differentiate (6) holding firm j's output fixed. We get,

$$\frac{dq_i}{dD_i} = \frac{R_i^i(q_i, q_j, \hat{z}_i) \cdot \dfrac{d\hat{z}_i}{dD_i} \cdot f(\hat{z}_i)}{V_{ii}^i} \tag{8}$$

This, in effect, tells us how an increase in debt causes firm i's reaction function to shift. Note that V_{ii}^i is negative by virtue of (7). Also, from (5), given that $\tilde{z}_i$ is defined so that R^i is increasing in $\tilde{z}_i$, we have $\dfrac{d\hat{z}_i}{dD_i} > 0$. Thus, the direction in which the reaction function shifts depends on the sign of the term $R_i^i(q_i, q_j, \hat{z}_i)$.

From equation (6), note that if $R_i^i(q_i, q_j, \tilde{z}_i)$ is increasing (decreasing) in $\tilde{z}_i$, i.e. $R_{iz}^i > 0$ ($R_{iz}^i < 0$), then $R_i^i(q_i, q_j, \hat{z}_i)$ must be negative (positive) otherwise the integral cannot 'sum' to zero.

Brander and Lewis (1986) focus attention on the case $R_{iz}^i(q_i, q_j, \tilde{z}_i) > 0$. To see that this is reasonable, let us consider two plausible scenarios. Assume that production is carried on under constant marginal cost. Under *demand uncertainty* assume that the price for firm i's product is given by $p_i(q_i, q_j, \tilde{z}_i) = p_i(q_i, q_j) + \tilde{z}_i$. Then, gross profit can be expressed as,

$$R^i(q_i, q_j, \tilde{z}_i) = [p_i(q_i, q_j) + \tilde{z}_i - c_i]q_i$$

and consequently, $R_{iz}^i(q_i, q_j, \tilde{z}_i) > 0$. With *cost uncertainty* assume marginal cost is $c_i = c - \tilde{z}_i$, so that gross profits are,

$$R^i(q_i, q_j, \tilde{z}_i) = (p_i(q_i, q_j) - c + \tilde{z}_i)q_i.$$

and consequently, again, $R^i_{iz}(q_i, q_j, \tilde{z}_i) > 0$. Thus, there are 'reasonable' scenarios under which the assumption $R^i_{iz}(q_i, q_j, \tilde{z}_i) > 0$ holds, and by virtue of equation (8), this implies that $\frac{dq_i}{dD_i} > 0$, i.e. an outward shift of the reaction curve. This is the 'strategic effect' of debt. It can be shown that this strategic effect of debt implies that both firms will choose some debt in equilibrium. In equilibrium, both firms would produce more and have lower profits than if neither had any debt.

More interesting are the implications the model has regarding the consequences of a *unilateral* increase in the debt level of a firm. As we shall discuss later, several researchers have attempted to investigate the consequences of events such as leveraged buy-outs (explained later) which are associated with large debt increases for a firm. The BL model has the implication that an increase in debt would cause a firm to produce more and gain market share. Industry prices would drop, and the effect on the profitability of rival firms would be negative.

4. ROBUSTNESS OF THE BL IMPLICATIONS

Several papers have questioned the robustness of the implications of the BL model regarding the impact of financial structure on product market outcomes. We review a few of these here.

4.1 Prices Versus Quantities

As is well known from the work of Bulow, Geneokopoulus and Klemperer (1985), results in models of oligopoly may be sensitive to whether the decision variables are strategic 'substitutes' or 'complements'. The BL model is no exception. Assume that the firms compete in prices, instead of quantities, as assumed in the BL model.[8] Then, a simple re-labelling of variables yields the following equation, analogous to equation (8),

[8]A more detailed analysis is given in Dasgupta and Titman (1996) and Showalter (1995).

$$\frac{dp_i}{dD_i} = \frac{R_i^i(p_i, p_j, \hat{z}_i) \cdot \dfrac{d\hat{z}_i}{dD_i} \cdot f(\hat{z}_i)}{V_{ii}^i} \tag{9}$$

Once again, the sign of this term depends on $R_i^i(p_i, p_j, \hat{z}_i)$, and is positive (negative) if the latter is negative (positive). An expression analogous to (6) implies that $R_i^i(p_i, p_j, \hat{z}_i)$ is negative (positive) if $R_{iz}^i(p_i, p_j, z_i)$ is positive (negative). Suppose now that uncertainty is with respect to the demand intercept, so that,

$$R^i(p_i, p_j, \tilde{z}_i) = (p_i - c_i)(q(p_i, p_j) + \tilde{z}_i)$$

It is easily checked that $R_{iz}^i > 0$, so that $\dfrac{dp_i}{dD_i} > 0$. Thus, debt will cause the price charged by firm i to rise. Since prices are strategic complements, this will also cause firm j to raise its price. Thus, the effect of an increase in the level of debt is to *raise* product prices, contrary to the BL model. It can be shown in this case, as in BL, that firms will optimally choose debt.

Quite a different conclusion emerges if firms compete in prices, but the uncertainty is with respect to the marginal cost of production. If the uncertainty affects marginal cost additively, the profit function is as follows,

$$R^i(p_i, p_j, \tilde{z}_i) = (p_i - c_i + z_i)q(p_i, p_j)$$

In this case, $R_{iz}^i(p_i, p_j, \tilde{z}_i) = \dfrac{\partial q(p_i, p_j)}{\partial p_i} < 0$. Accordingly, $R_i^i(p_i, p_j, \hat{z}) > 0$ and consequently, $\dfrac{dp_i}{dD_i} < 0$. Thus, the effect of an increase in the debt level in this case will be to lower prices. It is true that neither firm will choose debt in this case if product market concerns are the only reason to choose debt; however, leverage changes[9] may occur for a variety of reasons, and in these cases, prices will drop (rise) if leverage increases (decreases).

To conclude, even in the framework of the BL model, the conclusion as to the impact of debt on prices is quite sensitive to the nature of

[9]The word 'leverage' is sometimes synonymous with debt. Debt has the effect of magnifying the effect of earnings changes on the payoff to equity holders, hence, the term 'leverage'.

competition (i.e. whether firms compete in prices or quantities) and the nature of uncertainty.

4.2 THE MATURITY PERIOD OF DEBT

4.2.1 Long-Term Debt

Glazer (1994) has pointed out that the BL conclusions are driven by the assumption that repayment of the debt is imminent (or that the debt is short-term). He considers a two-period model. The debt is due at the end of period 2. Firms choose outputs at the beginning of period 1, and again at the beginning of period 2. Cash flows are realized at the end of period 1, and again at the end of period 2. There are covenants imposed by debt holders that prevent the firm from paying out period 1 cash flows as dividends to shareholders.[10] Importantly, even in this two-period model the firms can choose debt only once, at the beginning of period 1. It is also quite important to the model that period 1 profits cannot be re-invested, i.e. they must remain as cash in the balance sheet.

The basic idea is the following. If firm i chooses debt, then it will have a credible threat to be aggressive in the second period, as in Brander and Lewis (1986). Knowing this, its rival firm j in period 1 will find it in its interest to reduce firm i's *effective leverage* in period 2 by increasing i's profit in period 1 (which is carried over to period 2). In other words, firm j will cooperate in period 1 by reducing its output in period 1. This would imply that prices would be higher immediately after leverage increases, contrary to BL.

To see things a bit more formally, let us denote period 1 outputs by x_i and x_j, and period 2 outputs by y_i and y_j. Denote period 1 operating profits by $P^i(x_i, x_j)$ for i and similarly for j. Assume $P^i(x_i, x_j) \geq 0$, $P^i_j < 0$, $P^i_{ii} < 0$ and $P^i_{ij} < 0$. Period 2 profits are denoted by $R^i(y_i, y_j, z_i)$, where z_i is a random variable. $R^i(y_i, y_j, z_i)$ satisfies all the assumptions in the BL model, and in particular, we focus on the case $R^i_{iz} > 0$.

Let $\overline{D}_i$ denote the face value of the debt raised at the beginning of period 1, due at the end of period 2. For given x_i, x_j, y_i, y_j, the payment to the shareholders of firm i is,

[10]This makes debt different from other fixed claims against the firm, such as wage payments that the firm is committed to paying.

$$v^i(x_i, x_j, y_i, y_j, z_i) = \text{Max } \{P^i(x_i, x_j) + R^i(y_i, y_j, z_i) - \overline{D}_i,\ 0\}.$$

Let $D^i(x_i, x_j) = \text{Max } [\overline{D}_i - P^i(x_i, x_j), 0]$ denote the second period debt, i.e. the portion of the debt that remains uncovered after the first period. To simplify the analysis, assume that the debt obligation is large enough that period 1 profit is always insufficient to repay the debt in full, i.e. $D^i > 0$. The expected payoff to the shareholders is given by,

$$V^i(x_i, x_j, y_i, y_j) = \int_{\hat{z}_i}^{\bar{z}} (R^i(y_i, y_j, z_i) - D^i(x_i, x_j))\, dF(z_i) \qquad (10)$$

whereas in BL, $\hat{z}_i$ is defined by,

$$R^i(y_i, y_j, \hat{z}_i) - D^i(x_i, x_j) = 0$$

The period 2 problem is the maximization of the expression in equation (10) for given D^i with respect to y_i. This problem is completely identical to BL and (assuming $R^i_{iz} > 0$), we immediately have (i) $\frac{dy_i}{dD^i} > 0$ and (ii) $\frac{dy_j}{dD^i} < 0$.

To see the impact of debt on the first period output choices, it is helpful to consider the following expressions (which are derived after using the envelope theorem),

$$\frac{dV^i}{dD^i} = \int_{\hat{z}_i}^{\bar{z}} [R^i_j(y^e_i, y^e_j, z_i)\, \frac{dy^e_j}{dD^i} - 1]\, dF(z)$$

and

$$\frac{dV^i}{dD^j} = \int_{\hat{z}_i}^{\bar{z}} [R^i_j(y^e_i, y^e_j, z_i)\, \frac{dy^e_j}{dD^j} - 1]\, dF(z)$$

where the subscript *e* denotes equilibrium quantities. The first expression is ambiguous in sign, but the second expression is negative, since $R^i_j < 0$ and $\frac{dy^e_j}{dD^j} > 0$.

The period 1 output choice by firm 1 satisfies the following condition,

$$\frac{dV^i}{dx_i} = \frac{dV^i}{dD^i} \cdot \frac{dD^i}{dx_i} + \frac{dV^i}{dD^j} \cdot \frac{dD^j}{dx_i} \qquad (11)$$

$$= \frac{dV^i}{dD^i} \cdot (-P^i_i(x_i, x_j)) + \frac{dV^i}{dD^j} \cdot (-P^j_i(x_j, x_i)) = 0 \qquad (12)$$

We can now study the effect of debt on period 1 output choice by the firms. Suppose firm *j* is equity financed. Then from the definition of

D^j, since D^j is identically zero, we have $\frac{dD^j}{dx_i} = 0$. It then follows from questions (11) and (12) that firm i's optimal period 1 output for any output x_j by firm j satisfies $P_i^i\,(x_i, x_j) = 0$. Let $B(x_j)$ denote this best response to firm j's output (i.e. it is firm i's reaction function). We shall now show that if firm j has risky debt, $x_i < B\,(x_j)$ i.e. firm i will contract its period 1 output for any level of output by firm j.

To see this, suppose, to the contrary, that $x_i \geq B(x_j)$. Consider the possibility $x_i > B(x_j)$ first. It follows from the concavity of i's period 1 profit function that there must be another output $x_i' < B(x_j)$ such that $P^i(x_i', x_j) = P^i(x_i, x_j)$, which in turn implies $D^i(x_i', x_j) = D^i(x_i, x_j)$. Moreover, $P^j(x_i', x_j) > P(x_i, x_j)$, which implies $D^j(x_i', x_j) < D^j(x_i, x_j)$. It then follows from the fact that $\frac{dV^i}{dD^j} < 0$, that x_i' gives shareholders of firm i higher profit than x_i. To see that $x_i = B(x_j)$ is not possible, notice that since at this level of output $P_i^i(x_i, x_j) = 0$, but $P_i^j(x_j, x_i)$ is negative, and $\frac{dV^i}{dD^j} < 0$, equation (12) implies a contradiction.

When both firms have risky debt, it follows that in *symmetric equilibrium*, both firms will produce less in the first period than under equity financing, so that prices will be higher.[11]

4.2.2 *Predation*

In contrast to Glazer (1994) who focuses on long-term debt, it can be argued that short term debt (as in BL) may have different implications about product market behaviour, once the possibility of future period profits is incorporated into the model. In BL, not only is the debt for one period, but there is also no second (or later) period production.

[11]Glazer (1994) does not explicitly consider the question of optimal debt choices. It is true, however, that it will never be the case in his model that neither firm has debt. Notice also, that in view of our discussion in the section 'Prices versus Quantities', since the driving force of the model is the second period BL effect, the effect on period 1 prices is sensitive to the nature of competition and uncertainty.

[12]In the section 'Future Financing Needs', we discuss a model by Chevalier and Scharfstein (1994) which focuses on a different model of competition and arrives at the opposite conclusion when short-term debt is present.

Consider now the following possibility. Firm *i* finances with short-term debt. Firm *j* realizes that if firm *i* defaults on its debt payments, then it may be forced into bankruptcy, in which case firm *j* will reap higher future profits. In other words, firm *i* may invite 'predation' by its rival if it finances with short-term debt.[12]

Poitevin (1989) addresses the issue of how predation can emerge in a context similar to the one described above, and why a firm would finance with debt, even though predation is anticipated. Let us briefly discuss the latter issue first. Poitevin assumes that one of the firms is an 'old' firm (firm '*O*') about which there is relatively good quality information in the financial markets. The other firm is a 'new' firm (firm '*N*') about which this information is lacking. The information asymmetry here concerns the marginal cost of production of the new firm, which can be either high or low. This marginal cost is private information of the firm and unknown to the financial market (the market has priors on the probability distribution of 'types').

Poitevin assumes that

(i) both the old and the new firm have to finance the same fixed cost through either debt or equity before production,

(ii) under full information about costs, the high cost new firm would not be able to produce profitably, and

(iii) if the market could not identify the types, the high cost new firm would be able to achieve a 'mis-pricing gain' through the issue of equity sufficient to make the project profitable.

In this adverse selection framework similar to that of Myers and Majluf (1984), the low cost incumbent would not issue equity because its equity issue would be underpriced (the market believes that only the high marginal cost firm will issue equity). Thus, it can avoid this mis-pricing loss by issuing debt, even though debt may invite a predatory response from its rival.[13]

We now turn to an analysis of predation, given that firm *N* issues debt. We shall assume that the financing choice at the prior stage has correctly identified the type of the firm, so that at the

[13]Notice that the old firm can finance with equity without mis-pricing, because its 'type' (i.e. marginal cost) is known. Gertner, Gibbons and Scharfstein (1988), in a related paper, consider the possibility that a firm's financing choice may convey information not only to financial markets, but also to its rivals in product markets. They show how this 'two-audience' signalling feature affects the nature of equilibrium (i.e. whether separating or pooling) at the financing stage.

production stage, the marginal cost is known. Production profit of each firm is given by,

$$S^i(a_i, q_i, c_i, q_j) = P(Q)q_i - c_i q_i + a_i, \qquad i = N, O, \; i \neq j$$

where $P(Q)$ is the demand curve, and $Q = q_N + q_O$. a_i is a firm-specific random demand intercept, drawn from a distribution $F(a)$ with support $[\underline{a}, \overline{a}]$.

It is assumed that if either firm is bankrupt, the other receives a net additional benefit B. The critical value $\hat{a}_i$ such that firm i is solvent for $a > \hat{a}_i$ is given by,

$$S^i(\hat{a}_i, q_i, c_i, q_j) + D_i + E_i - K + F(\hat{a}_j)B = D_i(1 + r_i) \qquad (13)$$

where D_i and E_i denote the amounts raised through issuing debt and equity by firm i prior to the production stage, K is the fixed cost of production, and r_i the interest rate on debt paid by firm i (this is endogenously determined in the model and will reflect the default probability). $\hat{a}_j$ is the analogous critical value of a for firm j, and is determined by an analogous expression. The expression implicitly assumes that the lender cannot observe whether the rival firm j is bankrupt, and will be willing to lend $F(\hat{a}_j)B$ in exchange of B if it helps avoid bankruptcy.

We shall confine our discussion to showing that firm N's leverage makes O more aggressive (i.e. its reaction function will shift outwards). O's optimal output is obtained by maximizing the following expression w.r.t. q_O,

$$\int_{\hat{a}_O}^{\overline{a}} [S^O(a_O, q_O, c_O, q_N) + D_O + E_O - K + F(\hat{a}_N)B - D_O(1 + r_O)] \, dF(a)$$

The first-order condition is,

$$[P'(Q)q_O + P(Q) - c_O + f(\hat{a}_N)B \frac{d(\hat{a}_N)}{dq_O}] \cdot (1 - F(\hat{a}_O)) = 0 \qquad (14)$$

If firm N were completely equity financed (but its type correctly identified) then we can set $F(\hat{a}_N) = 0$ and the first order condition would be given by,

$$P'(Q)q_O + P(Q) - c_O = 0 \qquad (15)$$

[14]Notice that the incentive for predation exists regardless of whether $D_O > 0$ or not.

Notice from equation (13) that $\frac{d(\hat{a}_N)}{dq_O} = -P'(Q)q_N > 0$. It then follows from comparing (14) and (15) that firm O's output for any given level of N's output will be higher when the latter firm is debt financed. This is predation, and product prices will be lower and firm N will lose market share to its rival.[14]

4.2.3 Related Literature

The idea that a financially 'vulnerable' firm may be subject to predation dates back to McGee (1958) and Telser (1966). These authors simply assumed that an entrant is more resource constrained than an incumbent firm. Thus, the incumbent preys on the entrant by engaging it in price wars, thereby exhausting its resources and forcing it out of the market. Benoit (1984) also assumes that the entrant is financially able to sustain a price war for only a finite number of periods. However, with perfect capital markets, if staying in the business is profitable, there is no reason why the entrant should be unable to raise the necessary resources.

Bolton and Scharfstein (1992) formally model the idea that when financial markets cannot observe the true state of profitability of a firm, predation may be profitable.[15] They also explicitly consider how the possibility of predation may affect the financial contract between the firm and investors. The structure of the model is as follows. There are two firms—the incumbent, which has a 'deep pocket' i.e. enough internal funds that it does not have to take recourse to the financial markets, and an entrant, which must borrow funds from investors. Funds are needed to finance a fixed cost of production F in each of two periods. The product market interaction between the entrant and the incumbent is not formally modelled. Predation takes the form of the incumbent spending a fixed amount c of its resources, which affects the probability distribution of the entrant's output.

Consider first the financial contract between the entrant and the investors in the absence of predation. In each period, the entrant's profit π can take either of two values, π_1 and π_2, where $\pi_2 > \pi_1$, and Prob. $[\pi = \pi_1] = \theta$ in each period, i.e. the profits are uncorrelated across the two periods. It is assumed that,

(i) $\theta\pi_1 + (1 - \theta)\pi_2 = \bar{\pi} > F$, and

[15] See also Fudenberg and Tirole (1986).

(ii) $\pi_1 < F$.

The first assumption is simply that the investment has positive net present value in each period, while the second assumption is quite crucial and will be discussed below. The actual cash profits in each period cannot be verified, and the repayments made by the entrant cannot be made contingent on the realization of π. The investor has all the bargaining power and offers the entrant a 'take or leave' contract. Appealing to the revelation principle, the contract specifies the repayments by the entrant as functions of the reported profit by the entrant and induces truthful reporting.

Essentially, the contract has three features:

(a) a repayment R_i in period 1 if the entrant reports state π_i, $i = 1, 2$

(b) a probability β_i of obtaining refinancing in period 2 if state i is reported in period 1, and

(c) a repayment R_{ij} in period 2 if entrant reports i in period 1, j in period 2, and obtains refinancing. Bolton and Scharfstein show that the optimal contract involves $\beta_2 = 1$, $\beta_1 = 0$, $R_1 = \pi_1$, $R_2 = \bar{\pi}$ and $R_{ij} = \pi_1$ for $i, j = 1, 2$.

To understand the optimal contract, notice first that the incentive to misreport in period 1 (i.e. report π_1 when π_2 is realized) is minimized by spreading the gap between β_2 and β_1—and hence, the optimal values of 1 and 0, respectively. Notice also that in a one period model, two things would be true. First, since the issue of refinancing does not exist, the firm would always report π_1, and second, because of this, since $F > \pi_1$ the investors will never provide financing. The second period repayments are set equal to π_1 essentially because of the first fact, since there is no termination threat at this point. For the first period, R_1 obviously cannot be set above π_1. Setting $R_1 = \pi_1$ implies that if $R_2 = \bar{\pi}$, the gain from misrepresenting if π_2 is realized is $\pi_2 - \pi_1$ (since $\beta_1 = 0$), which is the same as the gain from truthful reporting (given $\beta_2 = 1$), which is $\pi_2 - \bar{\pi} + (\bar{\pi} - \pi_1) = \pi_2 - \pi_1$. Thus, truthful reporting is optimal. Notice that the commitment to not refinance if π_1 is reported leads to some inefficiency, since production is profitable in period 2. However, it is impossible to renegotiate around this inefficiency since $\pi_1 < F$ and the most that investors can obtain is π_1.

Consider now the possibility of predation. Predation takes the following form: at a cost c the incumbent can raise, from θ to μ, the probability that the entrant's profit is π_1 in period 1. Such an activity helps the incumbent, since it increases the probability (given the contract between the entrant and the investors described above) that the entrant will not receive refinancing. This will enable the incumbent to reap monopoly profits rather than duopoly profits in period 2.

At issue, however, is whether the investors can adjust the contract to make predation unprofitable, and how the contract should be adjusted. Clearly, predation hurts the investors as well, since it increases the risk of not being able to cover *F*. There are two scenarios. Suppose that the contract between the investors and the entrant is observable. Then, to make predation unprofitable, the investors can do either of two things. They may either make it more difficult for the entrant to obtain refinancing when the good state is realized (i.e. lower β_2), or they may make it easier to get refinancing when the bad state is realized (raise β_1). Either of these will reduce the return from predation.

Bolton and Scharfstein obtain the result that the optimal response that deters predation is to lower β_2, i.e. make refinancing more tight, rather than make it more lenient. The intuition for this result has to do with the assumption that $\pi_1 < F$, i.e. refinancing is a negative NPV activity for the investor. When the contract is unobservable to the incumbent, predation cannot be prevented in equilibrium, and the optimal contract is as described in the absence of predation.

4.3 Future Financing Needs

A major shortcoming of the BL model is that it does not explicitly model the investment need of the firm. If the time *0* decision is a *pure capital structure decision*, i.e. a decision about an appropriate debt-equity ratio which could come about, for example, through a debt-for-equity or equity-for-debt swap, then implicitly, it is being assumed that there is enough production capacity to sustain the desired production level. Alternatively, one could assume that the funds raised are used to finance production capacity. However, it is noteworthy that the capacity choice decision in not modelled in BL.

In any event, the BL model is particularly unsuitable to analyze the consequences of events such as leveraged buy-outs (LBOs) or leveraged recapitalizations. These are events in which a dramatic change in the debt-equity ratio comes about as a firm uses debt financing to buy up outstanding shares. These are no immediate implications for production capacity. To finance *future growth in production*, the firm will have to raise funds in the future by issuing debt or equity.

In situations like this, a problem similar to the Myers underinvestment problem discussed in section 2.2 arises. The pricing and production decisions of the firm will take into account the fact that the future beneficial consequences of these decisions will partly be passed on to the existing debt holders also. Unlike the previous class of models discussed above, which follow BL in emphasizing the 'risk shifting aspect' of debt, the focus now is on a version of the 'underinvestment' problem.

Dasgupta and Titman (DT) (1998) analyze this problem in the context of models of competition put forward by Klemperer (1987), and Froot and Klemperer (1989). The basic idea of this model is that the prices firms charge today affect today's market share, which in turn, matters for future profits, either because of network externalities or consumer switching costs. Thus, firms have an incentive to 'invest' in market share by charging lower prices today than the myopic profit maximizing prices. The presence of debt, however, affects the trade-off because debt increases *future borrowing costs*, and hence, the discount rate for future profits. As a result, firms charge higher prices today.

To see how the argument works, we will first consider the case of a *monopoly* producer who sets quantity in each of two periods[16]. Period 1 profit depends only on period 1 quantity, but period 2 profit depends on period 1 quantity as well as period 2 quantity. This latter assumption can be justified, for example, if there are network externalities, or if there is a fringe of customers who are uninformed about the good, and learn about it only through those who try it in the first period. We shall assume that period 1 output affects a parameter θ of the period 2 profit function: $x_2 = x_2(\theta(q_1), q_2)$, and that $\frac{\partial x_2}{\partial \theta} > 0$ and $\frac{d\theta}{dq_1} > 0$, where x_i will be used to denote profit in period i and q_i quantity produced in period i.

The timing assumptions are as follows. At the beginning of period 1, the firm makes a pure capital structure decision, issuing debt to buy back equity or vice versa. It then chooses its period 1 price or quantity. Period 1 cash flows are then realized. At the end of period 1, the firm has to finance new investment I to sustain period 2 production. We assume that period 1 cash flows are insufficient to meet this investment need, so the

[16]For monopoly, it obviously does not matter whether the firm sets quantity or price.

firm has to raise new finance at the beginning of period 2. The firm then chooses period 2 price. At the end of period 2, further cash flows are realized, debt holders are paid off if the firm has any debt, and the firm is liquidated. The cash flows consist of period 2 operating cash flows, plus a liquidation cash flow $\tilde{I}$.

The liquidation cash flow is random, and drawn from a distribution $F(\tilde{I})$ with density $f(\tilde{I})$ and support $[0, \bar{I}]$. This random liquidation value is the only source of uncertainty in the model.

For an all-equity firm, the two period profits are given by[17],

$$\Pi(q_i, q_2) = x_1(q_1) + x_2(\theta(q_1), q_2) + E\tilde{I} - I \tag{16}$$

where E is the expectations operator. Notice that the period 2 output decision is a function of θ[18], so we can write $x_2\,[\theta(q_1), q_2)] = x_2\,[\theta(q_1)]$, with some abuse of notation. Thus, the period 1 decision problem of the firm is to choose q_1 to maximize,

$$x_1(q_1) + x_2(\theta(q_1)) + E\tilde{I} - I$$

The first order condition is,

$$\frac{dx_1}{dq_1} + \frac{dx_2}{d\theta}\frac{d\theta}{dq_1} = 0 \tag{17}$$

Clearly, $\dfrac{dx_1}{dq_1} < 0$, i.e. the firm overproduces relative to the myopic period 1 profit maximizing output—a result that is hardly surprising.

Consider now the effect of senior debt being issued at the beginning of peirod 1. This debt is senior, in the sense that these debt holders have a prior claim on the firm's cash flows over equity, or any subsequent debt or equity issued. We assume that the presence of senior debt comes with covenants which prevent the payout of period 1 cash flows to equity holders as dividends.

To finance the investment need I, an amount $I - x_1$ has to be raised either through the issue of junior debt or equity. The analysis of these

[17]The shortfall $I - x_1$ may be financed through either debt or equity issues at the end of period 1. Since the buyers of these new securities will have to be promised the amount $I - x_1$ in expected value, this is deducted from the expected cash flow in period 2.

[18]The period 2 output decision obviously solves $\dfrac{\partial x_2\,(\theta(q_1), q_2)}{\partial q_2} = 0$.

two financing alternatives is more or less similar, and we focus on junior debt financing here.

Let y denote the face value of junior debt required to finance the intermediate period investment. Then assuming that the newly issued debt is priced competitively, we have,

$$I - x_1 = y[1 - F(d + y - x_2)] + \int_{d-x_2}^{d+y-x_2} (\tilde{I} + x_2 - d)\, dF \qquad (18)$$

Notice that this pricing equation reflects the fact that the debt issued to finance intermediate period investment is junior to the existing debt, as the new debt holders get anything if and only if the period 2 cash flows are enough to pay the senior claim d.

Now, the firm's two-period profit is,

$$\Pi = \int_{d+y-x_2}^{\bar{I}} (x_2 - d - y + \tilde{I})\, dF$$

$$= x_1 + (x_2 - d)[1 - F(d - x_2)] + E\tilde{I} - \int_0^{d-x_2} \tilde{I}\, dF - I \qquad (19)$$

$$= x_1 + \int_{d-x_2}^{\bar{I}} (\tilde{I} + x_2 - d)\, dF - I \qquad (20)$$

where we have used equation (18) in deriving (19).

To analyze the firm's equilibrium output choices, we begin, as usual, with the last period. At the beginning of period 2, notice that both the face value of senior and junior debt (D and y, respectively) are fixed. Hence, for a given θ, the firm chooses q_2 to maximize $\int_{d+y-x_2}^{\bar{I}} [x_2 + \tilde{I} - d - y]$. The first order condition is given by,

$$\frac{\partial x_2(\theta, q_2)}{\partial q_2} = 0. \qquad (21)$$

It is therefore obvious that the second period output, *as a function of* $\theta(q_1)$, is exactly the same as when the firm is completely equity financed.

Consider now the choice of period 1 output. Differentiating (20) w.r.t. q_1, we get,

$$\frac{\partial x_1}{\partial q_1} + \frac{\partial x_2}{\partial \theta}\frac{\partial \theta}{\partial q_1} \cdot [1 - F(d - x_2)] = 0. \qquad (22)$$

It is immediately clear from a comparison of equations (17) and (22) that the effect of senior debt is to lower period 1 production and raise period 1 price. Thus, far from being expansionary as in BL, debt has a contractionary effect on output.

In the case of a monopoly producer, there is no difference between choosing quantity or price. The effect of debt is to distort output (and price) from their first best levels, and lower firm value. This is immediate because, given that the debt claims are fairly priced, the value of the firm (equivalently, the expected cash flows to the shareholders at the beginning of period 1) is given by equation (16), and this is maximized by the level of output corresponding to equation (17).

Extension of this model to duopoly is straightforward[19]. Assume now that [as in Froot and Klemperer (1989)] firms compete in period 1 for market share, which matters for period 2 profits. When firms compete in quantities, the effect of leverage will be to shift the reaction function inwards (for any given output of the rival, debt will lead to contraction of output, as in the above analysis of monopoly). This will cause period 1 equilibrium prices to rise. Leverage will have a positive effect on the rival firm's value and a negative effect on own value. If the firms compete in prices, however, since prices are strategic complements (i.e. reaction functions are positively sloped), both firms will raise prices as the firm that increases its leverage will have its reaction function shift out. Here, leverage will have a positive 'strategic effect' due to the fact that the rival firm will raise its price. Leverage now has a positive effect on both the rival firm's value as well as own value.

It is important to note the differences of the model outlined above with the BL model. First, unlike the BL framework, the DT model gives unambiguous implications in some key respects, e.g. irrespective of whether the firms compete in prices or quantities, prices rise and the rival firm's profits increase following an increase in leverage. Second, the model does not require bankruptcy to be *imminent* for there to be any impact on prices or outputs. Third, the firm does not have to be uninformed about the current state of demand or costs for debt to have any impact on prices and quantities; in fact, the DT model assumes that the firm is perfectly informed about current (as well as future) demand and costs.

Chevalier and Scharfstein (1994) also take off from Klemperer (1993) and examine the role of financing constraints in the context of

[19]For a detailed analysis, see Dasgupta and Titman (1998).

a model of pricing for market share. Their basic purpose is to examine how financing constraints affect the cyclical behaviour of price-cost mark-ups. Financially constrained firms finance their investments through debt—agency problems dictate that in their model, this debt must be due at the end of the first period. However, period 1 cash flows are uncertain, so in some states, the firm will be liquidated as it is unable to pay off the debt. The possibility that it may not survive into the second period makes the period 2 less important. So the incentive for pricing for market share is less, and firms raise their period 1 prices when they have to issue debt. Chevalier and Scharfstein (1994) go on to demonstrate that in this scenario, mark-ups will be countercyclical, a prediction they verify empirically as well.

4.4 Product Quality

Titman (1984) was the first to propose the idea that a firm's liquidation decision may impose costs on other stake holders, especially customers, workers or input suppliers who make specific investments in the relationship. Titman (1984) showed that a firm may optimally choose a capital structure to commit to an efficient liquidation policy[20]. Anecdotal evidence supports the view that customers may be reluctant to do business with firms that are threatened with bankruptcy. This suggests that firms facing impending bankruptcy, or highly leveraged firms in declining industries, will lose market share to their rivals and lower prices of their products. Later, we shall discuss empirical evidence in support of this prediction.

Maksimovic and Titman (1991) and Dasgupta and Titman (1996) study the incentives of levered firms to maintain the quality of their products. Evidence from the U.S. airline industry suggests that the financial position of firms may affect their incentives to maintain product quality[21]. Maksimovic and Titman (1991) show that when a firm is unconstrained by dividend restricting covenants, they may prefer to increase current cash flows by cutting quality rather than investing in quality, since the benefits of this investment may pass on to senior debt holders. Even when dividend restrictions are in place, a

[20]Titman and Wessels (1988) find that firms in industries which may be expected to have unique or specialized products have lower debt.

[21]The case of Beech-Nut, manufacturers of body food, which sold adulterated apple juice when faced with financial distress, provides additional evidence.

firm that must borrow to cover its operating expenses will have similar incentives. Dasgupta and Titman (1996) show how, in a model of price competition among duopolists of the type introduced by Klemperer (see Klemperer, 1993), financing decisions, pricing decisions, and product quality choices interact. For example, following an increase in leverage, a firm may need to drop prices and increase its market share in order to convince customers that it will maintain product quality.

To see how a combination of outstanding senior debt and either insufficient operating cash flows or lack of dividend restrictions may bring about a decline in a firm's incentive to invest in product promotion, product quality or R&D, consider the following simple model.

The duopolists must spend x_i at the beginning of the period $i = 1, 2$ to earn profits $R^i(p_i, p_j, x_i)$ at the end of the period. Firm 1 is unlevered, but firm 2 has outstanding senior debt D, due at the end of the period. The firm will be liquidated at the end of the period, and the liquidation value can be either 0 or L. Let Prob $[L] = \pi$, and suppose that L is high enough that the firm is never bankrupt if L is realized, and D is sufficiently large that the firm is always bankrupt if 0 is realized. Suppose that firm j cannot observe the level of x_i chosen by frm i, i.e. we can regard the prices and the levels of x_i to be chosen simultaneously.

Assume first that each firm has sufficiently large cash holdings X at the beginning of the period to finance x_i, and that firm 2 (and obviously firm 1 as well) faces no dividend restrictions.

Ignoring discounting, firm 1, the unlevered firm, evidently chooses x_1 and p_1 to maximize,

$$R^1(p_1, p_2, x_1) - x_1 + X.$$

On the other hand, firm 2's equity holders will get $R^2(p_2, p_1, x_2) - D$ only with probability π, i.e. if it is not bankrupt (otherwise, debt holders get everything). Thus, firm 2 will maximize,

$$\pi[R^2(p_2, p_1, x_2) - D] - x_2 + X. \qquad (23)$$

Here, we have assumed that $X - x_2$ is paid out to shareholders[22]. Suppose instead that for firm 2, $X = 0$ and there are dividend restrictions in place. In this case, firm 2 must issue junior debt to finance x_2. Let

[22]With dividend restrictions, the payoff would be $\pi[R^2(p_2, p_1, x_2) - D - x_2 + X]$ and the problem of choosing x_2 is the same as that of an unlevered firm.

the face value of this debt be y. The junior debt holders get paid if and only if L is realized. Accordingly, fair pricing requires,

$$x_2 = \pi y.$$

Firm 2 thus maximizes,

$$\pi[R^2(p_2, p_1, x_2) - D - y] = \pi[R^2(p_2, p_1, x_2) - D] - x_2 \qquad (24)$$

Notice that both (23) and (24) are isomorphic to maximizing,

$$R^2(p_2, p_1, x_2) - \frac{1}{\pi} x_2$$

Since $\pi < 1$, effectively, firm 2 faces a higher cost of product promotion. In more fully specified models, it can be shown that leverage will cause the firm to cut down on product promotion, lower prices, and lose market share.

5. EMPIRICAL EVIDENCE

Empirical work on the interaction between financing choices and product market outcomes is relatively new. We discuss below the main stylized facts that this literature has uncovered, and their relationship to the various models of pricing strategy and financing that we have reviewed above.

5.1 Leveraged Buy-Outs and Recaps

Most of the work has focused on the effect of 'dramatic' increases in leverage by firms in certain industries which have undergone LBOs (leveraged buy-outs) or leveraged recapitalizations[23]. While this provides an ideal experiment to study how competition 'shakes out' after sudden increases in debt levels, some limitations have also to be noted. First, since LBOs are pure capital restructurings and the proceeds of the debt issue are used to buy back outstanding shares rather than to

[23] A leveraged buy-out is the purchase of the outstanding stock of a company by a small group of investors (which may include the current management of the company), financed largely by debt. A leveraged recapitalization involves paying a large cash dividend to 'outside' shareholders with borrowed funds, with the 'inside' shareholders receiving new shares of stock. Since it leaves the firm with large amount of debt and more concentrated ownership, it is a defensive measure against takeover threats.

finance investment, aggressive output expansion by firms, as implied by Brander and Lewis (1986), is limited by existing production capacity. If firms have to finance new investment to grow, then the presence of the newly acquired debt is likely to make a model such as Dasgupta and Titman (1998) or Chevalier and Scharfstein (1994) more applicable. In other words, these studies are unsuited to test the validity of a class of models of product market behaviour and financing choice. A second limitation is that the decision to do an LBO may itself be endogenous to the particular product market outcome that is anticipated in a given market.

Chevalier (1995a, 1995b) studies the effect of debt on product market competition by focusing on U.S. supermarket chains operating in local markets. Many large supermarket chains in the U.S. undertook LBOs in the late eighties. The supermarket industry is well suited for the study for a number of reasons. First, since supermarket competition takes place at the local level, Chevalier is able to study supermarket competition across markets. Second, at the local level, the supermarket industry is highly concentrated, with a four-firm concentration ratio of 58 per cent in 1982 for the average metropolitan area. Finally, since 1992, electronic supermarket scanner data is available to make possible some comparisons based on *firm level data* on prices, as opposed to city-level data.

Chevalier (1995a) studies the effect of the LBO of one of four major supermarket stores on the stock returns of other supermarkets. She finds that rivals who compete in some local markets with the firms undergoing LBO experience positive abnormal stock returns, while those rivals who do not directly compete experience insignificant abnormal returns. She also finds that following LBO by a firm, non-LBO incumbents in a given market are more likely to expand stores, and the larger the market share of LBO incumbents, the larger is this tendency. On the other hand, LBO incumbents do not show any significant tendency to expand following LBO by rivals.

Chevalier (1995b) examines the effect of LBOs on product prices. First, using city-level data, she finds that market price changes following LBOs are positively related to the store share of prior LBO firms in the city, but negatively related to the share of the largest non-LBO firm in the city. Using firm-level data, she also documents that firms that have undergone LBOs in a local market consistently charge higher prices than non-LBO firms.

Phillips (1995) studies four industries—fibreglass, tractor trailer, polyethylene and gypsum. These industries were chosen because they are relatively concentrated and have multiple firms that had sharply increased their leverage following leveraged recapitalizations. He documents that in the first three industries, firms that increased leverage lose market share or fail to gain market share following exit by smaller rivals. Accounting data indicate that operating margins increase and sales decrease for the firms undergoing leverage changes. Industry output levels contract and prices increase, after controlling for changes in input prices. All three industries are characterized by relatively leveraged rival firms. In contrast, in the Gypsum industry, the largest unleveraged firms significantly increased market share. Industry output increased and product prices dropped.

Kovenock and Phillips (1995) examine recapitalization decisions in ten commodity industries. They use a logistic regression to test whether firm productivity, industry demand factors and industry concentration affects the decision to recapitalize. They find that the decision to recapitalize is negatively related to the total factor productivity of the least productive plant, positively related to industry concentration, and negatively related to increase in demand. Kovenock and Phillips (1994) report that recapitalizing firms are more likely to close plants than non-recapitalizing firms, more likely to close plants in concentrated industries, and less likely to invest. Rivals are less likely to close plants and more likely to invest when the market share of leveraged firms is higher.

All the studies discussed above are broadly consistent with the view that product market competition becomes 'softer' following dramatic leverage increases. The evidence in Chevalier (1995a, 1995b) that competing firms gain in value following an LBO but not non-competing firms, and that LBO firms charge higher prices than the non-LBO firms, the evidence in Phillips (1995) that for the first three industries prices rise, output falls and the leverage-increasing firm loses market share, are all consistent with 'pricing-for-market-share' based models, e.g. Chevalier and Scharfstein (1994) and Dasgupta and Titman (1998). Interestingly, both Chevalier (1995b) and Phillips (1995) find evidence that when there are major relatively unleveraged firms, prices may drop. Chevalier (1995b) suggests that this might imply predatory pricing. Dasgupta and Titman (1998) show that if the dominant firm is a price leader, it may have an incentive to cut prices following LBO by a rival.

Both Chevalier (1995a) and Kovenock and Phillips (1994, 1995) find evidence that LBOs are sometimes accompanied by plant closing by the LBO firms, and expansion by rivals. This is consistent with the model of Chevalier and Scharfstein, which explicity considers the plant-closing possibility and shows that this may cause industry prices to rise. The results of Kovenock and Phillips (1995) suggest that agency problems of the type discussed by Jensen (1986), Stulz (1990) and Hart (1991) may be an important factor behind LBOs[24]. The fact that leveraged recapitalizations are more likely to lead to plant closing in concentrated industries suggests that these agency problems are more acute when the discipline of competition is less.

5.2 Bankruptcy and Financial Distress

In contrast to the above studies, Opler and Titman (1994) and Borenstein and Rose (1995) study the effect of financial distress on highly leveraged firms. Opler and Titman (1994) examine whether firms with high leverage are more likely to experience performance losses in industry downturns than less leveraged firms. They look at industries which had negative median sales growth and median stock return below 30 per cent between 1972 and 1991. They find that the highly leveraged firms in these industries lose market share to their less leveraged competitors. These effects are stronger in concentrated industries and for highly leveraged firms that are more R&D intensive. Similar results are obtained for other measures of performance, such as stock price changes and operating income.

Borenstein and Rose (1995) study the effect of bankruptcy announcements on pricing behaviour in the U.S. airline industry. They study data from seven Chapter 11 bankruptcy filings by large U.S. airlines between 1989–1992. They find that airlines that file for bankruptcy cut their prices 90 to 180 days before the filing by an average of 5.6 per cent, and prices continue to decline for the next nine months. Competitors' prices rise moderately. They also find that bankrupt airlines experience statistically significant declines in market share, in spite of their lower prices.

Both these studies provide ideal environments for testing the BL model. The BL effect should be most important when bankruptcy is imminent, and existing capacity is adequate for sustaining the optimal output levels. This would seem to be particularly the case in Opler and

[24]The idea in these papers is that debt desciplines managers by forcing them to sell off unprofitable divisions to meet debt and interest payments.

Titman (1994), who study industries in decline. According to BL, the highly levered firms in these industries should gain market share at the expense of their less levered counterparts.

Opler and Titman (1994), in fact, find exactly the opposite. As they point out, the loss in market share for the highly levered firms could be for three different reasons. They could be (i) customer driven, following the arguments in section (4.4), (ii) competitor driven, suggesting that less financially constrained firms predate on the more financially constrained ones, or (iii) manager driven, reflecting efficient downsizing. The fact that the loss of performance is stronger in industries that are more concentrated suggests that the effects may be competitor driven; the fact that they are stronger if the firms engage in R&D (suggesting unique products) suggests that they may be customer driven as well.

However, the fact that operating income decreases for the highly levered firms suggests that they are probably not manager driven (i.e. managers are not selling off loss making units). Likewise, the findings of Borenstein and Rose (1995) also reveal little of the BL effect; in fact, all their findings are easily explained in terms of a simple model of product promotion such as the one discussed in section (4.4).

6. CONCLUSIONS

This survey has been necessarily selective. We have focused on how financing decisions affect product markets. Relatively little work has been done on the following important areas, and we have left them out as they are too thin to survey at this point. Maksimovic (1988) remains the only work on financing choices in the context of a dynamic oligopoly. An early paper by Allen (1985) addressed the important issue of why *ex-ante* identical firms in an industry may choose different capital structures. Maksimovic and Zechner (1989) also address this issue [see also Williams (1995)]. Bhattacharyya and Leach (1992) and Wong (1995) examine how product market characteristics may affect a firm's required return relevant in capital budgeting decisions. Dasgupta and Wong (1996) discuss the relevance of product market considerations for the choice between private debt (e.g. bank debt) and public debt. Dasgupta and Shin (1995) consider the issue of how capital structure may affect the incentives of firms to share information through trade associations.

There is also an emerging literature on how leverage affects bilateral outcomes in factor and product markets. In the eighties, leveraged buyouts were held to have enabled firms to renegotiate wage contracts with workers. Debt is supposed to be useful in bilateral bargaining. Consistent with this view, Bronars and Deere (1991) find that firms which face higher threats of unionization in the U.S. have more debt.

Theoretical models which explore this and related issues are Dasgupta and Sengupta (1993), and Perotti and Spier (1993). On the other hand, Dasgupta and Kim (1996) have found that U.S. manufacturing firms, which depend on a few major customers for their sales, have lower leverage, suggesting that the possibility of hold-up may make the firm financially more vulnerable and its optimal response may be to reduce leverage. In the end, whether debt is a help or hindrance in bilateral bargaining may well depend on the outside options of the bargaining parties, and more work in this area is needed.

References

Allen, F. (1985), 'Capital Structure and Imperfect Competition in Product Markets', University of Pennsylvania Discussion Paper No. 189.

Benoit, J. (1984), 'Financially Constrained Entry in a Game with Incomplete Information', *Rand Journal of Economics* 15, pp. 90–499.

Bhattacharyya, S. and C. Leach (1993), 'Product and Financial Market Interactions: Risk Spillovers and the Valuation of Rents', mimeo.

Bolton, P. and D. Scharfstein (1990), 'A Theory of Predation Based on Agency Problems in Financial Contracting', *American Economic Review*, 80, pp. 93–106.

Borenstein, S. and N. Rose (1995), 'Bankruptcy and Pricing Behavior in U.S. Airlines Markets', *American Economic Review* (AEA papers and proceedings), pp. 397–402.

Brander, J.A. and T.R. Lewis (1986), 'Oligopoly and Financial Structure: The Limited Liability Effect', *Amerian Economic Review*, 76, pp. 956–70.

——— (1988), 'Bankruptcy Costs and the Theory of Oligopoly', *Canadian Journal of Economics*, 21(2), pp. 221–43.

Brander, J.A. and B. Spencer (1984), 'Strategic Commitment with R&D: The Symmetric Case', *Bell Journal of Economics*, 14, pp. 225–35.

Bronars, S. and D. Deere (1991), 'The Threat of Unionization, the Use of Debt, and the Preservation of Shareholder Wealth', *Quarterly Journal of Economics*, 16, pp. 231–54.

Bulow J., J. Geanakoplos and P. Klemperer (1985), 'Multimarket Oligopoly: Stractegic Substitutes and Complements', *Journal of Political Economy*, 93, pp. 488–511.

Chevalier, J.A. (1995a), 'Capital Structure and Product Market Competition: Empirical Evidence from the Supermarket Industry', *American Economic Review*, June, pp. 415–35.

——— (1995b), 'Do LBO Supermarkets Charge More? An Empirical Analysis of the Effects of LBOs on Supermarket Pricing', *Journal of Finance,* 4, pp. 1095–112.

Chevalier, J.A. and D. Scharfstein (1994), 'Capital Market Imperfections and Counter-Cyclical Markups: Theory and Evidence', National Bureau of Economic Research, Working Paper No. 4614.

Dasgupta, S. and Y. Kim (1995), 'Big Customers, Bargaining, and Capital Structure', HKUST, mimeo.

Dasgupta, S. and K. Sengupta (1993), 'Sunk Investment, Bargaining, and Choice of Capital Structure', *International Economic Review*, 34, pp. 203–20.

Dasgupta, S. and S. Titman (1996), 'Pricing Strategy and Financing Policy', National Bureau of Economic Research, Working Paper No. 5498.

——— (1998), 'Pricing Strategy and Financing Policy, forthcoming, *Review of Financial Studies.*

Dasgupta, S. and J. Shin,'Information Sharing, Information Free-Riding and Capital Structure in Oligopolies', forthcoming, *International Journal of Industrial Organization.*

Dasgupta, S. and K.P. Wong (1996), 'Private Debt, Public Debt, and Product Market Competition', HKUST mimeo.

Froot, K. and P. Klemperer (1989), 'Exchange Rate Pass-Through When Markert Share Matters', *American Economic Review*, 79, pp. 637–53.

Fudenberg, D. and J. Tirole (1986), 'A 'Signal-Jamming' Theory of Predation', *Rand Journal of Economics*, 17, pp. 366–76.

Gertner, R., R. Gibbons, and D. Scharfstein (1988), 'Simultaneous Signalling to the Capital and Product Markets', *Rand Journal of Economics* 19, pp. 173–90.

Glazer, J. (1994), 'The Strategic Effects of Long-Term Debt in Imperfect Competition', *Journal of Economic Theory*, 62, pp. 428–43.

Green, R. (1984), 'Investment Incentives, Debt, and Warrants', *Journal of Financial Economics*, 13, pp. 115–36.

Hart, O. (1991), 'Theories of Optimal Capital Structure: A Principal-Agent Perspective', in M. Blair (ed.), *The Deal Decade*, Washington D.C.: Brookings Institution.

Jensen, M., and W. Meckling (1976), 'The Theory of the Firm: Managerial Behavior, Agency Costs and Ownership Structure', *Journal of Financial Economics*, 3, pp. 305–60.

Kaplan, S. (1989), 'The Effects of Management Buyouts on Operating Performance and Value', *Journal of Financial Economics*, 24, pp. 217–54.

Klemperer, P. (1987), 'Markets with Consumer Switching Costs', *Quarterly Journal of Economics*, pp. 375–94.

——— (1993), 'Competition in Markets with Consumer Switching Costs: An Overview', Oxford University Working Paper, 1993.

Kovenock, D. and G. Phillips (1995), 'Capital Structure and Product-Market Rivalry: How do we reconcile Theory and Evidence?', *American Economic Review* (AEA Papers and Proceedings), pp. 403–8.

——— , 'Capital Structure and Product Market Behavior: An Examination of Plant Exit and Investment Decisions', mimeo, Purdue University.

Maksimovic, V. (1986), 'Optimal Capital Structure in Oligopolies', unpublished PhD dissertation, Harvard University.

——— (1988), 'Optimal Capital Structure in Repeated Oligopolies', *Rand Journal of Economics*, 19, pp. 389–407.

——— (1990), 'Product Market Imperfections and Loan Commitments', *Journal of Finance*, 45, pp. 1641–53.

Maksimovic, V. and J. Zechner (1991), 'Debt, Agency Costs, and Industry Equilibrium', *Journal of Finance*, pp. 1619–43.

Maksimovic, V. and S. Titman (1991), 'Financial Reputation and Reputation for Product Quality', *Review of Financial Studies*, 2, pp. 175–200.

Maksimovic, V. (1996), 'Financial Structure and Product Market Competition, in R. Jarrow, V. Maksimovic and W.T. Ziemba (eds), *Handbook of Finance,* Amsterdam: North Holland.

Myers, S. (1977), 'Determinants of Corporate Borrowing', *Journal of Financial Economics*, 9, pp. 147–75.

Opler, T. and S. Titman (1994), 'Financial Distress and Corporate Performance', *Journal of Finance*, 49, pp. 1015–40.

Perotti, E. and K. Spier (1993), 'Capital Structure as a Bargaining Tool: The Role of Leverage in Contract Renegotiation', *American Economic Review*, pp. 1131–41.

Phillips, G. (1995), 'Increased Debt and Product Market Competition: An Empirical Analysis', *Journal of Financial Economics*, 37, pp. 189–238.

Showalter, D. (1995), 'Oligopoly and Financial Structure: Comment', *American Economic Review*, pp. 647–53

Stulz, R. (1990), 'Managerial Discretion and Optimal Financing Policies', *Journal of Financial Economics*, 26, pp. 3–27.

Telser, L. (1963), 'Cutthroat Competition and the Long Purse', *Journal of Law and Economics*, 9, pp. 259–77.

Titman, S. (1984), 'The Effect of Capital Structure on the Firm's Liquidation Decision', *Journal of Financial Economics*, 13, pp. 137–52.

——— and R. Wessels (1988), 'The Determinants of Capital Structure Choice', *Journal of Finance*, 43, pp. 1–19.

Williams, J. (1995), 'Agency, Capital Structure and Equilibrium', *Review of Financial Studies*, 8, pp. 431–74.

Wong, K.P. (1995), 'Cournot Oligopoly and Systematic Risk', *Journal of Economics and Business*, 47, pp. 385–95.

Zechner, J. (1996), 'Financial Market-Product Market Interactions in Industry Equilibrium: Implications for Information Acquisition Decisions', *European Economic Review*.

8

Private Lending to Sovereign Debtors

BHASWAR MOITRA*

1. INTRODUCTION

After the first major oil price rise in 1973–74, several member countries of OPEC placed the bulk of their massive current account surpluses in foreign assets. Roughly fifty per cent of these assets were bank deposits, primarily in the Euro currency market. At the same time, most non-oil producing developing countries were faced with sharply rising current account deficits. Given the low real rates of interest prevailing in the developed countries at the time, the large international banks found it profitable to reinvest these surplus funds deposited with them in loans to developing countries. For the rest of the decade, bank lending to developing countries continued to increase. In fact, after the second round of oil price increases in 1978–79, the pace accelerated, so that the total bank exposure in 1981 was twice the level of exposure in 1979.

Much of the lending was carried out through syndicated loans organized by a core of twenty five to fifty large (first tier) banks in developed countries, with about three thousand other smaller banks occasionally joining the syndicates. Curiously enough, of the forty or so Less Developed Countries (LDCs) that borrowed commercially from international banks, the bulk of the loans went to four countries. Bank managers, violating norms of prudent behaviour, treated loans made for separate projects in a country as separate loans in spite of the fact that these loans were guaranteed by the same agency (the government of the borrowing country).

By the end of the decade, however, the world economic environment had changed. By the latter part of the decade of the 1970s, large scale capital flight from these countries was rampant as domestic residents

*I wish to thank, without implicating, Smita Adhikari who taught me a lot about this subject over the years that she was writing her doctoral dissertation, and Nilanjana Gupta who graciously read through this essay and suggested several changes that, I believe, have made it more readable.

shifted their wealth offshore. Over the next few years, recessions in the developed nations led to a drop in export earnings for many of the borrower nations. At the same time, rising oil prices increased their import bills, and rising world interest rates increased their debt service obligations. By the end of 1981, many of the developing countries who had borrowed to fund investment projects, or consumption, or simply to cover massive governmental budget deficits caused by economic mismanagement, were in serious trouble as it became more and more obvious that they would not be able to meet their debt service obligations.

In August 1982, the Mexican government declared a moratorium on external debt service payments. Although this moratorium lasted for only about four months, as Mexico managed to renegotiate its payments schedule with its private creditors by December 1982, it led to a crisis of confidence among the lender banks and new bank lending to developing countries dropped dramatically. As a result, many LDCs who were depending on these loans to finance their scheduled payments on existing debt, were placed in a position where they were no longer able to meet their current obligations. The financial world was in the middle of a debt crisis.

While there were few actual defaults, many debtor nations renegotiated their loans, and in the years that followed, new private sector bank lending to LDCs remained at a fairly low level. The debt crisis is not over yet and it will take years perhaps, to return to a situation where private lenders have enough confidence to lend enthusiastically to developing countries.

Looked at in isolation, the entire cycle—from enthusiastic lending to the crisis in confidence, and finally, the sharp withdrawal of lenders from the market—would seem like an aberration that caused a lot of damage to both lenders and the borrower nations, who, in many instances, lost decades of development as they were forced into adopting severe austerity measures to adjust to the post-crisis scenario. A look at the history of private international lending, however, reveals that this sort of credit cycle has been the norm from at least the end of the eighteenth century. The distinctive feature of this last cycle is that almost all of the money lent was lent by private banks [Lindert and Morton (1989)][1].

This paper deals with the theoretical and empirical knowledge accumulated on the subject over the last twenty years. The central

[1]See also the *World Bank Development Report 1985* for a very useful survey of the history of private international lending.

theoretical issues are laid out in the paper, even though it often moves beyond the models set up, in order to introduce real world features to make it more relevant and explain many things that have remained unexplained, so far, in the formal literature.

2. AN IMPORTANT DISTINCTION AND THE ESSENTIAL PROBLEM

Suppose a bank is asked to lend Rs 10,000 to an entrepreneur for one year at an interest rate of ten per cent. The entrepreneur plans to use the money to buy a small printing business. Let us also suppose that given the wear and tear on his equipment, his business will have no market value at the end of the year.

However, if his luck is good, he will earn a gross operating profit of Rs 20,000, which is sufficient for him to repay his loan with interest, and still have money left to spend at the Saturday races. On the other hand, if his luck is bad, his gross operating profit will be Rs 2000. This is hardly enough to repay his loan, even if he wants to do so, and the bank can get at most Rs 2000 in this case. In the hard luck scenario, we say that the borrower is faced with a 'repayment problem' because he does not have the ability to pay.

There is, however, another possibility that is more frightening for the bank. Suppose that at the end of the year, the entrepreneur decamps with the till. In that case, the bank will get nothing under either scenario. What we have here is a problem of 'moral hazard': after the contract is signed and the bank hands over the money, the entrepreneur can take an action that leads to a situation that is against the bank's interest, and the bank can do nothing to prevent it.

Prudent bankers, thus, ask for sufficient collateral to insure themselves against such undesirable outcomes. Of course, the bank may have to go through long drawn out legal procedures before it can liquidate the collateral and get its money. But in the end, the existence of an efficient judicial system that the bank can appeal to, helps to reduce much of the risk for the banker. What is of critical importance then is the existence of a set of efficient institutions that can, by and large, enforce contracts[2].

[2]Of course, the institution that is used to enforce contracts does not have to be legal. Village moneylenders rarely appeal to the courts or the police. I am told that some modern retail bankers in India adopt methods that moneylenders have perfected over the years.

When a lender lends to a borrower who lives in the same country then usually, contract disputes can be settled in the country's courts. However, if the borrower is outside the jurisdiction of the courts of the lender's country, then it becomes difficult (if not impossible) to enforce contracts through the legal mechanism. This is the distinctive feature of sovereign debt: the lender has no legal means of ensuring that contracts are not violated. The point is important and to drive it home, I quote Grossman and Van Huyck (1988) who state it with great clarity.

> Private debts are subject to laws regarding bankruptcy and enforcement of collateral. Sovereign debts, in contrast, are above the law. Indeed, we can regard the power to abrogate commitments without having to answer to a higher authority to be the essential property of sovereignity. (Given this definition, historical cases in which one sovereign or its agents seized the assets of another apparent sovereign who is failing to service its debts involve infringement of sovereignity.)[3]

The question then is: why would a private lender voluntarily enter into the business of cross border lending at all? After all, a sovereign borrower, like any other debtor, may not have the ability to pay when payments become due. And the temptation to avoid repayment may actually be stronger. But as we have seen, such lending does occur. This merits an explanation. In the next section we try to provide just that.

3. A SIMPLE MODEL OF SOVEREIGN BORROWING

In this section we construct a very simple model of borrowing by a sovereign debtor. The objective is to provide some understanding of the kinds of reasons that often generate enough confidence among private lenders to make them willing to lend voluntarily to governments of other countries. The model is a drastically edited version of one constructed by Eaton and Gersovitz (1981). However, in order to preserve the pedagogical lucidity, some of the mathematical intricacies have been dispensed with.

Suppose a country's GNP can take two values, Y_1 and Y_2 (where $Y_1 < Y_2$), and that it takes the first value in odd years and the second in even years. The country's utility function is given by,

$$U(C_i) = \Sigma_{t=i}\, u(c_t) \tag{1}$$

where $C_i = (c_i, c_{i+1}, c_{i+2}, \ldots)$ is the infinite dimensional vector of consumption level, starting from year i, $u(\cdot)$ is the per period utility function and $\delta \in (0, 1)$ is the discount factor. Let $u'(\cdot) > 0$ and

[3]Grossman and Van Huyck (1988), p. 1088.

$u''(\cdot) < 0$. Consider first the case where the country has no access to foreign financial markets. This means that it cannot smoothen out its consumption stream by borrowing in the lean years and repaying in the good years. Then, from the perspective of any arbitrarily chosen odd year, say year 1, the utility of the country's consumption stream starting at year 1, is given by,

$$U(C_1) = u(Y_1) + \delta u(Y_2) + \delta^2 u(Y_1) + \delta^3 u(Y_2) + \delta^4 u(Y_1) + \ldots$$

$$= \frac{1}{1-\delta^2}[u(Y_1) + \delta u(Y_2)] \tag{2}$$

since $\quad C_1 = (Y_1, Y_2, Y_1, Y_2, \ldots)$.

Suppose now, that the country is allowed access to the international financial markets, where it has the option of taking one period loans, or of making one period loans, at the interest rate $r > 0$. By borrowing in the lean periods and repaying in the good periods, it can smoothen out its consumption stream, and thus, attain a higher level of utility than before. The question is, how much will the country borrow in each lean period?

Let us start by assuming that the country intends to repay its loan fully, and in time, every time it borrows. Notice first, that the future, viewed from the perspective of any arbitrarily chosen lean year, is the same as that viewed from the perspective of any other lean year. So that, at the optimum, the level of borrowing in lean year i should be the same as the level of borrowing in lean year j, for all distinct values of i and j. This considerably simplifies our next step, which is to determine the country's desired stream of borrowings. Let b be the common level of borrowing in each lean year. Then, the level of utility that the country can attain over its lifetime (starting at period 1) is,

$$u(Y_1 + b) + \delta u(Y_2 - (1+r)b) + \delta^2 u(Y_1 + b) + \delta^3 u(Y_2 - (1+r)b) + \ldots$$

$$= \frac{1}{1-\delta^2}[u(Y_1 + b) + \delta u(Y_2 - (1+r)b)] \equiv V(b). \tag{3}$$

The optimal level of borrowing in each period is then given by the solution to,

$$\underset{b}{\text{argmax}}\ V(b)$$

$$\text{subject to } Y_1 + b \geq 0 \text{ and } Y_2 - (1+r)b \geq 0. \tag{4}$$

Assume that a unique solution exists, and let it be $b = b^*$. The country's desired borrowing stream starting in period 1 is:

$$b^*, 0, b^*, 0, b^*, 0, \ldots$$

Unfortunately, the lenders have no way of knowing that the country does intend to repay (with interest) in each good period what it had borrowed in the last lean period.

As we saw in the last section, what we have here is a 'moral hazard' problem. Since the debt is owed by a sovereign government, attaching of assets is not possible without violating sovereign rights. Yet, without some sort of credible threat of retaliation, or some credible promise to reward those with a record of timely and full repayment, it is in the country's best interest to default on its repayments. One possible kind of threat that, perhaps, strictly speaking, violates the sovereignty principle, is that a complete and permanent debarment from the international credit market will be enforced immediately if a default occurs. Even this may not be enough to ensure that the country will adhere to its repayment plans if it is allowed to borrow the amount b^*. Let us see why.

Consider the country's options in period 2. It has borrowed some amount b in period 1 and has to make a payment of $(1 + r)b$ in period 2 if it wants to maintain its access to the international credit market. It can choose to default now, or it can choose to repay. The decision to default cuts it off from the international credit market for ever. This means that it will not be able to borrow again in the international market.

But there is more to it than just that. It also means that it can never lend in the international market. If this part of the threat did not exist, then it would always be better for the country to default in period 2 than to repay. For, in that case, the country could default and lend $(1 + r)b$ in period 2. This would give it $(1 + r)^2b$ in period 3, when it could consume $Y_1 + (1 + r)^2b$. In period 4 it can once again lend $(1 + r)b$ and, hence, consume $Y_1 + (1 + r)^2b$ in period 5. It is easy to see that this would yield a higher utility than the utility that would be derived from maintaining the reputation of a borrower who always repays his debts.

The argument, however, is still not complete. While it is true that continued access to the international credit market as a lender after a default makes the decision to default superior to the decision to borrow in each lean period and repay in the next for ever, is it superior to the decision to repay now and continue on a path of borrowing in odd numbered periods, and repaying in even numbered periods, till some odd numbered period $T + 1$ in the future, before defaulting in period

$T+2$? In this context it will be shown that if the country defers the decision to default for T periods, then it will never default. Consider the country's decision problem in period $T+2$. Since the model is stationary and the horizon is infinite, the future, from the perspective of period $T+2$ is identical to the future as it was viewed from the perspective of period 2. So the rationale that justified defering default for T periods in period 2 is the same one that will justify the decision to defer default for T periods in period $T+2$. Repeated use of this argument shows that the country will never default if it decides to postpone default in period 2.

Under what circumstances will a country that has borrowed the amount b in period 1 not default in period 2? It will not default if and only if the utility payoff from defaulting and surviving without borrowing or lending thereafter, falls short of the utility payoff from following a path of borrowing the amount b in every lean period and repaying in the next period. That is, default is not profitable if and only if,

$$u(Y_2) + \frac{\delta}{1-\delta^2}[u(Y_1) + \delta u(Y_2)] \leq u(Y_2 - (1+r)b) + \frac{\delta}{1-\delta^2}[u(Y_1 + b) + \delta u(Y_2 - (1+r)b)] \qquad (5)$$

Clearly, the equality holds if $b = 0$. For simplicity, let us assume that the right hand side is strictly concave and has a single peak over the domain $(0, \infty)$. Then there is at most one finite and positive value of b (call it $\bar{b}$) where this equality holds. For all values of $b \in [0, \bar{b}]$, the right hand side of the inequality exceeds the left hand side. This means that if the desired level of borrowing does not exceed $\bar{b}$, and the threat of disbarment is believable, then the country will not default[4]. If, however,

[4]Things are a bit different if the imposition of penalties is not costless. Suppose the creditor has to spend a positive amount, say C, to impose penalties on a recalcitrant borrower. Then he is better off accepting a payment $b - C$ (which is smaller than b) than he is going to be if he holds out for the amount b and imposes a penalty if it is not paid. In fact, for the creditor it is better to write off the debt and not impose a penalty than to impose a costly penalty. Knowing this, the debtor will seek to renegotiate the payment, once the loan is made, and will drive the creditor down to accepting a zero payment. In the language of theory, any agreement that stipulates a positive repayment is not 'renegotiation proof' if (a) the creditor has to pay for imposition of penalties and (b) gains nothing (as in this model) if the penalty is imposed. For more on these lines see the seminal paper by Bulow and Rogoff (1989a).

b is greater than $\bar{b}$, the left hand side of the inequality is greater than the right hand side so that, for any borrowing level above $\bar{b}$, the 'moral hazard' problem exists. We call $\bar{b}$ the maximum credible level of borrowing. Given full information about the country's preferences and its income in each period, lenders will not be willing to lend a total amount exceeding $\bar{b}$.

Even though the model constructed is abstract and shorn of much of the real world details that make sovereign international borrowing such a risky affair[5], it is instructive because it sets up a framework on the basis of which some real world issues can be explored. The first thing to observe is that it may be very difficult for lenders to know the exact preferences and future earning streams of the borrowers. The earning stream of a country may depend on a whole host of factors, some of which are beyond the control of both, the lender and the borrower. For example, as governments change, the time preferences of the decision makers in the borrowing countries may change. This could affect both, the *inclination* as well as the *capability* of repayment of the debtor.

The first part of the assertion is easy to see in the context of our model. Suppose, that at the beginning of period 1, lenders know that the debtor government's discount factor is δ_1 and lend the corresponding maximum credible amount of loan b_1. Suppose further, that at the beginning of period 2 there is a new government which has a lower level of time preference, so that its discount factor δ_2 is smaller than δ_1. Check that $b'(\delta)$ is negative. This means that $b_1(1 + r)$ will not be repaid by the new government.

The second part of the assertion is not immediately obvious from the model. But suppose, a country's future earning stream depends to a great extent on its productive capacity. Suppose a government run by a cabal of thieves comes to power after a loan has been taken. They rob the land of its wealth and move to Monaco with the spoils. The country's productive capacity falls and when repayment is due, the

[5] I am afraid that the model may have reminded some readers of Macbeth's famous lines:

> It is a tale
> Told by an idiot, full of sound and fury,
> Signifying nothing.
>
> [*Macbeth* V: 5: 26–28.]

country cannot pay. This is a possibility that the lenders will have to bear in mind at the time of making the loans[6].

Generalization of the model to incorporate such difficulties is possible, although such a model would have to make the assumption that the lender has some probabilistic notion about the time preferences of the country's future governments and about its future earning streams[7]. There is also the problem that emerges because countries typically borrow from a number of lenders. Thus, a typical lender may not have a very good idea about the total debt that the country has already incurred before it lends to the country, so that even if the total safe borrowing limit is known, the lender does not know how close the country is to this limit. Kletzer (1984) addresses this issue.

An issue that lies at the heart of the problem of sovereign debt is that voluntary lending by private lenders to sovereign borrowers will never occur unless there is an implicit belief of a reasonably high probability that the money lent will ultimately be repaid. Underlying such a faith is the belief that debtors will not default because they fear that default will be met by some sort of penalty that will be imposed on them if they default, or that default will not occur because debtors hope to gain from developing a reputation for faithful repayment. This line of thought is fairly common in the literature on sovereign debt problems[8]. The particular type of sanction postulated seems to be an intuitively plausible sort of threat of this sort[9].

Delving deeper into the nature of this threat yields some interesting dividends. As seen before, there are two components to the threat: first, the defaulter nation will not be able to lend again in the private international credit market; and second, it will never be able to borrow in these markets after a default. The question is: how are these threats going to be carried out?

One way to carry out the first threat is to impound all existing financial assets, held in the home countries of the lenders by the

[6]Examples of such behaviour are commonplace.

[7]Eaton and Gersovitz (1981) model a stochastic future earning stream, as do a whole host of other papers. I have avoided such a framework to keep it simple.

[8]See Eaton and Gersovitz (1981), Allen (1982), Krugman (1985), Eaton, Gersovitz and Stiglitz (1986), Bulow and Rogoff (1989), Fernandez and Rosenthal (1990) among others.

[9]In much of the theortical literature on the debt crisis, threats of this sort have been used to explain both, lending and the limits to prudent lending. See footnote 4 for some references.

defaulting nation, after a default. This includes all financial assets acquired before and after the default. But this clearly violates the sovereign rights of the debtor[10] and may require the intervention of the courts and the governments of the lenders' home countries. While there are instances where assets of recalcitrant debtors have been frozen, such instances are rare. Further, in many cases, citizens of debtor nations that have defaulted have stashed away very large sums in financial and other assets in developed countries. Such funds, however, remain untouched, perhaps because it is difficult to convince a court that impounding such assets is legally justifiable.

Implementation of the second part of the sanction may be just as tricky, but lenders have found some ways around the difficulties. A country typically borrows over time from several lenders. In principle, it can default on its loans from one or more of these lenders and still be able to borrow from other lenders, unless lenders collude to blacklist a borrower who has defaulted on any loan in the past. Of course, such an agreement may be difficult to enforce and, hence, implementation of this part of the sanction may be impossible. Lenders have, at least partially, solved this problem by including cross-default clauses and seniority clauses in the loan agreements that they sign[11].

It seems appropriate now to look at the history of private international lending to see if defaulters have been punished and faithful borrowers rewarded[12]. In the past, some countries who defaulted in the bond lending era, like Egypt (1882) and Mexico (1859–61), suffered invasions and temporary losses of sovereignity. Brazil in the 1890s agreed to give up all its customs receipts and to impose a moratorium on its internal and external debt issues to appease its foreign creditors.

Lindert and Morton (1989) assert that before 1918 the majority of defaulters suffered no harm. In the widespread defaults on LDC loans in the 1930s, defaulters suffered cut-backs in trade credits. What is, however, more interesting is that for decades thereafter, lenders suffered from a widespread aversion to LDC debt, irrespective of whether a

[10]See Fernandez and Rosenthal (1990) for more on this issue.

[11]A cross default clause makes a country a defaulter on a loan if it defaults on any loan made by a lender named in the cross default agreement. A seniority clause guarantees that if a country repays only a part of its total debt, then senior creditors (i.e. typically, creditors who have lent earlier) will get paid first.

[12]This section is based on Lindert and Morton (1989) and the World Bank's *World Development Report 1985*. If serious historians find my thumbnail sketch appallingly naive I extend my apologies.

country had defaulted in the past or not. In the years 1974–82, lenders, in the words of Lindert and Morton, 'paid no attention to the past history of defaults' and the interest premiums charged were the same for borrowers who had defaulted in the past as for those who had not[13]. In the post-crisis years, the contraction in privately supplied credit seems to have affected almost all LDCs, irrespective of their history of default.

This chapter contends that lenders move in packs, concentrating on certain regions of the globe. When one or more countries in a region default, there is a crisis of confidence and lenders begin to withdraw from the region. This leads to a 'domino effect', as country after country faces payment difficulties and renegotiation of payments becomes the order of the day. Ultimately, lenders withdraw totally and do not return till the crisis is a distant event recorded in history books that the new generation of fund managers choose to ignore.

The question that still reamins unanswered is, why do lenders lend to LDCs? The reason, perhaps, is that there is a sense that borrower nations will put up with a lot of pain before declaring their inability to carry on with the repayment schedule. Why do sovereign borrowers try to avoid default when default stares them in the face? The answer lies in the fact that the perceived cost of default is ultimately quite high. For countries that are fairly open to international trade, the loss of trade credits can be fairly expensive. There is also the fear that suspension of payments can lead to a drop in the level of support that the country receives from the international agencies and foreign aid agencies, together with a loss of support on foreign policy that smaller nations often need from major countries like the USA and its allies.

There is also the question of the domestic fallout from a default. Under the straitened circumstances that typically precede a payment crisis, a large section of the population may be unwilling to suffer the privations caused by heavy repayment requirements. There are others who are dependent heavily on international trade or investments, who oppose default because they stand to lose from reductions in trade credits or other borrowing facilities. A government contemplating a repayment moratorium has to balance these forces.

Why then, do countries default? In the deterministic world of our model, unless lenders make an error in calculation, there should be no

[13]Sule Ozler (1993), however, is of the view that in the last phase of heavy lending, banks ignored only the very distant history of default.

default. So, defaults can only occur in a world of uncertainty and imperfect information. The consensus among experts in the field is that defaults occur because of three sorts of reasons. The first reason is that the country has accumulated debts that are not repayable under the best of circumstances. The second reason is that the country is faced with unforeseen events that affect its ability to pay. The third reason is that the money borrowed has been misused, in the sense that it has not added to the country's productive capacity. The model in the next section shows how unforeseen events can alter a country's status from that of a 'good' debtor to that of a problem debtor. The model is subsequently used to look at some of the major suggestions for ending the debt crisis.

4. DEBT CRISIS AND AFTER

As in the last section, this section begins with a stylized model on the basis of which some relatively complex issues are explored[14].

At any point in time, a country may have a stock of debt that it has inherited from the past, which it is expected to repay in accordance with some schedules of repayment that have been agreed upon earlier. However, the country's ability to adhere to the repayment schedules depends on a host of factors, some of which may be outside its control.

Thus, in a given year, it may not have the ability to pay the scheduled amount. If lenders are confident that, given time, it can make good on the shortfall in payment, then the existing creditors may be willing to defer repayment by treating the shortfall as a new loan. Alternatively, new lenders may be found, from whom money can be borrowed to pay the entire amount that is due to the existing creditors. In contrast, the country is said to be facing a *liquidity crisis* if the existing and potential creditors are not confident that the country can repay its debt, even if it is given time. For, in that case, the country cannot borrow to meet its current obligations and defaulting on payments will be the only option available to it[15].

Basu (1994) provides an interesting model that captures the essential

[14]This model is a somewhat simpler version of a model developed in Adhikari and Moitra (1996).

[15]Notice that in this case the country cannot borrow, even if it offers a higher rate of interest. A higher interest rate will increase its payment obligations and lenders are unsure about its ability to repay even at the existing interest rate.

fragility of a borrower nation's situation. The line between the lenders' confidence in the ability of a nation to repay and their belief that it will be unable to repay is often fairly thin, and a switch from the former to the latter can lead to disaster for the nation's economy. The following model tries to capture some of these ideas.

Consider a country whose government has borrowed internationally in the past. Repayments on debt incurred in one year are due at the beginning of the next. If the country is unable to repay the full amount due in a given year, then the shortfall in payment may be refinanced as a new one-year loan at the market rate of interest. Of course, such refinancing will be available only if the creditors are confident that the country can make the payment in the future.

Suppose the government plans to repay its debts out of its revenue collections after paying for domestic expenses. Let R_s be the government's revenue in year s, net of all its expenses except its payments on its international debt. Then,

$$R_s = T_s + A_s \tag{6}$$

where T_s is the revenue from taxes placed on the domestic production sector and A_s is its revenue from other sources minus its total expenditure (except debt repayments). For the moment, assume that A_s remains unchanged over time, so that for all S, A_s equals some fixed value A_0[16].

For simplicity of exposition, let there be one representative producer and let input prices, measured in units of the single good produced, be fixed. Production requires payment in advance for inputs. Given productive capacity, technology and input prices, output depends on the quantity of working capital that is available to the producer. Given working capital C, let the relationship between a given quantity of (C) and the maximum output (Y) that can be produced, be given by,

$$Y = g(C) \tag{7}$$

with $$g'(C) > 0 \text{ and } g''(C) < 0.$$

Then,

$$R_s = A_0 + T_s = A_0 + t_s\, g(C_s) \tag{8}$$

(where t_s is the tax rate imposed in year s)
is the revenue in year s if the working capital used is C_s.

[16]We shall have more to say on this a bit later.

Assume that the economy is financially open, so that the producer can borrow his working capital either domestically, or outside at the world rate of interest r. Dropping time subscripts for the moment, the producer's profit function is given by,

$$\pi = (1 - t)g(C) - (1 + r)C \tag{9}$$

At the beginning of each year, the government selects the tax rate t. The producer observes the tax rate and selects his profit maximizing level of working capital $C^*(t, r)$ given by the solution to,

$$(1 - t)g'(C) = (1 + r) \tag{10}$$

Then, the maximum revenue that government can raise through the tax on output, given r, is,

$$T(r) = \max_{t} tg\,(C^*(t, r)) \tag{11}$$

so that the government's maximum repayment potential is,

$$R_s^* = A_0 + T(r) = R^* \tag{12}$$

and its net repayment is,

$$P_s = \min\,[D_s, R_s^*] \tag{13}$$

Hence, the debt repayment obligation at the beginning of year $s + 1$ is,

$$D_{s+1} = \max\,[0, (D_s - R_s^*(r))(1 + r)] \tag{14}$$

It follows then, that,

$$D_{s+1} = 0 \qquad \text{if } Ds \leq R^*$$

and

$$D_{s+1} > 0 \qquad \text{otherwise} \tag{15}$$

Figure 8.1 shows the graph of D_{s+1} as a function of D_s for two values of r, r_1 and r_2. For each value of r, D_{s+1} equals zero for all values of D_s less than or equal to $R^*(r)$. Thereafter, it rises as D_s rises. Notice that the slope of this function is $(1 + r)$ for $D_s > R^*$, so that there exists a debt level $D^*(r)$, at which the outstanding debt remains unchanged over time if the interest rate does not change. It is not very difficult to check that $R^*(r)$ falls as r rises. This means that if $r_2 > r_1$ then $D^*(r_1) > D^*(r_2)$.

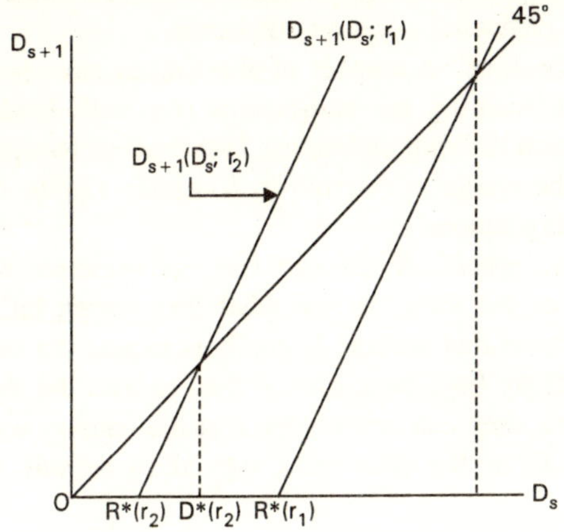

FIGURE 8.1 Second Period Debt Repayment Obligation as a Function of Interest Rates in Period 1 (r_1) and Period 2 (r_2).

If the initial debt level is less than this critical level and if the interest rate does not rise above the current level, the country will be able to repay its debt in a finite number of years. The caveat, of course, is that creditors have to keep re-lending till the country clears the entire debt. If creditors do not expect the interest rate to rise for a sufficiently large number of years, then, of course, this lending should be forthcoming. On the other hand, if the outstanding debt in the current period exceeds D^*, then at the current interest rate, the debt burden will explode over time, even if the creditors agree to re-lend the shortfall in payments every year.

Suppose now, that a country has an outstanding payment of $D_0 \in [D^*(r_2), D^*(r_1)]$. At the beginning of the current year the interest rate rises from r_1 to r_2. If this interest rate is expected to persist for ever, then the debt is never repayable. At a somewhat more heuristic level, if lenders expect the higher interest rate to persist for some time, or to go up even further before coming down, the debt may never be repayable, even if they carry on re-lending the shortfall in payments each year. The important point is that no one knows with complete certainty how long the higher interest rate will persist.

Which brings us back to the point where we had started: if lenders believe that interest rates will not fall in the forseeable future, then no new loans will be forthcoming to finance current shortfalls in payment, and we have a payments crisis on our hands.

What is to be done? A number of alternatives have been suggested as means for extricating the participants (i.e. both lenders and borrowers) from such difficult situations. Two lines of thought are briefly sketched and the reader is referred to Krugman (1988, 1989a, b) for more detailed expositions.

There is one school of thought that recommends that creditors forgive a part of the debt. To see what they mean, let us return to the model set up in this section. If creditors expect the interest rate r_2 to persist for a long time then, even if they re-lend the shortfall at the new interest rate, they can never hope that the country will be able to settle its debts. If, on the other hand, they allow default, they can get, at most,

$$R^*(r_2) < D^*(r_2) < D^*(r_1)$$

In this case, a one time reduction in debt to $D^*(r_2) - \varepsilon$ (where ε is some arbitrarily small positive number) makes the renegotiated debt level repayable if the interest rate does not rise any further, and leads to an outcome that is preferable to both parties[17]. [See Figure 8.1[18].]

An alternative strategy that is often suggested involves collective lending by existing lenders, so as to push back the day of reckoning. To get to the heart of the argument, let us adopt a two period framework. At the beginning of period 1 a country has an outstanding debt D, but is able to transfer at most $x_1 < D$. In the next period, the maximum potential repayment is uncertain: with probability p, it is equal to x_H; and with probability $(1-p)$, it is equal to x_L, where $x_H > x_L$. The creditors have one of two options: they can lend the amount $D - x_1$ to the country and prevent default; or they can allow default to occur. In the latter case, they are unlikely to collect the entire amount x_1 as disorderly default can involve costs for the creditors before they can collect their share of the payments. Let $Z < x_1$ be the amount they can collect. Suppose that they decide to lend. Then lenders can negotiate with the borrower to decide how much is paid in each state. In the extreme case, where the creditors have all the bargaining power, they can force a contract that gives them

[17]The debtor would prefer this, as this would allow it to avoid possible default penalties which can be fairly steep.

[18]Bulow and Rogoff (1989) and Fernandez and Rosenthal (1990) are two papers that use bargaining models to look at this issue.

x_H in the good state and x_L in the bad state. In that case, the present value of their receipts is,

$$P = x_1 + [px_H + (1 - p)\, x_L]/(1 + r) \tag{16}$$

where r is the current interest rate. It is useful to distinguish between two cases.

CASE 1. $P \geq D$

In this case, lenders should be more than willing to lend the amount $D - x_1$. In fact, even new lenders should be willing to lend this amount to the country[19]

CASE 2. $P \leq D$

This case is tricky, since,

$$px_H + (1 - p)\, x_L < (D - x_1)\,(1 + r) \tag{17}$$

for, this means that new lenders will not be willing to lend. For the existing creditors, however, treating the shortfall as a new loan makes sense. By doing this they get $x_1 > Z$ in the first year and if the borrower has no bargaining power, in the next period they get x_H if the state is good, and x_L if the state is bad.

Either scenario is better than getting Z alone in the first year. For the existing creditors, postponing the default in this way is a way of defending the value of their existing claims.

The argument stated above seems to provide a clear cut justification for re-lending by the existing creditors. Here, we introduce a wrinkle that can make defensive lending a bit less attractive. Suppose that the probability p of achieving x_H in the second period is positively related to the adjustment effort made by the borrower nation to meet its repayment obligations. In the framework of our model, this is equivalent to raising A_0. At a more mundane level, this may involve cutting down governmental expenditure on programmes that are deemed to be wasteful. Quite often, such reductions, especially if they involve efforts to downgrade or to completely eliminate distributional programmes that require governmental subsidies, meet with stiff resistance adjustment efforts, and also often require the country to run large non-interest

[19] I am assuming that lenders are risk neutral.

current account surpluses, which may require sharp cuts in the imports of essential final goods or inputs for non-traded goods. This can impose severe costs on the domestic populace.

The point here is that painful adjustment efforts will be resisted by the residents of the borrower nation if they see no gain from it[20]. Thus, if the entire gain from adjustment is expropriated for the repayment of debts, ensuring adjustment after the contract is signed will be difficult. In that case p will fall, i.e. the probability of getting x_H will fall. Creditors may, therefore, have to forego picking up all of x_H in the event that the good state occurs to induce the adjustment effort. The difficulty here lies in judging how much adjustment effort will be forthcoming for each unit reduction in the claim made if the good state occurs[21].

Most of the plans for finding a way out of the debt crisis revolve around these extremes. In practice, what is required is a workable design for engineering debt forgiveness. Programmes like the 'Brady Plan' try to do just that. Even here, several subtle problems emerge. For more on this, the reader is encouraged to begin by reading the *Journal of Economic Perspectives*, Volume 4, Number 1, (1990), the survey article by Eaton and Fernandez (1995), and chapter six in Obstfeld and Rogoff (1996).

CONCLUSIONS

This essay tries to provide a fairly non-technical introduction to the literature on private lending to sovereign debtors. The term sovereign debt has been used in a narrow sense to include only the debt incurred by a sovereign government or debt that is guaranteed by one. Would the story be very different were it to include the unguaranteed debt of private firms? It is commonly believed that in the end, lenders lend to private firms across their borders only if there is some sort of faith that in a crunch the borrowers' governments can be coaxed into settling the claim. See, for example, Diaz-Alejandro (1985).

Before concluding, the chapter notes that a country faced with a shortage of savings or foreign exchange, quite often has very powerful reasons for borrowing abroad commercially. There is, however, more

[20]In the 1980s, Chile, under a strong autocratic regime, could afford to tighten its belt in ways that were not open to regimes that were either democratic or less well-entrenched autocracies.

[21]See also Corden (1988) and Cohen (1993).

to international borrowing than a simple transfer of savings from countries where the return on investment is low to countries where the return is higher. This chapter has merely tried to introduce the reader to the complications involved that are not usually spelled out in an undergraduate level course on development economics.

References

Adhikari, S. and B. Moitra (1997), 'Interest Rate Changes and Capital Flight: The Origins of a Debt Crisis', manuscript, Jadavpur University.

Basu, K. (1991), 'The International Debt Problem, Credit Rationing and Loan Pushing: Theory and Decision', *Princeton Studies in International Finance*, 79.

——— (1993), 'On the Suddenness of the International Debt Crisis', *Sankhya: The Indian Journal of Statistics*, 55(B3), pp. 291–6.

Bulow, J. and K. Rogoff (1988), 'Multilateral Negotiations for Rescheduling Developing Country Debt', *International Monetary Fund Staff Papers*, 35 pp. 644–57.

——— (1989a), 'A Constant Recontracting Model of Sovereign Debt', *Journal of Political Economy*, 97, pp. 155–78.

——— (1989b), 'Sovereign Debt: Is to Forgive to Forget?', *American Economic Review*, 79, pp. 43–50.

Calvo, G.A. and G.L. Kaminsky (1991), 'Debt Relief and Debt Resheduling: The Optimal-Contract Approach', *Journal of Development Economics*, 36, pp. 5–36.

Cohen, D. (1993), 'Low Investment and Large LDC Debt in the 1980s', *American Economic Review*, 83(3), pp. 437–49.

Congdon, T. (1988), *The Debt Threat*, New York: Basil Blackwell.

Corden, W. Max (1988), 'Debt Relief and Adjustment Incentives', *International Monetary Funds Staff Papers*, 35 pp. 628–43.

Diaz-Alejandro, C. (1985), 'Good-Bye Financial Repression, Hello Financial Crash', *Journal of Development Economics*, 19, pp. 1–24.

Eaton, J. (1987), 'Public Debt Guarantees and Private Capital Flight', *World Bank Economic Review*, 1, pp. 337–95.

——— (1990), 'Debt Relief and the International Enforcement of Loan Contracts', *Journal of Economic Perspective*, 4(1), pp. 43–56.

——— (1993), 'Sovereign Debt: A Primer', *The World Bank Economic Review*, 7, pp. 137–72.

Eaton, J. and M. Gersovitz (1981), 'Debt with Potential Repudiation: Theoretical and Empirical Analysis', *Review of Economic Studies*, 48, pp. 289–309.

Eaton, J., M. Gersovitz and J. Stiglitz (1986), 'The Pure Theory of Country Risk', *European Economic Review*, 30(3), pp. 481–513.

Eaton, J. and Taylor (1986), 'Developing Country Finance and Debt', *Journal of Development Economics*, 22, pp. 209–65.

Eaton, J. and R. Fernandez (1995), 'Sovereign Debt', in G. Grossman and K. Rogoff (eds), *Handbook of International Economics*, vol. 3, Amsterdam: North Holland.

Fernandez, R. and R. Rosenthal (1990), 'Strategic Models of Sovereign-Debt Renegotiations', *Review of Economic Studies*, 57, pp. 331–49.

Grossman, H.I. and J.B. Van Huyck (1988), 'Sovereign Debt as a Contingent Claim: Excusable Default, Repudiation and Reputation', *American Economic Review*, 78(5), pp. 1088–97.

Smith, G.W. and J.T. Cuddington (eds), (1985), 'International Debt and the Developing Countries', World Bank, Washington, DC.

Helpman, E. (1990), 'The Simple Analytics of Debt-Equity Swaps', *American Economic Review*, 79(3), pp. 440–51.

Kindleberger, C.P. (1978), *Manias, Panics, and Crashes: A History of Financial Crises*, New York.

Kletzer, K. (1984), 'Asymmetries of Information and LDC Borrowing with Sovereign Risk', *Economic Journal*, 94, pp. 287–307.

Krugman, P. (1988), 'Financing vs. Forgiving a Debt Overhang', *Journal of Development Economics*, 29, pp. 253–68.

——— (1989a), 'Private Capital Flows to Problem Debtors', in J.D. Sachs (ed.), *Developing Country Debt and the World Economy*, Chicago-London: University of Chicago Press.

——— (1989b), 'Market-Based Debt-Reduction Schemes', in J.A. Frenkel *et al.* (eds.), *Analytical Issues in Debt*, Washington D.C. International Monetary Fund.

Lindert, P.H. and P.J. Morton (1989), 'How Sovereign Debt has Worked', in J.D. Sachs (ed.), *Developing Country Debt and the World Economy*, Chicago–London: University of Chicago Press.

McDonald, D.C. (1982), 'Debt Capacity and Developing Country Borrowing: A Survey of the Literature', *International Monetary Fund Staff Papers*, 29, pp. 603–46.

Obstfeld, M. and K. Rogoff (1996), *Foundations of International Macroeconomics,* Cambridge, Massachuseths: MIT Press.

Ozler, Sule (1993), 'Have Commercial Banks Ignored History?', *American Economic Review*, 83(3), pp. 608–20.

Rosenthal (1991), 'On the Incentives Associated with Sovereign Debt', *International Economic Review.*

Sachs, J.D. (ed.), (1989) *Developing Country Debt and the World Economy*, Chicago–London: University of Chicago Press.

Sachs, J. and D. Cohen (1986), 'Growth and External Debt Under Risk of Debt Repudiation', *European Economic Review*, 30, pp. 529–60.

Sachs, J. and H. Huizinga (1987), 'U.S. Commercial Banks and the Developing-Country Debt Crisis', *Brooking Papers on Economic Activity*, 2, pp. 555–601.

World Bank, *World Development Report* (1985).

Institutions

Institutions: An Introduction

One of the most exciting recent developments in economics is the explicit study of institutions. In its broadest sense, an institution may be regarded as a contextual device within which social and economic relationships are framed. From this point of view, a village economy that engages in reciprocal transactions (such as inter-household insurance), supported by the threat of social sanctions in the event of non-compliance is just as much an institution as a formal legal system that defines acceptable contracts and enforces them.

The study of social and economic institutions may be divided into two methodological categories. One might be interested in analyzing the effect of a given institution, such as a legal system, a constitution, or social norms. Or one might be interested in the normative question of institutional design. Starting with the seminal work of writers such as Leonid Hurwicz and Eric Maskin, this falls under the subject of implementation. The two chapters on institutions in this volume are examples of work in each of these two categories.

Dealers, Markets and Exchanges

Gautam Bose's chapter represents a selective study of different institutional arrangements that facilitate intermediation of trading processes, but one that yields general insights. In the standard Walrasian framework, the entire question of how trade is conducted is relegated to the hands of a fictional auctioneer, who helpfully adjusts prices to equate supply and demand. Yet, many transactions are costly, and are intermediated through retail stores or middlemen. Matching a potential buyer (of some good, service, or input) to a potential seller of that same product may be a non-trivial exercise, and the act of arbitrage which accomplishes such matching needs to be studied.

Bose discusses two aspects of the intermediation process. One aspect is that intermediation acts as an absorber of costly delays: it provides immediacy in exchange. For instance, intermediaries on a stock exchange might provide immediacy in return for a price: the bid-ask spread. Because delays have important macroeconomic implications, an institution of intermediation that reduces delay will affect economic welfare. Bose shows that if both intermediation and private meetings are permitted, those agents with greater potential gains from trade will take the intermediation route, while the remaining agents will wait for private trades. To be sure, this does not mean that the intermediated equilibrium Pareto-dominates its non-intermediated counterpart: agents who choose private trade under the intermediated equilibrium will be worse off, owing to the reduced frequency of trades.

The second aspect of the intermediation process addressed by Bose is its role in screening or sorting. Returning to the example of the stock exchange, it may be that large traders wish to meet other large traders (in order to reduce the incidence of transaction-specific fixed costs). Institutions such as the stock exchange might accomplish this separation by charging a suitable entry fee for trading on the floor; large traders would then be willing to pay the fee while small traders trade 'outside' or over-the-counter. The crucial question here is whether an efficiency-enhancing separation can be achieved; the fee must be large enough to deter an outsider from entering, while not being so high that the insider is discouraged from paying it. Bose discusses these issues elegantly (his own contribution to this literature, it should be added, is significant).

Implementation

It is fair to say that the modern theory of implementation owes its origin to the problem of public goods provision. In public goods economies, it is straightforward to characterize efficiency provided that preferences are known to the social planner.* But the requirement that preferences must be known is very strong. In general, appropriate incentives must be provided to elicit this information, or more generally, mechanisms must be designed that induce the agents to act in a way which leads to efficiency. Remarkable progress has been made in this direction.† To

*A classic reference is E. Lindahl (1919), 'Just Taxation—A Positive Solution', reprinted in; *Classics in the Theory of Public Finance*, (1967), Eds, R. Musgrave and A. Peacock, New York: Martins Press.

†See, for instance, J. Green and J.J. Laffont (1979), *Incentives in Public Decision Making*, Amsterdam: North-Holland, and J.J. Laffont (1987), 'Incentives and the Allocation of Public Goods', in *Handbook of Public Economics*, Vol. 2, Eds, A. Auerbach and M. Feldstein, Amsterdam: North-Holland.

use Sonnenschein's words, 'one does not so lightly say that it is not possible to design cooperation.‡

It becomes clear very quickly that public goods provision is an instance of a more general situation in which a planner has a 'social choice correspondence'; a mapping from agent preferences to social outcomes. However, the planner does not know what these preferences are, and must provide incentives for them to be indirectly or directly revealed: this is the problem of implementation. Bhaskar Dutta has played an important role in obtaining many of the key results in this literature. In his contribution to this volume, he surveys a class of conditions, known as 'preference reversal conditions', that can be used as litmus tests for determining whether a given social choice correspondence is implementable or not. Naturally, these conditions vary with the equilibrium concept that is used to describe agent behaviour. Dutta provides a unified treatment of both the conditions themselves, and the way in which they vary with the equilibrium concept.

‡H. Sonnenschein (1983), 'The Economics of Incentives: An Introductory Account', in *Frontiers of Research in Economic Theory: The Nancy L. Schwartz Memorial Lectures, 1983–1997*, (1998), Eds, D. Jacobs, E. Kalai and M. Kamien, Cambridge: Cambridge University Press.

9

Dealers, Markets, and Exchanges
A Study of Intermediation

GAUTAM BOSE

1. INTRODUCTION

The question of intermediation and of institutional rules for trading has received far less attention in economic theory than is properly its due. The two dominant approaches to equilibrium analysis—the Edgeworthian and the Walrasian—both ignore trading processes. In the Edgeworthian approach, trades are proposed and blocked by extended coalitions of agents, but procedures for constructing such coalitions are not explicitly analysed. In the Walrasian approach, intermediation is assumed to be perfect, *a priori*, and hence, does not attract analytical attention.

However, the most casual observation makes it abundantly clear that institutionalized processes and intermediation are pervasive characteristics of modern markets. In a contemporary economy, almost all trade in physical goods takes place through intermediaries such as retail stores or sales agencies. Even for services which are directly rendered by producers to final users, the buyer and seller are often matched by an intermediary. Travel agencies, corporate 'head hunters', and financial planners are some obvious examples.

The anlaysis of trading processes is of interest for two reasons. Once we drop the Walrasian construct of the auctioneer (and thus, of perfect intermediation), we are able to meaningfully address questions of price dispersion arising from this kind of friction, and thus, gain better understanding of the structure of markets. We can also ask whether the institutions of trade make the market more efficient, and whether the conditions under which this happens are compatible with intermediaries making a profit. This is the micro perspective. From a macro viewpoint, it is interesting to ask whether variations in the structure of trade can be responsible for coordination failures of a Keynesian type, and can, therefore, account for inefficient equilibria.

This chapter attempts to provide a very selective outline of a literature concerned with the above questions. The observations integrated below have been chosen for analytical coherence, and to a large extent, reflect the author's own preferences; there is no presumption of survey-like completeness. Nor has there been any attempt to provide technical detail. Instead, principal points have been illustrated through fairly general examples. Nevertheless, the treatment uncovers some major concerns, and points out some interesting insights.

The explanation for the existence of intermediation which suggests itself most immediately to economists is one which postulates non-convexities in the technology of exchange, i.e. increasing returns to scale. If conducting a transaction, for example, has a fixed cost independent of the scale or diversity of the bundles of goods transacted, and intermediation can economize on the number of transactions, then a set of intermediated transactions will be more efficient than the corresponding unintermediated ones. While economies of scale are certainly important and valid reasons for intermediation to arise, this does not constitute the focus of the present.

In his study of the New York Stock Exchange, Demsetz (1968) pointed out that an important function performed by intermediaries is that they provide immediacy in exchange. For traders who come to the market to exchange goods, the act of exchange itself is incidental to broader pursuits (e.g. production and consumption), and therefore, a delay in effecting exchange is costly. This creates a role for a mediator who is willing to absorb the delay in return for a price. The price of mediation is captured by the 'bid-ask spread'.

In his seminal 1982 paper, Diamond showed that equilibrium delays in exchange can affect production decisions, and thus, have significant macroeconomic consequences. One of the two themes that are explored below is that intermediaries, by providing immediacy (or at least by altering the 'thickness' of the market), can variously, reduce search costs, influence production decisions, and in general, can affect economic welfare.

Not all agencies which facilitate trade do so by absorbing delay. Many are matchmakers, primarily serving the purpose of bringing together pairs (or coalitions) or agents who have a preference for dealing with each other. Singles bars come to mind. This function is more delicate if there are potential pairings in which preference is not mutual.

An example of such a separating function is found in gambling establishments frequented by both professional card-sharps and vacationers. The former may well like to be matched with the latter, but the preference is not reciprocated. The casino mediates by placing different betting limits on different tables. Tables with low limits attract the tourist, but are not worthwhile for the professional.

The second theme investigated below is this screening function of trading institutions.

When the intermediary absorbs delay, he trades separately with each partner; when he screens he simply brings together the right pair of partners, who then conduct trade directly. In either case, the terms of trade may be determined in different ways. In the standard Walrasian approach, prices are determined by competitive pressure—essentially outside the ambit of the individual transaction. In the alternative sequential bargaining framework (Rubinstein 1982, Rubinstein and Wolinsky 1985), matched traders are 'locked in' to each other to some extent, and it is costly to regain access to the competitive market. The latter framework adds more structure to the transaction process than does the former, and it is well known that the equilibrium outcome can often be very sensitive to the exact specification of the process through which bargaining takes place.

Section 'Continuous-Time Models' investigates the immediacy and screening functions of intermediation in the context of a market where prices are determined outside the individual transaction, as in a competitive market. Section 2 takes up the case of bargaining markets. In light of the fact that the two structures often yield very different answers to similar questions, it is satisfying to find that the basic intuitions underlined in this chapter hold up in both frameworks, and may thus, be considered fairly robust.

Only section 1.3 presents new material. The rest of the material is culled from existing works, and citations are provided in appropriate places. However, I have in been made no attempt to reproduce specific models, choosing instead, to bring out the various results by introducing variations within a single structure. Inevitably, this structure is not adequate for a complete presentation of all results that the various authors have deemed important or interesting. Nor does it pretend to represent the perspectives and concerns of those authors.

Such representation is not the aim of this chapter. Instead, it is an attempt at exposition, within a relatively simple framework, of the precise role trading institutions play in the exchange process. Its main purpose is to present a relatively coherent picture to the non-specialist, and especially, to the inquisitive student. In this pedagogic purpose it would be successful, if it even imperfectly imitates the art of the great teacher this volume intends to honour.

2. CONTINUOUS-TIME MODELS

Consider the following version of Diamond's 'coconut' model (Diamond 1982). In an economy there are a large number of agents. At any instant of time, each agent either has a unit of a homogeneous good for sale, or is looking for an opportunity to produce a unit of the good. For the moment, we ignore production and concentrate on the exchange aspect of the model. The need for exchange is driven by a 'taboo' that an individual agent cannot consume the unit he has himself produced. Without unnecessarily complicating the model, this captures the fact that in modern economies one typically consumes very little of one's own output, and the need for exchange is paramount.

The agent who has a unit of the good for sale, proceeds to the market-place, where he will exchange his unit with any other agent who he may meet. He encounters other agents according to a Poisson process with rate λ. Once he meets another agent, the transaction is concluded and consumption occurs immediately. He gets an instantaneous utility of x from consumption of x units, and discounts the future at an instantaneous rate r. The expected discounted utility of returning to production is v. This will depend on the efficiency of the exchange process itself, but here we will take it as given. We assume, for the present, that the rate of exchange is one-to-one in private (unmediated) trades. On arriving at the marketplace, then, the agent's expected utility is,

$$w = \int_0^\infty \lambda e^{-\lambda t} e^{-rt}(1 + v)\, dt = \frac{\lambda}{r+\lambda}(1 + v) \qquad (1)$$

where t is the time elapsed after his arrival, and $\lambda e^{-\lambda t}$ is the density function for the arrival time of first trading partner.

2.1 The Service of Immediacy

Now suppose that there is an intermediary who waits in the market with some amount of the good, and offers an instantaneous trade in which he will pay $q < 1$ units of his good in exchange for the one held by the newly-arrived agent. The latter will be willing to take the lower price as long as $q + v \geq \frac{\lambda}{r+\lambda}(1+v)$, which implies,

$$q \geq \frac{\lambda}{r+\lambda} - \frac{r}{r+\lambda} v \tag{2}$$

i.e. as long as the intermediary's 'bid-ask spread' or mediation charge $1 - q$ is less than or equal to $\frac{r}{r+\lambda}(1+v)$.

The above example is a restricted one. Once we introduce the intermediary and exchanges are speeded up, the value of v will change, and the arrival rate of agents seeking traders will also increase, since now agents spend less of their time seeking trades, and therefore, more in producing goods. Also, as long as intermediation yields a higher (lower) expected utility compared to production, erstwhile producers can be expected to enter the intermediation sector, and a full equilibrium analysis will take account of this. Some of these issues have been investigated in Bhattacharya and Hagerty (1989), and the author pursues them in greater detail elsewhere. However, even in this limited framework, the model yields an important insight, which agrees with Demsetz (1968).

PROPOSITION 1: The bid-ask spread will be higher when the market is 'thinner', i.e. the rate of arrival λ is smaller, and also when the agents are more impatient, i.e. r is higher.

2.2 HETEROGENEOUS AGENTS

In the previous example, all agents were assumed to be identical, and hence, all would utilize the intermediary as long as the latter set an appropriate bid-ask spread. To introduce variation among the agents, suppose that different agents face different costs in their productive enterprises. This affects the discounted future utility of entering production, v—agents with higher costs have lower v, and vice versa. Let $F(v)$ be the distribution of v in the population. Given a specific cost of intermediation, an agent who obtains a sufficiently high reward from returning to production—i.e. can produce at low cost—will seek intermediation, whereas another agent who does not gain as much may wait to find a partner for a direct trade.

We assume that agents who look for direct trade do not meet those who go to the mediator. Then, given that a fraction π goes to the marketplace, the expected utility of such an agent is $\frac{\pi\lambda}{r + \pi\lambda}(1 + v)$. For a given price q offered by the intermediary, let v_q be the cutoff level of v, such that agents with $v > v_q$ go to the intermediary, while the rest go to the market. The proportion of agents with $v < v_q$ is $F(v_q)$. Thus, v_q is defined by,

$$q + v_q = \frac{\lambda F(v_q)}{r + \lambda F(v_q)}(1 + v_q) \tag{3}$$

The right-hand-side of (3) is the RHS of (1) with λ replaced by $\lambda F(v_q)$, i.e. the market payoff when the arrival rate is suitably adjusted. Since we have not placed any restrictions on $F(\cdot)$, there may be multiple solutions to (3) which differ in their welfare properties.

If there is a single profit-maximizing intermediary, he makes a profit of $[(1 - q)(1 - F(v_q)]$ by setting a price q; thus, he will choose q to maximize this quantity subject to the constraint (3). If $F(\cdot)$ is continuous, it can be shown easily that this profit-maximization problem has a well-defined solution in which profits are positive, and in which v_q lies in the interior of its support.

Several observations are now in order. Subsets of the following results are found in various forms in Gehrig (1990), Moresy (1991), Yavas (1993), and in Bose and Pingle (1995), on which the above exposition is partially based, Since the above papers employ a fairly varied complement of models, it seems that these results are reasonably robust to modelling variations.

PROPOSITION 2: In an equilibrium where trade is conducted through both intermediation and through private meetings, the agents with greater gains from trade deal with intermediaries, while those with lesser gains wait for private trades.

PROPOSITION 3: In such an equilibrium, there are at least two prices at which trades are conducted in the market—(at least) one price for the intermediated trades, and (at least) another for the private exchanges.

PROPOSITION 4: The equilibrium with intermediation is, in general, not Pareto-comparable with the unintermediated one—some traders gain, i.e. the ones who go to the intermediary, while others lose, i.e. the ones that remain in the marketplace.

The last result needs some qualification. The traders who remain in the marketplace certainly obtain a lower expected utility, since the rate of arrivals in the marketplace falls, and hence, the cost of waiting increases. However, one can construct non-artificial equilibria in which the agents who go to the intermediary are also worse off compared to the situation in which all agents trade on the market. However, given that a fraction of agents actually go to the intermediary, these agents are better off than they would be if they had looked for direct trades. This is because, given the division of traders between the direct market and the intermediary, the rate of arrivals in the direct market is lower than it would have been if the intermediary was absent. However, the mediated equilibrium in this case would collapse if a sufficiently large number of agents migrated from the intermediary to the direct market (see Pagano 1989).

2.3 Screening

Next, let us move on to a case where there are different types of agents, some of whom have preferences regarding the agents they would like to meet. We want to show that, with proper pricing, an intermediary can effect a separation between traders. In this example, the intermediary does not directly buy and sell goods. Instead, he provides a separate market for one type of agents. There is a price for entering this market. Agents who are particularly eager to meet a specific type of trading partner turn out to be willing to pay the price, while the others do not.

To motivate this, suppose that there are two types: 'large' traders, each of whom bring two units of the good, and 'small' traders, each with one unit of the good. Large traders comprise a fraction π of the population, and small traders comprise the remaining $1 - \pi$. Agents arrive at a rate λ as before, so the arrival rates of large and small traders are $\lambda\pi$ and $\lambda(1 - \pi)$ respectively.

The endowment of the traders is private information, which is revealed when two traders meet. We assume that there is a cost c for traders to exchange this information, which is incurred, regardless of whether the traders subsequently conduct an exchange or not. The existence of this cost induces an adverse selection problem for the large traders. If a large trader meets another large trader, then they can exchange their entire endowments in one transaction. However, if a large trader meets a small trader, then he can exchange, at the most, one of his two units, and must wait for another match to complete his transaction. Since the 'meeting' cost must be paid anyway, the large trader will, in fact, trade half his endowment when he meets a small trader, for, then he is sure to conclude trading after one more meeting.

We assume that a trader must wait to complete his exchanges before he can consume, and he pays the costs at this time. Traders retire after they complete consumption; in this example we dispose of the future utility v. Nothing significant hinges on these assumptions.

To establish the intuition of what follows, suppose that the large traders could build a separate trading 'floor' for themselves, from which their smaller counterparts would be debarred. The question for which we want an answer is: under what conditions and at what cost would they be willing to do so? Separating themselves would reduce the frequency of meetings, and thus, extend the expected time to complete trades. But at the same time, it would reduce the cost to each trader of conducting a complete transaction. Thus, separation would be more attractive if large traders are a bigger proportion of the population, and if the cost per meeting is high.

The determination of the price for entry to the trading floor is of some interest. Assuming an equilibrium in which all large traders trade on the floor, while all small traders trade 'outside' (or over-the-counter), the price for entry to the floor must be smaller than the improvement in payoff which a large trader gets by entering. But if trading on the floor is thicker than trading outside, then small traders may also be willing to pay the price to enter. Thus, the price must also be larger than the increase in payoff which a small trader would get if he did so. Whether or not a separation can be effected depends on whether the upper and lower limits are compatible.

To formalize this, the expected payoff of each type of agent in the unseparated market must first be computed. For the small trader, this is simply $W_0^S = \dfrac{\lambda}{r+\lambda}(1-c)$, derived as in (1). For the large trader, the instantaneous payoff depends on whether the first trader he meets is large or small. In the former case—which has probability π—it is $(2-c)$, and trade is concluded with the arrival of the first trader. The latter case has probability $1-\pi$, trade is concluded with arrival of the second trader, and the payoff is $(2-2c)$. Noting that the density function for the time of the second arrival is $\lambda^2 te^{-\lambda t}$, we get the expected payoff,

$$W_0^L = \pi(2-c)\int_0^\infty \lambda e^{-\lambda t}e^{-rt}\,dt + (1-\pi)(2-2c)\int_0^\infty \lambda^2 t e^{-\lambda t}e^{-rt}\,dt$$

$$= \frac{\lambda\pi}{\lambda + r}(2-c) + \frac{\lambda^2(1-\pi)}{(\lambda+r)^2}(2-2c) \qquad (4)$$

Now, suppose the types were separated, then the arrival rate on the floor would be $\lambda\pi$, and large traders would complete their trades in one transaction, which gives the expected payoff,

$$W_F^L = \frac{\lambda\pi}{\lambda\pi + r}(2-c) \qquad (5)$$

The amount which a large trader will be willing to pay to establish a separate floor and trade on it is given by $W_F^L - W_0^L$. Some algebra yields that the condition for this to be positive is,

$$c > \frac{2(1-\pi)r}{(1-\pi)r + (\lambda\pi + r)} \qquad (6)$$

However, once the floor is established, and all large traders do trade on it, the amount an individual trader will be willing to pay to trade on it is greater than $W_F^L - W_0^L$. This follows from the fact that the expected payoff to a large trader from trading with only small traders is lower than the expected payoff in the undivided market.

We can similarly calculate the amount small traders would be willing to pay to prevent a separate floor from being established, and the amount they would themselves be willing to pay to trade on the floor, once it is established. The latter is important, since this is the minimum price which must be charged for trading on the floor if the small traders are to be kept out. This price is positive only if $\pi > \frac{1}{2}$, i.e. there are more large traders than small ones, since to the small traders, it is only the thickness of the market that matters, not the size of traders trading on the market.

PROPOSITION 5: An intermediary can effect a separation between different types of traders purely by charging the right price for entry into a separate trading establishment.

It also follows that, by its nature, such intermediation cannot be open to price-competition. In this case, the intermediary performs only a screening function; he possesses no special information or skills, nor does he provide the service of immediacy.[1]

3. DISCRETE-TIME MODELS

We now move on to trading processes in which the terms of exchange are determined by bargaining. While retaining the same basic model, it is convenient to redefine time as having a discrete structure. We must also allow the price in private exchanges to be variable. To facilitate the latter, we will pretend that all agents have some amount of a second good called 'money', and when an exchange is conducted at a price ratio different from unity, the difference is settled by a transfer of money from one agent to the other. The analysis of the models discussed here is somewhat more detailed and complicated, so, the discussion is kept at a more informal level.

We consider an economy in which, at any given time, there are a large number M of traders, to which may be added another number K of middlemen. Time runs forever and is divided into periods, and in each period a number e of new traders enter the economy. Agents—whether traders or middlemen—are matched with other traders and middlemen according to some rule (to be specified). Without loss of generality, we assume that one unit of surplus is generated when an exchange takes place between two traders. Such exchanges may be mediated or unmediated. A mediated exchange will actually require two transactions. The distribution of surplus within a transaction is effected by transferring an amount of money from one agent to the other. Once a trader concludes his part of an exchange, he leaves the economy.

If a matched pair cannot agree to the terms of the transaction, then they go back to the market and are matched again with different partners in the next period. The expected value of this constitutes the threat point for each agent. Agents discount future utility, so there is pressure to conclude an agreement. In principle, prices are determined by strategic bargaining (Rubinstein 1982), which, in practice, reduces to the following rule: first each agent takes an amount equal to his expected value of disagreement (his threat point), and then any remaining surplus is divided equally between the two. It follows that disagree-

[1]The result that large traders trade on the floor while small traders trade on a parallel market is also obtained in Pagano (1989), though in a different context and model.

ment would occur if and only if the threat points add up to more than the available surplus.

We investigate the properties of a steady state in this economy. In what follows, we assume the existence of equilibria—the interested reader may consult the references for proofs of this. Since e traders enter the economy in each period, in a steady state, the same numbers must also leave the economy in each period. Middlemen remain in the economy forever. Thus $\frac{1}{2}e$ pairs of agents must conclude agreements (directly or through intermediaries). The fraction of traders leaving the economy is e/M. The smaller is this fraction, the larger is the expected delay that an individual trader faces in effecting exchange. Since the future is discounted, delay implies a potential welfare loss for the economy.

In the most efficient outcome, all entrants conclude an exchange and leave in each period, so $M = e$. Thus, the steady-state size of the trader population is a measure of the efficiency of the matching process. Accordingly, intermediaries can be said to improve the performance of the economy if they result in a reduction of this steady-state size of the population.[2] The first model below describes intermediation which improves the rate of exchanges by thickening the market, the second one shows that, by introducing a 'trading floor' with an entry fee, certain traders, who would otherwise wait to be matched with specific partners, can be screened out, thus, increasing the rate of agreements.

3.1 Thickening the Market

Consider an economy where matching is imperfect. There are potentially two types of agents in the economy, *bona fide* traders and middlemen. The sizes of the two populations are denoted L and K respectively. The probability that a trader will meet another trader is given by a function $\alpha(L)$, $\alpha(L)L$, which has the property that the total number of agents who find matches, $\alpha(L)L$ is increasing in L. The probability that a middleman will meet a trader is $\gamma(K, L)$, which is

[2]A reduction in M does not necessarily correspond to a Pareto-improvement. First, not all agents may gain in a mediated equilibrium compared to an unmediated one; secondly, the intermediaries—who are non-existent in an unmediated equilibrium—will normally realise a profit in a mediated equilibrium.

declining in K. The potential maximum number of middlemen is $\overline{K}$. Middlemen trade in the economy exactly on the same terms as the buyers and sellers, and discount the future at the same rate. The only asymmetry is in the matching probabilities, as described above.

First consider the economy without middlemen. Let the number of traders in equilibrium be L'. Then a steady-state requires that,

$$\alpha(L')L' = e \qquad (7)$$

Now, suppose instead, that there are a number K of middlemen who are active in equilibrium. Let the number of traders in this equilibrium be L. Then,

$$\alpha(L)L + \gamma(K, L)K = e \qquad (8)$$

Comparing (7) and (8), it follows immediately that $\alpha(L)L < \alpha(L')L'$, which implies that $L < L'$. Thus, if middlemen are active, each trader waits a shorter time to conclude an exchange than he would if middlemen were not active. So, middlemen improve the efficiency of the exchange process. However, this does not mean that agents are better off in the presence of middlemen, since middlemen make a profit by trading (Rubinstein and Wolinsky, p. 592).

It also turns out that middlemen will be active in equilibrium only if the efficiency of a middleman in making contracts with traders is at least as great as the efficiency of an ordinary trader, i.e. if $\gamma(K, L) \geq \alpha(L)$. This corresponds to the requirement that a middleman's expected profit must be non-negative. Then it follows that, since $\gamma(K, \cdot)$ declines as K increases, middlemen will enter the economy only if $\gamma(0, L) > \alpha(L)$. They will continue to enter until γ falls to equality with α, or until $K = \overline{K}$, i.e. all potential middlemen have entered.

The model in this section is based on Rubinstein and Wolinsky (1987). This is the only known analysis of intermediation in the literature, in which intermediaries enter completely symmetrically with other traders.

PROPOSITION 6: Propositions 1, 3 and 4 (stated in the previous section) all hold in this model. Proposition 2 does not apply because traders cannot choose to meet or avoid intermediaries.

3.2 MORE SCREENING

Next, suppose that matching is perfect, i.e. in each period every trader will randomly meet exactly one other trader. Thus, all entering traders can potentially conclude exchanges in each period. Thus, there is no scope for intermediaries to speed up exchanges by providing immediacy. However, there is still scope for a trading insitution to arise, which improves the overall efficiency of the economy.

Let us now assume that a fraction s of the entering traders in each period is more impatient than the rest. In other words, of the e entering traders, se have a discount factor μ while the remaining $(1 - s)e$ have a discount factor δ, and $\delta > \mu$. The asymmetry in the discounting introduces an asymmetry in the bargaining process. The impatient traders lose more in the case that a match ends in disagreement, since they value the future less relative to the present. Thus, in a meeting between a patient and an impatient trader, the former will get a larger share of the surplus than the latter.[3] In a meeting between two patient traders or between two impatient traders, there is no asymmetry, so if there is agreement, the surplus must be equally divided.

It follows, therefore, that the impatient traders have an interest in avoiding the patient ones, while the latter are especially eager to meet them. Indeed, meeting an impatient trader is more desirable to both types of traders. Thus an increase in the density of impatient traders in the population raises the expected value prior to matching for both types. This means that a match involving at least one impatient trader will always conclude in agreement, since his partner could not do better by going back to the market.

However, if the density of impatient traders in the economy is sufficiently high, then a match between two patient ones may not conclude in agreement, since both of them may expect to do better by going back to the market than they would by equally sharing the surplus. Accordingly, it turns out that if the fraction s is sufficiently high, then at least some matches between patient traders end in diagreement—patient traders who meet each other prefer to disagree and wait to meet impatient partners. In the resulting steady-state equilibrium, the fraction of impatient traders in the steady-state population is, therefore, depressed below s.

A device like the trading floor of Section 1.3 again turns out to be effective in restoring efficiency in this case. Given that the price for entering the floor is correctly set, there is an equilibrium in which all impatient traders trade on the floor, and all the patient traders trade

[3]This holds whether the terms of the trade are determined by a Nash assignment, as in the last section, or by strategic bargaining.

outside. Then, since patient traders cannot meet impatient ones, no trader has an incentive to wait, and all traders conclude exchanges in each period.

The price for entry to the floor must satisfy two conditions. First, since an indvidual patient trader can get a better payoff by entering the floor (where he will certainly meet an impatient partner) than he does outside (where his partner is also invariably patient), the price of entry must be high enough to discourage entry by patient traders. Secondly, though an impatient trader gets a lower payoff by trading outside, the price of entry to the floor must be low enough that the net benefit of trading on the floor does not fall below that of trading outside. The two conditions coincide, fixing the price uniquely.

The above model is based on Bose (1996). It is similar in spirit to the model presented in Section 1.3. There, the large traders went to the floor to avoid the extra cost generated by meetings with small traders. In many real-life situations, however, the extra cost may not be as benignly generated. A person often goes to a formal trading establishment rather than to a decentralized bazaar, because he is apprehensive of falling prey to 'sharks', who might take advantage of his inferior bargaining ability or greater impatience, to drive a hard bargain. The higher price at the formal establishments discourages the bargain-hunters, and therefore, reduces this risk, attracting that segment of traders who would be at a disadvantage on the pairwise trading market. In equilibrium, the weaker agents go to the formal trading sector, while the stronger agents trade through pairwise matching (see also Bose and Pingle 1995).

PROPOSITION 7: Proposition 5 holds.

It is interesting to note, in particular, that there is again no possibility of price-competition among potential providers of the trading institution.

4. CONCLUSIONS

This chapter has tried to provide a very simplified and contained account of two specific types of activities which facilitate exchange. One is that of an intermediary who acts as a go-between for traders who would not otherwise meet each other (or would take longer to do so). The other is that of an institutional arrangement which prevents undesirable meetings which would otherwise have occurred. From an

Edgeworthian perspective, both can be viewed as activities which enable specific coalitions to form—one by bringing traders into a coalition, and the other by filtering unwanted traders out of it. Such filtering is necessary because in the markets that we consider, only allocations which are arrived at following certain trading procedures (e.g. the matching and bargaining procedures) can be achieved. A blocking coalition cannot enforce a particular allocation simply by threatening to defect, if that allocation cannot be generated by the trading rules within the grand coalition. Actual defection takes place, but a mechanism is necessary to co-ordinate this defection.

There are various relevant topics which have not been included in the interest of compactness and cogency. Most prominent among these are models with search. When traders can actively search for trading partners, the existence of an intermediary affects the trading outcome when traders use his services. This is expected. However, the existence of the intermediary affects search intensities, even when the traders do not use his services, which is somewhat surprising (Yavas 1992, 1993). Apart from this, however, models in which search is a choice variable do not seem to generate fundamentally different insights (Gehrig 1990, Moresy 1991).

The other point worthy of note is that intermediation generates an externality, so that the amount of intermediation that is privately provided even in competitive equilibrium will, in general, not be socially optimal. These and other questions require further study; our understanding of the phenomenon of intermediation is still very rudimentary.

References

Bhattacharya, S. and K. Hagerty (1989), 'Dealerships, Trading Externalities, and General Equilibrium', in E.C. Prescott and N. Wallace (eds), *Contractual Arrangements for Intertemporal Trade*, Minnesota Studies in Macroeconomics, 1, Minnesota.

Bose, Gautam and Mark Pingle (1995), *Economic Theory*, Stores, 6, pp. 251–62.

Bose, Gautam (1996), 'Bargaining Economics with Patient and Impatient Agents: Equilibria and Intermediation', *Games and Economic Behavior*, 14, pp. 149–72.

Demsetz, Harold (1968), 'The Cost of Transacting', *Quarterly Journal of Economics*, pp. 33–53.

Diamond, P. (1982), 'Aggregate Demand Management in Search Equilibrium', *Journal of Political Economy*, 90, pp. 881–94.

Gehrig, T. (1993), 'Intermediation in Search Markets', *Journal of Economics and Management Strategy*, pp. 97–120.

Moresy, S. (1991), 'Intermediation in Markets with Sequential Bargaining and Heterogeneous Buyers and Sellers', mimeo.

Pagano, Marco (1989), 'Trading Volume and Asset Liquidity', *Quarterly Journal of Economics*, pp. 255–74.

Rubinstein, A. (1982), 'Perfect Equilibrium in a Bargaining Model', *Econometrica*, 50, pp. 97–110.

Rubinstein, A. and A. Wolinsky (1987), 'Middlemen', *Quarterly Journal of Economics*, 102, pp. 581–93.

Yavas, Abdullah (1992), 'Marketmakers versus Matchmakers', *Journal of Financial Intermediation*, 2, pp. 33–58.

——— (1996), 'Search and Trading in Intermediated Markets', *Journal of Economics and Management Strategy*, pp. 195–216.

10

Implementation and Preference Reversals

BHASKAR DUTTA*

INTRODUCTION

The theory of implementation is concerned with the extent to which social goals can be achieved or *implemented* through decentralized decision-making procedures. The social goals are represented by a *social choice correspondence* while the decentralized procedure is given by a *mechanism* or *game form*. A game form, together with a profile of agents' preferences, defines a game in normal form. Given any particular equilibrium of a normal form game, a game form implements a particular set of social goals if its *equilibrium correspondence* coincides with the social choice correspondence.

Typically, the social goals of the planner will depend on the characteristics of individuals which are often *private* information. It is natural to assume that individuals will voluntarily reveal their private information only if it is in their interest to do so. However, the objective or goal of the 'planner' need not *coincide* with those of the individual agents. So, the mechanism must induce individual agents to correctly reveal privately held information for public use. The need to induce agents to reveal the necessary information may, therefore, act as a constraint both on the choice of procedures which can be used as decentralized decision procedures, as well as on the type of objective functions which can be achieved or implemented.

A variety of problems fits this general description. The examples given below represent a small sample of implementation problems.

EXAMPLE 1: PUBLIC GOODS PROVISION

A set of agents have to choose *one* project out of a set K of feasible

*I am most grateful to Debraj Ray for innumerable helpful suggestions.

projects. Each agent has a preference ordering over K, say indicating the maximum willingness to pay for any project. The cost associated with each project is common knowledge, but the individuals' willingness to pay for different projects is private information. The choice problem is to select which project to choose from K, and how to assign the cost shares to the different individuals. For example, suppose the planner wants to select that project which maximises the difference between the sum of the agents' willingness to pay and the cost of production, and to assign costs in proportion to the individuals' willingness to pay for the chosen project. Suppose $K = \{x, y\}$, the set of agents is $\{1, 2\}$ with valuations $v_1(x) = 3, v_1(y) = 0, v_2(x) = 2$, $v_2(y) = 1$, while both x and y cost 1 unit. Then, the planner wants to choose x with cost shares $c_1 = \frac{3}{5}$, $c_2 = \frac{2}{5}$. Clearly, agent 1 can avoid paying for the public good by declaring (say) $v_1(x) = v_1(y) = 0$. It is obvious that agent 2 also has no incentive to declare his or her true willingness to pay.

EXAMPLE 2: FAIR DIVISION PROBLEM

Two brothers have inherited an estate consisting of one unit each of two divisible goods x and y. The utility function of the two brothers is given by,

$$u_i(x_i, y_i) = x_i^{\alpha_i} y_i^{1-\alpha_i} \tag{1.1}$$

where x_i, y_i denote the consumption of goods x and y by individual i and α_i is some number in (0, 1).

The brothers cannot come to an agreement about the division of the estate, and approach an arbitrator A. A is well-versed with the principles of fair division, and feels that a just resolution of the problem is provided by choosing the *Walrasian allocation from equal division of the endowment.*

A. knows that the individuals have utility functions of the form (1.1), but does not know the values of the coefficients α_i. To simplify the problem, let us assume that he knows that $\alpha_1 \in \{\frac{1}{2}, \frac{5}{8}\}$ and $\alpha_2 \in \{\frac{1}{2}, \frac{3}{4}\}$.

	$\alpha_2 = \frac{3}{4}$	$\alpha_2 = \frac{1}{2}$
$\alpha_1 = \frac{5}{8}$	$(\frac{5}{11}, \frac{3}{5}), (\frac{6}{11}, \frac{2}{5})$	$(\frac{5}{9}, \frac{3}{7}), (\frac{4}{9}, \frac{4}{7})$
$\alpha_1 = \frac{1}{2}$	$(\frac{2}{5}, \frac{2}{3}), (\frac{3}{5}, \frac{1}{3})$	$(\frac{1}{2}, \frac{1}{2}), (\frac{1}{2}, \frac{1}{2})$

A. cannot simply ask the individuals to reveal the values of α_i because they will not always tell the truth. For example, suppose the true parameters are $\alpha_1^* = \frac{1}{2}$, and $\alpha_2^* = \frac{3}{4}$. If 2 tells the truth, then 1 is better off announcing $\alpha_1 = \frac{5}{8}$, since he prefers $(\frac{5}{11}, \frac{3}{5})$ to $(\frac{2}{5}, \frac{2}{3})$.

EXAMPLE 3: VOTING

There are 3 agents and 3 outcomes $\{a, b, c\}$. Agents have preference orderings defined over the set of outcomes. A social choice rule aggregates the individual preferences to choose a socially optimal outcome.

Suppose the rule specifies that the optimal outcome is the majority winner if it exists, and individual 1's best outcome otherwise. Let the individual preference profile be,

$$P_1 : (a\ c\ b)$$

$$P_2 : (b\ c\ a)$$

$$P_3 : (c\ a\ b).$$

(Here, 1 prefers a to c to b, and so on.)

Then, the optimal outcome is c. But, suppose 1 expresses the preference ordering $P_1' : (a\ b\ c)$. Then, the outcome is a, since no majority winner exists in this case. Since $a\ P_1\ b$, 1 gains by declaring the false preference ordering.

The purpose of this paper is to provide a brief and elementary introduction to the vast literature on implementation. I make no attempt to cover the wide array of issues which have been discussed in the literature. Instead, focus on a class of *preference reversal* conditions (on social choice correspondences) which have played a central role in the theory of implementation, and try to provide a heuristic explanation of why these conditions are so important.

The plan of the chapter is as follows. In the next section, the formal framework underlying the theory of implementation is described. Section 3 discusses some of the main preference reversal conditions, while Section 4 discusses why these conditions are important. Section 5 concludes.

2. THE FORMAL FRAMEWORK

Consider an environment with a *finite* set $I = \{1, \ldots, n\}$ of *agents*, with $n \geq 2$ and a set X of feasible outcomes.

Given any individual set, $\{B_i\}_{i \in I}$, $B = \Pi_{i \in I} B_i$, $B_{-i} = \Pi_{j \neq i} B_j$. In general, lower case letters will denote elements of sets which are represented by the corresponding upper case letters. So, $b \in B$, $b_i \in B_i$, $b_{-i} \in B_{-i}$.

The set of *states of the world* is given by Θ with generic element θ. In state θ, agent i has a preference ordering $R_i(\theta)$ on the set X. Let $P_i(\theta)$ and $I_i(\theta)$ denote the strict preference and indifference relations corresponding to θ. An n-tuple of preference orderings will be called a *profile* and denoted $R(\theta)$. In Example 1, the state of the world will be the vector of individual willingness to pay, while in Example 2, it will be the vector (α_1, α_2).

A *social choice correspondence* (*scc*) is a mapping $f: \Theta \rightarrow X$ that specifies a non-empty choice set $f(\theta) \subseteq X$ for each state θ. An *scc* which is always *single valued* will be called a *social choice function* (*scf*).

The *scc* represents the goals of the planner. Given any $\theta, f(\theta)$ is the set of outcomes which the planner wants to achieve. For example, in Example 1, one possible *scc* is to choose that project which maximizes the sum of individuals' willingness to pay, net of the project cost, and then distribute the cost in proportion to willingness to pay. In Example 2, the Walrasian allocation from equal division is the *scc*.

An implementation problem arises because θ is private information to the agents. As we have seen from the examples, the planner cannot simply ask agents to announce their private information. She has to take recourse to more sophisticated schemes.

A *mechanism* or *game form* g consists of a pair (S, π), where S is the product of individual strategy sets S_i and π is the outcome function mapping each vector of individual strategies into an outcome in A. The game form represents the decentralized decision procedure.

A game form g together with each profile of preferences constitutes a *game*. The planner specifies a particular game form g in the hope that the equilibria (according to the *relevant* equilibrium concept) of the game $(g, R(\theta))$ will coincide with $f(\theta)$ for each $\theta \in \Theta$. A more formal definition follows. Let E^* be some solution concept for each of the games $(g, R(\theta))$. Then, $E^*(g, \theta)$ denotes the set of E^*-equilibria of the game (g, θ), for each g and each θ.

DEFINITION 1: An *scc* f is implementable in E^*-equilibrium if there is a game form g such that for every $\theta \in \Theta$, $\{x \mid \pi(s) = x \text{ for some } s \in E^*(g, \theta)\} = f(\theta)$.

In this paper, I will discuss results related to implementation in Nash equilibrium, undominated Nash equilibrium and sub-game perfect equilibrium. Of course, these are just a few of the alternative solution concepts (or special cases of E^*) used in the theory of Nash implementation.

The underlying philosophy of implementation theory is that the ends justify the means. The planner knows that individuals will not reveal their private information to her unless it is in their interest to do so. If she believes that E^* is the appropriate equilibrium (that is, E^* describes or predicts the behaviour of agents accurately), then it is sufficient for her to be able to devise a game whose E^*-equilibrium will coincide with her goals. Note that her interest in the mechanism or game form is restricted solely to the properties of its equilibrium correspondence. Other properties of the game form are irrelevant. However, Moore (1992) and Dutta (1998) discuss why it may be desirable to impose some minimal restrictions on the game form.

3. PREFERENCE REVERSALS

In this section I define some of the preference reversal conditions which are pivotal in the theory of implementation. As will be clear from the discussion in the next section, it is easy to construct game forms whose equilibria are all socially optimal. It is much more difficult to ensure that socially inoptimal outcomes *cannot* be supported as equilibria of the mechanism. The role of the preference reversal conditions is precisely to rule out the possibility of inoptimal outcomes from turning out to be equilibria. Of course, the more stringent the equilibrium concept, the smaller is the set of equilibria, and hence, the easier it is to ensure that socially undesirable outcomes do not turn out to be weaker. It is not surprising that the preference reversal conditions become progressively weaker as the equilibrium concept is strengthened.

However, an important qualification needs to be made. If the equilibrium concept is too demanding, then it becomes difficult to fulfill the *other* half of implementation, namely ensuring that socially optimal outcomes can be sustained as equilibria. This is true, for instance, of implementation in strong Nash equilibrium.[1]

The first preference-reversal condition was introduced by Maskin (1977) in his seminal paper.

DEFINITION 2: f satisfies *monotonicity* if for all $\theta, \phi \in \Theta$, $x \in f(\theta) \setminus f(\phi)$ implies that there is $i \in I$, $y \in X$ such that $xR_i(\theta)y$ and $yP_i(\phi)x$.

Monotonicity says the following. Suppose $a \in f(\theta)$, but $a \notin f(\phi)$, where ϕ is another state. In that case, there must have been some preference reversal. That is, the relative position of a must have worsened in someone's ranking. This particular notion of *preference reversal* is expressed conveniently in the following way. For every triple (a, θ, ϕ) where $a \in f(\theta) \setminus f(\phi)$, define i to be a *test agent* and (a, y) to be a *test pair* (relative to the test agent) if $aR_i(\theta)y$ and $yP_i(\theta)a$. If f is monotonic, then a test agent and test pair always exist.

Although monotonicity seems a very reasonable condition, it has a lot of bite. In particular, there is *no* (Maskin) monotonic, non-dictatorial *social choice function* if X has at least 3 alternatives, and all logically possible preference profiles are in the domain of the social choice function.[2] In the pure voting context, it is even difficult to construct monotonic social choice correspondences. For instance, monotonicity rules out practically all *scoring rules* such as the Borda count or Plurality rule. The following example shows that *majority-type* rules are also not monotonic.

EXAMPLE 4

Let $I = \{1, 2, 3\}$, $X = \{a, b, c\}$. Let f be any *scc* which selects the majority winner if it exists,[3] and *any* subset of X if there is no majority winner. Consider the following profile of preferences in state θ.

$R_1(\theta)$	$R_2(\theta)$	$R_3(\theta)$
a	b	c
b	c	a
c	a	b

[1]See Dutta and Sen (1991b) for characterization results on implementation in strong Nash equilibrium.

[2]If X has only 2 alternatives, then all 'reasonable' rules satisfy monotonicity.

[3]Assume, for simplicity, that individual preferences are strict, so that any majority winner must be unique.

This is the familiar profile resulting in the 'voting paradox', and no majority winner exists. Without loss of generality, suppose that $a \in f(\theta)$. Suppose $\phi \in \Theta$ is such that $R_i(\theta) = R_i(\phi)$ for $i \neq 2$, and $cP_2(\phi)bP_2(\phi)a$. Then, c is the majority winner in ϕ, and so $f(\phi) = \{c\}$. In other words, $a \in f(\theta) \setminus f(\phi)$. Noting that there has been no preference reversal involving a, it is clear that f violates monotonicity.

However, it is easier to construct monotonic rules in *economic environments*. Consider, for instance, the class of *public ownership economies*, in which an *aggregate endowment* ω of L goods is jointly owned by the set of agents I. Here, X is the set of feasible allocations corresponding to ω. Given any allocation x, let x_i denote the commodity bundle allocated to i. Agents have preferences $R_i(\theta)$ over $\Re^L_+$. An allocation $x \in X$ is *envy-free* in state θ if for all $i, j \in I$, $x_i R_i(\theta) x_j$. The *envy-free* correspondence, f^E selects the set of envy-free allocations in each state $\theta \in \Theta$. It is easy to check that f^E is monotonic.

The most familiar *scc* in private ownership economies is the Walrasian correspondence. Unfortunately, the Walrasian correspondence itself does not satisfy Monotonicity. This is shown in Figure 10.1. Here, ω is the initial endowment vector, while I_1I_1 and I_2I_2 are indifference curves of agents 1 and 2 respectively in state θ. Clearly, $x = (x_1, x_2) \in f^W(\theta)$, where f^W denotes the Walrasian correspondence. Consider some other state ϕ in which the indifference curve of agent 2 passing through x remains unchanged. The indifference curve of agent 1 through x is given

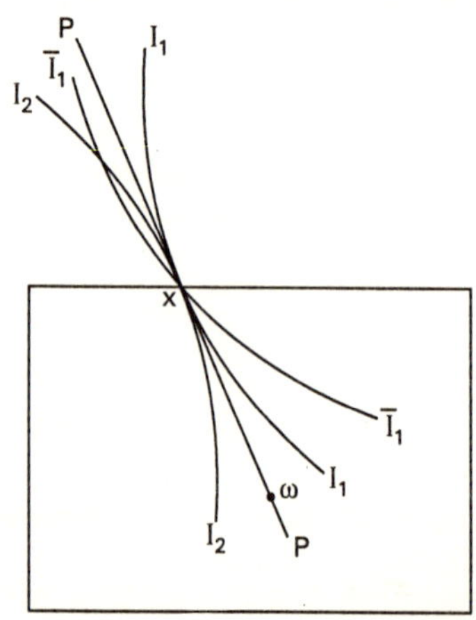

FIGURE 10.1 Violation of Monotonicity.

by $\overline{I_1 I_1}$. Since x_1 is no longer the most-preferred bundle of agent 1 in her budget set, $x \notin f^W(\phi)$. So, $x \in f^W(\theta) \setminus f^W(\phi)$. Notice, however, that there has been no preference reversal involving x amongst the set of feasible allocations.

It should also be clear that f^W can violate monotonicity only if some *boundary* allocation is Walrasian. In other words, if there is some restriction on individual preferences which ensures that all Walrasian allocations are in the *interior* of the Edgeworth box, then f^W will satisfy monotonicity.[4]

Notice also that if allocations such as x were socially optimal in state ϕ, then f^W would satisfy Monotonicity. This indicates why the *Constrained Walrasian Correspondence*, f^{CW}, satisfies monotonicity.[5] Formally f^{CW} is defined as follows.

DEFINITION 3: $x \in f^{CW}(\theta)$ if there is a price vector p such that for all agents i, x_i is $R_i(\theta)$-maximal in the constrained budget set

$$CB_i(p) = \{z \in \Re^L_+ \mid pz \leq p\omega_i,\ z \leq \omega\}$$

Notice that for all $\theta \in \Theta$, $f^W(\theta) \subseteq f^{CW}(\theta)$. Moreover, the two correspondences coincide whenever f^W is contained in the interior of the Edgeworth box.

The next section shows the crucial role palyed by Monotonicity in the context of Nash implementation. The next condition, due to Abreu and Sen (1990), plays an analogous role in subgame perfect implementation.

DEFINITION 4: f satisfies condition α if there exists $B \subseteq X$ with range $f \subseteq B$ such that for all θ, ϕ, if $x \in f(\theta) \setminus f(\phi)$, then there exists a finite sequence of allocations in B, $a_0 = x$, $a_1, \ldots, a_l$, a_{l+1} and a sequence of agents, $j(0), j(1), \ldots, j(l)$ such that

(i) $a_k R_{j(k)}(\theta) a_{k+1}$ for $k = 0, 1, \ldots, l-1$.
(ii) $a_l R_{j(l)}(\theta) a_{l+1}$ and $a_{l+1} P_{j(l)}(\phi) a_l$.
(iii) a_k is not $R_{j(k)}(\phi)$— *maximal* for $j(k)$ in B.
(iv) $j(l) \neq j(l-1)$ or $l = 0$ if a_{l+1} is $R_i(\phi)$—*maximal* in B for all $i \neq j(l)$.

[4]For instance, if all permissible utility functions are Cobb-Douglas, then f^W satisfies monotonicity.

[5]The *Core correspondence* also satisfies monotonicity.

In order to understand condition α, consider the simplest case where $X = \text{range} f$. Obviously, given any extensive form mechanism Γ, the subgame perfect equilibria of Γ corresponding to two different preference profiles can differ only if there is a preference reversal for some agent. Conditions (i) and (ii) above make this explicit—individual $j(l)$ is the *test agent*, whose preferences are reversed over the *test pair* (a_l, a_{l+1}). The rest of Condition α specifies that the outcome x must be linked to a_l in a particular way.

The difference between monotonicity and condition α is that in the case of the former, if $x \in f(\theta) \setminus f(\phi)$, then the preference reversal has to involve the outcome a. But, so far as condition α is concerned, it is sufficient if the preference reversal takes place over *some* pair of alternatives. Of course, there has to be an 'appropriate' connection between the test pair and x. Notice that if f satisfies monotonicity, then there exist *two-element* sequences which satisfy condition α.

Condition α is considerably weaker than monotonicity. For instance, Moore and Repullo (1988) show that any selection from the Walrasian correspondence satisfies the condition. However, several well-known voting rules do not satisfy condition α. The following example illustrates why the plurality rule does not satisfy the condition.

EXAMPLE 5

Let $X = \{x, y, z\}$, $I = \{1, 2, 3\}$, and $\Theta = \{\theta, \phi\}$. The preference orderings of the 3 agents are given below.

$R_1(\theta) = R_1(\phi)$	$R_2(\theta) = R_2(\phi)$	$R_3(\theta)$	$R_3(\phi)$
x	y	z	y
y	z	y	z
z	x	x	x

Suppose the *scc* is the plurality rule f^p which selects the outcome(s) which is (are) the first choice of the most number of agents. So, we have $f^p(\theta) = \{x, y, z\}$ and $f^p(\phi) = \{y\}$. Hence, $x \in f^p(\theta) \setminus f^p(\phi)$. f^p violates condition α because for all sequences $j(0), \ldots, j(l)$ and $x = a_0, \ldots, a_{l+1}, x$ is $R_{j(0)}(\phi)$-maximal.

Perhaps, the weakest preference reversal condition is due to Palfrey and Srivastava (1991), who showed that this is the relevant condition for implementation in *undominated Nash equilibrium*.

DEFINITION 5: f satisfies *Property Q* if for all $\theta, \phi \in \Theta$, if $x \in f(\theta) \setminus f(\phi)$, then one of the following is true:

(i) There exist $i \in I$, $a, b \in X$ such that $aP_i(\theta)b$ and $bR_i(\phi)a$, and there exist $c, d \in X$ with $cP_i(\phi)d$.

(ii) There exist $i \in I$, $a, b \in X$ with $aR_i(\theta)b$ and $bP_i(\phi)a$.

Notice that Property Q is satisfied if the *test agent* has different preferences over the test pair, and if he is not completely indifferent at ϕ. Further, there need not be *any* connection at all between the test pair and x. Clearly, it is much weaker than Condition α. Indeed, Property Q is satisfied by *all sccs* if individual preferences are assumed to be strict.

As we will see in the next section, the mechanism used by Palfrey and Srivastava (1991) to show that Property Q is 'almost' sufficient for implementation in undominated equilibrium was not particularly desirable. Jackson, Palfrey and Srivastava (1994) (henceforth JPS) also analysed implementation in undominated Nash equilibrium, but with a restriction on the class of permissible mechanisms so as to rule out such undesirable mechanisms. Obviously, this meant that a stronger condition was needed. This condition is defined below.

DEFINITION 6: f is chained if whenever $x \in f(\theta) \setminus f(\phi)$, there exist a test agent i and a test pair (y_1, y_2) such that $y_1P_i(\theta)y_2$ and $y_2P_i(\phi)y_1$ where either of the following conditions is true:

(A) $y_1 = x$

(B) There exist agent $j \neq i$ and alternatives z_1 and $z_2 \notin \{x, z_1\}$ such that,

(B1) $z_2P_j(\phi)x$, $z_2P_i(\phi)z_1$;

(B2) $z_1 = x$ or $xP_j(\theta)z_1$.

Part A of the chained condition is the (Maskin) monotonicity condition. Part B, which is more complicated, requires the existence of two agents who are linked in a special way. Notice that agent i satisfies the preference reversal condition specified in Property Q since i's preferences differ over the pair (y_1, y_2) in states θ, ϕ.

While the chained condition is implied by monotonicity (and in turn implies Q), there is no logical connection between it and condition α. JPS show that f^p, the plurality correspondence, is chained whereas we have already seen that it violates Condition α. JPS also construct an example of a *scc* which is not chained, but which satisfies Condition α.

4. THE ROLE OF PREFERENCE REVERSAL CONDITIONS

In this section I describe the main characterization results on implementation using the three equilibrium concepts mentioned above. I also describe some typical mechanisms used in the literature, so as to explain the role of the preference reversal conditions defined earlier.

Maskin's (1977) classic paper has laid the foundation for subsequent work in 'Nash implementation'. The canonical mechanism, often called a Maskin game form, is a variant of the original mechanism proposed by him.

Before describing this mechanism, I define another condition on an *scc*.

DEFINITION 7: A *scc* f satisfies *No Veto Power* if for all $a \in A$, for all $\theta \in \Theta$, if $|\{i \in I \mid aR_i(\theta)b \text{ for all } b \neq a\}| \geq n - 1$, then $a \in f(\theta)$.

No Veto Power requires that if an outcome a is top-ranked in A for at least $(n - 1)$ agents in some state θ, then $a \in f(\theta)$. Notice that in economies with private goods, no allocation can be simultaneously maximal for two or more agents. Hence, if there are three or more agents, then No Veto Power is trivially satisfied in such economies.

Maskin (1977) proved the following:

THEOREM 1: If a *scc* f is Nash implementable, then it satisfies Monotonicity. Moreover, if $n \geq 3$ and if f satisfies Monotonicity and No Veto Power, then f is implementable in Nash equilibrium.[6]

Why is monotonicity a necessary condition for Nash implementation? Suppose a *scc* f is Nash implementable by means of the game form g. Let $x \in f(\theta) \setminus f(\phi)$. Since x is in $f(\theta)$, there must be some equilibrium of the game $(g, R(\theta))$ resulting in x. Let s be the required Nash equilibrium. However, x cannot be a Nash equilibrium of $(g, R(\phi))$ since x is not in $f(\phi)$. So, there must be some individual i who can deviate profitably from s_i to say $\bar{s}_i$ when the preference profile is $R(\phi)$. Letting $\pi(s_{-i}, \bar{s}_i) = y$, we have i as the test agent and (x, y) as the test pair. This explains why monotonicity is necessary.

In order to give an idea of why Monotonicity and No Veto Power

[6]The general necessary and sufficient conditions are given in Moore and Repullo (1990). Also the two-person case requires an additional condition. See Dutta and Sen (1991a) and Moore and Repullo (1990).

are sufficient for Nash implementation, I will describe heuristically why the canonical mechanism 'works'.

Let f be any *scc* satisfying Monotonicity and No Veto Power. Construct the following mechanism. For each agent i, a typical message or strategy consists of an announcement of a state of the world θ, an outcome a, and an integer in $[1, n]$. The outcome function is specified by the following rules:

(R.1): If all agents announce the same state θ, together with the same outcome $a \in f(\theta)$, then the outcome is a.

(R.2): If all but one agent announces the same θ and $a \in f(\theta)$, but the remaining agent i announces (ϕ, b) then the outcome is a unless (i) $a \notin f(\phi)$ and (ii) i is the test agent and (a, b) is the test pair. In this case, the outcome is b.

(R.3): In all other cases, the outcome is the one announced by i^*, where $i^* = \text{mod}_n \sum_{j \in I} k_j$, k_j being the integer announced by j.

Why does this mechanism implement f? First, notice that if all individuals unanimously announce the *true* state θ and the same $a \in f(\theta)$, then this will constitute a Nash equilibrium with outcome a. This is because any individual i's deviation from this announcement will only permit him or her to attain elements which are no better than a according to $R_i(\theta)$.

To complete the heuristic demonstration, we have to show that all Nash equilibria corresponding to state θ lead to outcomes in $f(\theta)$. Let us check for possible candidate equilibria. The regime described by (R.3) in which the winner of the so-called *modulo game* picks an element from A cannot have any equilibrium *unless* all individuals unanimously prefer an outcome a to all other outcomes. But, then No Veto Power will assure that a is in $f(\theta)$. Consider an n-tuple of announcements covered by (R.2). In this case, $(n - 1)$ individuals are making a common announcement, while i is the 'deviant'. Now, any of these $(n - 1)$ individuals can also deviate and precipitate (and win) the modulo game. If no such deviation is profitable, then all the $(n - 1)$ individuals must prefer the current outcome a to all other outcomes in A. Again, No Veto Power ensures that $a \in f(\theta)$.

The remaining case is if *all* individuals unanimously announce (ϕ, a) and $a \in f(\phi)$. If $a \in f(\theta)$, then there is nothing to prove. If $a \notin f(\theta)$, then there is a test agent i and test pair (a, b) such that $bP_i(\theta)a$ and $aR_i(\phi)b$. Then, i can announce (θ, b), in which case the outcome is b. Since $bP_i(\theta)a$, the original announcement is not a Nash equilibrium.

From this description of the canonical mechanism, it is clear that the difficult half of (Nash) implementation is to ensure that outcomes which are not socially optimal do not constitute Nash equilibria. The modulo game helps in knocking out these undesirable equilibria unless all players are making a unanimous announcement. In the latter case, the fact that agents announce the entire profile of preferences allows the planner to reconstruct players' lower contour sets. Monotonicity then ensures that unanimous falsehood cannot be an equilibrium.

I have remarked earlier that the preference reversal condition becomes progressively weaker as the equilibrium condition is strengthened. This also suggests that it should be possible to implement a larger class of social choice rules in *refinements* of Nash equilibrium since it will then be easier to knock out 'undesirable' or socially inoptimal outcomes as equilibria. In other words, the *scc* need only satisfy a *weaker* preference-reversal condition in order to be implemented.

I will illustrate why it is possible to implement a larger class of choice rules with *some* refinements of Nash equilibrium, by discussing the implementation in undominated Nash equilibrium and sub-game perfect equilibrium as follows.

I take up first the case of undominated Nash equilibrium. Palfrey and Srivastava (1991) proved the following result.

THEOREM 2: Suppose $n \geq 3$, and the *scc* f satisfies Property Q. Then, f is implementable in undominated Nash equilibrium.

The proof of the theorem in the general case is quite long and involved. Here, I will give an outline of the proof for the case when individual preferences are always *strict*,[7] and there is a *uniformly worst outcome*. The latter assumption means that there is $w \in X$ such that $xP_i(\theta)w$ for all $i \in I$, for all $\theta \in \Theta$ and for all $x \in f(\theta)$.

The mechanism used in this case is a close cousin of the canonical mechanism used in Nash implementation. The strategy set of each agent i is $S_i = X \times \Theta \times \Theta \times \{-0, 1, \ldots, n\}$. For each $\theta \in \Theta$, if $x \in f(\theta)$, then the strategy vector supporting x as an equilibrium is the one in which each agent announces $(x, \theta, \theta, 0)$. A modulo game is also used in the

[7]Note that in this case Property Q is satisfied by all choice rules.

case of hybrid announcements, i.e. when less than $(n-1)$ agents make the (same) equilibrium announcement.

Suppose now that there is $x \in f(\theta) \setminus f(\phi)$. From what has been said before, the unanimous announcement of $(x, \theta, \theta, 0)$ is an undominated Nash equilibrium (UNE) when the state of the world is θ. But, this strategy vector *cannot be* a UNE when the true realization of preferences is ϕ. This is where the mechanism departs from the Maskin game form. Let i be the test agent and (y_1, y_2) be the test pair at (θ, ϕ), so that $y_1 P_i(\theta) y_2$ and $y_2 P_i(\phi) y_1$. The outcome function is so defined that $s_i = (x, \theta, \theta, 0)$ is *weakly dominated* for i by $\bar{s}_i = (x, \theta, \phi, 0)$. This is done by the following specification of the outcome function,

$$\pi(s_i, s_{-i}) = x$$

$$\pi(s_i, \bar{s}_{-i}) = y_1$$

$$\pi(\bar{s}_i, s_{-i}) = x$$

$$\pi(\bar{s}_i, \bar{s}_{-i}) = y_2$$

Here, $\bar{s}_j = (x, \theta, \phi, -1)$ for all $j \neq i$. The rest of the construction ensures that agent i never loses by using $\bar{s}_i$ rather than s_i when the true state is ϕ. Hence, $\bar{s}_i$ weakly dominates s_i for agent i at state ϕ since $y_2 P_i(\phi) y_1$. Of course, since $y_1 P_i(\theta) y_2$, $\bar{s}_i$ *does not* weakly dominate s_i at θ.

Since s_i is weakly dominated at ϕ, the unanimous announcement of $(x, \theta, \theta, 0)$ cannot be a UNE at ϕ, *even if it is a Nash equilibrium.* Of course, we must also ensure that $(\bar{s}_i, s_i)$ does not become a UNE at ϕ. Judicious use of the worst outcome w ensures this.

However, in the general case, where no such worst outcome exists, this requires the use of what has come to be called a *tailchasing device.* This involves the creation of an infinite sequence of strategies such that each strategy in the sequence is weakly dominated by its successor!

Constructions such as the tailchasing device have been criticized. In particular, Jackson (1992) points out that if tailchasing is incorporated in the mechanism, then it may not be a reasonable assumption to assume that agents do not use dominated strategies. This is part of the general criticism that the equilibrium concept cannot be independent of the mechanism. For instance, if the mechanism is such that at some strategy profile, an agent does not have a best response to the other agents' strategies, then it is not legitimate to assume that Nash equilibrium is a good predictor of agents' behaviour.[8]

A mechanism is called *bounded* if every (weakly) dominated strategy is dominated by at least one undominated strategy. This obviously means that *all* finite mechanisms (that is, mechanisms in which each agent's strategy set is finite) are bounded. However, even infinite mechanisms can be bounded. The following example illustrates why it is unreasonable to assume that agents will not use dominated strategies if the mechanism is unbounded.

EXAMPLE 6

Let $I = \{1, 2\}$, $X = \{a, b\}$. Consider a mechanism in which both agents have a countable set of strategies. The outcome function is described by means of the following table. (Here, agent 1's strategies are represented by different rows, while 2's strategies are the different columns.)

b	a	a	a	a	...	a	...
a	b	a	a	a	...	a	...
a	b	b	a	a	...	a	...
a	b	b	b	a	...	a	...
.	.	.	.	.	...	.	...
.	.	.	.	.	...	.	...
.	.	.	.	.	...	.	...

Now, suppose $bP_1(\theta)a$. Let s_1^k denote the strategy of agent 1 associated with row k and s_2^k the strategy of agent 2 associated with column k. Then, the only undominated strategy of player 1, when his preferences are given by $P_1(\theta)$ is s_1^1. This is because for all $k \geq 2$, strategy s_1^k is weakly dominated by s_1^{k+1}. Notice, however, that s_1^1 gives the outcome b *only* when player 2 uses s_2^1. Since $bP_1(\theta)a$, it is counter-intuitive to assert that 1 will use s_1^1 rather than, say, s_1^k where k is a very large integer. After all, s_1^k does *strictly* better than s_1^1 against $(k - 1)$ strategies of player 2!

JPS restrict mechanisms to be bounded and also to have the *best response property*, i.e. the property that all agents always have a best

[8]See also, Moore (1992) and Dutta (1998) for discussions of some of the recent criticisms of the *mechanisms* used in implementation.

response to other agents' strategies. They prove the following result for implementation in UNE.

THEOREM 3: If $n \geq 3$, X is finite and f satisfies No Veto Power and is chained, then f is implementable in UNE by a bounded mechanism with the best response property.

This chapter does not go into a discussion of the proof of this theorem since it is quite complicated, although the canonical mechanism used here is in the same family as the Maskin game form.

I now turn to a discussion of implementation in subgame perfect equilibrium. As I mentioned earlier, Abreu and Sen (1990) proved the most general theorem for this case. Their result is given below.

THEOREM 4: If f is implementable in subgame perfect equilibrium, then f satisfies Condition α. Moreover, if $n \geq 3$, f satisfies No Veto Power and condition α, then f is implementable in subgame perfect equilibrium.

The proof of necessity of Condition α is long and somewhat tedious. However, I give a sketch of the proof of sufficiency below. The essential idea here is that sequential rationality can be used in conjunction with condition α to replace monotonicity.

Consider any f satisfying Condition α. Recall that for any $x \in f(\theta) \setminus f(\phi)$, there exist sequences $j(\theta, \phi, x)$ of individuals $\{j(0), \ldots, j(l)\}$ and $a(\theta, \phi, x)$ of outcomes $\{a(0), \ldots, a(l+1)\}$ with $x = a(0)$ satisfying Condition α. The mechanism consists of $(l + 1)$ stages. In stage 0, each agent i announces a triplet (θ_i, x_i, n_i) where $x_i \in f(\theta_i)$ and n_i is some integer. If $(n - 1)$ agents announce the same pair $(x, f(\theta))$, the outcome is x unless the remaining agent j announces ϕ, where $x \in f(\theta) \setminus f(\phi)$ and $j = j(0)$ in the sequence $j(\theta, \phi, x)$. In this case, go to stage 1. In all other cases, the agent announcing the highest integer gets to choose an outcome from the set B.

In subsequent stages k, where $k = 1, \ldots, l$, each agent can either 'raise a flag' or announce a non-negative integer. In stage k, if at least $(n - 1)$ agents raise a flag, then $j(k - 1)$ can select any outcome in B. If at least $(n - 1)$ agents announce zero, the outcome is a_k, unless $j(k)$ does not announce zero. In the latter case, go to the next stage or choose $a_{(l+1)}$ if $k = l$. In all other cases, the agent announcing the highest integer gets to choose any outcome from B.

Although the mechanism seems involved, the proof is quite

transparent. Suppose θ is the true state. Then, the strategy profile in which agents unanimously announce $(x, \theta, 0)$ in stage 0 and zero in all subsequent stages, is a subgame perfect equilibrium yielding $x \in f(\theta)$ as the outcome. To see this, consider any deviation. At any stage k, only player $j(k)$ can change the outcome from a_k to a_{k+1}. But by hypothesis, $a_k P_{j(k)}(\theta) a_{(k+1)}$. So, $j(k)$ does not gain by deviating.

What about the converse? There are *two* possible kinds of subgame perfect equilibria. The first kind consist of strategy announcements in which agents do not make a unanimous announcement. Since any one of $(n-1)$ agents can secure his or her best outcome in B by winning the 'integer' game, the outcome must be $R_i(\theta)$-optimal in B for at least $(n-1)$ agents. No Veto Power guarantees that the outcome is in $f(\theta)$ in this case.

The second possibility is that agents make a unanimous announcement of (x, ϕ), but $x \notin f(\theta)$.[9] Consider a deviation by $j(0)$ in the sequence $j(\phi, \theta, x)$, and let $j(0)$ announce θ, the true state of the world. Then, Condition α can be used to show that in the game beginning after $j(0)$'s deviation, all equilibrium outcomes must be $R_{j(0)}(\theta)$-maximal in B. Hence, $j(0)$ will deviate.

5. CONCLUSION

In the previous sections I have provided a brief account of some of the main results in the theory of implementation under complete information. In particular, I have emphasized the role of a class of preference-reversal conditions. Each equilibrium concept seems to give rise to a particular preference-reversal condition, which turns out to be a necessary condition for implementation. Often, the appropriate preference-reversal condition, in conjunction with No Veto Power, is also sufficient.

Within this class, (Maskin) Monotonicity, which is necessary for Nash implementation, is the most restrictive. Indeed, if all possible preference profiles are in the domain of the choice rule, then no single-valued rule can satisfy this condition. It is particularly difficult to construct *voting rules* satisfying monotonicity. However, in economic environments, some familiar rules such as the Envy-free and core correspondences are monotonic.

[9] Recall that monotonicity is required precisely for this case of unanimous falsehood in the context of Nash implementation.

Since the main function of the preference reversal conditions is to ensure that socially inoptimal outcomes cannot be supported as equilibria, implementation under *refinements* of Nash equilibrium typically leads to *weaker* preference reversal conditions. However, even some of these weaker conditions rule out several common voting correspondences.

References

Abreu, D. and A. Sen (1990), 'Sub-game Perfect Implementation: A Necessary and Almost Sufficient Condition', *Journal of Economic Theory*, 50, pp. 285–99.

Dutta, B. (1996), 'Reasonable Mechanisms and Nash Implementation', to appear in K.J. Arrow, A.K. Sen and K. Suzumura (eds), *Social Choice Theory Re-examined*, London: Macmillan.

Dutta, B. and A. Sen (1991a), 'A Necessary and Sufficient Condition for Two Person Nash Implementation', *Review of Economic Studies*, 58, pp. 121–8.

——— (1991b), 'Implementation under Strong Equilibrium: A Complete Characterization', *Journal of Mathematical Economics*, 20, pp. 49–67.

Jackson, M. (1992), 'Implementation in Undominated Strategies: A Look at Bounded Mechanisms', *Review of Economic Studies*, 59, pp. 757–75.

Jackson, M. and H. Moulin (1992), 'Implementing a Public Project and Sharing its Cost', *Journal of Economic Theory*, 57, pp. 124–40.

Jackson, M., T. Palfrey, and S. Srivastava (1992), 'Undominated Nash Implementation in Bounded Mechanisms', *Games and Economic Behavior*, 6, pp. 474–501.

Maskin, E. (1977), 'Nash Equilibrium and Welfare Optimality', mimeo.

Moore, J. (1992), 'Implementation in Environments with Complete Information', in J.J. Laffont (ed.), *Advances in Economic Theory*, Sixth World Congress, Vol. I, Cambridge: Cambridge University Press.

Moore, J. and R. Repullo (1988), 'Subgame Perfect Implementation', *Econometrica*, 56, pp. 1191–220.

——— (1990), 'Nash Implementation: A Full Characterization', *Econometrica*, 58, pp. 1083–1100.

Palfrey, T. and S. Srivastava (1991), 'Nash Implementation using Undominated Strategies', *Econometrica*, 59, pp. 479–501.

Index